VENICE &
BEYOND

ALEXEI J. COHEN

CONTENTS

Discover Venice & Beyond.......5

My Favorite Experiences 6

Explore Venice & Beyond........16

Before You Go 24

Venice...............................32

& Beyond

Venice's Lagoon Islands.........135

Padua 159

Vicenza...............................175

Verona................................190

Lake Garda 211

Ravenna.............................255

Essentials..........................268

Index.................................296

1. a plate of razor clams from Massimo Gusto

2. Cannaregio, Jewish Ghetto

3. arch at Basilica di San Vitale in Ravenna

4. Verona

5. street food in Venice

6. gondola on the Grand Canal

DISCOVER
VENICE & BEYOND

It's hard not to feel the romance of Venice. Founded after the fall of the Roman Empire, this island city's glorious past is still evident within the mosaic-encrusted Basilica di San Marco and inside Palazzo Ducale, where *doges* ruled over much of the Mediterranean.

Geography forced the city to look outward and prosper by trading with the world. The result of all that commercial and cultural exchange is still evident in Venice's art, architecture, and cuisine.

Today, the gondolas that glide up and down the Grand Canal infuse the city with otherworldly charm. Flavors and smells borrowed from the Orient enrich local kitchens. Venetians toast with *prosecco* and snack on delectable finger foods known as *cicchetti,* and there's seafood on nearly every menu. Artisans keep the traditions of glassblowing and lace making alive, and the city's *vaporetti* (ferries) put the lagoon islands of Murano and Burano enticingly within reach.

Beyond Venice are a string of magnificent cities founded by the Romans, each with its own unique flavor. The old university town of Padua offers dramatic frescoes and a lively happy-hour crowd. Vicenza is the adoptive city of one of Italy's greatest architects, Andrea Palladio, whose distinctive style elevates this market town. Ancient Roman ruins fill Verona, as do Shakespeare fans who come to pay homage to the world's most famous lovers.

Farther afield, Lake Garda provides an entirely different atmosphere with alpine views that grow increasingly dramatic the farther north you travel. Italy's largest lake is surrounded by picturesque towns that are suited to outdoor pursuits and the enjoyment of nature. South of Venice, along the Adriatic coast, lies the mosaic capital of Ravenna, flanked by a cluster of golden-sand beaches.

Whichever direction you choose, your trip to Venice is sure to be filled with delicious food, inspiring artwork, and unforgettable experiences.

MY FAVORITE
EXPERIENCES

1 **Cruising Venice's Canals** by gondola, *vaporetto,* or *traghetto* (page 72).

2 Taking in the thousands of golden mosaics that decorate **St. Mark's Basilica,** Venice's holiest site, where the city's patron saint is buried (page 46).

3 Sampling *cicchetti* at historic *bacari* (bars) surrounded by local Venetians (page 86).

4 Wandering the vast complex of the **Doge's Palace** to discover a darker side of Venice (page 48).

5 Learning the techniques of **Venetian glassblowing** at the furnaces of **Murano** (page 144).

6 Filling up on local wine to go at one of **Venice's** *vinerie* (page 95).

>>>

7 Marveling at Giotto's transformation of Western art inside Padua's **Scrovegni Chapel** (page 163).

8 Listening to opera al fresco in **Verona's ancient Arena** (page 196).

>>>

9 Taking a panoramic cable car ride to the top of **Monte Baldo,** then paragliding off the summit (page 241).

>>>

10 Appreciating Ravenna's stunning **mosaics,** best viewed on a guided nighttime tour (page 260).

11 Taking a slow cruise down the **Brenta Canal** from Venice to Padua, with frequent stops at Palladian villas (page 172).

12 Discovering the architectural genius of Andrea Palladio at **Teatro Olimpico,** the world's first covered theater (page 179).

EXPLORE
VENICE & BEYOND

To be fair, an entire lifetime isn't enough to explore Venice, but three days is a good start, after which there's plenty more to explore on dry land. From Venice, **Padua, Vicenza,** and **Verona** can all be easily reached in rapid succession (or individually) by train. Follow an overnight stay in any of these towns with an excursion around the southern part of **Lake Garda,** which is also accessible by rail or road. **Ravenna** is also well worth visiting but a separate mission. The journey to this ancient mosaic town south of Venice is longer but brings its own artistic rewards that more than compensate for the added distance.

St. Mark's Basilica in Venice

LOCAL TIP: WAKE UP!

The best time to experience Venice is **early morning,** so resist the urge to stay in bed. Morning is when locals still outnumber tourists, cruise ships have yet to dock, high-speed trains haven't arrived, and thousands of visitors inside and outside the city are still sleeping. If you're up and about by **7 or 8am,** you'll notice a whirlwind of activity that only happens early in the day: university students on their way to classes, parents accompanying children to school, bakers carting loaves to clients, fruit vendors laying out their stands, retirees walking dogs, musicians on their way to the conservatory, ladies dragging trolleys to the butcher, laborers hammering at streets, and swallows flying in the sky above. Mornings are best for visiting major monuments, too, and the lines to the bell tower and Basilica di San Marco are still reasonably short at 9am, before they open to the public.

You can catch the show at any large *campo* (square) like Santa Margherita or San Polo. When you've had your fill, head to a *bacaro* (bar) or café for a late breakfast.

BEST OF VENICE

Many visitors spend as little as one day in Venice, but it really shouldn't be rushed. Each *sestiere* (neighborhood) has its own character, and exploring these is the most enjoyable activity of all. Three or four days will allow you to join the masses flocking to San Marco and the *campanile*, discover the secrets of the Doge's Palace, and stroll through remote parts of the city where tour groups rarely tread. It will also provide sufficient time to explore the lagoon islands of Burano and Murano or the Lido and follow any path you choose without having to worry about time.

>DAY 1

- From the train station, sail down the **Grand Canal** to **Piazza San Marco.** Walk around the famous square, and visit **Basilica di San Marco** for a look at its glittering mosaics and the **Doge's Palace,** where you'll discover a darker side of Venice.

- Ride the number 2 *vaporetto* to **Isola di San Giorgio,** where you can climb the bell tower for stunning views.

- Explore Venetian Renaissance masterpieces in **Galleria dell'Accademia.**

- End your first day in Venice eating and drinking on the animated **Campo Santo Stefano.**

fisherman mending his net on a backstreet of Burano

storefront, Burano

>DAY 2

- Wake up early so you can see the city come to life before crowds start to gather. **Pasticceria Rizzardini** is a good option for coffee and pastries.

- After breakfast, head to the lively **fish market,** then cross the **Rialto Bridge** before it gets too crowded. Join the locals for lunch at a *trattoria.* **Cantina do Mori** is a good option.

- Take in Tintoretto canvases at **Scuola Grande di San Rocco,** then stroll **Strada Nuova** with a **gelato** in hand.

- Order *cicchetti* (Venetian finger food) along with a spritz or *prosecco* from one of the bars on **Fondamenta della Misericordia.**

>DAY 3

- Stay in Venice to explore the city **like a local** or purchase a *vaporetto* day pass (€20) and take a day trip out to **Venice's lagoon and islands.**

- Hop on the number 4.1 *vaporetto* from Fondamente Nove and ride one stop to Isola di San Michele. There you can explore the haunting cemetery **Cimitero di San Michele,** where thousands of Venetians are buried.

- Continue to **Murano** to view a **glassmaking demonstration.**

- Take the next *vaporetto* to **Burano,** where you can stroll the picturesque streets and enjoy a canal-side lunch.

- Your last island stop before heading back to Venice is **Torcello,** home to an **ancient church** with panoramic views and **Locanda Cipriani** *trattoria,* an old Hemingway haunt.

If You Want...	Destination	Why Go?	Distance/Travel Time from Venice	How Long to Stay
Unique souvenirs	Murano (page 140)	Visit a glassmaking workshop for a demonstration and pick up a few unique creations.	15 minutes by *vaporetto*	2 hours
	Burano (page 146)	Shop for locally made lace and admire the island's colorful homes.	40-50 minutes by *vaporetto*	1-2 hours
Art and architecture	Padua (page 159)	View Giotto's groundbreaking frescoes and peruse lively markets.	25 mi/40 km 1 hour by train 35 minutes by car	1 day
	Vicenza (page 175)	Discover Palladian architecture at this UNESCO World Heritage Site.	47 mi/75 km 45-75 minutes by train 1 hour by car	1 day
Beaches	Lido (page 154)	Steal away from Venice to lie on the beach or take a scenic seaside stroll.	10 minutes-1 hour by *vaporetto*	half day
	Ravenna (page 255)	Combine relaxing on wide sandy beaches of the Adriatic with a night tour of early Christian and Byzantine mosaics.	90 mi/144 km 3 hours by train 1 hour by car	overnight
Roman history	Verona (page 190)	See some of the finest ancient ruins outside Rome, and explore the city Shakespeare's star-crossed lovers made famous.	70 mi/112 km 70-90 minutes by train 70 minutes by car	overnight
Tranquility	Torcello (page 151)	Stroll along a canal and through rural scenery away from the crowds.	1 hour by *vaporetto*	half day
	Lake Garda (page 211)	Roman ruins, lakeside beaches, and plenty of recreational activities make for a peaceful break from the city.	87 mi/140 km 1.5-2 hours by train 1.5 hours by car	2 days

PADUA-VICENZA-VERONA

The Veneto region beyond Venice was a vital frontier for the Romans, who founded the cities of Padua, Vicenza, and Verona, along with an extensive road network. Today, it's easy to hop on the train for day trips from Venice, and you can link towns together for a fun multiday excursion. (Store your luggage in Venice's train station if you want to pack light for your outing.) Venice influenced each of these towns, and seeing and tasting the unique ways that cultural inheritance took root in each one makes this journey particularly interesting.

Make reservations for Padua's most famous sight, the **Scrovegni Chapel,** in advance. Also note that many of Padua's and Vicenza's museums are closed on Monday, though the Scrovegni Chapel is open daily.

>DAY 1 (OPTIONAL): CRUISING THE BRENTA CANAL

■ If your time is limited, skip this day by simply hopping a train in Venice to arrive in Padua in just an hour. But if you can, it's worth cruising the Brenta Canal from Venice to Padua with **Il Burchiello** (www. ilburchiello.it). Cruises depart near Piazza San Marco on Tuesday, Thursday, and Saturday at 8am, arriving in Padua at 7pm. Along the way, you'll enjoy wonderful countryside views, plus guided tours of some of the **Palladian villas** lining the canal. You can stow luggage onboard for €20 per bag. When you arrive in Padua, check into your hotel room (you'll stay here for a total of two nights).

>DAY 2: PADUA

■ If you're arriving by train from Venice, plan to be in Padua by around 10am.

■ Make a beeline for the **Scrovegni Chapel** (reservations required). You'll get 15 minutes inside the chapel, where you can see how Giotto redefined Western art.

■ Visit the market on **Piazza delle Erbe,** have lunch, and head over to **Basilica Sant'Antonio,** Padua's most exotic church.

■ Order a spritz and kick back on **Piazza dei Signori,** Padua's liveliest square, before turning in for the night.

Brenta Canal, Padua

TRAVEL LIKE A LOCAL

Venice attracts millions of visitors every year and is at serious risk of becoming a victim of its own success. For that reason it's essential to treat Venice with special care and ensure everyone has the opportunity to enjoy the city. Following the rules is a good way to start. Some of these are guidelines to follow as a courtesy, and others are laws that can result in a fine if broken. It's a privilege to visit Venice and preserving it should be a priority for everyone.

- **Walk on the right and avoid causing jams.** This is especially pertinent when you're stopping to windowshop, snap photos on bridges, or examine restaurant menus on crowded streets leading to the main tourist attractions.

- **Make way for two-wheeled trolleys.** These are used to transport food, merchandise, waste, and luggage around the city. It's especially important on mornings when deliveries are made and zigzagging heavy loads through tourists makes work even harder.

- **Do not sit on bridge steps.** Doing so creates unnecessary and annoying obstructions. At night or in quiet areas where few people pass, this rule can be overlooked.

- **Respect places of worship.** Tourists may outnumber parishioners but that doesn't mean anything goes inside churches. Dress respectfully in clothing that covers your shoulders and knees, keep voices low, leave food and drink outside, and do not use a flash or tripod when taking pictures.

- **Avoid sunbathing.** It may be tempting to remove clothing and sit or lie on the stones of Venice but it's considered disrespectful. (Bare-chested men may even be fined!) You're better off hopping a ferry and enjoying sand and sea on the beaches of the Lido.

- **Do not drag luggage over bridges.** Lift suitcases and trolleys to avoid damaging steps. If you're traveling with a heavy load, hire one of the porters waiting outside the train station (prices start at €10 per bag).

- **Remove backpacks on *vaporetti*.** Carry bags in your hands. This is less to deter pickpockets (which are rare in Venice) than to maximize space and avoid disturbing fellow passengers.

- **Never discard waste in streets or canals.** This includes cigarette butts, unwanted food, and everything else. There aren't many trash cans in Venice but you can always walk into a bar and use their bin.

- **Do not feed the pigeons.** It's forbidden and isn't a joking matter. Not only can pigeon droppings come back to haunt you, but also their corrosiveness damages buildings over time.

- **Do not swim in canals.** Local newspapers regularly report tourists diving into canals. It may be funny to some, but it's illegal and there are better ways to explore the city's waterways. Also, canals aren't that clean and leave an odor you don't want to bring home.

>DAY 3: VICENZA

- Timing is important in Vicenza: You'll want to be at the Basilica Palladiana just before noon, when the bells in the adjacent tower chime, and at Teatro Olimpico at 3pm for the sound and light show. Fortunately, Vicenza is a short (15-30 minutes) train ride from Padua, and trains depart every 20 minutes.

trompe l'oeil fresco inside Villa Valmarana

- When you arrive at the train station in Vicenza, **stow your luggage** for the day (it's free!) at the tourist office in Piazza Matteotti.

- The **Palladio Museum** should be your first stop, as it's a great place to learn about the architect who had such a strong influence on the town and region.

- Head south to **Basilica Palladiana** for views from the terrace. The bells in the adjacent tower chime at noon.

>DAY 4: VERONA

Romance, Roman ruins, and Renaissance palaces fill this vibrant city, where eating well is a point of pride and artisans can be found at work on every street.

- Circle the **Arena di Verona,** the third largest amphitheater from antiquity.

- Head to **Casa di Giulietta,** where it's said a real-life Juliet waited for her Romeo.

- Explore **Teatro Olimpico,** the first covered theater in the world, where a light and sound show takes place at 3pm.

- Discover two impressive **villas, Villa Valmarana** and **Villa La Rotonda,** south of town, before collecting your luggage at the tourist office and hopping a train to Verona. There are three or four departures per hour that can take 25-60 minutes, depending on the service. You'll be there by dinnertime.

- Ride a funicular up to the **San Pietro Panoramic Point** for impressive views.

- Enjoy an *aperitivo* before boarding a train back to Venice or continuing on to Lake Garda. Trains leave several times an hour, and the last one departs at 10:20pm. The journey takes an hour and 10 minutes on the Frecciarossa service.

LAKE GARDA

Lake Garda offers visitors an opportunity to experience an entirely different part of Italy, with cultural and gastronomic traditions influenced by the Alps. Desenzano, on the southern shore of the lake, is on the rail line that runs between Venice and Milan, making it easy to reach from Venice, Verona, Vicenza, or Padua. From there, many charming lakeside towns can be reached by ferry, bus, or car.

▶DAY 1: DESENZANO AND SIRMIONE

- After breakfast at your hotel in Desenzano, hop a ferry to **Sirmione** to explore a **castle** and **Roman ruins.**

- Back in Desenzano, have lunch and take a **stroll along the waterfront.**

- Enjoy a top-notch dinner before dancing and drinks at **Coco Beach.**

▶DAY 2: MALCESINE

- Hop a fast ferry from Desenzano to this scenic town on the northern part of Lake Garda.

- Head to the center of town, where you can take a **cable car** to the peak of **Monte Baldo.** Spend the morning **hiking** or **paragliding** from the summit.

- Spend the afternoon at **Lido Paina beach.**

- Enjoy a dinner of local flavors at **Ristorante Vecchia Malcesine.**

view of Sirmione and Lake Garda from Scaligero Castle

BEFORE YOU GO

WHEN TO GO

Venice is among the most visited cities in the world. Deciding when to go will have a significant impact on your experience.

SUMMER

Summer sees a dramatic increase in arrivals, with **July** and **August** at the apex of the tourist season. Airlines and hotels take advantage of demand to raise their rates, and temperatures rise to sweltering. Avoid visiting in July and August if you can. If you can't, book ahead and purchase **sightseeing passes** like the **Venezia Unica** (Venice) to speed up entry to monuments. The majority of Italians take their vacations in August, which means many small businesses close and it can feel like tourists outnumber locals.

One advantage of arriving in summer is, there are lots of **events** planned. The cultural calendar is full of outdoor concerts, festivals, and street fairs that make a visit even more exciting than usual.

SPRING AND FALL

Late spring and early fall are ideal times to visit. **May** and **September** are especially pleasant. Not only are there fewer tourists, but also temperatures are comfortable, daylight is long, and precipitation is low. Hotels charge midseason rates, and locals are engaged in their usual routines. Autumn is harvest season, so in September, food-related festivals are beginning and newly picked grapes are transformed into wine.

WHAT YOU NEED TO KNOW

- **Currency:** Euro (€)

- **Conversion rate:** €1=$1.14 USD; €1=£0.88GBP

- **Entry requirements:** European Union citizens can travel visa-free to Italy with a valid identity card or passport. The UK's exit from the EU may affect travelers from Britain. Travelers from the United States, Canada, Australia, and New Zealand do not need a visa for visits of less than 90 days, but a passport is required. For travelers from South Africa, a visa is required; there is a fee, and the application process takes two weeks.

- **Emergency number:** 118

- **Time zone:** GMT+1

- **Electrical system:** 220-volt system. (Plugs have two round prongs.)

- **Opening hours:** Small businesses often close 1pm-3pm. Many shops close on Sunday, and restaurants and museums are not usually open on Monday.

WINTER

November and **December** are the rainiest months and can be very cold in Venice. Christmas and New Year festivities attract a wave of visitors over the holidays, as does **Carnevale** in February. Outside of those holidays, accommodations and airfare are more affordable in winter, and getting into the most famous sights in January can take minutes rather than hours.

DAILY REMINDERS

IN VENICE

Some sights in Venice, like the Doge's Palace, are open daily. Others, including the Guggenheim Foundation and Galleria dell'Accademia, are closed or close early on **Monday.** Museums shut on January 1, May 1, and December 25. Opening hours are usually extended March–October and reduced during the winter. Most museums stop selling tickets one hour before closing and are least crowded very early or very late. Outdoor markets operate in the morning and are closed on weekends. The Burano Island market is open on Monday, Wednesday, and Saturday mornings.

BEYOND VENICE

Many sights in Padua and Vicenza are closed **Monday** (though Padua's most popular sight, the Scrovegni Chapel, is open daily). In Verona, many sights are closed Monday morning.

GETTING THERE

Venice's **Aeroporto di Venezia** (VCE, Via Galileo Galilei 30, tel. 041/260-6111, www.veniceairport. it) receives some flights from outside Europe, including North America. There are no direct flights from Australia, New Zealand, or South Africa.

Verona Villafranca Airport (VRN, www.aeroportoverona.it) has a handful of European flights, including daily arrivals from London Gatwick and Stansted, but most overseas visitors fly into Milan or Venice.

hiking above Lake Garda, Monte Baldo

GETTING AROUND

IN VENICE

Venice is a **pedestrian-only** city, and those who aren't used to doing a lot of walking may be surprised how tired they are at the end of the day. Venetian streets are the antithesis of the linear, which can be frustrating if you need to get anywhere fast. Fortunately, there are plenty of clear yellow signs pointing to the Rialto, San Marco, and other major monuments. Still, be prepared to get lost; it's part of the fun.

Public transportation in Venice isn't cheap. A single ferry ticket that's valid for 75 minutes costs €7.50, so you're better off investing in a single-day or multiday *vaporetto* **pass.** You can buy them in advance from **Venezia Unica** (www.veneziaunica.it) or at ferry stations and sales points around the city. They come in one-day (€20), two-day (€30), three-day (€40), and seven-day (€60) versions, and provide a fast, enjoyable way to explore Venice and outlying lagoon islands. The clock starts ticking when you validate your ticket at a dockside machine, which means you can use a 24-hour pass over a two-day period if you like. Forgetting to validate a ticket can result in a heavy fine and controls are frequent. Route maps are available for download from Venezia Unica and posted at each stop.

Some of the best views in Venice are from the outdoor seats at

Piazza San Marco

small port along Lake Garda

the bow and stern you'll find on the number 2, 4.1, 4.2, 5.1, 5.2, 12, and 13 ferries.

BEYOND VENICE

Train is the best way of getting around the Veneto region, and all the destinations covered in this guide can be conveniently reached by train from Venice. Stations are located within walking distance of city centers, and tickets are inexpensive. They can be reserved in advance, but frequent service makes it as easy to purchase at the time of departure. **Trenitalia** (www.trenitalia. it) operates commuter, regional,

and intercity trains throughout Italy. There are also a half-dozen car rental companies in Piazza Roma near Santa Lucia train station, and road is another viable option. Padua, Vicenza, Verona, and Lake Garda are located off the A4 highway, and paid parking is available.

Within each day trip destination, walking is the best way of reaching historic landmarks. Bicycles are popular with locals, and renting a bike is a fun way to cover more ground. There are many bike paths and pedestrian routes to enjoy, especially in small towns and along Lake Garda.

BUDGETING

- **Espresso:** €1

- **Beer:** €3 (small), €5 (large)

- **Glass of wine:** €3-5

- **Sandwich:** €3-5

- **Lunch or dinner:** €25-35 per person

- **Hotel:** €90-150 d

- **Car rental:** €70-100 per day for a mid-size vehicle

- **Gasoline:** €1.90 per liter (€1.75 per liter for diesel)

- **Parking:** €1 per hour

- *Traghetto* **crossing:** €2

- **24-hour** *Vaporetto* **pass:** €20

- **Gondola ride:** €80

- **One-way train fare:** €5-20 from Venice to Padua, Vicenza, and Verona

WHAT TO PACK

Beware of overpacking, especially if you're visiting enough destinations to get tired of hauling your luggage, unpacking, and repacking. It's probably best to leave expensive watches and jewelry at home, but do make sure you have backup copies of important documentation: You can email yourself any important credit card codes or customer service numbers as backup in case you lose your wallet.

- **Luggage:** A wheeled suitcase makes getting around airports and hotels easier. Backpacks or handbags are good for daily excursions; choose day bags with zippers to dissuade pickpockets.

A money belt can be useful for storing cash and valuables.

- **Paperwork:** Hotel staff will ask to see your passport when you check in. You'll need your passport and a driver's license to rent a moped or car. An international driving permit is not required but can prevent confusion if you're pulled over.

- **Clothing, shoes, and accessories:** Select comfortable clothes that can be mixed and matched. Layers are important in spring and fall when mornings are chilly, and temperatures change throughout the day. Formal clothes may be necessary if you plan on doing any fine dining or clubbing. Remember that knees and shoulders must be covered when entering religious buildings. Sunglasses are essential during the summer, especially if you'll be doing any driving, and hats are useful. You'll probably do a lot of walking, so bring at least two comfortable pairs of shoes.

- **Toiletries and medication:** A high-SPF sunscreen is vital during summer. If you take medication, make sure to bring enough and carry a copy of your prescription in case you need a refill. If you forget something, pharmacies in Italy are good sources for toiletries and over-the-counter medicines. Most hotels provide hair dryers, but if you're staying in a B&B or a hostel, you may want to pack one; it should be adaptable to Italy's 220 voltage. **Hand sanitizer** can be useful to remove bacteria while you're on the go.

- **Electronics:** Devices run on 220 volts in Italy, and plugs have two round prongs. Electronic devices that need recharging require an adapter. Simple U.S.-to-European **travel adapters** are available for less than $10 at electronic stores (and for double that at airports). They're harder to find in Italy, but many hotels supply them to guests free of charge. An extra memory card is useful for digital photographers, and a portable battery charger can prevent phones and other devices from going dark.

- **Binoculars** are helpful to spot details on grand church facades and to see cityscapes from the tops of bell towers.

Lido beach

SIGHTSEEING PASSES

Other than the monuments in Piazza San Marco and the pedestrian jam over Rialto Bridge, major sights such as museums, galleries, and historic buildings in Venice are not overly crowded. If you don't plan to visit more than a couple of sights, you can rely on single-entry tickets; otherwise, invest in a sightseeing pass. Beware, though: Purchasing too comprehensive a card for too short a visit can add unnecessary pressure to see it all. When choosing a card, consider your tolerance for museums as well as length of stay. You can purchase passes online and print them out at home, or buy them from the main tourist office in Piazzale Roma, automated ticketing machines outside the train station, or authorized shops around the city.

Venezia Unica (www.veneziaunica.it) is Venice's official tourism website and offers many different passes:

- **Silver City Pass** (€30): Covers Doge's Palace, three civic museums in St. Mark's Square, plus entry to three churches of your choosing. It's a good basic card for a multiday visit.

- **Gold City Pass** (€81): Covers Doge's Palace, 10 civic museums, 16 churches, and the Jewish Museum, plus unlimited three-day *vaporetto* ferry boat access.

- **The Platinum Pass** (€126): Includes all of the above over a seven-day period (transport is still only for three days), plus a guided lagoon

shops and restaurants along the Grand Canal in Venice

IN VENICE

Reservations are required for the **Secret Itineraries** (daily, 9:55am, 10:45am, and 11:35am, €20) or **Hidden Treasures** (daily, 11:45am, €20) tours of the **Doge's Palace,** which is the most visited sight in Venice. Reserve online (www.palazzoducale. visitmuve.it) or by telephone (+39 0414/273-0892 outside of Italy or 848/082-000 inside).

Hour-long in-depth tours (tel. 041/240-5440, €85) of the **Guggenheim Foundation** (www.guggenheim-venice.it) can also be reserved.

Advance **hotel reservations** are essential at peak times like Carnevale in February, the Venice Film Festival in September, and major holidays.

OUTSIDE VENICE

Entry to Padua's **Scrovegni Chapel** must be reserved in advance, as visitor numbers are limited. Opera lovers flock to Verona during the **summer music festival** (late June-early Sept.) and fill up hotel rooms and restaurants fast.

tour and casino entry. This is the most comprehensive pass you can get.

- **Saint Mark's Square Pass** (€20): Allows access to the Doge's Palace and three museums within Piazza San Marco. Single tickets are not sold. The pass is valid three months and does not include the clock tower or *campanile.*

- **Museum Pass** (€24): Covers Venice's 11 civic museums, including the Doge's Palace, Correr Museum, and Glass Museum in Murano. It's available at all participating museums and valid for six months.

- **Island Pass** (€12): Glass Museum in Murano and Lace Museum in Burano.

- **Chorus Card** (www.chorusvenezia. org, €12): Provides entry to 16 of the city's churches, including Chiesa del Redentore in Giudecca and Basilica Santa Maria Gloriosa dei Frari. Entry to St. Mark's

Basilica is free. Most member churches are open Monday to Saturday 10am-4:30pm, and the card can be purchased from any of the churches or online. Church entry without the card is €3.

- **Chorus Pass Family** (€24): Valid for two adults and any number of children under 18. Kids under 11 are free.

Children under 5 and visitors with disabilities can enter sights for free, while youths aged 6-25 and seniors over 65 receive discounts to most museums and monuments in Venice. Private institutions like the Guggenheim and Palazzo Grassi have slightly different discount policies, and it's always worth asking at ticket offices before paying. **Rolling Venice Card** (€6, www.veneziaunica.it) provides discounted *vaporetto* travel for ages 6-29. Under 6s always travel free and don't need a card.

VENICE

Orientation.............. 37
Itinerary Ideas 39
Sights 43
Food 75
Nightlife and
  Entertainment.......... 91
Shopping 103
Recreation and
  Activities 115
Accommodations 121
Information and
  Services 127
Transportation 129

Venice is unlike any city in the world, an improbable place founded on islets in a flood-prone lagoon.

Historically, commerce was king, and individual freedoms existed like nowhere else. At one time, Venice was the most populated city in the world, and everyone who was anyone did business or indulged here. Germans, Jews, Spaniards, Turks, French, and Arabs were all welcome. Nationality mattered less than money, and even the Vatican didn't have much sway in the lagoon.

HIGHLIGHTS

✪ **ST. MARK'S BASILICA:** Thousands of golden mosaics line the ceilings of this stunning cathedral (page 46).

✪ **DOGE'S PALACE:** No building in Venice has more history than this one. Step inside to discover what made Venice great over the centuries—and what happened to anyone who broke the law (page 48).

✪ **RIALTO BRIDGE:** This famous bridge is the center of Venetian commerce, with markets, food stalls, and shops of all kinds on and around it (page 54).

✪ **GUGGENHEIM FOUNDATION:** Leave historic Venice behind and fast-forward a few centuries at this unique gallery of 20th-century masterpieces (page 56).

✪ *VAPORETTO* **FERRIES:** Navigate canals with a single or multiday pass to experience another side of the city and the lagoon islands. These public ferries are more useful than gondolas—and often just as romantic as a gondola ride (page 73).

✪ *CICCHETTI* **APPETIZERS:** Enter a traditional *bacaro* bar to enjoy a tempting selection of Venetian finger food, accompanied by sparkling *prosecco* wine (page 86).

✪ **SHOPPING FOR CARNIVAL MASKS:** Browsing for papier-mâché disguises is a fun way to bring home a memorable souvenir that's an iconic symbol of the city (page 107).

Venice's economy relied on the sea and on trade with Europe, Asia, and the Middle East. Along with the goods that came in and out of its ports, Venice was exposed to new ideas, architecture, flavors, and culture. That East-meets-West crossroads atmosphere is still alive today, from the Arabesque shape of windows overlooking the Grand Canal to the spices used in local kitchens.

The greatest sight in Venice is not a museum or a monument but the city itself. Buildings may be slowly decaying, but Venice has lost none of its golden-age flair, and hundreds of artisans, shopkeepers, fishermen, and chefs preserve the Venetian way of life. Gondolas still glide along canals, bells still toll the daylight hours, and glass is still blown. The absence of cars and the extraordinary presence of boats make everything about the city even more magical. The best way to experience Venice is to put away your map, resist the urge to photograph every sight, and lose yourself in the city. Whichever byway, bridge, or canal you follow, it's impossible to stray from the enchanting labyrinth that is Venice. Regardless of how many tourists surround you there is always an alley or *sotoportego* leading to an intimate, deserted corner of the city. Let Venice lead you in unexpected directions and when you get thirsty or

Venice

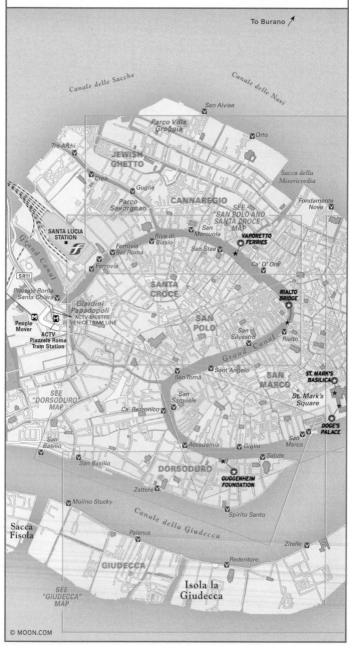

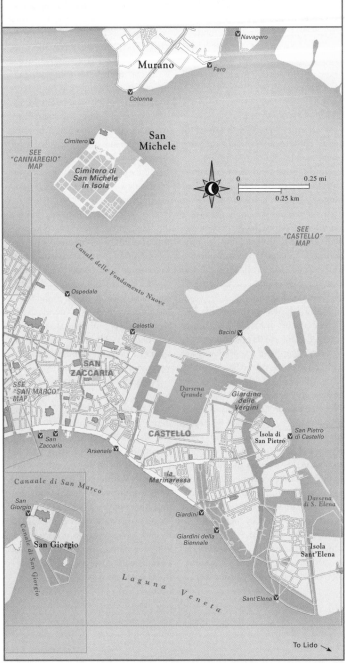

Navagero

Murano

Faro

Colonna

Cimitero

San Michele

SEE "CANNAREGIO" MAP

Cimitero di San Michele in Isola

0   0.25 mi

0   0.25 km

SEE "CASTELLO" MAP

Canale delle Fondamento Nuove

Ospedale

Celestia

Bacini

SAN ZACCARIA

SEE "SAN MARCO" MAP

Darsena Grande

Giardino delle Vergini

Isola di San Pietro

San Pietro di Castello

San Zaccaria

CASTELLO

Arsenale

la Marinaressa

Canaale di San Marco

San Giorgio

San Giorgio

Darsena di S. Elena

Canale di San Giorgio

Giardini

Giardini della Biennale

Isola Sant'Elena

Laguna Veneta

Sant'Elena

To Lido

35

require sustenance do as the locals do and enter a *bacaro* bar for a glass of *prosecco* and Venetian finger food.

Consider yourself warned: There is a risk of falling in love with Venice, and if you do you will spend the rest of your life longing to return.

HISTORY

Like all cities Venice is the result of many coincidences. It just so happened that the Roman Empire was in decline, Germanic tribes were entering the Italian peninsula, and local people needed a place to survive. In Tuscany and most of Italy they built walls but in Venice the sea became the wall. The small fishing villages on the mainland were no longer safe and the best refuge from Vandals were the maze of small islets scattered around the Venetian Lagoon.

Many islands were settled, but Venice is the one that eventually emerged thanks to its position and geography. Soggy land was gradually urbanized over the centuries and trade with Adriatic port cities and exotic Eastern empires allowed it to flourish. The city was organized into a semidemocratic republic ruled by *doges*, who were king-like figures with great power and privilege; they were guided by a council of advisers and supported by influential Venetian families. There were 120 *doges* in all and many of their portraits appear within the Doge's Palace from where they reigned.

After the body of St. Mark was smuggled to the city in an attempt to gain prestige and religious clout, pilgrims from across Europe began flooding into Venice. Visitors have been welcomed ever since, and along with trade were fundamental in the city's rise. Goods, language, and ideas from Asia Minor left a unique cultural impression that still permeates the city today. New palaces were built, basilicas consecrated, canals dug, and sailing ships launched. At its height Venice had a population of 160,000 and controlled large stretches of the Mediterranean from Crete to Lebanon. Vast wealth was accumulated and invested in art and architecture.

It wasn't all good times, though, and frequent plagues led to the decimation of the population and the formation of charitable associations known as the Scuole Grande that cared for the sick and opened the city's first hospitals. They built grand meeting halls like the Scuole Grande di San Rocco and commissioned the decoration of interiors by Renaissance artists such as Titian and Tintoretto, who developed a unique Venetian style and were capable of covering canvases like no one else.

A thousand years of independence came to an end in 1797 when Napoleon captured the city, and the Venetian Republic—already past its heyday and slowly degenerating—went out with a whimper. But a city like Venice could never decline for long, and it was only a matter of time before it was rediscovered and glorified by 19th-century intellectuals, writers, and musicians. Soon the entire world knew about Venice and has been trying to get there ever since.

Orientation

The city is divided into six *sestiere* (neighborhoods). All but one of these border the Grand Canal, which snakes through Venice like a backward S. There are no towering landmarks or hills to facilitate navigation and getting a sense of direction isn't easy. Hundreds of canals and bridges don't help matters and have a disorienting effect. Few streets run straight other than **Strada Nuova** and the *fondamente* embankments overlooking the lagoon. When you need to get somewhere quickly follow the yellow signs to major destinations like the train station or Rialto Bridge that lies in the center of the city.

SAN MARCO

Many of Venice's sights are concentrated in San Marco. It's the administrative and religious hub where you'll find symbols of the city like the **Basilica di San Marco** and **Palazzo Ducale,** both located in the grand **Piazza San Marco,** which attracts the most visitors. Nearby there are five-star hotels, luxury boutiques, and **historic cafés** where exorbitantly priced coffee comes with a spectacular view.

Piazza San Marco

Classical ensembles regularly play Vivaldi in the local churches and opera can be heard at **Teatro La Fenice.** The neighborhood is easily reached on foot along clearly indicated routes from the Rialto or Accademia Bridges, or from the sea, which is how 18th-century travelers arrived (and purists still do).

DORSODURO

Dorsoduro lies on the western side of the Grand Canal. It's a residential *sestiere* with fewer shops and a large university community that gathers in **Campo Santa Margherita** on weekends. Some of the best museums and galleries are located here. The views from **Punta della Dogana** are superb and it's where visitors watch aquatic traffic motoring through the Grand Canal and listen to street musicians. The **Fondamenta Zattere** promenade runs along the entire southern edge of the neighborhood and leads to quiet streets and canals where gondoliers bring their boats for repair, and stumbling across reasonably priced *trattorie* and outdoor cafés is easy.

SAN POLO AND SANTA CROCE

Santa Croce lies opposite the Santa Maria train station and can be reached over the **Ponte degli Scalzi** and **Costituzione** bridges to the left and right of the train station. It's the smallest of the six *sestiere* and remains underexplored by visitors intent on reaching San Marco. Stray from the main thoroughfare to discover back streets, empty churches, and impressive palaces facing the Grand Canal. **Ca' Pesaro** is one of the finest of these and houses the city's museum of modern art.

San Polo is the commercial center of Venice; it was one of the first areas settled due to its slightly elevated terrain. Shakespeare refers to it in *The Merchant of Venice,* and there are still lively markets where Venetians buy fish, vegetables, and fruit and tourists shop for glass and lace. The *sestiere* was named after the church of San Polo in the *campo* of the same name. The closer you get to the Rialto the busier things become. Crossing the city's most famous bridge can be agonizingly slow in summer, while the district's religious and artistic sights—Santa Maria Gloriosa Dei Frari and Scuola Grande di San Rocco—are often deserted. It's also home to the largest concentration of *bacari* bars and a small but active nightlife.

CANNAREGIO

Cannaregio is the first *sestiere* most travelers set foot on and home to the Santa Lucia Train Station. The gateway to the area is Rio Terra Lista di Spagna, which is lined with souvenir shops and leads to Strada Nuova. That street is usually packed with visitors on their way to the Rialto. Other than this busy thoroughfare, much of the neighborhood is quiet and it's a good place to learn how to row a Venetian boat or go stand-up paddling. The bars and restaurants lining Fondamenta della Misericordia are animated with a mix of residents and visitors at night, and ferries depart from Fondamente Nuove to the islands of Murano and Burano all day long.

CASTELLO

Streets become narrower the closer you get to Castello and regularly intersect tiny squares where locals congregate. The neighborhood is one of the largest and least-visited *sestieri* in the city—except during the Venice Biennale, when art lovers converge here. It's also where Venetian galleons were built in the Arsenale shipyards and period vessels can be seen inside the Museo Storico Navale. There are several lovely churches and some of the best workshops in the city where masks are still patiently made by hand. At the southern edge of Castello is the wide Riva degli Schiavone embankment lined with ferry boats, souvenir stands, and outdoor cafés with great views of the lagoon.

GIUDECCA

Although the island of Giudecca is technically considered part of Dorsoduro, it has its own distinct atmosphere. That's because it's the only part of Venice that can't be reached on foot and few tourists visit the island. There aren't many blockbuster attractions here other than the Chiesa del Redentore and a long embankment overlooking the Giudecca Canal. Nevertheless, in recent decades this traditionally blue-collar neighborhood of laborers and fishermen has been gradually gentrified. Abandoned factories have been transformed into luxury lofts and five-star hotels. The Palanca ferry station is a good place to disembark and explore the mix of modern and 19th-century architecture. At the eastern end lies the island of San Giorgio, which has a bell tower with a panoramic view of the city.

Itinerary Ideas

Millions of visitors spend less than 24 hours in Venice every year but to really discover the city and appreciate its particularities you'll need at least a couple of days.

VENICE ON DAY 1

Spend your first day in Venice exploring San Marco followed by a ferry ride to Isola di San Giorgio for lagoon views from the city's second-highest bell tower.

1 Sightseeing starts as soon as you step out of Santa Lucia train station. Hop on the number 1 or 2 *vaporetto* at the landing outside the station and sail down the **Grand Canal.**

2 Disembark at **Piazza San Marco** and walk around the square. Enter Basilica di San Marco and take the secret tour of the Doge's Palace next door to learn how the Bridge of Sighs got its name.

3 Ride the 2 *vaporetto* to **Isola di San Giorgio.** Climb the bell tower for a view as stunning as the one from the Campanile, but without the long lines.

4 Continue to Giudecca and the panoramic promenade that stretches along the entire northern side of this quiet island. **Majer,** near the Palanca water station, makes a good caffeine stop.

5 Ride the 2 *vaporetto* ferry to Dorsoduro and stop at **Al Bottegon** for *prosecco* in a plastic cup and an assortment of *cicchetti* snacks while watching gondolas being repaired in the dry dock opposite.

6 Continue to the **Galleria dell'Accademia** to brush up on Venetian Renaissance masterpieces or check out modern art at the Guggenheim Foundation nearby.

7 Browse for souvenirs at the workshops and galleries along **Calle del Bastion,** then walk to the tip of the Dorsoduro neighborhood to watch boats entering the Grand Canal.

8 Ride a *vaporetto* or navigate your way on foot to **Campo Santo Stefano** and enjoy the rest of the evening eating and drinking in this animated square.

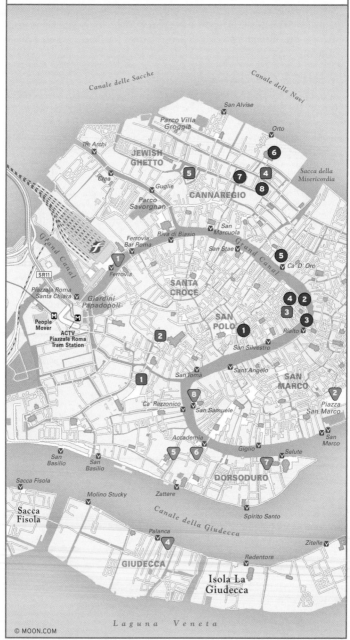

Venice Itinerary Ideas

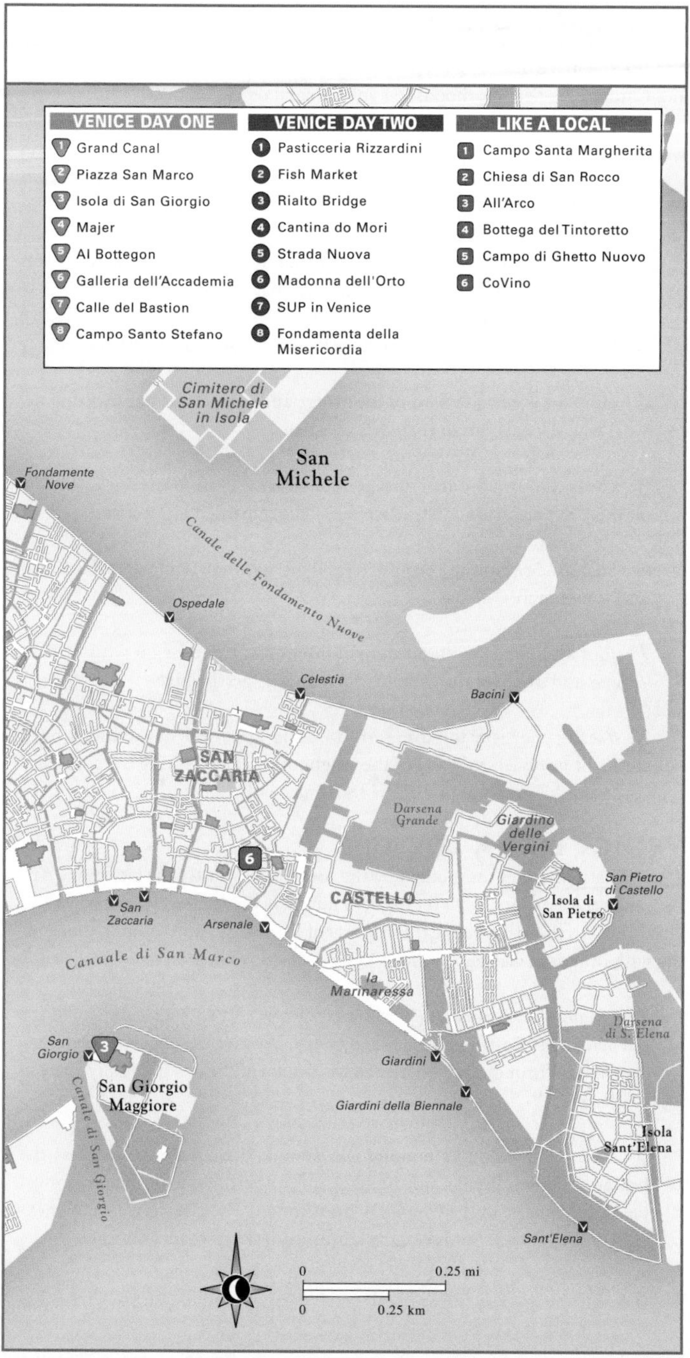

VENICE DAY ONE	VENICE DAY TWO	LIKE A LOCAL
1 Grand Canal	1 Pasticceria Rizzardini	1 Campo Santa Margherita
2 Piazza San Marco	2 Fish Market	2 Chiesa di San Rocco
3 Isola di San Giorgio	3 Rialto Bridge	3 All'Arco
4 Majer	4 Cantina do Mori	4 Bottega del Tintoretto
5 Al Bottegon	5 Strada Nuova	5 Campo di Ghetto Nuovo
6 Galleria dell'Accademia	6 Madonna dell'Orto	6 CoVino
7 Calle del Bastion	7 SUP in Venice	
8 Campo Santo Stefano	8 Fondamenta della Misericordia	

Cimitero di
San Michele
in Isola

San
Michele

Fondamente
Nove

Canale delle Fondamento Nuove

Ospedale

Celestia

Bacini

SAN
ZACCARIA

Darsena
Grande

Giardino
delle
Vergini

San Pietro
di Castello

CASTELLO

Isola di
San Pietro

San
Zaccaria

Arsenale

Canaale di San Marco

la
Marinaressa

Darsena
di S. Elena

San
Giorgio

Giardini

San Giorgio
Maggiore

Giardini della Biennale

Isola
Sant'Elena

Canale di San Giorgio

Sant'Elena

| 0 | | 0.25 mi |
| 0 | 0.25 km | |

VENICE ON DAY 2

Explore the maze of streets around the Rialto Bridge, along with the San Polo and Cannaregio neighborhoods, on your second day in Venice.

1 Get up early and observe the city coming to life. Order coffee at the counter of **Pasticceria Rizzardini** accompanied by *pan del doge* or *Mori di Venezia* pastries.

2 Head to the **fish market** to watch the mongers in action and stroll among visitors and locals thinking about what to cook and eat.

3 Explore the **Rialto Bridge** before it gets overwhelmed with tourists.

4 Hunt for a *trattoria* west of the bridge and choose one like **Cantina do Mori** where locals gather regularly at lunch.

5 Cross the Grand Canal on a gondola ferry (€2) from the dock near the markets and stroll along **Strada Nuova** accompanied by a gelato.

6 Step inside **Madonna dell'Orto** and discover how Tintoretto decorated his local church.

7 Join an hour-long stand-up paddle tour of Cannaregio with **SUP in Venice** and discover the canals from a unique perspective.

8 Zigzag your way to **Fondamenta della Misericordia.** Order a beer, spritz, or *prosecco* from any of the neighborhood bars lining the canal and get an outdoor table at one of the *trattorie* nearby.

VENICE LIKE A LOCAL

True Venetians are outnumbered by the tourists who enter the city every day. Although they are rare, what they lack in numbers they make up for in style and charisma. On this day you'll explore parts of Dorsoduro and Cannaregio, ending with dinner in Castello—one of Venice's most residential neighborhoods.

1 Do not delay getting up. Grab a front-row seat to Venice on one of the red benches in **Campo Santa Margherita.** Watch early-morning commuters passing through the square and the drama of the city gradually coming to life.

2 Exit the campo north along Rio Terà de la Scoazzera and cross the bridges into San Polo to pay homage to Tintoretto, one of the city's most beloved painters, in the **Chiesa di San Rocco.** The church is located next to Scuola di Rocco, but is equally stunning, less crowded, and free.

3 Take a *cicchetti* break at **All'Arco** near the Rialto Bridge and don't hesitate to indulge in a mid-morning *prosecco*. Order a selection of small finger-food snacks and enjoy them standing at the bar next to the locals.

4 Ride the *traghetto* ferry (€2) across the Grand Canal to Cannaregio and zigzag your way to **Bottega del Tintoretto.** Pop into the workshop where the painter once worked and have a look at what modern artists are up to. Ask them about their creations and learn their techniques.

5 Walk up Fondamento dela Sensa and over to **Campo di Ghetto Nuovo,** the center of the Jewish Ghetto. Take a seat on a marble bench in the shade to watch locals and visitors passing through this lovely lopsided square.

6 Head south into Castello or take a *vaporetto* shortcut to **CoVino** for when you feel the first pangs of hunger. Ask for the wine menu and order a bottle from the Veneto region along with the daily special.

Sights

Each neighborhood in Venice has a distinct character that's a result of the city's history and its present-day inhabitants. Take time to explore the streets—and especially the squares—where life tends to congregate. These squares can be large and vibrant or small and intimate settings where Venetians go to shop, socialize, and stretch their legs. You're as likely to see extraordinary things here as anywhere else, and the journey to a destination can be as gratifying as the destination itself.

SAN MARCO

San Marco is the thumb-shaped *sestiere* that extends from the entrance of the Grand Canal all the way around to the Rialto. It's home of the famous Piazza San Marco and the number one destination in Venice.

ST. MARK'S SQUARE
(Piazza San Marco)

Piazza San Marco, the largest square in the city, is the administrative and religious heart of Venice, where citizens and pilgrims have gathered for centuries. The sprawling open space is bordered on one end by the **Basilica di San Marco** and **Palazzo Ducale,** where leaders of the city resided and reigned. The remaining three sides are made up of **Museo Correr** and the colonnaded palaces that housed the Procurators of St. Mark, who were responsible for looking after the basilica. A little off-center are the *campanile* **bell tower** and **Torre dell'Orologio** clock tower, where Venetians once came to observe the time and visitors now get great views of the city.

Today, the *piazza* is animated with competing quartets playing on outdoor stages at elegant cafés, tour groups waiting to enter Palazzo Ducale, fearless seagulls searching for their next meal, and itinerant sunglass vendors hoping to make a sale. They may also offer birdseed that you should decline, as pigeons damage buildings and feeding them is prohibited. All the sights

San Marco

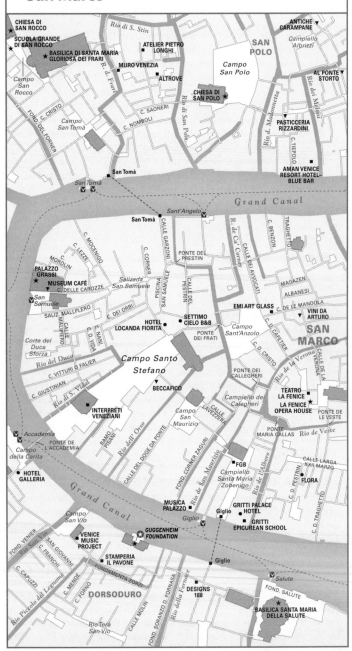

★ CHIESA DI
SAN ROCCO

SCUOLA GRANDE
DI SAN ROCCO

★ BASILICA DI SANTA MARIA
GLORIOSA DEI FRARI

■ ATELIER PIETRO
LONGHI

■ MURO VENEZIA

■ ALTROVE

CHIESA DI
SAN POLO ★

Rio di S. Stin

SAN
POLO

*Campo
San Polo*

*Campiello
Albrizzi*

AL PONTE ▼
STORTO

Rio dei Meloni

PASTICCERIA
RIZZARDINI ■

Rio d. Madonnetta

Rio di San Polo

*Campo
San
Rocco*

Fond. del Forner

C. Cristo

*Campo
San Tomà*

C. SAONERI

C. NOMBOLI

R. d. Frari

C. TIEPOLO

AMAN VENICE
RESORT HOTEL-
BLUE BAR ■

San Tomà ■

San Tomà
▽ ▽

Grand Canal

San Tomà ■

Sant'Angelo ▽

CALLE GARZONI

R. de Ca' Corner

CALLE BENZON

TRAGHETTO

PONTE DEL
PRESTIN

CALLE DEI AVVOCATI

MAGAZEN

ALBANESI

C. DE LE MANDOLA

VINI DA
ARTURO ▼

SAN
MARCO

C. MOCENIGO

MOROLIN

C. LEZZE

C. CORNER

SALIZADA
SAN SAMUELE

PISCINA

SAN SAMUELE

CALLE DEL
PESTRIN

EMI ART GLASS ■

C. D. CAFETIER

PALAZZO
GRASSI ★

MUSEUM CAFÉ

C. DELLE CAROZZE

*San
Samuele* ■

SALIZ. MALIPIERO

C. DEI ORBI

CALLE
MALIPIERO

C. D. NANI

C. D. VIDA

*Corte del
Duca
Sforza*

Rio del Duca

C. VITTURI O FALIER

C. GIUSTINIAN

Rio di S. Vidal

INTERPRETI
VENEZIANI ★

▽ *Accademia*

▽

PONTE DE
L'ACCADEMIA

*Campo
della Carità*

● HOTEL
GALLERIA

SETTIMO
CIELO B&B ■

HOTEL
LOCANDA FIORITA ●

PONTE
DEI FRATI

*Campo
Sant'Anzolo*

C. D. CRISTO

Rio de la Verona

*Campo Santo
Stefano*

▼ BECCAFICO

PONTE DEI
CALLEGHERI

*Campiello dei
Calegheri*

CALLE DE LA
VERONA

TEATRO
LA FENICE ★

LA FENICE
OPERA HOUSE ★

PONTE DE
LE VESTE

RAMO
PISANI

*Campo
San Maurizio*

CALLE
L'AVEZZERA

Rio dell'Orso

CALLE DEL DOGE DA PONTE

FOND. CORNER ZAGURI

PONTE
MARIA CALLAS

Rio de Verde

FGB ■

*Campiello
Santa Maria
Zobenigo*

FLORA ●

CALLE LARGA
XXII MARZO

C. D. PESTRIN

Rio de l'Alboro

Grand Canal

*Campo
San Vio*

FOND. VENIER

Rio San Vio

C. SAN GIOVANNI

C. FRANCHI

C. CAPUZZI

C. MENDE

C. FORNO

MUSICA
PALAZZO ■

GUGGENHEIM
FOUNDATION ★

VENICE
MUSIC
PROJECT ■

STAMPERIA
IL PAVONE ■

FONDAMENTA ZORZI

Giglio ▽

Giglio ■

GRITTI PALACE
HOTEL ■

GRITTI
EPICUREAN SCHOOL ■

Giglio ▽

DORSODURO

C. TOFFO

Rio Piccolo del Legname

*Rio Terà
San Vio*

CALLE MOLIN

Rio delle Fornace

FOND. SORANZO O FORNASA

DESIGNS
188 ■

Salute ▽

FOND. SALUTE

BASILICA SANTA MARIA
DELLA SALUTE ★

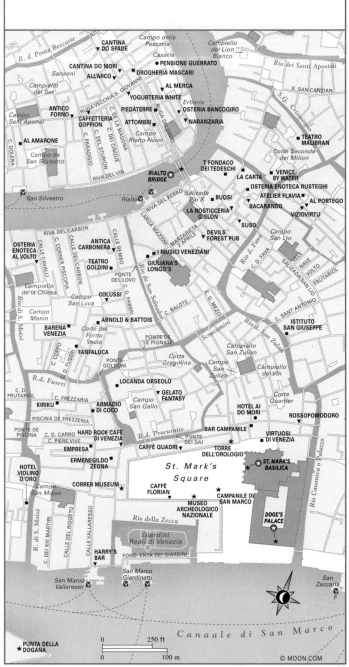

St. Mark's Basilica and Doge's Palace

(except the bell and clock towers) are accessible with the **Saint Mark's Square Pass** (€20), and some, like the Basilica and **Bibliotheca Marciana**, are partially free.

The *piazza* can be entered from several different directions. Each has its particular charm. You can take the direct route from the Rialto through the clock tower archway or approach from the Ponte dell'Accademia bridge along the winding streets leading to Museo Correr. The most dramatic approach, however, is by boat, which was the most common way of reaching the *piazza* before the train station was built.

TOP EXPERIENCE

✪ ST. MARK'S BASILICA
(Basilica di San Marco)

Piazza San Marco 328, tel. 041/270-8311, www.basilicasanmarco.it, Mon.-Sat. 9:30am-5pm and Sun. 2pm-4:30pm, free

Basilica di San Marco, founded in 832, was built to house the remains of St. Mark, which were looted from Egypt in a pork-laden basket (to deter Muslim customs officials) after two enterprising merchants decided that Mark should be the patron saint of their city. The basilica was influenced by Greek, Byzantine, and Islamic art and architecture. The five domes are reminiscent of a mosque, and the floor plan is a Greek cross. Mosaics above the entrance recount the saint's arrival to the city, and a team of four bronze horses plundered from Constantinople stand triumphantly above the central portal.

Inside, golden mosaics embellish over 40,000 square feet (3,716 square meters) of the cavernous church. The uneven marble floor is also decorated in exotic patterns, and it's clear how much the ground has shifted over the centuries. Biblical tales like the *Descent of the Holy Ghost* are beautifully illustrated on the dome interiors. Just behind the altar is the

Pala d'Oro, or Golden Ball, which was created by the city's goldsmiths and adorned with hundreds of precious gems. The chapel is connected to the church and although a velvet rope separates it from the rest of the basilica, you can get a good look at the interior in relative peace. Over the centuries the basilica was decorated with columns, marble, sculptures, gold, and other spoils of war brought back by the city's merchants' ships after the sack of Constantinople and other military victories.

Also inside the Basilica is the **Museo di San Marco** (Basilica di San Marco, tel. 041/270-8311, 9:30am-5pm, €5), dedicated to mosaics, textiles, and ancient relics such as the original *quadriga* statue of four bronze horses. A detour here provides access to the second-story balcony overlooking Piazza San Marco. This is where *doges* and dignitaries greeted crowds on special occasions and visitors now gather to get a great view of the square below. If you watched the final episode of *The Young Pope* it will already be familiar. The basilica's **Treasury** (9:35am-5pm, €3) and **Pala d'Oro** (9:35am-5pm, €2), a stunning gold and gem-encrusted altarpiece begun in the 10th century by Byzantine jewelers, can also be visited.

mosaics inside St. Mark's Basilica

There's no better time to experience the basilica than during **Sunday mass** (6:45pm), when lights are switched on and thousands of mosaics are fully illuminated. The ceremony isn't intended for tourists, so if you aren't religious, be prepared to sit through a 45-minute sermon conducted in Latin and Italian. Masses are held every morning, but only the Sunday evening service includes spotlights.

When visiting the basilica, remember to dress appropriately (no bare shoulders or knees) and keep quiet, and no photos or filming are allowed. Free one-hour **tours** (tel. 041/241-3817, Mon-Fri. 11am, 2:30pm, 4pm) are organized on a month-by-month basis in English by the Pastoral and Pilgrimage Office of Venice. They start in the basilica atrium and reservations are not necessary, although you may want to call and ensure there will be one that day, as the schedule fluctuates throughout the year.

If the line at the main entrance is too long, try entering the church through the prayer door on the side of the church in Campo Leoni. The facade and other parts of the basilica are often undergoing restoration and may be partially covered or closed.

facade of St. Mark's Basilica

❂ DOGE'S PALACE
(Palazzo Ducale)

Piazza San Marco 1, tel. 041/271-5911, www.palazzoducale.visitmuve.it, Apr.-Oct. 8:30am-7pm, Nov.-Mar. 8:30am-5:30pm, St. Mark's Square Pass €20 or Museum Pass €24, audio guide €5

To understand Venice requires visiting Palazzo Ducale. This imposing palace on the southeastern corner of Piazza San Marco is where the *doge* resided and the Venetian senate met to make the decisions that ensured the city was a leading power for centuries. It's a White House and Capitol Hill rolled into one. It's also where dignitaries were received, powerful men slept, and prisoners were kept.

The palace is an immense U-shaped complex with stunning facades and sumptuous interiors. The exterior is wrapped in a columned arcade that supports an intricate *loggia*. The upper stories are covered in smooth brick decorated in a diamond pattern. *Doges* once addressed citizens gathered below from the ornate balconies. Inside, there's a vast courtyard, grand reception rooms, a chapel, luxurious sleeping quarters, prison cells, and a museum. This is where you'll find several of the world's largest oil paintings by the likes of Tintoretto, Titian, and Veronese.

The fixed itinerary leads visitors through grand chambers where the city counselors gathered and an extensive armory stocked with swords and early firearms used by the *doge's* guards and auxiliary troops. *Sala dei Consigli*, the next stop, is one of the biggest rooms in Europe. It's where *doges* were elected, and up to 2,000 counselors met every Sunday to express their grievances. Paintings depicting Venice's greatest triumphs and the portraits of 76 *doges* cover

Doge's Palace

WHAT'S A DOGE?

Doge is a title that derives from the Latin *dux,* or commander (duke in English). It was used in Venice from AD 697 until the fall of the Republic in 1797. During those thousand years, the position evolved from primitive military leader to something close to a king and eventually a mere figurehead.

Becoming a *doge* was nearly as complicated as becoming a pope. The elaborate and complicated rules of the election system were intended to dissuade any overeager aristocrats from taking shortcuts to power. Each *doge* was, however, required to pay for his furnishings and expenses, which meant only the richest Venetians could aspire to the position. In the city's 15th-century heyday the *doge's* primary responsibility was representing Venice during public ceremonies and proceeding over diplomatic relations with other states. He could recommend foreign policy but his advice was not always taken and he wasn't allowed to meet with ambassadors without the presence of his counselors.

Eventually the election of *doges* became the responsibility of a council of aristocrats, and the independence of *doges* was severely limited. They could not marry foreign princesses, abdicate, write or receive letters without the presence of a witness, conduct business, own land outside the palace, or leave the city without special permission. Toward the end of the Republic the position was limited to presiding over the government without any real control, and by then a *doge* was simply a fancy magistrate whose gondola was no nicer than those of the other nobles. The biggest benefit was residing in the most prestigious palace in town. The only power that was never stripped was commander in chief of the navy in times of war.

Doges can be seen in many paintings inside Palazzo Ducale and are often portrayed wearing scarlet robes with a fur collar and an oddly shaped hat. Power was gradually siphoned away from the *doge* by an emerging merchant class who distrusted too much power in one place. The sculpture of a *doge* bowing in submission to a lion (above the palace entrance nearest the basilica) is the expression of that distrust and a constant reminder of who was serving whom.

the ceiling and walls. The hall is lined with wooden benches and no matter how crowded the palace gets there's always room to sit and admire it here.

Sala dei Consigli is exited through a small doorway that leads to the cramped *Palazzo dei Prigioni* prisons. The narrow stone passageway crosses the **Bridge of Sighs,** where prisoners were once led to the gallows and through a long series of cells and chambers that make it clear how the Republic deterred anyone from breaking the law. This is where Casanova was briefly detained and less fortunate prisoners met their end. The itinerary ends in a bookshop and café near the main courtyard.

The Doge's Palace is the most visited monument in Venice. Lines form early, but if you arrive at 9am the efficient ticket office is nearly empty. If you want a behind-the-scenes look at the palace, reserve the **Secret Itineraries** (daily, 9:55am, 10:45am, and 11:35am, €20) or **Hidden Treasures** (daily, 11:45am, €20) tour. These 75-minute guided walks through lesser-known parts of the *palazzo* are conducted in English. They cost the same as a regular ticket and afterward you're free to visit the rest of the building. Reservations are required and can be made online (www.palazzoducale. visitmuve.it) or by telephone (+39 0414/273-0892 outside of Italy or 848/082-000 inside). Visitors entering the palace are checked with metal detectors. Leave large backpacks and bags at your hotel; otherwise, they'll have to be checked in at the cloakroom on the right side of the courtyard.

CAMPANILE DI SAN MARCO

Piazza San Marco, www.basilicasanmarco.it,
daily Apr. 16-Oct. 8:30am-9pm, Nov.-Apr. 15
9:30am-5:30pm, €8

The Campanile di San Marco, or bell tower, is nearly 328 feet (100 meters) high and would be the oldest in the city if it hadn't collapsed in 1902. Fortunately, it was entirely rebuilt to 12th-century specs and an elevator was added to facilitate getting to the top. Only one of the original five bells survived the crash but they were all eventually replaced. Each has a name and had a specific purpose. *Marangona*, the main bell, signaled the start and end of the working day while the *Trottiera* called patricians to the Doge's Palace and *Renghiera*, the smallest bell, announced executions. They still ring out today but only to tell time and celebrate holidays. Galileo demonstrated his first telescope here in 1609 and the lightning conductor fitted on the roof a century and half later was the first of its kind.

From the upper terrace there's an unobstructed view of the city and lagoon islands. The elevator has a capacity of 16 passengers, and the terrace accommodates 20-25 visitors at a time. There are coin-operated binoculars at the top and you can stay up as long as you like. Tickets are available inside the bell tower, which may be closed in the event of high winds, flooding, or adverse weather.

Lines to enter the bell tower can be long and if you don't feel like waiting, ride the number 2 *vaporetto* across the mouth of the Grand Canal to Isola di San Giorgio. There's another bell tower there that's less crowded and provides equally satisfying views of the city.

TORRE DELL'OROLOGIO

Piazza San Marco, tel. 848/082-000
or tel. 041/4273-0892 from abroad,
www.torreorologio.visitmuve.it, €12, €7
with Museum Pass or St. Mark's Square Pass

In the 15th century, knowing the time meant looking at the sun or listening to church bells. The Torre dell'Orologio clock tower in the northeastern corner of Piazza San Marco changed all that with Renaissance high-tech ingenuity.

The blue facade of the enormous astronomical clock contains rotating panels that tell the hour, day, lunar phase, and zodiac sign. It was a great innovation, even if it didn't have a minute hand, and provided essential information for sailors, senators, and merchants, all of whom came to rely on the clock and checked it regularly. Visitors gather hourly in front of the tower to see the bronze sculptures on top strike a large bell. The statue on the left strikes two minutes before the hour to represent time that has passed, while the statue on the right hammers two minutes after the hour to signify the time to come.

You can observe the clock tower for free from the square or reserve a tour of the inside and discover what keeps

Campanile di San Marco

it ticking. Reservations must be made in advance or on the same day at the Correr Museum ticket office, where the 50-minute visit begins. English-speaking tours are held Monday to Wednesday at 10am and 11am and Thursday to Sunday at 2pm and 3pm. Tour groups do not exceed 12 visitors.

CORRER MUSEUM
(Museo Correr)

Piazza San Marco 52, tel. 041/240-5211, www.correr.visitmuve.it, daily Apr.-Oct. 10am-7pm, Nov.-Mar. 10am-5pm, St. Mark's Square Pass or Museum Pass

Museo Correr is a behemoth of a museum on the western edge of Piazza San Marco. The 17th-century palace contains over 70 rooms. Most people head straight to the rooms filled with Venetian Gothic art, but you could also discover where an Austrian princess resided, admire 19th-century sculpture, or learn some Venetian history.

The Quadreria picture gallery located on the second floor is filled with religious effigies, portraits of aristocrats, and scenes documenting everyday Venetians like the *Two Ladies of Venice* in room 15. The neoclassical rooms on the same floor display the marble sculptures of Antonio Canova, a skilled artist-diplomat who managed to bring back much of the art shipped off to Paris after Napoleon captured the city.

Before Museo Correr became a museum it was a royal residence and hosted Empress Sissi of Austria during her mid-18th-century visit to Venice. The Imperial Apartments are a miniature Versailles and include a throne room, dining area, audience hall, study, bedroom, and boudoir complete with period furnishings. The Civilita di Venezia rooms downstairs provide insight into how the city once operated and are organized by themes including the *doge,* military, maritime trade, and daily life. Most rooms contain explanation panels in English. Tours (€100/1-4 people) are available.

The museum cafeteria is one of the least expensive places to have a coffee or light snack in Piazza San Marco. The views are great and the drink-sandwich combo only costs €10. The Bibliotheca Marciana (Piazzetta San Marco 7, Mon.-Fri. 8am-7pm and Sat. 8pm-1:30pm, free) can be entered through the museum. The library contains a monumental reading room decorated by Tiziano, Tintoretto, and Veronese. Tours (tel. 041/240-7238, mazzariol@marciana.venezia.sbn.it, St. Mark's Square Pass or Museum Pass) in Italian last 50 minutes and can be arranged in advance.

MUSEO ARCHEOLOGICO NAZIONALE

Piazzetta San Marco 17, tel. 041/522-5978, Apr.-Oct. 10am-7pm, Nov.-Mar. 10am-5pm, St. Mark's Square Pass or Museum Pass

Museo Archeologico Nazionale is the smallest museum on the square and the least visited. The collection of Greek and Roman sculptures, ceramics, coins, and stones dates back to the 1st century BC and was amassed by wealthy Venetian families who eventually donated the antiquities to the state. It can be visited in under an hour and skipped entirely if you've already seen ancient sculptures in Rome. Access is through the Napoleonic wing of the Correr Museum.

LA FENICE OPERA HOUSE
(Teatro La Fenice)

Campo San Fantin, tel. 041/786-672, www.festfenice.com, Mon.-Fri. 9:30am-5pm and Sat.-Sun. 9:30am-1:30pm, €10 with audio guide

Opera is an Italian invention, and the

theaters where Rossini, Verdi, and other great composers premiered their works are legendary. Teatro La Fenice is among the most prestigious and has staged thousands of hours of melodies since it was opened in 1792. It has seen more than its share of drama and twice burned down only to be rebuilt, most recently in 1996. The simple neoclassical exterior gives little hint of the opulent five-tiered seating inside. Unless you attend a performance, the best way to visit the theater is with the self-guided **audio tour** in English that lasts 45 minutes and includes a visit to a permanent exhibit dedicated to Maria Callas. Music lovers can go backstage, see contemporary sets, sit in the royal box, and learn about singers like Callas who frequently sang here. Venetian audiences have very high standards and even the greatest performers have been booed on this stage.

CAMPO SANTO STEFANO

The largest *campo* in San Marco is a vibrant intersection where visitors pause on their way to and from Piazza San Marco and local children run free. It was once used for bullfights, masked balls, and processions during *Carnevale* and is lined with modest *palazzo* and outdoor cafés. The statue in the center honors Niccolò Tommaseo, one of the city's hometown writers, and the steps at the base are usually occupied with people watchers. The Gothic church of Santo Stefano has a simple brick facade and a ceiling shaped like a ship's keel. There's a small museum (tel. 041/522-2362, Mon.-Sat. 10am-5pm, €3 or Chorus Card) in the adjacent cloister with a *Last Supper* painted by Tintoretto. On the other side of the *campo* is the Chiesa di San Vidale, where classical concerts are held every

Campo Santo Stefano

Venice would be a dark and dreary place without its *campi*. These oddly shaped squares provide light and space for locals to commune, children to play, and pigeons to gather. They come in all sizes and are recognizable by the wellheads, flagpoles, and red benches that characterize them. Tourists walk quickly through, but these aren't just stone paving between destinations—they are destinations in themselves, where you can observe daily life, fill up a bottle of water, and enjoy a spritz at an outdoor café.

There are dozens of *campi* in each neighborhood and they are difficult not to stumble upon. Some are large and busy at all hours, like **Campo Santo Stefano** (Dorsoduro), which is lined with eateries and popular with students from the nearby universities; others are semideserted and lacking in commerce, such as **Campo S. Agnese** (Dorsoduro), where the biggest attraction is the shade from the trees and the entertainment by the street musicians playing violins and accordions.

On the other side of the Grand Canal **Campo Santo Stefano** (San Marco) is a mix of the two types. It's flanked on either end by churches and sees a constant stream of visitors on their way to and from Piazza San Marco. At its outdoor tables you can enjoy a drink in the sun and try to distinguish Venetians from tourists (hint: Venetians walk a little faster, are dressed more elegantly, and know where they're going).

Some *campi* overlook canals like **Santa Maria Formosa** and **Campo San Lorenzo** (Castello), where gondoliers wait patiently for fares and lines form outside small gelato shops. They are natural pit stops for enjoying a gelato or browsing vegetable stalls in search of fresh fruit. **Campo San Polo** (San Polo) is one of the biggest and nearly empty most of the year—except during the Venice Film Festival when a giant screen is set up and spectators watch the latest international releases outdoors and enjoy pints of beer at the *pizzeria* on the corner.

There's a *campo* for everyone, whether you prefer a boisterous or desolate atmosphere, and whichever you choose you'll be able to admire the beauty of the city from a unique urban setting.

evening. The repertoire nearly always includes Vivaldi.

PALAZZO GRASSI

Campo San Samuele 3231, tel. 041/200-1057, www.palazzograssi.it, Wed.-Mon. 10am-7pm, €18 with Punta della Dogana

Palazzo Grassi was purchased by French billionaire and art collector Francois Pinault in 2005. It was the last palace built before the end of the Republic and he hired Japanese architect Tadao Hando to transform the dilapidated building into a minimalist shrine to contemporary art. Exhibitions alternate every six months and include pieces from the philanthropist's personal collection along with retrospectives of established artists like Damien Hirst and Cindy Sherman. The building itself is something to look at, especially the second floor with its large airy rooms, ornate ceilings, and view of the canal. There are free lockers downstairs, an exceptionally good museum café, and plenty of knowledgeable staff ready to answer questions.

There are free **guided tours** in Italian every Saturday at 3pm; group tours are available the rest of the week by reservation (tel. 041/271-9031, visite@palazzograssi.it, €85, €160 for Palazzo Grassi and Punta della Dogana). The ticket includes entry to Pinault's second contemporary art emporium across the Grand Canal at **Punta della Dogana**. A handy map available from the box office makes getting from one to the other easy. It's a 15-minute walk along some of the most scenic streets in the city.

Rialto Bridge

✪ RIALTO BRIDGE

There are four bridges spanning the Grand Canal, but the Rialto is the grandest, and the one everyone wants to cross. It's divided into three lanes, the outermost of which provide good views of the canal in both directions. It's flanked with shops and is a magnet for commercial activity. The bridge is crowded throughout the day and can be difficult to cross let alone enjoy. Early mornings and late evenings are the best time to appreciate the harmonious stonework and twin archways in the middle without being bumped. The Rialto can also be viewed from the embankments on both sides of the Grand Canal and looks better than ever after the renovation was completed in 2018.

There's been a succession of bridges on the same spot since the 13th century and each increased in size as the city grew in power and wealth. The current version of the Rialto was the result of a competition held in 1524 to replace a wooden bridge. Although Palladio and Michelangelo were among the participants, a little-known local architect named Antonio de Ponte (*ponte* coincidentally means bridge in Italian) got the job. He completed the project in less than three years using stone and a single 157-foot (48-meter) arch to span the canal. Critics at the time predicted the audacious design would collapse but until now the Rialto has passed the test of time.

DORSODURO

ACCADEMIA
(Galleria dell'Accademia)

Campo della Carità 1050, tel. 041/522-2247, www.gallerieaccademia.it, Mon. 8:15am-2pm, Tues.-Sun. 8:15am-7:15pm, €15

Galleria dell'Accademia contains the greatest collection of Venetian art in the world and traces the evolution of the city's changing tastes from the Middle Ages to the 18th century. Paintings by Mantegna, Titian, Tintoretto, and Veronese can all be found inside the former church that opened to the public in 1817.

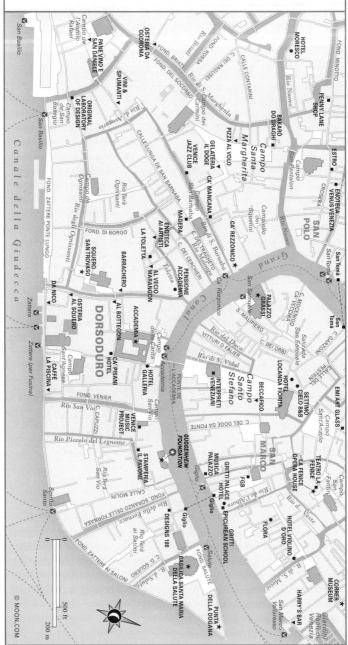

Dorsoduro

The collection spans five centuries and is arranged chronologically. There is no better place to gaze upon Venetian masters, which explains why the museum is the third most visited in the city. Even the lesser-known works demonstrate brilliance and the Venetian love of vibrant colors and light. One of the most interesting pieces is Veronese's *Last Supper,* which includes dogs, midgets, and drunkards. It was deemed too racy for the time and nearly got the artist locked up. He eventually passed the censors by changing the title of the work to *Feast in the House of Levi* (room 10).

Bags must be checked (€1) and fire regulations limit the number of visitors allowed into the museum at any one time. That can lead to a 30-45-minute wait in summer that is reduced by reserving tickets in advance at the museum website for a small fee. The audio guide (€6) reveals the story behind every canvas.

At the time of writing, the building was undergoing partial renovation, and many paintings are under wraps until the museum completes its makeover in 2020. Nevertheless, the Accademia is still worth visiting.

✪ GUGGENHEIM FOUNDATION

Fondamenta Venier 704 or 701,
tel. 041/240-5411, www.guggenheim-venice.
it, daily 10am-6pm, €15

America's savviest art patron, Peggy Guggenheim, moved to Venice in 1949 and assembled a vast collection of modern art in Palazzo Venier. The Guggenheim Foundation is her legacy and a lasting gift to art lovers. It's located along the Grand Canal in a modest 18th-century *palazzo* where she lived and encouraged artists to ignore boundaries until her death in 1979. The all-star cast of painters includes Chagall, Dali, Duchamp, and Miro, and other giants of 20th-century art.

The museum is entered through narrow stone archways that can be easily missed and lead to a peaceful sculpture garden. The villa is smaller than you might expect and filled with eager visitors getting close-up views of Pollocks and Picassos. A historic photograph in each room shows how things looked in Peggy's time. Most of the furniture is gone but the artwork remains. If you have any questions about the art or the heiress, ask the multilingual interns stationed around the foundation. You can also enjoy the view of the canal from the terrace at the front of the building.

the Guggenheim Foundation

Visitors can pick up an audio guide (€7) or join free 10-minute talks (daily 11am and 5pm) that focus on a single painting. Brief explanations about the life and times of Peggy Guggenheim (daily noon and 4pm) in Italian and English are given every day. Hour-long in-depth tours (tel. 041/240-5440, €85) can also be reserved. The café is bright but slightly overpriced and the foundation gift shop is down the street on Fondamenta Venier.

BASILICA SANTA MARIA DELLA SALUTE

Campo della Salute 1,
www.basilicasalutevenezia.it, daily
9:30am-noon and 3pm-5:30pm, free

Basilica Santa Maria della Salute dominates the entrance to the Grand Canal and has dazzled visitors with its white baroque facade since it was erected in the 17th century. The basilica was commissioned by the Venetian senate in gratitude for ending a plague that devastated the city and consists of an octagonal plan topped by an enormous dome that can be seen throughout the lagoon. The monumental steps are a wonderful place to sit and watch boats traveling up and down the canal.

Inside are works by Titian and Tintoretto as well as a small gallery museum (€4) in the sacristy to the left of the altar. There are free afternoon concerts that start at 3:30pm when the church organist, Paolo Talamini, plays the massive instrument alone or accompanied by a chorus. Venetians are still thankful to the Virgin Mary for ending the plague and every year on November 21 they show their respect.

Basilica Santa Maria della Salute

A pontoon bridge is assembled from San Marco and locals come to light votive candles and gondoliers have their oars blessed.

PUNTA DELLA DOGANA

Campo della Salute 2, tel. 041/200-1057,
Wed.-Mon. 10am-7pm, €18 with
Palazzo Grassi

The area known as Punta della Dogana was in disrepair until Francois Pinault purchased this iconic building and transformed it into the second piece of his contemporary art empire, also known as Punta della Dogana. The triangle-shaped former customhouse and warehouse was an important entry point for commercial vessels and salt can still be seen encrusted on the brick walls inside. Tadao Hando gave the interior a Zen makeover and today his trademark gray prevails throughout the immense gallery. There are a dozen spacious rooms exhibiting photography, installations, video, and sculpture on a rotating basis. Much of the art leaves an impression and challenges the senses. At the end of the complex are a bar, museum shop, and stairs leading to the lookout tower where spotters once scanned the lagoon for incoming ships. There are guided tours (free) in Italian every Saturday at 3pm; group tours are available the rest of the week by reservation (tel. 041/271-9031, www.palazzograssi. it, €85, €160 for Palazzo Grassi and Punta della Dogana).

Also located in the area known as Punta della Dogana, the **Fondamenta Salute** embankment leads to the easternmost tip of Dorsoduro and one of the best views of the city. It's a great point to stop and admire Venice. Afterward, avoid backtracking and follow **Fondamenta Zattere** along the wide promenade facing Giudecca.

SQUERO SAN TROVASO

Fondamenta Bonlini 1097, tel. 041/522-9146

Although the number of gondoliers is in decline, new boats are still built and old ones need repair, fresh paint, and regular maintenance. Squero San Trovaso is one of four remaining gondola shipyards where that work is done.

The best view of the small alpine-like huts and teams of workers hammering, sawing, and painting away is from Fondamenta Nani, which links the Grand Canal with the Giudecca Canal. There are usually several gondolas in dry dock being cared for by a team of workers. It can take up to a year to complete a new gondola, and each artisan has his own specialty handed down from generation to generation. Although there are occasional tours, they prefer if you watch from afar unless you're interested in buying a boat. Osteria Al Squero is perfectly positioned for observing the shipyard and is popular with visitors and locals who gather to watch the action and enjoy a drink.

CA' REZZONICO

Fondamenta Rezzonico 3136,
tel. 041/241-0100, Wed.-Mon. 10am-6pm,
€10 or Museum Pass, audio guide €4

Like most palatial estates lining the Grand Canal, Ca' Rezzonico had a series of illustrious owners who wanted to demonstrate their power through art and architecture. Some of them went bankrupt in the process, and the palace changed hands many times before becoming the temporary home of Robert Browning and later Cole Porter. It was purchased by the city in 1935 and transformed into a house museum where you can discover how Venetian nobility once lived.

The audio guide is useful for deciphering the 18th-century paintings,

furnishings, and the Murano chandeliers decorating all three floors of the pristine *palazzo*. There are great views of the Grand Canal upstairs and a small shaded garden in back that's great for resting. Ca' Rezzonico is delightfully uncrowded and has its very own water stop, which makes it an easy and fun destination to reach.

CAMPO SANTA MARGHERITA

Campo Santa Margherita is a relief from history. There are no major monuments, no earth-shattering churches, and no reason not to relax in this square. It's simply a popular university hangout lined with pretty houses and neighborhood shops where regulars eat at affordable *trattoria*. Most mornings there's an animated fish and vegetable market, and there's always plenty of space on the red benches that dot the large rectangular square. The oddly positioned building at the southern end of the *campo* is the *scuola piccola* (confraternity) where local tanners once met.

SAN GIORGIO ISLAND
(Isola di San Giorgio)

San Giorgio is a small island in front of Piazza San Marco and next to Giudecca that can only be reached by *vaporetto*. It's worth making a detour here to climb the church of the same name (Chiesa di San Giorgio Maggiore) and visit a superb glass gallery. Isola di San Giorgio has one water station that can be reached with the number 2 *vaporetto*. It's one stop from Zattere in Giudecca and S. Zaccaria (F) near Piazza San Marco.

Chiesa di San Giorgio Maggiore

Isola di San Giorgio Maggiore,
daily 7am-6pm, free

Travelers who make the effort to reach

San Giorgio Island can visit the Chiesa di San Giorgio Maggiore and adjacent Benedictine monastery where Cosimo de Medici stayed while banished from Florence. The church is enormous and if the architect's intention was to make parishioners feel small, he succeeded. Supporting columns are massive and the unadorned ceilings nose-bleedingly high. There are several paintings by Tintoretto and few visitors on most mornings.

The main attraction is the view from the *campanile* (**bell tower**, €6) that lies opposite the entrance. On your way to the ticket office take a look at the choir behind the main altar with its intricately carved seating and Q*bert-like marble floor patterns. The *campanile* is slightly smaller than its San Marco counterpart but was also rebuilt after an unexpected collapse. Lines are shorter here and the stairs are out of order with little hope of

being restored, making an elevator the only way up. The panorama at the top is sweeping with Venice, the Lido, Murano, and a distant Burano all in view. This is a great place to observe the busy maritime traffic and the occasional cruise ship being tugged into the city. It can get very windy and you may be startled when the largest of the nine working bells rings out the hour or half hour.

The church and bell tower can be combined with a visit of the **Cini Foundation** (Isola di San Giorgio Maggiore, tel. 041/271-0217, www. cini.it, daily 10am-5pm, €13), which includes paintings, sculpture, and furniture. The foundation is located inside the former Benedictine monastery attached to Chiesa di San Giorgio Maggiore and has played an instrumental part in redeveloping the island and supporting local culture. To see the cloisters, garden, *Last Supper*,

San Giorgio Island

library, and labyrinth, visitors must join one of the guided audio tours that lasts 45 minutes and departs every hour on the hour.

Le Stanze del Vetro

Isola di San Giorgio Maggiore 1,
tel. 041/522-9138, Thurs.-Mon.
10am-7pm, free

It's incredible what can be done with glass and at Le Stanze del Vetro you can discover how ancient and modern craftspeople manipulate this incredibly versatile material. The gallery is located behind the church of San Giorgio and run by an association that organizes two exhibitions per year. Spring and early summer are dedicated to contemporary artists from around the world, while the rest of the year celebrates the city's own glass-making tradition. Exhibitions are free and shown in a bright, modern gallery that's a pleasure to visit. Documentary videos explain the creative process and a small gift shop sells Fabriano stationery and a few select pieces of glass.

SAN POLO AND SANTA CROCE

MUSEUM OF NATURAL HISTORY
(Museo di Storia Naturale)

Santa Croce, Salita Fontego 1730,
tel. 041/270-0370,
www.museiciviciveneziani.it, Jun.-Oct.
Tues.-Sun. 10am-6pm, Nov.-May Tues.-Fri.
9am-5pm and Sat.-Sun. 10am-6pm, €8
or Museum Pass

Venice's natural history museum, Museo di Storia Naturale, isn't just for kids interested in dinosaurs (although there are plenty of those)—it's also the best place to learn about lagoon fauna and biodiversity. Many exhibits are interactive and several rooms contain artifacts dating from the Iron Age.

The museum is housed in the former **Fondaco dei Turchi**, a warehouse once used by Turkish merchants. Foreign traders operating in the city often built their own designated warehouses. This allowed city officials to keep an eye on their movements and confiscate money and weapons upon arrival. No Christian women or children were allowed to enter the area, which was originally equipped with a bathhouse and Turkish eateries. The Fondaco was used for trade until 1838 and eventually transformed into a natural history museum after an extensive restoration.

Museum of Natural History

PALAZZO MOCENIGO

Santa Croce, Salizzada di San Stae 1992,
tel. 041/721-798, www.mocenigo.visitmuve.it,
Apr.-Oct., Tues.-Sun. 10am-5pm, Nov.-Mar.,
Tues.-Sun. 10am-4pm, €8 or Museum Pass

Palazzo Mocenigo provides a glimpse of Venetian aristocrat life. Part of this modest museum is dedicated to perfumes (first floor) and the rest to textiles and costumes. In the 18th century, Venice was continually importing new scents from the Orient and transforming them into scents for the city's well-to-do. Visitors can smell the most popular of these and visit a laboratory where this ancient craft was conducted. Upstairs is filled with fashionable Venetian clothing from yesteryear. The collection includes period ball gowns, waistcoats, hats, and shoes.

You can learn more about perfume making by joining one of the museum's olfactory workshops (two hours, includes tour of museum). Participants discover the basic concepts and classifications of fragrance and create their own personal scent. Workshops must be reserved at least four days in advance and are usually held weekdays from 10am to noon. The cost is €80-100 per person depending on the number of participants, which never exceeds twelve.

The wealthy Mocenigo family who inhabited the *palazzo* included a number of *doges* and financed the building of the **San Stae** church down the street from their residence. The grand classical facade is anything but modest and opens out on the Grand Canal where people wait on the watery steps for the next *vaporetto* to arrive.

RIALTO FISH AND PRODUCE MARKETS

There are markets in squares around the city where everyday Venetian life goes on as it always has, but the Rialto markets are the original center of commerce. The area even has its own *vaporetto* stop. If you disembark at *Rialto Mercato* any morning you'll discover the animated covered **fish market** (daily 7am-2pm). It doesn't get any fresher than this and a stroll beneath the shaded colonnades reveals chefs, housewives, and old-timers bantering with vivacious fishmongers. There are more kinds of fish and crustaceans here than at any supermarket, and having a look is the perfect preview for lunch or dinner. Adjacent to the fish market are the green stalls of the **fruit and vegetable market** (daily,

7am-8pm) selling the latest harvest from the Veneto region and beyond.

You can make a quick getaway to and from the markets on board the **traghetto ferry** that shuttles locals and visitors across the Grand Canal in a modified gondola. It departs every 10 minutes or whenever filled, from the northeastern corner of the fish market. This is one of the best rides in Venice and only costs €2.

BASILICA DI SANTA MARIA GLORIOSA DEI FRARI

San Polo, Campo dei Frari 3072,
www.basilicadeifrari.it, tel. 041/272-8611,
Mon.-Sat. 9am-5:30pm, Sun. 1pm-5:30pm,
€3 or Chorus Pass, audio guide €2

The Basilica di San Marco may be Venice's most famous church, but Basilica di Santa Maria Gloriosa dei Frari is the biggest—and that's not the only thing it has going for it. Inside the plain brick facade favored by Franciscan monks are works by Venetian masters including Vivarini, Bellini, and Titian, who died of the plague and is buried here along with several *doges*. A monument dedicated to him stands near the entrance on the right while the enormous *Annunciation* he painted hangs over the altar. It's not just paintings that stand out—it's the overall craftsmanship visible in the choir stalls, tombs,

Basilica di Santa Maria Gloriosa dei Frari

San Polo and Santa Croce

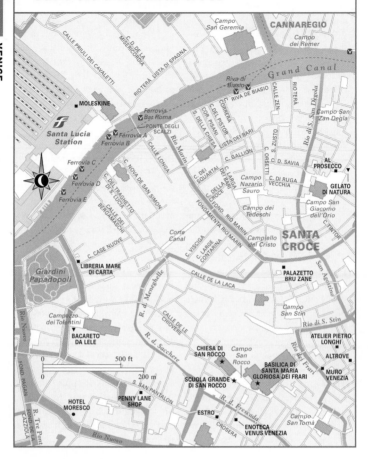

murals, and wooden sculptures. The 15th-century choir in the center of the church is a masterpiece of carpentry, with 50 carved panels illustrating everyday life in Venice.

SCUOLA GRANDE DI SAN ROCCO

San Polo, Campo di San Rocco 3052, tel. 041/523-4864, www.scuolagrandesanrocco.org, daily 9:30am-5:30pm, €10, audio guide €5

Scuola Grande di San Rocco was the last confraternity founded and the best preserved in Venice. The interior avoided looting during Napoleon's sojourn in the city in 1797 and is filled with 73 paintings by Tintoretto alone. The ambitious artist won the competition to paint the first canvas inside by famously installing a completed work rather than the sketch judges were expecting. He avoided a prison sentence by donating the painting and later became a member of the *scuola* where

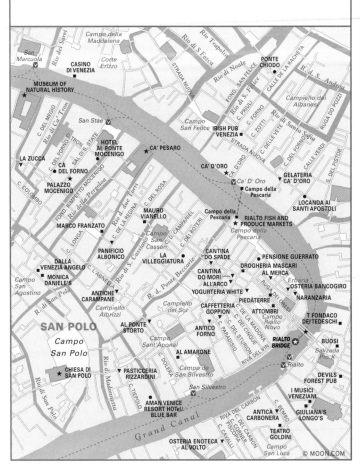

he spent the next 23 years decorating the institution.

Enormous wall and ceiling paintings fill the rectangular *Sala Terrena* on the ground floor that was open to the public and where religious ceremonies were held, and upstairs in the *Sala dell'Albergo* where members still gather. Tintoretto began work on the *Sala Capitolare* next door in 1574. Most of the paintings are religious in nature and recount stories from the New Testament, including the *Fall of Man* and the *Sacrifice of Isaac,* and New Testament themes like the *Last Supper.* The *Sala dell'Albergo* contains Tintoretto's competition-winning entry *St. Roch in Glory* and a stunning *Crucifixion.* An explanation of the paintings is available in English at the entrance.

CHIESA DI SAN ROCCO

Campo San Rocco, daily 9:30am-1pm and 3pm-5:30pm, Sun. mass 11am, free

The Tintoretto tour can continue

TINTORETTO: THE LITTLE TANNER

The name Jacobo Robisti (1519-1594) doesn't ring a lot of bells but you may have heard of **Tintoretto.** It means little tanner, a nickname the artist earned as a child working in his father's tannery. The boy was always ambitious and grew up to be one of the most remarkable painters of his age. His reputation was greatly enhanced by the writings of John Ruskin (1819-1900), who was a great admirer and marveled at the size and visual depth of the canvases. The best places to appreciate these are **Chiesa della Madonna dell'Orto** and the **Scuolo di San Rocco** where the painter audaciously won a competition by bypassing regulations, submitting and installing a completed work rather than a sketch. The Scuola contains 73 works from the painter in the immense ground- and first-floor halls where Venetians met. Subjects are religious in nature and cover both the Old and New Testaments. At a time of widespread illiteracy these were vital ways to illustrate the Bible and remind citizens of the power of man and god. The first painting he completed for the scuola is across the square in the church of San Rocco.

Unlike Rome and Florence, Venice's damp climate was unsuited for fresco painting and wood or canvas were preferred by artists. This was advantageous to painters like Tintoretto who could work in his studio located along the Fondament dei Mori, saving him the kind of grueling backaches Michelangelo endured working on the Sistine Chapel. That didn't mean Tintoretto's paintings were any smaller than those of his Renaissance contemporaries. He mastered the ability to cover colossal spaces with scores of dramatic figures in epic scenes. Unlike many artists who traveled around Italy painting for patrons, Tintoretto remained in Venice his entire life, which may explain why he isn't the most famous Renaissance painter. Even in his hometown he generated contrasting opinions but worked steadily throughout his life and left behind an enormous artistic inheritance that can be seen in churches, palaces, *scuole,* and museums throughout Venice. He was buried in the church of Madonna dell'Orto and it's not uncommon to find fresh flowers on his tomb, presumably laid by one of his modern-day fans.

at the Chiesa di San Rocco opposite the Scuola Grande. The church is owned by the confraternity and contains several paintings that predate the artist's work in the main building. The first of these is *San Rocco che Visita gli Appestati* and depicts the life of St. Roch assisting victims of the plague. The church and school were both named after the saint and the brotherhood was very active in plague relief.

The church is a great place to escape summer heat and observe masterpieces. Canvases are dark yet vivid, and to the right of the altar the future saint is portrayed in a squalid prison cell tending to victims. It's a crowded scene populated by suffering men and women, a dog in the foreground, and a corpse who didn't make it. There is another immense canvas on the opposite side and several more currently undergoing restoration. The guardian might be convinced to let you have a peek at these if you demonstrate interest and discretion.

Another notable aspect of the church is the cantoria. These Baroque structures were added to many churches during the 18th century as a stage for organs and singers. This one was removed and lost for nearly a century until it was accidently discovered in a school gym. The Scuola spent years and millions of euros (it was *lire* at the time) restoring it with the help of local apprentices. If you look at the two-story construction from the altar it blends in perfectly and the columns at the entrance appear as solid as the walls behind them. Once you touch them it's clear they're hollow and made of wood. The restored cantoria is often used and there are frequent free concerts.

Opening times vary according to restoration that's expected to be completed in 2020.

CAMPO SAN POLO

Campo San Polo became the largest square in the *sestiere* when a canal was filled and paved over. The parallel lines of white stone on the curved end of the square indicate exactly where the waterway once ran. Venetians have used the square for horse racing, bullfights, and masked *Carnevale* parties for centuries. Today it's a playground for children and a peaceful retreat for residents who sit on the red benches in the shade of a half-dozen trees. There's a newsstand at one end near the flagpole that gets used on special occasions. From July to September the *campo* is transformed into an open-air cinema (€5-8, or 6 films for €24) and throughout the Venice Film Festival movies are projected after their Lido premieres.

Chiesa di San Polo

Salita San Polo, Mon.-Sat. 10:30am-4:30pm, €3 or Chorus Pass

Chiesa di San Polo, located in the *campo*, is even older than the square and was founded by Doge Pietro Gradonico in AD 737 with significant modifications in the 14th and 15th centuries. The church doesn't face the square and visitors must walk around the corner to reach the entrance and see the bell tower with the two stone lions carved into its base that represent the city.

CA' PESARO

Santa Croce, Fondamenta de Ca' Pesaro 2076, tel. 041/721-127,

www.capesaro.visitmuve.it, Tues.-Sun. 10am-6pm, €10 or Museum Pass

Ca' Pesaro isn't just a pretty facade along the Grand Canal. It's home to two remarkable museums in one stunning 17th-century *palazzo*. The first two floors are occupied by the Galleria Internazionale d'Arte Moderna with works by Chagall, Kandinsky, Klee, Matisse, and Moore. Paintings from early editions of the Venice Art Biennale also ended up hanging here. Highlights include *Giudetta II* by Klimt and a version of *The Thinker* by Rodin. Guided two-hour tours (education@fmcvenezia.it, €100/1-4 people) of the collection explore the artistic trends and innovations of the 20th century.

Upstairs, the Museo d'Arte Orientale displays more than 30,000 artworks and artifacts Prince Enrico di Borbone gathered during his grand tour of Asia. It's the largest collection of Edo-era objects outside of Japan and a drastic departure from the Venetian landscape. There are kimonos, lacquer furnishings, porcelain, paintings, shadow puppets, weaponry, and everyday personal items. The dark wood-paneled rooms also contain jade-and-gold-painted shells from China. A short video in Italian and English explains the origins of the collection.

A single ticket provides entry to both museums. A small cafeteria on the ground floor serves both museums, and a cloakroom and bookshop are located near the main entrance.

CANNAREGIO

GRAND CANAL
(Canal Grande)

The Grand Canal is the busiest and most important waterway in Venice. It snakes through the center of the city

SCHOOLS OF VENICE

Scuole or schools were (and in some cases, still are) important institutions in Venice. The word shouldn't be confused with its modern definition; it takes the Greek meaning of *association or confraternity*. Historically, doges and ruling nobles of Venetian society were more interested in politics, trade, and war than they were in their citizens' well being. The first scuola were founded in the 11th century in reaction to this, as a way to assist the poor and provide plague relief to citizens and foreigners residing in the city.

Scuole are secular organizations. There were six great schools or *scuole grande* and hundreds of little schools or *scuole piccole*. The latter represented the interests of the various trades active in the city and acted a little like modern unions. They also settled disputes between members, regulated trade standards, and oversaw apprenticeship. The *scuole grande* were concerned with charitable activities and ensured the city survived plagues and recurrent crises that regularly befell Venice.

The *scuole grande* grew from small, meager groups into wealthy bastions, each with its own meeting house and church or chapel. The desire to impress and outdo one another meant a lot of time and money was invested into the embellishment of facades and interiors where the public and members met. Leading artists were commissioned and no expense was spared. Napoleon closed most of the schools during his occupation of the city in 1797 and sent a lot of art back to the Louvre in Paris. The only exception was Scuola Grande di San Rocco, which the emperor allowed to go on assisting the devasted population.

Today, San Rocco continues its charitable mission and carries on many traditions that were initiated centuries ago. New members must still be presented by an existing member and receive a majority of votes to be accepted. During the annual ceremony, a golden ball is used to ensure brothers don't leave the meeting early. Everyone is given a numbered ticket and at the end, members are called one by one to pick from an urn filled with hundreds of bronze metal balls and a single golden ball. If the *palla d'oro* is not selected (due to absentee members) the gold is donated to charity.

from Stazione Santa Lucia station to Piazza San Marco. The canal is lined with prestigious *palazzi*, churches, and former warehouses. It's always animated, especially on weekday mornings when boats of all kinds move up and down making deliveries, removing trash, and shuttling residents and visitors between 23 *vaporetto* stops. There is no continuous embankment along the canal, but there are partial promenades near the train station, north and south of the Rialto Bridge, and at the entrance to the canal itself in front of Santa Maria della Salute church and Piazza San Marco. You can get inviting glimpses of the canal from the four bridges that cross it or the many streets that lead to it, but the only way to see it all is by *vaporetto*, gondola, or renting a boat.

JEWISH GHETTO

The word *ghetto* derives from the Venetian *geto,* a part of Cannaregio where iron foundries were located. It became associated with Jews during the 14th century when they were ordered to live in the area. Their lives were closely regulated: Although they could leave during the day, guards stationed along the canals made sure residents remained in the ghetto at night. It wasn't until Napoleon arrived in 1797 that the gates were removed and Jews allowed to live anywhere they liked. A small but vibrant Jewish community is still based here and worship in synagogues that are among the oldest in Italy.

Campo di Ghetto Nuovo is the center of the neighborhood. It's a large, unevenly shaped *campo* with a

Cannaregio

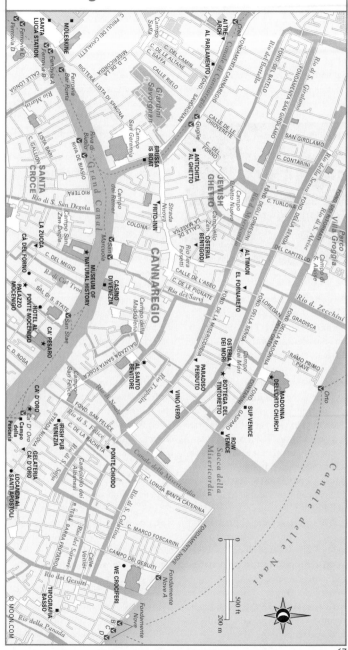

SANTA LUCIA STATION
MOLESKINE
Ferrovia G
Ferrovia D
Ferrovia A
Ferrovia B
CALLE LONGA
Rio Marin
Ferrovia
Bar Roma
LISTA DI SPAGNA
C. D. PRIULI DEI CAVALLETTI
MISERICORDIA FOND.
C. DE LA SAFFA
C. DELLE ALTANE
C. DEL CAMIN
ALTRE
ARCHI
AL PARLAMENTO
Crea
Campo di Cannaregio
Campo Saffa
FONDAMENTA CANNAREGIO
Canale di Cannaregio
Rio del Batèllo
FOND. DEL BATÈLO
FONDAMENTA SAN GIROLAMO
Rio di S. Girolamo
FOND. DELLA SENSA
SAN GIROLAMO
C. CONTARINI
Rio della Sensa
FOND. Gh. TURLONA
FOND. DELLA SENSA
DEL CAPITELLO
Campo di S. Alvise
Villa Groggia
Parco
FONDAMENTA SAN ALVISE
Rio di S. Alvise
FOND. DELLA MADONNA
Rio d. Zecchini

RIOTERA LISTA DI SPAGNA
FONDAMENTA FOND. SAVORGNAN
Giardini Savorgnan
CALLE RIELLO
CALLE DE LE CHIOVERETE
Riva di Biasio
RIVA DE BIASIO
Riva di Biasio
Campo San Geremia
Campo dei Reniér
C. D. GALLION
LISTA BARI
SANTA CROCE
Grand Canal
Rio di S. San Degola
Campo San Zan Degola
LA ZUCCA
CA' DEL FORNO
C. DEL MEGIO
R. di Ca' Tron
MUSEUM OF NATURAL HISTORY
SAL DI S. STAE
San Stae
PALAZZO MOCENIGO
PONTE MOCENIGO
HOTEL AL PONTE MOCENIGO
CA' PESARO
C. D. ROSA
CA' D'ORO
Campo della Pescaria
IRISH PUB SANTA VENEZIA
GELATERIA CA' D'ORO
STRADA NUOVA
STRADA NUOVA
LOCANDA AI SANTI APOSTOLI

BRUSSA IS BOAT
ANTICHITÀ AL GHETTO
CALLE DEL FORNO
Guglie
FRITO-INN
Strada Nuova
COLONA
San Marcuola
Rio Marcuola
Campo San Maddalena
SALIZADA SANTA FOSCA
GALIZADA SANTA FOSCA
Campo San Felice
FOND. SAN FELICE
Rio di S. Felice
C. DE LA RACHETA
CASINÒ DI VENEZIA
CA' ZUCCA
AL SANTO BEVITORE
Rio della Misericordia
Campiello dei Alberti
PONTE CHIODO

JEWISH GHETTO
Campo Ghetto Nuovo
Campo Ghetto Nuovo
Campiello Zen
CALLE DE LA MASENA
OSTERIA BENTIGODI
Rio Tera Farsetti
CALLE DE L'ASEO
C. DE LE PIGNATE
Rio dei Sarvi
AL TIMON
EL FORNARETO
FOND. DE LA MISERICORDIA
FOND. DELLA SENSA
Campo dei Mori
OSTERIA DEI MORI
BOTTEGA DEL TINTORETTO
PARADISO PERDUTO
VINO VERO
Rio della Sensa
FOND. DELLA MISERICORDIA
FOND. GRADISCA
RAMO PRIMO PIAVE
RAMO PRIMO PIAVE
MADONNA DELL'ORTO CHURCH
SUP VENICE
FOND. GASPARO
ROW VENICE
Sacca della Misericordia
Orto

Canale delle Navi

C. LONGA SANTA CATERINA
Rio della Misericordia
Canale della Misericordia
R. dei Servi
Rio di S. Catarina
Calle Venier
C. MARCO FOSCARINI
Rio dei Gesuiti
Rio della Panada
CAMPO DEI GESUITI
WE CROCIFERI
TIPOGRAFIA BASSO
Fondamente Nove A
Fondamente Nove
Fondamente Nove B
C
D

© MOON.COM

0   500 ft
0   200 m

handful of trees and marble benches where workers and visitors pause for lunch. There are Holocaust memorials on several walls and a number of kosher restaurants lining the square. (These are closed Saturdays during Sabbath and it's best to visit on weekdays or Sundays if you want to sample Venetian kosher.)

Jewish quarter

The **Synagogue** and **Museo Ebraico** (Cannaregio, Campo Ghetto Nuovo, tel. 041/715-359, www.museoebraico.it, Jun.-Sept. Sun.-Fri. 10am-7pm, Oct.-May Sun.-Fri. 10am-5:30pm, €8 or €12 with tour, or City Pass) are in the southwestern corner in front of the old rainwater wells and the tall wooden flagpole. The museum is divided in two parts that illustrate Jewish traditions and recount the long history of Venetian Jews through objects, images, and firsthand accounts. **Tours** depart hourly starting from 10:30am and are conducted in Italian and English.

There are several approaches to the Ghetto, but the historic route is along **Calle Ghetto Vecchio.** When approaching from the train station follow Rio Terra Lista all the way to Ponte delle Guglie. Cross the bridge, turn left, and take the second right through the underpass that marks the main entrance to the Ghetto.

MADONNA DELL'ORTO CHURCH
(Chiesa della Madonna dell'Orto)

Cannaregio, Fondamenta Madonna dell'Orto, tel. 041/719-933, Mon.-Sat. 10am-5pm, Sun. noon-5pm, €3 or Chorus Pass

Chiesa Madonna dell'Orto is one of the largest churches in the *sestiere,* which may explain why German troops used it as a stable during World War II. It was in bad shape for decades until an Englishman (buried in the chapel near the altar) bequeathed funds to restore the church. The elegant facade and modest interior now look as good as they did when the church was built in the 14th century. It's a great example of Venice's take on Gothic architecture and was Tintoretto's local parish. The artist donated over a dozen large-scale biblical paintings to the church that draw a trickle of tourists. If you're lucky, one of the many dedicated volunteers will be on duty and can answer questions about the building or the artist. **Mass** is held daily at 9am weekdays and 11am on Sunday, but the organ that was intended for Teatro La Fenice is only played during weddings and funerals.

Tintoretto is buried inside the church, and there are often flowers lying on the marble plaque marking his grave. The artist lived and worked just over the bridge facing the church on Fondamenta dei Mori.

Bottega del Tintoretto

Cannaregio, Fondamenta dei Mori 3400, tel. 041/722-081, daily 10am-7pm, free

There's no museum or trace of the painter but it's still worth stopping by Bottega del Tintoretto to watch the artisans, sculptors, printers, and lithographers who now occupy the building. If you're interested in ink, bookbinding, and printing, Roberto and other members of his craft association will gladly explain their techniques.

CA' D'ORO

Cannaregio, Calle Ca' d'Oro 3932,
tel. 041/520-0345, www.cadoro.org,
Tues.-Sun. 10am-6pm, €11, audio guide €4

Venice never fully embraced Renaissance architecture, and instead maintained the Gothic status quo long after the movement had gone out of fashion in other cities. This explains the intricate facades lining the Grand Canal. If you're going to enter any of these ornate family residences, the Ca' d'Oro is a good option. The home dates from the 15th century but it's the later restoration that is visible today; it was donated to the city in 1916 along with an extensive collection of sculpture, tapestries, paintings, and pottery that's on display today.

The ground floor contains a small courtyard with the original well and early 20th-century mosaic paving that leads to a private dock. Temporary exhibitions of modern artists are staged in the former reception halls upstairs while the smaller rooms are lined with religious paintings, including Mantegna's *St. Sebastian*. The best feature of the building is the terrace that

Palazzo Ca' d'Oro on the Grand Canal

overlooks the waterway and allows visitors to observe the comings and goings along the Grand Canal below.

CASTELLO
SCUOLA GRANDE DI SAN MARCO

Castello, Fondamenta Mendicante 6776,
tel. 041/529-4323,
www.scuolagrandesanmarco.it,
Tues.-Sat. 9:30am-5:30pm, €5

With its ornate entrance and statue of Saint Mark, it's easy to mistake Scuola Grande di San Marco for a church, but the refined *palazzo* facing Campo Giovanni e Paolo isn't a religious building. Scuola Grande is a *scuola,* the Venetian version of the Lion's Club, founded by do-gooders in the 13th century and used as a fancy clubhouse until Napoleon abolished fraternal organizations in the city.

The *scuola* was reopened in 2013 and the facade is an eyeful. There are interesting uses of perspective, elaborate stonework that distinguishes Venetian Renaissance architecture from Florentine and Roman designs—and plenty of lions. The grand entrance on the left leads to a reception hall while the relatively modest doorway on the right provides access to the *albergo* and is usually closed. The interior was stripped of artwork after the brotherhood disbanded but the two main rooms upstairs regained their former opulence during a lengthy restoration. *Sala Capitolare* contains a collection of medical artifacts and several paintings by Tintoretto recounting the life of St. Mark. The walls in *Sala dell'Albergo* next door are also dedicated to the saint. Both rooms have massive engraved ceilings.

The square out front is one of the

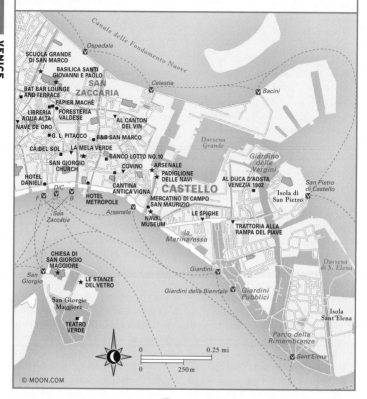

Castello

SCUOLA GRANDE
DI SAN MARCO

BASILICA SANTI
GIOVANNI E PAOLO

Ospedale

Canale delle Fondamento Nuove

SAN
ZACCARIA

Celestia

Bacini

BAT BAR LOUNGE
AND TERRACE

PAPIER MACHÉ

LIBRERIA   FORESTERIA
AQUA ALTA   VALDESE
NAVE DE ORO

AL CANTON
DEL VIN

G. L. PITACCO   B&B SAN MARCO

CÀ DEL SOL   LA MELA VERDE

SAN GIORGIO
CHURCH

BANCO LOTTO NO.10

COVINO   ARSENALE

HOTEL
DANIELI

D/C

PADIGLIONE
DELLE NAVI

CANTINA
ANTICA VIGNA

HOTEL
METROPOLE

Arsenale

Darsena
Grande

CASTELLO

AL DUCA D'AOSTA
VENEZIA 1902

MERCATINO DI CAMPO
SAN MAURIZIO

LE SPIGHE

Giardino
delle
Vergini

San Pietro
di Castello

Isola di
San Pietro

San
Zaccaria

NAVAL
MUSEUM

La
Marinaressa

TRATTORIA ALLA
RAMPA DEL PIAVE

CHIESA DI
SAN GIORGIO
MAGGIORE

San
Giorgio

LE STANZE
DEL VETRO

Giardini

Darsena
di S. Elena

San Giorgio
Maggiore

TEATRO
VERDE

Giardini della Biennale

Giardini
Pubblici

Isola
Sant'Elena

Parco della
Rimembranze

Sant'Elena

0   0.25 mi

0   250 m

© MOON.COM

nicest in Castello and a lovely place to linger. Café tables line the southern edge of the square underneath a bronze equestrian statue of a local mercenary and gelato can be purchased nearby.

Basilica Santi Giovanni e Paolo

Mon.-Sat. 9am-6pm and Sun. noon-6pm, €4

The cavernous Basilica Santi Giovanni e Paolo is the final resting place of many illustrious Venetians, with enormous stained-glass windows created in Murano that are best viewed from the inside. Mass is held at 8am and 6:30pm on weekdays and 9am, 11am, and 6:30pm on weekends.

SAN GIORGIO CHURCH (Chiesa di San Giorgio dei Greci)

Castello, Ponte dei Greci 3412, tel. 041/523-9569, Mon.-Sat. 9am-12:30pm and 2:30pm-4:30pm, Sun. 9am-1pm, free

Greeks have a long history in Venice. They were attracted to the city for its commercial ties to the Orient and tended to settle in Castello, and their numbers grew even larger after the Turks captured Constantinople in 1453. Eventually the Orthodox community wanted a church of its own. Permission to build the Chiesa di San Giorgio was granted in 1498. The single-nave structure was completed a century later in one of the most

VENICE
SIGHTS

tranquil parts of the city. The imposing bell tower cannot be visited, but a small museum can and contains a collection of colorful Byzantine icons.

ARSENALE

Castello, Campo del Arsenale,
tel. 041/241-2020, Mon.-Fri. 9am-6pm, free

Venice wouldn't have been possible without an imposing fleet of ships that controlled the Eastern Mediterranean and the islands of Crete and Cyprus. Those vessels were built in the Arsenale, the world's first large-scale shipyard. The Arsenale was active for seven centuries, employing over 2,000 workers at its peak, and takes up 15 percent of the city's land mass.

Today, it's used by the Italian Navy and as an exhibition space during the Venice Biennale. The best view of the complex is from the wooden bridge at the end of Fondamenta dell'Arsenale. Four immense stone lions guard the imposing twin-tower entrance and demonstrate just how important the site was to the city. Although there are plans to transform the Arsenale into a cultural center, most of the area is closed to the public and open during special exhibitions. What can be visited is entered near either of the two *vaporetto* stops (Celestia or Bacini Arsenale). Arriving on the 4.1 or 5.1 ferry not only makes a dramatic entrance but can save you walking to one of the most distant parts of the city.

NAVAL MUSEUM
(Museo Storico Navale)

Castello, Riva S. Bagio 2148,
tel. 041/244-1399, daily 10am-6pm, €10

To get an even better idea of Venice's seafaring past head to **Museo Storico Navale**, located near the Arsenale. This museum covers five floors and several centuries of history. The first

two are the most relevant and document how Venice created and retained its naval superiority. There are extensive collections of navigational instruments, uniforms, and models of the vessels used for trade and warfare. The museum was reopened last year after a structural makeover.

Padiglione Delle Navi

Rio della Tana Castello 2162/C,
tel. 041/2424, daily 8:45am-5pm, €5

Actual merchant ships, warships, and gondolas can be seen close-up in the adjacent Padiglione Delle Navi. A single ticket allows entry to both this museum and the Museo Storico Navale.

RIVA DEGLI SCHIAVONE

Venice has a split personality, one that's depressingly crowded and another that's melancholy and tranquil. Sometimes the two can be experienced in a single location, and depending on the hour you may love or hate Riva degli Schiavone. In the early morning and evening this wide promenade stretching from Piazza San Marco to the Biennale Gardens is nearly deserted and the dramatic views of the lagoon can be enjoyed in relative peace. In between those times the embankment is lined with pleasure boats, souvenir stands, and itinerant salespeople hawking cheap gadgets to tourists and cruise ship passengers. Choose your moment well, and remember that the further you get from Piazza San Marco the quieter things become until you eventually reach the solitude of Sant'Elena Island at the southeastern tip of Venice.

SANT'ELENA ISLAND
(Isola Sant'Elena)

There's little to see in the touristic sense on Sant'Elena Island—and that's

CRUISING VENICE'S CANALS

Venice is a city at one with the sea, and if you don't step on board a gondola, *vaporetto,* or water taxi you're missing out on the best part. The views from a boat help make sense of the city and seduce the eyes in a way walking cannot.

GONDOLA

Gondolas are so closely linked with Venice that it's hard to imagine one without the other, and a ride does live up to clichés. If you decide to hire a gondola, it's important to choose a good point of departure. There are eleven **gondola stations** as well as vessels docked in ones or twos around the city. Some, like those near San Marco, are so busy shuttling passengers under the Bridge of Sighs that a ride feels like being on a merry-go-round. You'll also share the experience with hundreds of eager onlookers and end up in who knows how many photographs. It's more romantic to depart from quieter *sestiere,* like Dorsoduro or Castello, where canals are uncluttered and you can glide past one of the last *squero* (gondola workshops) in Venice.

The profession is highly regulated, and prices are fixed at €80 for a 40-minute ride during the day and €100 after 7pm on a gondola that seats up to six passengers. The gondoliers themselves are romantic figures dressed in red- or blue-striped shirts and conscious of the historical role they play. Some will point out landmarks along the way while others will keep to themselves, silently navigating the canals. None are required to sing although a couple still do. The profession is often handed down from generation to generation and it's not uncommon for multiple members of the same family to practice this ancient trade. Today there are 453 gondoliers left and they are nearly all men although several women have obtained licenses in recent years. Getting one from the city council is a time-consuming and strenuous affair that can take up to ten years.

TRAGHETTO

Anyone who doesn't want to invest time or money in a full-fledged gondola excursion can get the condensed experience at the *traghetti* (gondola ferry) stations along the Grand Canal. There are three landings still in activity: **Santa Sofia** (weekdays 7:30am-7pm, weekends 8:45am-7pm), **San Tomà** (weekdays 7:30am-8pm, weekends 8:30am-7:30pm), and **Santa Maria del Giglio** (weekdays 7am-6pm, weekends 9am-7pm), where two-man teams shuttle residents and adventurous travelers across the Grand Canal in refitted gondolas. One of the ferry points is located in Cannaregio near the Ca d'Oro and connects the neighborhood with the fish market in San Polo close to the Rialto. The other two are near Piazza San Marco. Santa Maria del Giglio is especially convenient for reaching the Punta della

what makes it worth visiting. It's out of the way by Venetian standards and can take ages to reach on foot. It's easier to ride the *vaporetto* and get off at the Sant' Elena stop. The island is wrapped in a tree-lined park and most of the residential housing in the center was built in the 1920s. There are few businesses and only a couple of simple eateries serving unadulterated classics. On the westernmost point is the modest Chiesa di Sant'Elena, where the remains of Emperor Constantine's mother are preserved. Nearby are two marinas filled with private yachts and a rickety stadium where Venice's lower-league soccer team play.

aquatic traffic along the Grand Canal

Dogana lookout point in Dorsoduro. A single ride (€2) lasts less than five minutes and is the most thrilling way of crossing Venice's busiest canal.

✪ VAPORETTO

Vaporetto, the aquatic equivalent of buses, are typical Venetian ferries that carry up to 210 passengers and form the backbone of the city's public transportation network. They've been serving the city since the late 19th century and make getting around easy. They regularly serve water stops along the Grand Canal, around the city's circumference, and in outlying islands throughout the lagoon. *Vaporetto* can be crowded and finding a seat on deck is often difficult, but standing along the open railing provides an equally great view and is quite romantic, especially at night when there are far fewer passengers and the distant lights of the city take on mysterious tones. You can buy a single ticket (€7.50), but the best option is a 24-hour (€20) or 48-hour (€30) pass that allows unlimited travel. *Vaporetto* operate day and night, and make it fun to discover secluded parts of the city like Giudecca, Isola di San Giorgio, and the Biennale Gardens, all of which are impossible or difficult to reach on foot.

The number 1 or 2 *vaporetto* from Santa Lucia train station provide a dramatic introduction to the city. They make 16 stops along the Grand Canal all the way to Piazza San Marco in 30-40 minutes. There are 21 lines in all and maps can be downloaded from ACTV (www.actv.avmspa.it) or studied at individual stops. There is a dedicated night service (N) and many seasonal lines that operate during the summer.

GIUDECCA

There's another side to Venice and it's called Giudecca. It may be less beautiful and house fewer monuments than its more illustrious neighbors but it's also blissfully less crowded. Although part of Venice, Guidecca can only be reached by *vaporetto,* which keeps tour groups and day-trippers away. Here you get a real sense of what it feels like to live on an island and watch locals going about their business as though they didn't live in the world's most beautiful city.

The long embankment that runs along the northern edge of Giudecca is the main artery and provides great views of Dorsoduro. Most bars and

73

Giudecca

restaurants are clustered along here and the **Palanca** *vaporetto* stop is the liveliest bit. If you've made it this far you should explore the backstreets of the island (actually 13 islets in one) where you'll stumble upon churches, public housing, hostels, stray cats, a women's prison, a luxury rooftop bar, and some surprises in between.

The biggest surprise and the only time of year Giudecca attracts thousands of visitors is during the **Festa del Redentore** when the city celebrates the end of a medieval plague and a pontoon bridge is built across the Giudecca Canal.

REDENTORE CHURCH
(Chiesa del Redentore)

Campo del SS. Redentore 195,
tel. 041/275-0462, daily 10:30am-4:30pm,
€3 or Chorus Pass

Plagues were an everyday reality in 16th-century Venice, and when they hit they decimated the city's population. After nearly 50,000 people died from a plague in the early 1570s, it was natural to commemorate the end of the epidemic by building a church. Palladio was commissioned and Chiesa del Redentore was completed in 1580. The exquisitely proportioned facade looks out over the waterfront and is topped with a distinct white dome flanked by twin spires.

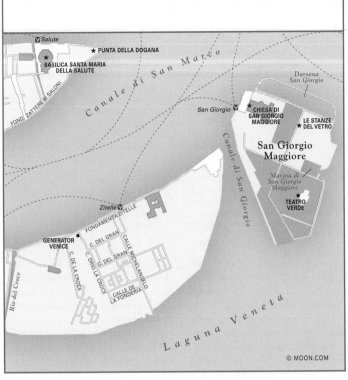

© MOON.COM

The church was decorated by Bassano and Tintoretto but it's the overall harmony of the space inside that makes it stunning. This is where the city's most popular festival takes place on the third Sunday in July, during which a pontoon footbridge is erected between Giudecca and Dorsoduro that attracts thousands of fervent Venetians.

Food

Venetian culinary traditions have a lot to do with geography and history. Unlike the landlocked cities of Rome and Florence, Venice has easy access to the sea. The fisheries you may have noticed as your train approached the city raise sea bass, sole, and sardines that are available at the central fish market, which also sells shrimp, crab, and other crustaceans that end up on plates around the city.

Venice's status as a seafaring power meant that exotic flavors and spices like pepper, clove, and cinnamon were imported from around the Mediterranean and adapted to local dishes. Long voyages meant food was prepared and preserved in creative

THE SMALLEST STREET IN VENICE

Venice has dozens of streets narrow enough to touch both walls at the same time. In these remote, dimly lit passages, silence reigns, and the city seems suddenly distant. Many are difficult to find and some are so small they don't appear on maps. Most travelers avoid these secret routes and choose more inviting directions, but the miniature streets of Venice are a remarkable and exciting part of the city's unique urban landscape.

There's debate on which *calle* is the tiniest but most locals agree **Calletta Varisco** (Cannaregio, near Campo Widman) holds the title. At its narrowest point the alley measures 21 inches (53 centimeters) across and turns two-way pedestrian traffic into a game of Twister. Fortunately, there are few people around and once you pass the Doric column time stands still. The *calle* dramatically ends in a canal and one might wonder why it was built in the first place. Dead ends, however, are an essential part of the city's transportation network. Where paving stops, water always begins.

Across the Grand Canal in San Polo **Calle Stretta,** 26 inches (66 centimeters) connects Campiello Albrizzi with the Furatola underpass. To the north in Santa Croce near the Riva de Biasio water stop is **Calle di Ca' Zusto,** barely 27 inches (68 centimeters) wide. **Calesela dell'Occhio Grosso** near Campo dell Gorne underneath the walls of the Arsenale is a mere 23 inches (58 centimeters) wide.

ways. Large communities of Jews, Greeks, and Turks also contributed a multicultural element to dishes that can still be tasted today.

Each *sestiere* is divided into smaller neighborhoods with their own church and, equally important, bakery where residents come for bread and local pastries. These are wonderful shops with large gas or electric ovens where dough is baked daily for residents.

DINING TIPS

Take care when choosing a restaurant in Venice. Many eateries near the train station and along busy routes to the Rialto and San Marco rely entirely on one-time tourist trade, and no Venetian with an appetite would ever eat there. Also, remember that fish is often priced by the 100 grams, which can result in an astronomical bill if you're not careful.

Expect the price of eating out in Venice to be higher than you may expect. This is due to added transportation costs, a limited number of venues, and high demand. Fish is pricier than meat, and it's hard to find a first course

under €10 or a second under €15. Fortunately there are many wonderful places to dine or snack and it's difficult not to be satisfied after an authentic Venetian meal.

A final note: All establishments are legally obliged to provide customers with a receipt. If they forget, remind them by asking for *il scontrino per favore* (Ill scon-TREE-no Pear fah-VOR-ay). By doing so, you're ensuring they pay taxes and doing all Italians a favor.

SAN MARCO
VENETIAN
Vini da Arturo

Calle Degli Assassini 3656, tel. 041/528-6974, Mon.-Sat. noon-2:30pm and 7pm-10:30pm, closed Aug., €15, cash only

With 20 seats, one waiter, and a chef, Ernesto Ballarin's small restaurant Vini da Arturo is a wonderful place to take a breather just north of Teatro Fenice. While many Venetian restaurants focus on fish, meat and vegetables are the stars here. There are tender filets of beef, breaded pork chops *(maiale alla Veneziana),* distinctive salads, and plenty of pasta *(spaghetti*

⭐ **BECCAFICO:** Enjoy fresh seafood with a Sicilian twist on an outdoor terrace overlooking one of the most vivacious squares in Venice (page 78).

⭐ **CAFFÈ FLORIAN:** This historic café facing Piazza San Marco dates back centuries—and has a faded elegance not even tourists can tarnish (page 79).

⭐ **AL BOTTEGON:** Enjoy one of the best *enoteche* in Venice from its wonderfully gritty interior or outside along the canal (page 80).

⭐ **DA NICO:** This century-old shop invented hazelnut and cacao-flavored *giandiotto* gelato. Its terrace has scenic canal views (page 81).

⭐ **ANTICHE CARAMPANE:** The best fish in the city is served in a simple but elegant atmosphere (page 84).

⭐ **CANTINA DO MORI:** Fresh fish, delivered daily, is transformed into delicious creamed cod and fried calamari, accompanied by *prosecco* (page 84).

⭐ **VINO VERO:** This hole-in-the-wall is packed with grape enthusiasts enjoying tempting *cicchetti* (page 89).

⭐ **BLUE BAR:** An elegant second-story bar at the Aman Venice Resort Hotel overlooking the Grand Canal (page 97).

---

alla gorgonzola). Framed photos of satisfied celebrities hang on the wood-paneled walls. If you're curious to see all the famous faces Ernesto has fed, ask to see the photo albums.

La Rosticceria Gislon

Calle della Bissa 5424a, tel. 041/522-3569, daily 9am-9:30pm, €10-€12

La Rosticceria Gislon is the Venetian version of a diner. You can sit at a table or the counter next to locals vying for sandwiches and roast fish and meat dishes served from large tins behind the counter. This is where the postman goes for lunch. Most tourists are intimidated by the confusion inside, but it's hard to find a more affordable lunch spot so close to the Rialto. If the downstairs area is too crowded, head upstairs.

Museum Café

Palazzo Grassi, Campo San Samuele 3231, Wed.-Mon. 10am-7pm, €18

The Museum Café, opened in 2018, is as stylish as the rest of Palazzo Grassi in which it's located, and an original lunch option. Several tables look out over the Grand Canal and the menu includes a vegetarian burger. Chef Marta Munerato, who trained under Gordon Ramsey and legendary Italian chef Gualtiero Marchesi, conjures up a daily special from scratch every morning. Expect stellar dishes at reasonable prices. Entry to the café requires a ticket to Palazzo Grassi, and combining lunch with a visit of the modern art gallery stimulates all the senses.

SEAFOOD
✪ Beccafico

Campo Santo Stefano 2801,
tel. 041/527-4879, daily noon-3pm
and 7pm-11pm, €15-20

Campo Santo Stefano is one of the most vivacious squares in Venice, and dining on the outdoor terrace of upscale Beccafico is a treat. The restaurant provides a Sicilian twist on local specialties. The fresh fish and crustaceans are the best reason to come. First courses like pasta with sardines and *zuppa di cozze* (mussel soup) are abundant and flavorful. The delicate seconds include grilled bream with citrus, stuffed swordfish, and large plates of fried fish and vegetables. Sicilian-style pizza is also served at lunch and the kitchen closes later than at most Venetian restaurants.

Antica Carbonera

Calle Bembo 4648, tel. 041/522-5479, daily
11:30am-3pm and 6:30pm-10:30pm, €15

Antica Carbonera has been maintaining Venetian gastronomic traditions since 1894. Portions are generous and served in copper skillets by an attentive staff. There are several dining rooms and the ground floor is decorated in salvaged nautical furnishings. It's cozy, especially if you sit in one of the booths lining the wall. Upstairs is a modern dining area and small terrace. The menu is all about fish, and *Cruditè di Giornata* (raw fish plate) includes fresh salmon, sea bream, bass, tuna, shrimp, and oysters. Pasta and desserts are all handmade daily at this historic *trattoria*.

CICCHETTI
Osteria Enoteca al Volto

Calle Cavalli 4081, tel. 041/522-8945,
daily 10am-3pm and 6pm-10pm, €10

Located on a quiet street near the Grand Canal, Osteria Enoteca al Volto can satisfy any *cicchetti* craving. There isn't much room inside the wood-paneled interior, and most visitors stand at the bar sipping glasses of wine and wondering whether to order the creamed cod or fried calamari on a stick. If you're lucky, one of the tables outside will be free and you can go back for seconds and thirds of the €3 house *prosecco*.

Bacarando

Calle dell'Orso 5495, tel. 041/523-8280,
daily 10:30am-11pm

Bacarando is one of the newer *bacari* bars in the city. It's spread out on two floors and features live music on Wednesday nights. There's seating outside in a pleasant courtyard where a range of *cicchetti* (€1-3) can be enjoyed with inexpensive wine.

PIZZA
Rossopomodoro

Calle Larga Rosa 404, tel. 041/243-8949,
daily 11:30am-11:30pm, €10

Not all chain restaurants should necessarily be avoided. If you feel like having a Neapolitan pizza in Venice, Rossopomodoro can satisfy a *Margherita* craving. You won't wait long at this large, modern restaurant, which has indoor and outdoor seating and a wood-burning oven in one corner where you can watch pizza being prepared. Toppings are fresh and prices reasonable given the proximity to Piazza San Marco.

BAKERIES
Colussi

Campo San Luca 4579, tel. 041/522-2659,
Mon.-Sat. 8am-2pm and 4:30pm-7:30pm

The Colussi family has produced six generations of bakers and know what they're doing when it comes to bread.

Inside their marble-clad shop, Colussi, you'll find an array of fresh loaves and Venetian cookies including *Zaletti, Pan del Pescatore,* and *Buranelli.* Many are prepacked and make delicious gifts.

GELATO
Suso
Calle della Bissa 5453, tel. 348/564-6545, daily 10am-midnight, €4

Suso is a small *gelateria* amid the busy streets around the Rialto and can be difficult to find. Flavors change according to the season and they're one of the only shops in the city that offer edible cups and cacao-flavored cones. *Moro di Venezia* and chocolate are the local favorites.

Gelato Fantasy
Calle dei Fabbri 929, tel. 041/522-5993, daily 10am-11:30pm, €3

For a generous scoop from a takeout-only gelateria try Gelato Fantasy. Nutella is the house specialty but they also make great dark chocolate and strawberry. If you're undecided let the friendly, English-speaking staff guide you or choose at random. It's impossible to go wrong.

COFFEE
The cafés of San Marco are nearly as famous as the square itself and have shared in the history of the city. They're extremely elegant, with chandeliered interiors, plush furnishings, and uniformed waitstaff who have spent lifetimes serving visitors. Each café provides outdoor seating from where you can admire the monuments and listen to musicians playing classical music on small stages facing the square.

Location and history comes with a price tag. Do not expect to pay the same for an espresso or *prosecco* in Piazza San Marco as in other squares. A cup of coffee that usually sells for €2 can cost €7 or more. If you add a couple of drinks, some snacks, and a dessert you could be looking at a three-digit bill. Either you don't care and count it as a once-in-a-lifetime experience, or go inside and drink at the bar where there's as much atmosphere at a fraction of the cost. Prices vary, especially at institutions like Harry's Bar where Arturo Toscanini, Charlie Chaplin, and Orson Welles hung out.

✪ Caffè Florian
Piazza San Marco 57, tel. 041/520-5641, daily 9am-midnight, €5-€10 inside

Caffè Florian has been in business since getting to the New World meant a long journey on a wooden ship. The café once attracted Venice's nobles, politicians, and intellectuals. Today, the plush furnishings and uniformed staff provide an aura of elegance. The view of Piazza San Marco from the tables is wonderful, while the interior provides more intimacy. Inside there are distinctly themed rooms (Chinese, Oriental, Senate, and Illustrious) decorated in 18th-century style. This is where local patriots plotted independence from Austria and artists hatched the idea of a Venice Biennale.

Caffè Quadri
Piazza San Marco 121, tel. 041/522-2105, daily 10:30am-midnight, €5 inside

Caffè Quadri doesn't disappoint with its mirrored walls, high ceilings, and gold-leaf moldings. At the counter you'll find a limited selection of high-quality *cicchetti* (€2 each) that can be accompanied by a glass of *prosecco* or spritz (€4). The coffee is excellent and affordable unless you choose to be served sitting down.

Harry's Bar

Calle Vallaresso 1323, tel. 041/528-5777,
daily 10:30am-11pm, €15-€20

Harry's Bar opened in 1931 and attracted illustrious regulars like Hemingway, Charlie Chaplin, and Alfred Hitchcock. Today the regulars are mostly tourists soaking up the atmosphere at this landmark institution where you can sip expensive Bellini cocktails (€16) from wooden tables or at the counter. Food is available too, but it's equally pricey and nothing to write home about.

DORSODURO

VENETIAN

Osteria da Codroma

Fondamenta Briati 2540, tel. 041/524-6789,
Tues.-Sat. noon-2:30pm and 7pm-10pm, €14

One of the places local Venetians can still be found enjoying traditional recipes and tapas is Osteria da Codroma. Under soft lighting and white wooden beams you'll receive a warm welcome and are likely to be the only tourist in sight. Silver-haired septuagenarians and students from the nearby university occupy most of the dark rustic tables, enjoying *sardee in saor* (sardines with onions), marinated fish, spaghetti with cuttlefish ink, and other Venetian delicacies. The kitchen is actually located across the street, but that doesn't seem to bother waiters.

Enoteca Ai Artisti

Fondamenta della Toletta 1169a,
tel. 041/523-8944, Tues.-Sat.
12:45pm-2:30pm and 7pm-11pm, €14

Cozy Enoteca Ai Artisti is a little out of the way but worth finding. It's open from breakfast to dinner and serves creative *cicchetti* throughout the day. Fish is from the Rialto market and transformed into Venetian classics with an edge. The wine cellar is stocked with labels from small Italian vineyards and the menu changes daily. Tables are limited inside, so if you don't want to be left standing at the bar arrive early or make reservations for one of two dinnertime slots (7pm or 9pm). Afterward you can browse the shelves at La Toletta, one of the city's oldest bookshops down the street.

Pane Vino e San Daniele

Campo dell'Angelo Raffaele 1722,
tel. 041/523-7456, daily noon-2:30pm
and 7pm-10:30pm, €13

There is an entire menu of reasons to eat at Pane Vino e San Daniele. Devoted out-of-towners come for the grilled seasonal vegetables. Cured meat and steaks are some of the best but vegetarians have nothing to fear. The flowered terrace on a hidden square is the icing on the *tiramisu*. There is no English menu but staff is patient and happy to explain any dishes you may be curious about. Wine is a bit expensive but there's a good selection and several by-the-glass options.

Al Vecio Marangon

Calle della Toletta, tel. 041/277-8554,
daily noon-10pm, €9-12

Al Vecio Marangon has a lot going for it including a quiet side street, handwritten menu, working fireplace, rustic wooden interior, soft jazz, large portions, and low-priced Venetian fare. It's a small one-room *trattoria* and if you don't enjoy rubbing shoulders with other diners you probably won't like it here, but there are tables on the street outside.

CICCHETTI

✪ Al Bottegon

Fondamenta Nani 992, tel. 041/523-0034,
Mon.-Sat. 8am-8pm, €6-10

You can tell from the aging sign above

Al Bottegon that this *bacaro* has been around for a while. Inside, three generations of the Gastaldi family keep the institution running on good wine and addictive *cicchetti*. The grape selection is written on a chalkboard and features over 30 varieties that can be ordered by the glass or carafe. This is one of the best *enoteche* in the city and the perfect place to enjoy red, white, or *prosecco* in the wonderfully gritty interior or outside along the canal.

✪ Osteria Al Squero

Fondamenta Nani 943,

Thurs.-Tues. 11am-9pm, €6-€10

There's a reason Osteria Al Squero is always crowded. The *cicchetti* are good, the wine is cheap, and you can enjoy both on a canal overlooking the San Trovaso workshop where gondolas are repaired. Service is fast but you'll need to get in line and move toward the counter with determination. Once it's your turn don't hesitate. Choose a plateful of appetizers (4-5 make a good snack) and two glasses of *prosecco* to avoid a return trip. It's all quickly served on plastic plates and cups so have money ready and enjoy.

Barrachero

Fondamenta Bonlini 1078,

Mon.-Sat. 10am-11pm, €5-8

When nearby snack bars are full to the gills, head down the *fondamenta* and over the bridge to Barrachero. The name means "the drunk" in Cuban slang and the mother, son, and aunt team who run the place are happy to get travelers tipsy inside their little shop selling wine from a tap, mini sandwiches (€2), and fried specialties (€2-3). Order a glass and sit inside or out next to the canal, but be wary of aggressive seagulls that occasionally swoop down to steal food from distracted diners.

PIZZA
Pizza al Volo

Campo Santa Margherita 2944a,

tel. 041/522-5430, daily 11:30am-4pm

and 5pm-1:30am

Order a slice or an entire pie at Pizza al Volo, a takeaway *pizzeria* with an oven in view and plenty of toppings to choose from. It's a favorite with university students and travelers who appreciate large portions at low prices. You can satisfy an appetite here for under €5 without sacrificing quality—and enjoy the action in the square as you eat.

GELATO
✪ Da Nico

Fondamenta Zattere al Ponte Lungo 922,

tel. 041/522-5293,

Fri.-Wed. 6:45am-10pm, €4

Da Nico is famous for the hazelnut and cacao-flavored *giandiotto* gelato (€6) that was invented in Venice and has been served here for over 80 years. Besides the elegant interior there's a scenic terrace facing Canale della Giudecca where gelato connoisseurs gather to enjoy the 25 flavors on offer. The San Basilio ferry station is nearby, making this a sweet stop before or after a visit to Giudecca on board the number 2 *vaporetto*.

Gelateria il Doge

Rio Terà Canal 3058a, daily 9am-11pm, €3-5

Just off Campo Santa Margherita, Gelateria il Doge quenches sweet cravings. They scoop great gelato and refreshing Sicilian *granite* ices into cones or cups inside or from a street-front window. All-star flavors include coffee, hazelnut, *tiramisu*, and the house specialty, *Crema del Doge*.

VENETIAN CUISINE

Venice offers flavors unlike any others in Italy, a world away from Rome or Florence. The cuisine will surprise your taste buds and make you rethink your definition of Italian food.

spritz cocktail

APPETIZERS (ANTIPASTI)

- **Sarde in Saor:** Fried sardines served with caramelized onions cooked in a vinegar sauce.

- **Baccalà mantecato:** Boiled and whipped cod spread on thin slices of fresh bread. It's often also available as a second.

- **Insalata di mare:** Cuttlefish, shrimp, and celery salad dressed in lemon juice and olive oil.

FIRST COURSES (PRIMI)

- **Risotto:** Rice plays a major role in local diets and is usually served in *risi bisi* (rice and peas) or with *sparasi* (asparagus) in early spring and summer.

- **Spaghetti con le vongole:** Spaghetti and clams, available year-round.

- **Spaghetti al nero di seppia:** Pasta with cuttlefish ink, seasoned with parsley, wine, and garlic.

- Other first courses include *zuppa di pesce* (fish soup), *pasta e fagiole* (pasta and beans), and *bigoli in salsa* (a thicker version of spaghetti, served with a sardine-and-onion sauce).

SECOND COURSES (SECONDI)

Fish is the king of Venetian second courses, and restaurants use all available varieties to prepare a vast range of dishes. It comes fried, grilled, baked, creamed, or marinated, and is almost always fresh. To get an idea of what to expect, head to the Rialto and take a stroll through the fish market that supplies many of the city's restaurants. *Bisato su l'ara* (eel), cuttlefish, *sardelle* (sardines), lagoon clams, soft-shell crab, sea bass, gray mullet, monkfish, calamari, and octopus are all prepared in dishes that are difficult to find anywhere else.

- **Fritto misto:** A heaping mixed plate of fried shrimp, calamari, sardines, and squid. Served in restaurants and *bacari,* where it can be ordered to go.

- **Bacalà con polenta:** Cod that's creamed or slowly stewed in tomato sauce, and served with polenta.

- **Branzino al forno:** Sea bass baked with onions and tomatoes, topped with a lemon slice.

- **Fegato alla Veneziana:** Pork or veal liver with white onions. Often accompanied by polenta.

SIDES (CONTORNI)

Second courses are usually served unaccompanied by vegetables, so if you want a little variety, you'll need to order a *contorno*.

- **Carciofi impanati:** Breaded artichokes.

- **Patate alla Veneziana:** Beans, onions, and potatoes stewed in vegetable broth.

- **Melanzane alla Giudea:** Jewish-style fried eggplant dish.

- **Polenta:** Polenta is common in northern Italy, but in Venice it's made from white corn flour and has a smoother consistency than the yellow variety.

WINE (VINO) AND OTHER DRINKS

There are dozens of local appellations to choose from in the Veneto region. White grape varieties tend to do better due to the colder climate, but there are exceptions. House wine is generally a safe bet.

- **Bardolino:** Dry red wine from the hills around Verona with a hint of bitterness and delicate aftertaste. Goes well with meat.

- **Soave:** Popular white wine produced from garganega or trebbiano grapes. Perfect with an appetizer, or with pasta and fish.

- **Prosecco:** Widely produced sparkling white wine that's a valid alternative to champagne. Can be drunk as an aperitif, as a nightcap, or with a meal.

- **Spritz:** A mix of *prosecco*, Aperol or Campari bitters, and seltzer, served over ice.

DESSERT (DOLCI)

Venetian desserts have Jewish, Austrian, and Middle Eastern roots, and rely on cacao and nuts for sweetness and crunch. During the run-up to Carnival, fried pastries *(frittole)* stuffed with cream, raisins, or pine nuts appear in bakery windows, and most holidays are celebrated with a particular dessert. Fortunately, most sweets are available year-round.

- **Pan di Doge:** Almond-covered biscuits baked in honor of the doge.

- **Moro di Venezia:** A large brownie-like cookie, made from chocolate and hazelnuts, available in most bakeries.

- **Pinza Veneziana:** Rustic cake made with dried raisins and topped with pine nuts.

- **Burranei:** Unevenly shaped butter cookies coated with powdered sugar and found in every bakery and pastry shop.

COFFEE
Caffè La Piscina

Fondamenta Zattera Ai Gesuiti,
tel. 041/520-6466, Tues.-Sun. 11am-10:30pm

Something about Caffè La Piscina attracted poets, novelists, playwrights, and their admirers. John Ruskin spent the spring of 1877 at the hotel upstairs working on his classic book *The Stones of Venice*, and Rainer Maria Rilke was a regular at the bar. Although the name has changed since its 19th-century heyday, the emotions remain. One look at the view and it's easy to be inspired. Beyond the tables set on a pier is the mysterious low skyline of Giudecca.

SAN POLO AND SANTA CROCE
VENETIAN
✪ Antiche Carampane

San Polo, Rio Terà Rampani 1911,
tel. 041/524-0165, Tues.-Sat.
12:30pm-2:30pm and 7:30pm-11pm, €20

Being hard to find keeps Antiche Carampane real. There's no pizza, no tourist menu, and no watered-down traditions here—just some of the best fish in the city served in a simple but elegant atmosphere. If you haven't had a three-course meal in Italy yet this is the place to have one. The raw fish, spider crab (*grancevola*), and turbot fillet (*rombo*) are stalwarts of a menu that changes according to what's available at the fish market. Expect superb desserts you won't want to share and a small, carefully selected wine list. Getting a table here can be difficult, especially during the Venice Film Festival when stars like Uma Thurman and Audrey Tautou turn up.

Al Ponte Storto

San Polo, Calle Bianca Cappello 1278,
tel. 041/528-2144, daily noon-3pm and
6-10pm, €14-16

Al Ponte Storto is cozy without being quaint. Alberto is a jovial host who welcomes guests and runs the restaurant with his brother, who mans the kitchen. Mom fills in on weekends when necessary and entertains guests with her lovely broken English and stories of her glass workshop on Murano. The menu changes four or five times a year depending on what's in season and there's always a fixed option (€35) that includes an appetizer, first course, dessert, carafe of wine, water, and coffee. Dishes combine tradition with a few flights of fancy and portions are neither too big nor too small. *Aperitivo* starts at 6pm and includes an inviting array of Venetian finger food accompanied by wine or beer that can be enjoyed on the romantic little square overlooking the uneven bridge after which the *osteria* is named.

CICCHETTI
✪ Cantina Do Mori

San Polo, Ruga due Mori 429,
tel. 041/522-5401, Mon.-Sat. 8am-7:30pm, €7

The shelves at Cantina Do Mori are lined with large vats of red and white wine on tap. The long wooden counter fills up fast during *aperitivo* with clients jostling to order triangular *tramezzini* sandwiches stuffed with crab, shrimp, and other lagoon delicacies. Legend has it Casanova was a regular at this historic *bacaro,* where you can forget about itineraries and just enjoy Venice.

Cantina do Spade

San Polo, Calle do Spade 859,
tel. 041/521-0583, €12-15

Nearby, Cantina do Spade has a dark wood interior with a glass case filled with *cicchetti* that include fried calamari, stuffed zucchini flowers, creamed cod, and liver pâté. It's one of the few old-style *bacari,* with inside seating and plenty of red and white wine along with regional beer such as Pedavena lager.

All'Arco

San Polo, Calle Arco 436, tel. 041/520-5666, Mon.-Sat. 8:30am-3:30pm, €8

A popular spot with street-side seating and a rustic look is All'Arco. The friendly staff is always busy making plates of tempting appetizers that often include their famous boiled-beef sandwich. Most of the *cicchetti* come from the nearby fish market and the owner will happily explain any mystery ingredients. The only drawbacks are the lines and the early closing time.

Osteria Bancogiro

San Polo, Campo San Giacometto 122, tel. 041/523-2061, Tues.-Sun. 9am-midnight, €8-€12

There are several *bacari* in the squares adjacent to the Rialto. Osteria Bancogiro is under the portico where wealthy Venetians sent their servants to pay and collect outstanding debts. You can sample the miniature surprises chef Jacopo Scarso creates at the small bar, or sit down for something more substantial and equally delicious with a view of the Grand Canal.

Naranzaria

San Polo, Campo Erberia 130, tel. 041/724-1035, daily 10am-midnight, €8

For a great look at the Rialto and fabulous *cicchetti*—all priced at €2 and featuring salmon, cod, and tuna toppings—head to Naranzaria. You can stand at the bar or take a seat outside a stone's throw from the bridge. Every Sunday local groups play jazz, rock, and soul. This is also one of the rare *bacari* that stays open until midnight.

Al Merca

San Polo, Campo Bella Vienna 213, tel. 346/834-0660, Mon.-Thurs. 10am-2:30pm and 6pm-8pm, Fri.-Sat. 10am-2:30pm and 6pm-9:30pm, €5

Al Merca is in the adjacent *campo* and one of the smallest *bacaro* in the city. There's hardly room to enter and consider which of the miniature *panini* sandwiches to order. Most cost €3 and are filled with *prosciutto,* meatballs, salami, or creamed cod. There's a classic assortment of red and white wines, local beers, and spritz. Diners stand outside holding plates or reclining on the nearby steps.

✪ Bacareto da Lele

Santa Croce, Fondamenta dei Tolenti 183, tel. 347/846-9728, Mon.-Fri. 6am-8pm, Sat. 6am-2pm, €5

Bacareto da Lele is one institution that lives up to its reputation and is hard not to love. There's a crowd inside and out of this tiny *bacaro* that churns out over 2,000 mini sandwiches a day. Lele prepares them in the back while his son works the counter and keeps a stream of regulars, university students, and tourists satisfied. There are 6-7 sandwiches (€1 each) to choose from with different fillings and if you're undecided, sample one of everything. Red and white wine is listed on a blackboard and ordering a double glass (€2) will save you from waiting in line again. People eat standing along the canal or on the steps facing the little square. Lele opens and closes early but if you're searching for a late-night bite **Arcicchetti Bakaro** (daily 11am-11pm) next door serves tasty open-faced *cicchetti* until 11pm. Both are only ten minutes from the train station, which makes them a great gastronomic introduction or farewell to Venice.

✪ SAMPLING *CICCHETTI*

Venetian finger food

A gastronomic highlight of any Venetian vacation is sampling the delicious assortment of finger food known as **cicchetti**. Reminiscent of tapas, *cicchetti* consist of sliced bread topped with creamed fish, sautéed vegetables, cheese, and many other enticing ingredients. Chefs take advantage of the abundance of fresh calamari and octopus and often serve them raw or dipped in light batter and fried.

Cicchetti are served at **bacari**, traditional Venetian bars that also sell wine by the glass or pitcher. Most *bacari* are delightfully unglamorous institutions that have been around for generations. They're usually small and darkly lit with rustic interiors where patrons stand around socializing while

VEGETARIAN

Venice has a good number of vegetarian restaurants per capita, and going meatless here is easy.

La Zucca

Santa Croce, Calle dello Specier 1762, tel. 041/524-1570, Mon.-Sat. 12:30pm-2:30pm and 7pm-10:30pm, €14

La Zucca is a cozy *osteria* with a soothing wood-paneled interior and street-side seating. The kitchen prepares imaginative pasta dishes like *tagliatelle con carciofi e pecorino* and *lasagna con zucchine e mandorle*. Waiters are happy to list ingredients, and there are several fish and duck options for carnivores. Reservations are useful in high season.

PIZZA

Venetian pizza is thick and closer to *focaccia* than the thin kind served in Rome. *Pizzerie* and by-the-cut shops are not very common and those that do exist can be found along busy streets catering to tourists.

Antico Forno

San Polo, Ruga Rialto 973, tel. 041/520-4110, daily 11:30am-9:30pm, €4-7

Antico Forno specializes in reasonably priced takeaway pizza. Toppings aren't overly elaborate and the best sellers are the *marinara* and *margherita*. There's no seating inside but you can enjoy a slice in the tranquility of Campo di San Silvestro a couple of minutes away.

they eat and drink. Staff may be charmingly brusque, and most *bacari* open and close early. A crowded sidewalk near a *bacaro* is always a good sign.

To order, get the proprietor's attention and point to the *cicchetti* you'd like to try. They'll be served on a small tray or plastic plate and ready to eat immediately. Individual portions cost €1-2 and are an inexpensive way to sample a variety of local flavors. Be sure to order a glass of **prosecco**, Venetian sparkling white wine, to savor with your snacks.

Every neighborhood has a handful of *bacari*, though they are particularly plentiful in San Polo, where workers from the nearby markets take their breaks. You'll find many hidden along the narrow streets north of the Rialto. Once you've tried one, it's hard to resist a *bacari* binge. Start near the fish market and continue sampling *cicchetti* along the **Fondamenta della Misericordia** in Cannaregio, **Fondamenta Nani** in Dorsoduro, and lively squares like **Campo Santa Margherita**.

Here are some good destinations for *cicchetti* hopping:

- **Cantina Do Mori:** Legendary bacaro reputed to be where Casanova liked to start his evenings (page 84).

- **Al Timon:** A local hangout serving cold and hot *cicchetti* for €1 a shot indoors or outside overlooking a canal (page 89).

- **Vino Vero:** An addictive little bar serving gourmet cheese and meat platters that can easily substitute for dinner (page 89).

- **Al Bottegon:** Once you enter you may never want to leave this friendly *bacaro* with wines priced to drink (page 80).

- **Osteria Al Squero:** It may be crowded, but it's the only place to nibble on *cicchetti* while watching gondolas being repaired (page 81).

- **Bacareto da Lele:** Lele's is the quintessential *bacaro:* simple food, simple surroundings, and lots of smiling faces (page 85).

BAKERIES
Panificio Albonico

Santa Croce, Calle della Regina 2268b,
tel. 041/524-1102,
Mon.-Sat. 7:30am-7:30pm, €4

Panificio Albonico is on a narrow thoroughfare where walking sometimes gets difficult. This homey, wood-paneled bakery provides instant relief from the crowds and during *Carnevale* season they prepare all sorts of fried *frittelle* treats. The rest of the year you'll find olive buns, mini pizzas, and *pincia,* a traditional sweet bread that comes in many varieties, all of which the owners are happy to explain.

GELATO
Gelato di Natura

Santa Croce, Campo San Giacomo
dall'Orio 1628, tel. 340/286-7178,
daily 10:30am-11pm, €4

Before you proclaim your favorite *gelateria* in Venice visit Gelato di Natura, where Pierangelo has been churning out organic gelato since 1982. All the flavors are made fresh daily using top ingredients, including hazelnuts from Piedmont and Sicilian pistachios that are mixed with organic milk, eggs, and mascarpone. There's something for every palate inside this attractive shop with bilingual labels next to every vat. They also create mint, lemon, and pear sorbets on sticks as well as vegan and lactose-free options that don't sacrifice flavor.

Yogurteria White

San Polo, Ruga Vecchia S. Giovanni 480,
tel. 041/528-5109, daily 10am-11pm, €4

Yogurteria White is unlike any other *gelateria* in the city. It's a self-service shop with rows of machines where you can fill up cones or cups with gelato and frozen yogurt and decorate them with chocolate, praline, hazelnut, or syrup toppings. The gelato is creamy and fun to prepare but be careful not to get overzealous—price is by weight and quickly adds up.

COFFEE

The best thing about Italian coffee bars is that they nearly always serve delicious pastries to accompany a cappuccino or espresso.

Pasticceria Rizzardini

San Polo, Campiello Meloni 1415,
tel. 041/522-3835, €3

The pastry selection at Pasticceria Rizzardini is extensive, and once you've picked a *crostata* or *canolo* pastry you can order a coffee at the metal counter. It's standing room only inside this classic bar with few signs of modernity and plenty of local drama.

Caffetteria Goppion

San Polo, Ruga Rialto 644,
tel. 041/523-7031, Wed.-Mon. 7am-8pm, €3

Caffetteria Goppion combines years of experience with the quality coffee. The cheerful staff busily grinds beans and serves cups to locals and visitors waiting anxiously at the long counter. There are sweet and salty snacks throughout the day at this pleasant bar with large plate-glass windows through which you can observe the flow of daily Venetian life.

CANNAREGIO
VENETIAN
Osteria dei Mori

Campo dei Mori 3386, tel. 041/524-3677,
Wed.-Mon. 12:30pm-3:30pm and
7pm-midnight, €15

Tucked between Chiesa della Madonna dell'Orto and Fondamenta della Misericordia, Osteria dei Mori is usually filled with locals. The menu provides a good mix of meat and fish to which the Sicilian chef adds a dash of southern Italian flavor. Notable dishes include the fried fish and vegetable plate along with a memorable *baccalà mantecato* (creamed cod). Rubbing the steel nose of the statue outside is said to bring good luck.

SEAFOOD
Osteria Bentigodi

Calle Farnese 1423, Wed.-Mon.
12:30pm-2:30pm and 7pm-10:30pm, €15

Any place decorated with rolling pins, vinyl records, and a vintage hand-cranked cash machine deserves a visit. Fortunately, the food at Osteria Bentigodi lives up to the rustic and eclectic interior. Cuttlefish with polenta, Venetian sardines, and lightly fried fish come at a price worth paying.

Frito-Inn

Cannaregio, Campo San Leonardo 1587,
tel. 041/564-7451, Mon.-Fri. 10am-8pm
and Sat.-Sun. 10am-10pm, €8

Venetians like their fish fried, and the mother/daughter team at Frito-Inn are happy to oblige. This tiny joint around the corner from a busy street can be smelled before it's seen. They fry a range of fish and vegetables but the house specialty is the calamari and shrimp rolled in flour, fried in sunflower oil, and served in paper cones perfect for carrying away or eating on the chairs facing the small square.

CICCHETTI
⭐ Vino Vero

Fondamenta della Misericordia 2497,
tel. 041/275-0044, Tues.-Sun.
noon-midnight, Mon. 6pm-midnight, €6

Vino Vero is packed with a young crowd of grape enthusiasts. The wine list covers an entire wall and the *cicchetti* are temptingly lined up behind a glass case on the counter where clients jostle to be served. It's a small, modern space, but there are some stools outside and they serve *crostini* on ingenious wooden trays with glass holders that make it easy to eat and drink while standing.

⭐ Al Timon

Fondamenta dei Ormesini 2754,
tel. 041/524-6066, daily 6pm-1am, €10

Al Timon is a small *osteria* just north of the Ghetto that caters to snackers and diners. The best *cicchetti* in the neighborhood can be ordered at the counter while the restaurant prepares Venetian-Tuscan dishes. This is the place in Venice to try *bistecca alla fiorentina*. There's a row of canvas-backed chairs and tables facing the canal but the best seats are on the boat moored out front where musicians occasionally perform and large groups of friends gather.

PIZZA
Ai Tre Arch

Fondamenta Savorgnan 552,
tel. 041/716-438, daily noon-3pm
and 6:30pm-11pm, €12

Pizza isn't that common in Venice and most *pizzeria* also serve traditional dishes. Ai Tre Arch is an exception and prepares over 50 kinds of pizza, with original toppings that take a while to choose. Staff is friendly and

there are shaded tables overlooking the Canneragio Canal.

STREET FOOD

Fondamenta della Misericordia is a great destination day and night for street food and drink. The canal-side promenade is lined with restaurants, bars, and *bacari* where locals and visitors huddle outdoors enjoying good food and wine. Don't be intimidated by the chaotic lines—just jump right in and persevere until you're served. Go back and forth between these informal establishments and find your favorite.

Paradiso Perduto

Fondamenta della Misericordia 2540,
tel. 041/720-581, Thurs.-Mon.
11am-midnight, €10

At Paradiso Perduto there are usually people waiting to choose from the counter filled with plates of fried fish dishes. When it's your turn, point to as many delicacies as you can handle. Most of the internal seating fills up early but you can sit along the canal and enjoy a cup or carafe of house wine. There's a regular calendar of musical performances on the small stage inside.

BAKERIES AND CHOCOLATE
El Fornareto

Calle del Forno 2668,
tel. 041/522-5426, Mon.-Sat. 6am-1:30pm
and 4:30pm-7:30pm, €4

El Fornareto is one of Venice's oldest bakeries and equipped with a 19th-century oven in full view. If you're interested, Silvia will open it up and reveal the scorching interior where loaves of bread and pastries are baked. Mornings are the best time to visit— the bread is still warm and pastries haven't sold out yet.

GELATO
Gelateria Ca' d'Oro

Strada Nuova 4273b, daily 10:30am-9:30pm,
€2-5

There are fewer *gelateria* in Venice than in Rome or Florence, but the gelato is just as good and prepared with care and attention to ingredients. The local flavor is *Crema del Doge* (vanilla cream), which is available at Gelateria Ca' d'Oro alongside some of the shop's own unique creations. Cones and cups come in four sizes and can be enjoyed in the adjacent square off the main street.

CASTELLO
Al Portego

Calle della Malvasia 6014,
tel. 041/522-9038, daily 10:30am-2:30pm
and 5:30pm-10:30pm, €12

If you want to find a table at Al Portego you need to reserve in advance or arrive early. This small *osteria* five minutes from the Rialto is popular and tables fill up fast. Fortunately, you can sample their fish *cicchetti* while you wait. Once you sit down it can be difficult to get a waiter's attention, but service is friendly and prices are reasonable. It's a good place to try Venetian classics like *baccalà mantecato* and *bigoli* pasta prepared the old-fashioned way.

Trattoria alla Rampa del Piave

Via Garibaldi 1135, tel. 041/528-5365,
Mon.-Sat. 12:30pm-3pm and
7:30pm-10pm, €8

Castello is one of the less-visited parts of the city, which also makes it one of the least expensive. Trattoria alla Rampa del Piave is a case in point. The *trattoria* is located at the end of Via Garibaldi in front of a red flagpole and floating fruit and vegetable market. The decor is nothing special but the simple interior is often packed with locals taking advantage of the fixed-price lunch menu (€14). It's a good place to try *risi e bisi, polenta e baccala* (cod), and *spaghetti al nero.*

Le Spighe

Via Garibaldi 1341, Mon.-Sat.
10:30am-2:30pm and 5:30pm-7:30pm, €6

At this casual vegan eatery, Doriana sells organic dishes by the kilo and serves them at a convivial communal table.

Covino

Calle Pestrin Castello 3829a,
tel. 041/241-2705, Thurs.-Mon.
12:30pm-2:30pm and 7pm-10:30pm,
€15, cash only

Put expectations aside and make a reservation at Covino. This wonderfully intimate restaurant with a festive host provides a multitude of flavors that blend tradition with creativity. A fixed-price menu (€36) includes a choice of starter, second, and dessert. Depending on the season this could include tartare, sardines, baked cod, veal sausage, tiramisu, and chocolate. Tables are close together and the restaurant gets loud—but that's because everyone is having a good time.

BAKERIES AND CHOCOLATE
VizioVirtu

Calle Forner 5988, tel. 041/275-0149,
daily 10am-7pm, €5

VizioVirtu is a sweet hideaway on a busy corner with trisecting streets. Once you've passed through the well-worn wooden doors of this chocolate boutique, the world disappears. Virtuous Vice is an appropriate name, since this is where cacao gets transformed into tempting pralines waiting to be devoured. There's a large assortment of desserts, including many exotic flavors, gelatin candies, and homemade gelato. Just point and let Maria Angela place your treats in a small plastic sachet for takeaway.

GELATO
La Mela Verde
Fondamenta de l'Osmarin 4977a,
tel. 349/195-7924, daily 11am-11pm, €4

La Mela Verde is located on a pleasant canal near the Greek Orthodox church. The gelato and sorbet are made on site by a friendly staff who take the time to explain the flavor of the day and allow customers to sample before choosing between pistachio, *torroncino, limone,* and many others. They've also recently started serving chocolate-filled crepes.

GIUDECCA
SEAFOOD
Fewer tourists venture to Giudecca than other parts of Venice and as a consequence it has fewer places to eat. Most of these are located near the Palanca water stop.

Majer
Fondamenta Sant'Eufemia 461,
tel. 041/521-1162, daily 9am-11pm, €3-5

Majer is a reliable breakfast, lunch, or dinner eatery with seven locations around the city. The Giudecca branch is the latest and has been decked out in pleasant earth tones. They do their own baking and serve a great almond croissant and cappuccino that can be slowly sipped at the long wooden sharing table as you look out onto the canal and wait for the next *vaporetto* to arrive.

La Palanca
Fondamenta di Ponte Piccolo 448,
tel. 041/528-7719, Mon.-Sat. 7am-9pm,
€12-15

La Palanca is near the *vaporetto* station overlooking Dorsoduro. There's a good chance you'll be greeted by the jovial Andrea Barina and seated outdoors at one of the tables along the water under the shade of large umbrellas. The menu has five or six pasta dishes with or without fish and a dozen seconds including grilled calamari, *seppie con polenta,* creamed cod, and a daily fish special.

Nightlife and Entertainment

When the sun goes down, Venice is transformed. An exodus of tourists and workers drains swiftly out of the city, reducing a daytime population of 100,000 to less than half that number. The result is invigorating for anyone who stays behind to explore the city at night. Take a starlit stroll and enjoy the silence. If you want human contact you can find it, although anyone with images of Casanova-style decadence will be disappointed. You won't find discos or dancing, though there's no shortage of canal-side bars, lively squares, and rustic *enoteche* where wine flows until late. After-dinner diversions include listening to classical music, gambling at the casino, and sipping cocktails inside five-star hotels. The drink of choice is a white sparkling wine called *prosecco* that's produced in the Veneto region and could be mistaken for Champagne. It's poured everywhere across the city and accompanied with delicious finger food known as *cicchetti*. Also quintessential to Venice is *spritz*, a cocktail consisting of *prosecco,* Aperol or Campari bitters, and seltzer. A *spritz* or one glass of *prosecco* may be all the nightlife you need.

One of the most popular nighttime areas with Venetians and visitors is Campo Santa Margherita in Dorsoduro. The large rectangular square is dotted with bars that are filled from happy hour to the early hours. Campo Erberia overlooking the Ponte di Rialto in San Polo is also reliably animated. Sure signs of nightlife can always be found along Cannaregio's Fondamenta della Misericordia, lined with *bacari,* restaurants, and wine bars.

SAN MARCO

BARS
Devils Forest Pub
Calle dei Stagneri 5185, tel. 041/520-0623, daily 11am-midnight

The Devils Forest Pub is a favorite with American and English visitors who become remarkably agitated whenever soccer or rugby is playing on the large TVs. It can be fun to partake in the joy and pain of supporters even if you don't know the offside rule or how to score a *try.* Regardless of the results everyone enjoys the beer at this authentic-looking pub with Strongbow, Guinness, and Harp on tap and wooden booths in the back.

Bar Campanile
Calle Larga S. Marco 310, tel. 041/522-1491, daily 8am-1am

Bar Campanile is just north of Piazza San Marco and has a different personality depending on the time of day. In the morning it's about coffee, at lunch it's *tramezzini* sandwiches, and at night the cocktails kick off. Staff is friendly and *spritz* can be ordered any time, but if the Cuban bartender is around order the mojito. Prices are cheaper if you stand at the bar, where drinks are served with light snacks, although there's not much room after dark and it remains crowded with Venetians and visitors until closing. There are DJ sets on Saturdays.

Hard Rock Café di Venezia
Bacino Orseolo 1192, tel. 041/522-9665, daily 11:30am-12:30am

Even if most Hard Rock Cafés make you blush, the Hard Rock Café di Venezia is different. You can tell from the red Murano chandelier hanging from the ceiling and the Venetian tiles on the floor. The music is good, the drinks are strong, and the views *do* rock. The café is located near Piazza San Marco in an historic *palazzo* overlooking a gondolier station. It's the smallest Hard Rock in Europe, which makes it only half a travel sin.

WINE BARS
Osteria Enoteca Rusteghi
San Marco, Corte del Tentor 5513, tel. 338/760-6034, daily 11:30am-3pm and 6:30pm-3am, €12

Wine rarely goes without food in Italy and you can choose either at Osteria Enoteca Rusteghi. This wine bar hidden away in a tiny courtyard near the Rialto lies just beyond the tourist masses, where Giovanni D'Este keeps the art of Venetian hospitality alive. He's usually stationed behind the counter pouring difficult-to-find wines to clients who eagerly listen to his gastronomic tales. Most glasses are €6-8 and can be accompanied by *bruschetta*, cheese plates, and other appetizers. It's best after dark when locals take back their city.

HOTEL BARS
Gritti Palace Hotel
San Marco, Campo Santa Maria del Giglio, tel. 041/794-611, www.thegrittipalace.com

Inside the expensive Gritti Palace Hotel is the Longhi Bar (11am-1am), where you can order the cocktail of the same name and sit back amid the opulence of mirrored walls, 18th-century paintings, and antique settees. Hemingway called this the best hotel in the city and never passed up an opportunity to drink here. Today Cristiano Luciano does the mixing dressed in black-tie attire. The bar serves light fare along with Champagne and oysters on weekends. The house cocktail contains Campari, dry vermouth, China Martini, and orange. If you prefer to drink outdoors try the Riva Lounge on the terrace facing the Grand Canal.

OPERA AND CONCERTS
There are few large concert halls in Venice. Historically, most nobles had music played to them inside their homes, and today associations of musicians perform in churches and historic *palazzi*. These are informal performances in splendid settings that are accessible to all and a great way to begin or end an evening. Repertoires nearly always feature local favorite and homegrown Venetian Antonio Vivaldi, but Baroque and opera classics are also performed. *The Four Seasons* is at the top of the hit list and played nearly every evening at different venues. Tickets are reasonably priced given the quality of the music and the surroundings.

Teatro La Fenice
Campo San Fantin 1965, tel. 041/786-654, www.teatrolafenice.it, €39-180

Teatro La Fenice is one of the meccas of lyrical music, and if you enjoy opera—or even if you're just curious—this is the place to see it. The season runs from September to mid-July and nearly always includes crowd pleasers like *La Traviata* and *Madame Butterfly*, which are subtitled in Italian and English. Tickets aren't cheap and the most affordable seats in the upper galleries sell out fast. Most performances begin at 7pm and can last up to three hours with several intermissions. Jacket and tie are expected on opening nights, but semi-elegant will do after that; any unnecessary items must be checked into the cloakrooms. The theater also presents a varied symphonic program performed by its own philharmonic (www.filarmonica-fenice.it) and many illustrious guest conductors.

Teatro Goldini
Calle del Teatro 4650b, tel. 041/240-2011, www.teatrostabileveneto.it, €8-35

La Fenice may be the most famous theater in Venice but Teatro Goldini is the oldest still in existence and may have the best acoustics in town. The theater has a capacity of over 1,000 and an intimate four-tiered interior where drama takes center stage. Sundays are reserved for families and shows that everyone can enjoy.

Interpreti Veneziani
tel. 041/277-0561, www.interpretiveneziani. com, showtime 9pm, €30

The Interpreti Veneziani are one of the oldest chamber groups in the city and have recorded dozens of albums and toured extensively. The ensemble consists entirely of string players and performs in **Chiesa San Vidal** (Campo San Vidal/Santo Stefano) across from the Ponte dell'Accademia. Concerts are held daily during the summer and there's a high probability of listening to Vivaldi's *Four Seasons* as well as lesser-known compositions by the Venetian native. Tickets can be purchased directly at the church and performances begin at 9pm.

I Musici Veneziani

Scuola Grande di San Teodoro, Campo San Salvador 4810, tel. 041/521-0294, www.imusiciveneziani.com, 8:30pm, €24-€39

I Musici Veneziani are big fans of Vivaldi, whose works they regularly perform, but they're also passionate about Baroque and opera. They play the greatest hits by Verdi, Puccini, Rossini, and many others inside a *palazzo* with exceptional acoustics. All the musicians and singers dress in 17th-century regalia, which adds instant drama to every performance.

Virtuosi di Venezia

San Marco, Ateneo di San Basso, tel. 041/528-2825, www.virtuosidivenezia.com, 8:30pm, €29

Vivaldi sounds better in Venice and the Virtuosi di Venezia is one of the reasons why. This small chamber orchestra regularly pays tribute to the composer and performs both *The Four Seasons* along with opera medleys. The arias feature a talented tenor and mezzosoprano who sing in the Ateneo di San Basso overlooking Piazza San Marco.

Musica Palazzo

Palazzo Barbarigo Minotto, Fondamenta Duodo or Barbarigo 2504, tel. 340/971-7272, www.musicapalazzo.com, 8:30pm, €85

If you want to experience opera up close, to be inches from sopranos and listen to the classics in an intimate setting, then Musica Palazzo is the ticket. This talented ensemble leads audiences through itinerant performances set in the stunning rooms of a meticulously preserved villa facing the Grand Canal. Doors open at 8pm and shows last two hours. Smart casual dress is encouraged and tickets may be booked online.

DORSODURO

BARS

Bakarò Do Draghi

Calle della Chiesa 3665, daily 10am-2am

There are lots of bars in Campo Santa Margherita, but Bakarò Do Draghi is around the corner on the edge of the square. That doesn't mean it's not crowded—it is, and like many bars in Venice patrons often spill out onto the street. That's what happens in a city without cars, and it's an especially good thing at this colorful bar where it's impossible to go over budget ordering *spritz* served in large glasses and snacks that keep university students and young travelers merry.

WINE BARS

Estro

Calle Crosera 3778, tel. 041/476-4914, Wed.-Mon. noon-11pm, kitchen closes at 9:30pm

There are many reasons to love Estro, but best of all are the relaxed atmosphere, delicious food, and two enterprising brothers from Murano that make coming here enjoyable. The wine list includes over a hundred labels the pair have personally selected from small producers they never tire of touting. You can drink at the bar and select from a myriad of *tramezzino* sandwiches stuffed with boiled meat, creamed fish, and vegetables,

WINE TO GO

Some traditions only exist in Venice. One of those is the *cantina* or wine shop (sometimes also called vinerie), which has nothing to do with fancy labels or rows of expensive bottles. Inside these historic locales you'll find large vats from which plastic takeaway bottles are filled. Most of the wine is from the Veneto region and hauled to the city by boat. There's always a good selection of young red, white, and bubbly *prosecco* that's extremely drinkable and quite refreshing on a hot summer day. Prices are unbeatable and most of the customers are locals. There are about a dozen *cantina* scattered around the city, and you'll find at least one in every *sestiere*. Most have been in business for decades and have a dusty appearance that keeps tourists away. Don't let that put you off. Owners usually take long lunch breaks, shut by 8pm, and are closed on Sundays, so arrive early and enjoy one of Venice's enduring traditions.

wine shop

These shops deal exclusively in the sale of wine. It can't be consumed on the premises; instead it must be taken away and free bottles are provided.

The smaller option is a good investment and an opportunity to sample local wines fresh from the casks lining **Nave de Oro** (Castello, Calle del Mondo Novo 5786b, tel. 041/523-3056, Mon.-Sat. 9am-1pm and 5pm-7:45pm, Wed. 9am-1pm). The husband-and-wife owners have been providing *rosso, bianco,* and *frizzanti* to faithful customers and curious travelers since 1984.

Locals and curious travelers fill up bottles of wine from the half-dozen vats at **Al Canton del Vin** (Castello, Salizada Santa Giustina, tel. 041/277-0449, Mon.-Sat. 9am-1pm and 5pm-7:30). They'll provide you with plastic bottles if you arrive empty-handed and tempt you with soave or cabernet. It's cheap, extremely drinkable, and close to several pleasant squares where you can drink outdoors in peace.

Vini & Spumanti (Dorsoduro, Campo dei Carmini 2611, tel. 041/523-1979, Tues.-Fri. 9:30am-1pm and 4:30pm-8pm, Mon. and Sat. 9:30am-1pm) recently relocated to Campo dei Carmini, and the interior benefited from the move. It's one of the few *cantine* not located on a commercial street, which makes it a little hard to find. The little square, however, is lovely and faces a canal. There are steps nearby that encourage immediately sampling whatever wines you've chosen.

The name **Vini & Spumanti** (Dorsoduro, Calle de l'Avogaria 1614, 9am-1pm and 4pm-7pm, closed Wed. and Sun.) is actually very common among *cantine,* and Danilo has been running his shop nearby for decades. There are over 20 red, white, and bubbly varieties on tap that he happily fills in half-liter or liter-and-a-half plastic bottles. All varieties are produced in the Veneto region and very affordable.

Dorsoduro has one of the highest concentrations of *cantine,* and you'll find another at the western entrance of **Campo Santa Margherita.** Like most it doesn't have any signage outside and provides very little clue of what goes on inside. That doesn't stop it from doing a very busy trade. New vats come in every morning and are usually empty by closing time. Clients run the gamut, but the vicinity of the university makes it popular with students who gather in the square and get progressively louder as the evening wears on.

or select from the full menu featuring the fish of the day, vegetarian lasagna, and soups served in a rustic décor near Campo Santa Margherita.

Enoteca Venus Venezia

Calle San Rocco 3961, tel. 331/487-2166, Mon.-Sat. 10am-3pm and 5pm-11:30pm

The fun and friendly staff at Enoteca Venus Venezia don't take wine too seriously but they are serious about hospitality. This is a cozy little bar with a relaxing atmosphere where everyone seems to know each other and regulars can escape from tourists. There's a long list of wines and a surprising selection of whiskeys, as well as a wonderful glass case filled with inexpensive appetizers that are too tempting not to try.

OPERA AND CONCERTS
Venice Music Project

Chiesa Anglicana di St. George, Campo San Vio 729a, tel. 345/791-1948, www.venicemusicproject.it, €30

Venice Music Project was launched in 2013 by an ensemble of local musicians with a passion for Baroque and musical archeology. They hunt for forgotten manuscripts and perform long-lost compositions that haven't been played in hundreds of years using period instruments. It sounds great and helps maintain an important local tradition. The season runs March-June with Saturday and Sunday concerts that usually start at 5pm or 7pm. Bach, Vivaldi, Mozart, and Haydn are stalwarts of their repertoire along with many lesser-known artists who sound just as good. The church where they play is small with good acoustics and comfortable wooden pews.

Venice Jazz Club

Ponte dei Pugni 3102, tel. 340/150-4985, daily except Thurs. and Sun., 7pm until late, concerts 9pm-11pm, closed August

If you're searching for jazz (recorded or live) with a sense of history, check out the Venice Jazz Club. Nights are dedicated to standards, Latin, and Bossa Nova, the cocktails are good, and the wine is priced to uncork. The house quartet performs regularly and entry to live shows (€20) includes a drink. The club is only open weekends during the winter.

SAN POLO AND SANTA CROCE
WINE BARS
Muro Venezia

San Polo, Rio Terà Cazza 2604b/c, tel. 041/524-5310, www.murovenezia.com, daily noon-3pm and 7pm-10:30pm

There are a lot of reasons to stop by Muro Venezia but probably the best is that it's one of the liveliest places in the city after dark. Inside the intimate bar someone is usually playing guitar and dozens of people are drinking outside in the little square close to the Rialto. During the day it makes a good happy-hour pit stop, and on Saturdays at noon they start serving fried fish and chardonnay outdoors for an unbeatable €8.

Al Amarone

San Polo, Calle Sbianchesini 1131, tel. 041/523-1184, Thurs.-Tues. 10am-11pm

Al Amarone is an excellent place to learn about local Veneto wines. They serve over 30 red, white, and sparkling vintages by the regular and double glass in a spacious, contemporary setting. There are also a number of interesting tasting offers (five glasses each) with different themes meant to educate palates. Wine can be accompanied with reasonably priced finger food, cheese, and cured meat platters or a selection of hearty pasta dishes.

Al Prosecco

Santa Croce, Campo San Giacomo de l'Orio
tel. 041/524-0222, Mon.-Sat. 9am-9pm

Any enoteca named Al Prosecco should leave no doubt what to order. You can discover different varieties of Venetian bubbly along with organic wines while seated in a lively square. Food isn't an afterthought and abundant plates of cheese, grilled vegetables, and gourmet sandwiches are served.

HOTEL BARS
✪ Aman Venice Resort Hotel and Blue Bar

San Polo, Calle Tiepolo Baiamonte 1364,
tel. 041/270-7333, www.aman.com

The Aman Venice Resort Hotel, around the bend from the Rialto, is the only seven-star hotel in Venice. Its **Blue Bar** (always open) consists of three chandeliered rooms on the *piano nobile* (second or noble floor). It's a little like Versailles with modern furniture. You can have a seat anywhere but the middle mirrored room with ornate gold fittings, stylish couches, and three low tables overlooking the canal is the perfect backdrop for a proposal of any kind. There's no signature drink but the bartenders can mix nearly everything.

OPERA AND CONCERTS
Palazetto Bru Zane

San Polo, Corte del Calderer 2368,
tel. 041/521-1005, www.bru-zane.com,
box office Mon.-Fri. 2:30pm-5:30pm

Palazetto Bru Zane aims to keep 18th-century classical music alive and presents 30-40 concerts per season (Sept.-June) in a refurbished villa.

Concerts are small-scale (the hall seats 100) and feature emerging international ensembles playing chamber, symphonic, and choral works. Tickets are €15 and free guided tours of the elaborately decorated building are available in English on Thursday afternoons at 3:30pm.

CANNAREGIO
BARS
Al Santo Bevitore

Fondamenta de Ca' Vendramin 2393a,
tel. 041/717-560, daily 4pm-2am

For a pint in a no-nonsense Italian pub, pull up a stool at Al Santo Bevitore. The attraction isn't the décor but the long row of taps behind the bar. They're all connected to thirst-quenching kegs of stout, bitter, and ale. You can try local brews made from fermenting Japanese and New Zealand hops together, sip Belgian strong ales like La Chouffe (8 percent) and Kwak (8.4 percent), or cross the Channel for a pint of Punks Do It Better (4.3 percent). A small courtyard overlooks a canal and musicians occasionally give impromptu concerts on Monday nights.

Al Parlamento

Fondamenta Savorgnan 511,
tel. 041/244-0214, daily 7:30am-1:30am

Don't come to Venice expecting bars like the ones back home. In Venice a bar can be more than a place to drink. Al Parlamento is a good example of that: Although you can come to take advantage of their €5 happy hour from 6pm to 9pm you can also order seafood *risotto* and a couple of other dishes that will help you avoid a *spritz* hangover. The space has been refurbished with attention to design but hasn't lost its charm, and still has scenic outdoor tables overlooking the city's second-widest canal.

Irish Pub Venezia

Corte dei Pali 3847, tel. 041/099-0196, daily 10am-2am

There's no shame in going to a pub in Venice, especially if you carry your pint outside. At the originally named Irish Pub Venezia you can do just that with a glass of Kilkenny or Bitburger in a little courtyard away from the crowds of Strada Nuova. Inside you're likely to find the television tuned to rugby or *calcio* (soccer).

CASINOS
Casino di Venezia

tel. 041/529-7111, www.casinovenezia.it, daily 11am-2:45am, tables open at 4pm

Anyone who wants to try their luck in Venice can bet inside the oldest gambling house in the world. Casino di Venezia opened in 1638 and moved to Ca' Vendramin Calergi along the Grand Canal in the 1950s. If you don't know the rules to *Chemin de Fer, Punto Banco,* or *Midi Trenta* you can stick with roulette, blackjack, or the slot machines. Tables are spread over three floors. When you're ready to spend your earnings (or tire of losing), hit the sophisticated restaurant (Fri.-Sun. 7:30pm-11:30pm, €25-35), modern pizzeria (daily noon-3:30pm and 7pm-11:30pm, €15-20), or lounge bar with nighttime views of the Grand Canal. A jacket is required to enter the upstairs parlors but can be borrowed for free at the door. ID is also required and the €10 entry fee includes a chip, cloakroom service, and shuttle from the train station to the casino's private dock.

OPERA AND CONCERTS
Teatro Malibran

Campiello del Teatro 5873, tel. 041/965-1975, €10-100

Teatro Malibran may not be as grand as La Fenice but it has an equally glorious past. It's the site of over a hundred operatic debuts since being inaugurated in 1678 and is now used as the second stage for La Fenice productions and music recitals. These are newer works for the most part and an opportunity for audiences to discover contemporary operas and up-and-coming musicians. Ticket prices are more affordable than La Fenice and start at €10 for seats with partially blocked visibility.

CASTELLO
WINE BARS
Cantina Antica Vigna

Calle Crosera 3818, tel. 041/523-1318, Mon.-Sat. 8am-8pm and Sun. 9am-1:30pm

If you like your wine bars small and simple, Cantina Antica Vigna is the perfect spot. Nothing about this standing-room-only enoteca is fancy and that's what makes it special. That and owner Ferdinando Benettelli, who has a lot of stories to tell and isn't thrifty when it comes to pouring the local wine he's been serving for decades. Try either of the two white wines on tap at the wooden counter with a stuffed *tramezzino* sandwich—if there are any left.

HOTEL BARS
Hotel Danieli

Riva degli Schiavoni 4196, tel. 041/522-6480, www.danielihotelvenice.com

Hotel Danieli is located in a 14th-century *palazzo* overlooking the Grand Canal. The narrow front entrance leads to a lavish four-story lobby that has changed little in the last six centuries. Bar Dandolo (daily 9:30am-1am), located on the ground floor, is managed by Roberto Naccari, who mixes Vesper martinis and his own creations. Try the After Eight, a drink consisting of Ombra digestif, mint syrup, and double cream. There are comfortable armchairs and velvet loveseats in the intimate bar that's perfect for exchanging confidences. The dress code is smart casual and afternoon tea is served at 4pm sharp. The Danieli also has a rooftop bar with wonderful views of the lagoon. It's open from May until September and *aperitivo* is served 3pm-6:30pm.

Bat Bar Lounge and Terrace

Calle Borgolocco 6108, tel. 041/241-1064, daily noon-11pm

The Bat Bar Lounge and Terrace inside Hotel Ai Cavalieri may not be the most elegant, but bartenders Giovanni and Claudio know what they're doing and mix their drinks with passion and flair. Signature cocktails are €13 and include the easy-to-sip La Dogaressa (vodka, peach liquor, white vermouth, and rose water).

GIUDECCA

HOTEL BARS
Skyline Rooftop Bar

Fondamenta S. Biagio 810, tel. 041/272-3311, daily noon-1am, Stucky or Palanca water stop

The Skyline Rooftop Bar sounds cool because it is cool. This lounge bar on top of the Hilton hotel occupies a unique location, and the view from the converted factory is one of the best in the city and compensates for the commute. The bar shakes and stirs original drinks at reasonable prices given the surroundings and is perfect for a sunset *aperitivo* or nightcap.

Generator

Fondamenta Zitelle 86, tel. 041/877-8288, daily 8am-12:30am

Along the canal in the opposite direction you'll find Generator. The hostel bar may not be as fancy as the Hilton

but it's a whole lot hipper and nearly always filled with 20-something travelers from all over the world. It's the liveliest place to drink in Giudecca, where newly made friends hang out on sofas and play pool.

OPERA AND CONCERTS
Teatro Verde

Isola di San Giorgio, tel. 366/909-9241, www.liveinve.com, €30-70

Venice isn't just about classical music and if you're into musicians outside the pop mainstream like Kings of Convenience, Melody Gardot, or Patti Smith, Teatro Verde is the place to go. The outdoor amphitheater on the island of San Giorgio is worth the *vaporetto* trip. Concerts are staged throughout the summer and start at 9:15pm. Tickets can be purchased on-site or at any tourist office. Prices vary, but the cheapest seats come with the best views of the canal. Doors open at 7:30pm and there's a temporary restaurant and bar.

FESTIVALS AND EVENTS

SPRING

Su e Zo per i Ponti (Up and Down the Bridges, www.suezo.it) is a non-competitive footrace on the second Sunday in April through the streets and squares and over the bridges of Venice. The 7.5-mile (12-kilometer) event begins and ends in Piazza San Marco and the route changes every year. There's also a shorter 3.7-mile (6-kilometer) fun run that leaves from the train station. Both start at 10:30am and are open to all. The race attracts over 10,000 runners. You can register online (€7) or in person (€8) on the day of the race. There are several refreshment areas along the way, and all proceeds go to charity.

Vogalonga (third Sunday in May) is Venice's largest regatta, with over 6,000 participants rowing 1,600 vessels. All types of boats, from gondolas to kayaks, can enter this noncompetitive event. The course is 18.6 miles (30 kilometers) long and follows the major canals around Venice as well as lagoon islands like Murano and Burano before returning to the city and finishing at Punta della Salute.

Festa della Sensa, one of Venice's oldest celebrations, began around AD 1000 as a way of marking the city's maritime rise to dominance and conquest of the Adriatic. The *doge's* ship would lead boats out of the lagoon into the open sea where prayers were recited to San Nicolo, the patron saint of sailors. The dropping of a precious ring by the *doge* was later added as a symbolic marriage of the city with the sea. The ritual is reenacted on the last Sunday in May with great pomp. Today, the mayor leads the procession, which is best viewed from the northern shore of the Lido.

SUMMER

One of the most popular celebrations in Venice is La Festa del Redentore (third Sunday in July). It originated in 1576 when locals vowed to build a church if the plague that was devastating the city ended. The disease miraculously relented and Venetians have shown their gratitude ever since. During the day they walk over a pontoon bridge to the Chiesa del Redentore in Giudecca—which was built as promised—and at night thousands watch fireworks that illuminate the sky from 11pm onward. Riva degli Schiavone in Castello and Fondamenta Zattere in Dorsoduro offer the best views but provide little elbow room, especially if you arrive late. After the pyrotechnics, younger Venetians continue the celebrations on the beaches of the Lido. The day after a special morning mass is held in the church and the temporary bridge remains in place for several days, offering a rare opportunity to cross the Giudecca Canal on foot.

During late August and early September it's not uncommon to spot international film stars zipping around Venice on motorboats. They're here for the Venice Film Festival (tel. 041/521-8711, www.labiennale.org) that's been held on the Lido since 1932 and is one of the oldest festivals of its kind. In Venice the best film is awarded a golden lion and stars walk the red carpet at the art deco Palazzo del Cinema (Lido, Lungomare Guglielmo Marconi) facing the Adriatic. The theater has a 1,100-seat screening room where entries are projected day and night. Tickets are available once the program is announced and many showings are open to the general public. It's an opportunity to see great films in an exceptional environment and possibly glimpse a famous face. Exhibitions and collateral events are organized throughout the city during the 10-day festival, including an outdoor cinema in Campo San Polo.

FALL

Gondoliers have been competing with one another for centuries, and the Regata Storica (first Sun. in Sept.) fills both sides of the Grand Canal with thousands of spectators. The regatta is divided into four categories according to the type of vessel and number of oars used. A lucky few watch from *palazzi* balconies while everyone else maneuvers for space on the bridges or along the *fondamente*. The event begins at 4pm with a parade of boats manned by sailors in colorful 15th-century attire and led by someone dressed as a *doge*. Boats depart from the Giardini Publici (Castello) and row up the Grand Canal to the train station and back to the finish line opposite Palazzo Ca' Foscari. The climax of the event features gondolas oared by teams of two. Each heat has 9 or 10 competitors. The first four to place are awarded cash prizes and a red, white, green, or blue standard depending on how they finished. Winning is a big deal, but the most prestigious honor is the *Re del Remo* (King of the Oar) title that is achieved by winning five consecutive regattas. Only seven gondoliers have won it in the history of the race.

Venice may look old on the outside but it's often brand-new on the inside. That's the contrast mayor Riccardo Selvatico wanted to create when he founded the **Venice**

Biennale (Castello, Giardini Publici and Arsenale, tel. 041/521-8711, www.labiennale.org, Tues.-Sun. 10am-6pm, May-Nov. in odd years) in 1895. Initially dedicated to sculpture and painting, the event has evolved into the premier showcase for contemporary art and architecture. Today the event remains on the cutting edge and introduces leading artists from over 90 countries to a global audience of critics, enthusiasts, and collectors. The event has also expanded to include music, dance, theater, and cinema. Each edition has a curator responsible for choosing a theme and selecting participants.

The Biennale is centered on a cluster of pavilions in the Giardini Publici and Arsenal warehouses on the eastern tip of the Castello neighborhood. The Giardini Publici at the southeastern corner of the *sestiere* is the original exhibition space where countries built

rowers preparing for the Vogalonga regatta

a group of *Carnivale* goers

a handful of small pavilions in the gardens over the decades. Arsenal, five minutes north, was added later and provides large industrial spaces where conceptual artists let their imaginations run wild. The art isn't restricted, however, only to Castello—there are installations in galleries and museums around the city. If you like art, it's a great time to visit. If you aren't a fan, Venice goes on as usual.

The Biennale offers several ticket options including a single (€25) and two-day pass (€30) valid for both locations and available at either of the ticket offices located at the **Giardini Publici** (Viale dei Giardini Publici) and **Arsenale** (Campo della Tana). If you want to have the art explained there are daily **group tours** (€7 for single venue, €10 for both) that don't require advance reservations and are conducted in Italian and English. **Private tours** (tel. 041/521-8828, Mon.-Sat. 10am-5:30pm, €90) can also be arranged. An architectural version of the Biennale was launched in 1980

and is held in even years. It's nearly impossible, therefore, to miss out on cutting-edge art or architecture as the two alternate years and find ways to outdo each other every edition.

WINTER

Epiphany usually lands on January 6. It's a holiday throughout Italy but in Venice they celebrate *la Befana* a little differently. A huge stocking is hung from the Rialto and the **Regatta delle Befane** race is held. Participants are dressed as the legendary witch who gives children candy or coal depending on how they've behaved. The procession departs from the San Tomà dock at 11am and heads up the Grand Canal toward the Rialto. It's a short race that lasts less than 15 minutes. Afterward there's plenty of steaming *vin brulé* wine and an opportunity to meet *Babbo Natale* (Father Christmas).

Carnevale began in 11th-century Venice as a gluttonous celebration before the arrival of Lent and its period of abstinence. By its 18th-century licentious peak, beautiful, sophisticated, outlandish, and amusing characters all joined the party. Celebrants disguised their identities behind masks and costumes that temporarily eliminated social distinctions. Its later decadence brought about a 19th-century decline and eventual disappearance until it was revived in the 1970s. Travelers shouldn't come to Venice during *Carnevale* unless they want to take part. Streets are choked with spectators and orchestrated costume parades while most Venetians are either out of town or at private parties. Piazza San Marco is the center of the action but all the larger squares organize music and dancing. You can watch the gaiety, or better yet, dress up and join the fun. If you haven't packed a costume there are plenty of rental shops, but a simple mask and a little creativity is all you need to join the mayhem.

Carnevale season starts on the ninth Sunday before Easter and climaxes two weeks later on *martedi grasso* (Mardi Gras or Fat Tuesday). The exact dates vary each year according to when Easter falls but it generally takes place in February.

Shopping

Shakespeare never imagined writing a play called the *Merchant of Paris* or *London*. He wrote the *Merchant of Venice* because that's where the shops were. In the 16th century the streets, markets, and docks around the Rialto were jammed with traders. Merchants came from all over Europe to Venice—the most active port in the Mediterranean—to trade with their Ottoman, Indian, and Chinese counterparts. Pigments, leather, textiles, spices, perfumes, precious wood, and foodstuffs were exchanged for gold, silver, and armaments. Local workshops transformed these materials into valuable objects that brought the city wealth and fame.

Many trades have survived, making shopping in Venice an adventure. The most celebrated of these create glass, lace, and papier-mâché. Although the number of craftspeople has declined, they can still be found plying their skills across the city. Historic workshops are common in Dorsoduro, where both **Calle del Bastion** and **Calle della Chiesa** are dotted with one-room galleries where artisans work in the back and display textiles, prints, and jewelry in the front. You can find glass and lace in showroom boutiques and souvenir shops around San Marco, but if you want to go to the source you'll need to board a *vaporetto* and head out to the furnaces of Murano or the back streets of Burano where lacemaking refuses to die. Always ask permission before taking photos.

Venice only has one megastore, but many designer boutiques. Major brands cluster along the most trafficked areas, such as the streets north and west of **Piazza San Marco** or in the **Strada Nuova** in Cannaregio, which stretches from the train station all the way to the Rialto. Both sides of the Rialto Bridge are heavily commercialized, and the arcades and market stalls on the San Polo side are a

Venetian glass

Venice is famous for glass, lace, and papier-mâché masks, but that doesn't mean all the glass, lace, and paper masks you'll find in Venice were made in Venice. Local supply simply can't keep up with demand and has led many shop owners to import their wares from other parts of the world. Venetian merchants have been doing that for centuries, but if you've come all this way you may as well get the real deal. That will almost always cost more, but handmade has advantages like craftsmanship and originality that are worth paying extra.

GLASS

Glass production is centered in Murano but many furnaces supply boutiques in San Marco and offer one-of-a-kind glassware that's difficult to imitate. Genuine glass usually comes with certification (Vetro Artistico Murano, www.muranoglass.com) and large pieces are often signed. There's something for all budgets, from glazed jewelry to colorful vases and immense chandeliers. Many workshops are equipped with ovens where artisans create and sell what they make. That's always a good sign and an opportunity to observe and ask questions about the glassmaking process.

LACE

Lace or *merletti* hasn't resisted globalization as well as glass; by some estimates over 90 percent of the merchandise in Venice is made outside the city. The school that once taught lacemaking on the island of Burano closed years ago and most practitioners are in their fifties or older—but don't let that discourage you. Authentic Venetian hand-stitched lace can be hard to find, but it's still out there and recognizable by its imperfections and price tag.

MASKS

You'll spot masks being sold as soon as you step out of the train station, but most of these are cheap plastic lacking in personality. A papier-mâché mask takes time and, most of all, imagination to shape and hand paint. It's an art that has dwindled down to a small circle of dedicated practitioners. The few remaining shops are crammed floor to ceiling with sensational characters that stop window shoppers in their tracks and can provide a fantastic reminder of your journey to Venice.

good place to search for T-shirts, jewelry, and masks. **Rio Terra Lista di Spagna,** the gateway to Cannaregio, is lined with shops, but it's very touristy and best avoided.

Smaller Venetian shops are generally open from 9am to 1pm and 3pm to 7pm, though many sacrifice the traditional lunch break, especially during summer. Most shops close on Sundays and many remain closed on Monday mornings.

SAN MARCO

San Marco is one of the most commercial *sestiere* in Venice, but you don't have to scour the entire neighborhood when you can find it all in **Calle Frezzaria.** This narrow street just west of Piazza San Marco provides a mix of new and old boutiques where nothing is off the assembly line and quality, selection, and fun still matter. It's a pleasant walk with stores that are close to each other on a street that isn't overly crowded and is shaded most of the day. Elite fashion brands like Gucci and Prada can be admired nearby in Calle Larga XXII Marzo, while Merceria II Aprile leading to the Rialto is lined with affordable shops selling clothes, shoes, and accessories. The newly restored Fontego dei Tedeschi is a grand food hall and fashion mecca that attracts lots of tourists searching for luxury labels.

GLASS

The majority of glass shops are located in the busy commercial streets north and west of Piazza San Marco. Lower-end outlets sell fairly anonymous sculptures, jewelry, and trinkets; if you can't get to Murano, they make decent souvenirs. For something larger and more impressive, there are also dozens of higher-end boutiques in the area.

FGB
S. Maria del Giglio 2514, tel. 041/523-6556, daily 10am-6:30pm

It's hard to imagine a more inviting location than FGB. This glass workshop is housed within an ancient tower of which only the base has remained. Inside, a couple uses the *lume* technique to create jewelry and decorations. They heat colored glass rods up to 500 degrees and shape them into beads of different dimensions that are then used to make colorful earrings, bracelets, and necklaces. You can find a nice gift here for under €20.

EMI Art Glass
Calle della Mandola 3803, tel. 041/523-1326, Mon.-Sat. 10:30am-7:30pm

To help consumers distinguish between Murano-made and everything else, the glassmakers association created a special *Vetro Artistico Murano* label that only shops selling authentic local glass can display. You'll find it at EMI Art Glass, which sells blown vases, marine sculptures, and solid-glass objects that would look good on a mantle or shelf. Pieces are as expensive as they are heavy and shipping can be arranged.

Once you begin shopping for glass it may be hard to stop—but the more time you spend examining the goods, the better you'll become at distinguishing made in China from made in Murano.

MASKS AND COSTUMES
Atelier Flavia
Santa Marina, Corte Spechiera 6010, tel. 041/528-7429, www.veniceatelier.com, Mon.-Sat. 10am-6pm

The historically accurate costumes, papier-mâché masks, tuxedos, wigs, capes, hats, and shoes at Atelier Flavia could transform anyone. It's the ideal place to come before *Carnevale* for an *Eyes Wide Shut* (or any other) look. Costumes are available for rental or purchase. If you miss the festivities you can still rent a costume for an hour (€50 women/€80 men) and take as many pictures as you want in the adjacent streets or have a professional photographer (€320) immortalize you dressed as a Venetian.

PAPER GOODS
La Carta
San Marco 5547a, tel. 041/520-2325, daily 9:30am-7:30pm

In front of the post office, La Carta sells handmade paper and specializes in marbleized sheets, calendars, and agendas. If you forgot your diary at home this is the perfect place to buy a new one and start jotting down your impressions of Venice. There's also a decent selection of pens and pencils.

CLOTHING AND ACCESSORIES
Al Duca d'Aosta Venezia 1902
Campo San Zulian 606, tel. 041/523-0145, Mon.-Sat. 10am-7:30pm and Sun. 11am-7pm

Anyone with the instinct of a dandy will enjoy a trip to Al Duca d'Aosta Venezia 1902. This venerated gentleman's brand combines traditional British style with elegant Italian tailoring. It's where princes came for fashion that never fades and modern gentlemen come for wool jackets, cashmere sweaters, and cotton shirts that cross seasonal divides.

Giuliana's Longo's
Calle del Lovo 4813, tel. 041/522-6454, Mon.-Sat. 10am-7pm

Items at Giuliana's Longo's hat shop are made right here in Venice. In fact, Giuliana herself makes the hats she stocks. Inside her shop Panama,

gondolier, *Carnevale*, felt, and straw hats are haphazardly arranged in armoires and on antique hat stands. This little corner of hat history is about as far as you can get from mass production. Giuliana is usually working away at her little desk on one-of-a-kind pieces that all have their own personality. Try one on and see if the hat fits.

Barena Venezia
Calle Minelli 4260b, tel. 041/523-8457, Mon.-Sat. 10am-1pm, 4pm-7:30pm

If you want to dress like a Venetian, visit Barena Venezia. This men's and women's shop has been creating versatile and functional clothing since 1961. Coats, jackets, and sweaters are made using local textiles and are inspired by 20th-century lagoon style. Everything is comfortable and easy to wear.

Ermenegildo Zegna
Bocca di Piazza San Marco 1241, tel. 041/522-1204, daily 10am-7pm

Gentlemen ready for an Italian makeover can head to Ermenegildo Zegna. Customers are coddled by expert staff who also offer made-to-measure clothing, which can be delivered overseas.

Buosi
San Bortolomio 5382, tel. 041/520-8567, daily 10am-7:30pm

Buosi has kept Venetian men looking good since 1897. They sew shirts, jackets, trousers, and suits to measure and have a selection of ready-to-wear pieces including ties any man would want to receive.

Kiriku
Calle Frezzaria 1729, tel. 041/296-0619, Mon.-Sat. 10am-7:30pm

If you need an evening cocktail dress, skirt, or blouse—or even if you don't—Kiriku boutique is worth browsing.

✪ SHOPPING FOR MASKS

Throughout the 18th century, Venetians used masks to enjoy stigma-free decadence. Nobles wore masks to visit brothels, youth to escape from parents, the poor to frequent the rich, the rich to frequent the poor, aristocratic ladies to enter dark alleys, clergy to temporarily break vows, and so on. Famous Venetian Giacomo Casanova wore a mask as he went to meet his lovers at the Cantina Do Mori, where he was a regular.

Masks are still used today and are one of the most common sights at street-side stalls and gift shops around the city, where cheap versions can be had for €5-10. These have little to do with the papier-mâché originals carefully made in a dozen or so ateliers around the city. These versions sell for €30 to €300 and are based on classic molds that have been used for centuries. The most common is the white *Bauta* mask that allows the wearer to eat and drink while remaining hidden from view. It is worn by both men and women and often paired with a black *tabarro* cape. Another popular mask is the *Medico della Peste,* recognizable by the long nose that resembles a bird's beak. It was invented by a doctor in the 17th century who didn't want to be recognized by his patients dying from the plague and was later adopted by *Carnevale* goers. The *Colombina* is a half mask that covers eyes and cheeks. It continues to be favored by Venetian ladies and often comes painted in silver or gold and adorned with feathers and beads.

These and many other historical masks along with newer creations are available at workshops around the city where you can learn more about the origins of your disguise. Castello is a good neighborhood to start shopping for masks. Below are some shops to check out:

- **Cà del Sol** (page 113): The place to play 12th-century dress up with a patient owner who explains the traditions behind the different costumes on display.

- **Papier Maché** (page 114): Handmade, authentic masks created to order or purchased off the shelf. Prices are higher here but worth it.

- **Ca' Mancana** (page 109): Friendly, unpushy staff with a wide selection of masks for varying budgets.

The wall racks are filled with emerging designers that have a retro-chic style that looks and feels good. A small selection of bags, shoes, and accessories are in the back next to the white revolving armchair where patient partners recline and express their approval.

Empresa

Calle Frezzeria 1586, tel. 041/241-2687, Mon.-Sat. 10am-7:30pm and Sun. 11:30am-7:30pm

Leather and other materials for both men and women await at Empresa. You'll find great jackets and accessories in this finely decorated store, which is run by five friendly brothers who aren't in a rush to sell anything.

Their original pieces can add personality to any outfit.

Arnold & Battois

Calle Fuseri 4271, tel. 041/528-5944,
daily 10am-1pm and 3:30pm-7:30pm

Arnold & Battois creates handbags in unique shapes that turn heads and fashionable women adore. Seasonal collections are inspired by and entirely made in Venice. Leather is the material of choice and the designs are a result of experience and slow production.

Armadio di Coco

Calle Frezzeria 1797, tel. 041/523-6093,
Mon.-Sat. 10:30am-1:30pm and 3pm-7:30pm

Armadio di Coco is an elegant vintage shop that would make an ideal walk-in closet. Dior, Chanel, Fendi, Valentino, and other designer labels are there, along with bags, belts, shoes, and hats all neatly arranged on secondhand racks and shelves. The clothes may be used but it's nearly impossible to tell. Many have been given new hems and necklines by the young designer/owner, who wields thread and needles in her backroom workshop.

DEPARTMENT STORES
T Fondaco dei Tedeschi

Calle del Fontego dei Tedeschi,
daily 10am-8pm

There's only one department store in Venice and that's more than enough. T Fondaco dei Tedeschi is a four-story shrine to luxury Italian brands and a magnet for fashion-conscious shoppers. The building has a long history of commerce and was originally constructed by German merchants in the 13th century. Today the newly renovated interior is a pleasure for the eyes and the wardrobe. Even if you aren't interested in bags or shoes there's a tempting food court and great views

from the rooftop terrace. Reservations are required and can be made on-site or online. Visitors have 15 minutes to enjoy the skyline.

TOYS
Fanfaluca

Calle Fuseri 4339, tel. 041/847-6891,
Mon.-Sat. 8am-8pm

Fanfaluca is as fun for nostalgic adults as it is for kids. There's clothing, wooden toys, puppets, old-fashioned dolls, and plenty of stuffed animals. They carry difficult-to-find teddy bears, sheep, rabbits, and cows from the legendary Moulin Roty brand. These soft, colorful animals make great presents and become instant friends for toddlers. A majority of the store's items are handmade.

MARKETS
Mercatino di Campo San Maurizio

Campo San Maurizio, tel. 333/965-9994,
www.mercatinocamposanmaurizio.it,
Fri.-Sun., 9am-7pm

Mercatino di Campo San Maurizio, a seasonal antiques market, is perfect for aimless meandering. Dealers from across Italy show a trove of collectibles and curiosities from the 17th to the 20th centuries and all decades in between. A variety of Murano glass is on display along with silver dinnerware, military regalia from both World Wars, textiles, phonographs, vintage clothing, and more. Browsing the covered wooden stalls is fun whether you're a collector or just interested in history. If you spot something you like, inquire about date and origin before asking the price, which can often be negotiated down. The market is generally held the weekend before Easter and the second weekends of September, October, and December but dates vary slightly every year.

DORSODURO

There are fewer shops in Dorsoduro than other *sestiere* but the ones you will find are often owned by craftspeople who split their time making glass or paper creations and assisting costumers. If you haven't found the right souvenir yet, **Calle del Bastion,** the narrow street connecting the Guggenheim to Punta della Dogana, is a good place to start looking. It's lined with small art galleries, jewelry workshops, and a great stationery store.

While you're browsing, keep an eye out for Bence; the lute-playing Hungarian expat can be found in Campiello Barbaro or in the nearby passageway leading to Punta della Dogana. Compositions are his own and sound like a Baroque version of *Stairway to Heaven*. He makes his living from donations and sales of his CD (€10). Over the canal, another street musician is usually playing classical music using wine glasses filled with water. Vivaldi sounds surprisingly good played this way and crowds tend to gather in the little square facing a church. CDs are also available here.

GLASS
Designs 188
Calle del Bastion 188, tel. 041/523-9426, Mon.-Sat. 11am-7pm
The secret to Giorgio and Trina's 30-year marriage is having separate workshops where they create distinctive glass jewelry. Granted the shops are on the same street and Giorgio is often working the flame in his wife's studio, but that doesn't seem to effect marital longevity. Earrings, bracelets, and necklaces inside Designs 188 are all beautifully intricate and colorful,

which makes choosing hard. Prices are reasonable and if you want to contrast and compare head to Giorgio's shop (Calle del Bastion 167) down the street on the corner. In between are a number of modern **galleries** featuring paintings and other ingenious objects by local artists.

MASKS AND COSTUMES
Ca' Mancana
Calle de le Botteghe 3172, tel. 041/277-6142, daily 10am-8pm
Masks are everywhere in Venice but few shops sell their own handmade models. Ca' Mancana is one of the finest and uses traditional papier-mâché techniques to create both classic *Carnevale* and fantasy characters. Anyone can hide their identity for as little as €30. This is where Stanley Kubrick came when he wanted masks for *Eyes Wide Shut*. If you want to learn how masks are made or are traveling with kids, ask about the maskmaking **workshops** that last a couple of hours and keep young and old entertained.

PAPER GOODS
Stamperia il Pavone
Calle Venier dei Leoni 721, tel. 041/523-4517, daily 10am-5:30pm
Fabio Pelosin has worked for over 30 years inside Stamperia il Pavone hand-decorating paper he uses to cover notebooks, photo albums, bookmarks, pencils, frames, and boxes. The process can be observed through the little window that divides the small showroom from the workshop where Fabio or his assistant can be found working on new creations. He begins by drawing a motif, which he then carves into a wooden block. The stamp is then covered with paint and applied to paper. The unique results make

colorful souvenirs you won't find anywhere else.

handmade stationery

BOOKS
La Toletta
Sacca della Toletta 1214, tel. 041/523-2034, Mon.-Sat. 9am-7:30pm, Sun. 11am-7pm
You can never have too many books, and even if you don't read Italian you can judge by the covers at La Toletta and choose a novel or nonfiction work for your bookcase back home. There are different sections to browse in this shop, which opened in 1933 and has retained a vintage 1970s look. Talks and lectures are regularly scheduled on weekends.

CLOTHING
Original Laboratory of Design
Fondamenta San Basilio 1643, daily 10am-7pm
Original Laboratory of Design sounds pretentious, but it's really just vintage women's clothing with a customized twist. Designer Federica and her artistic collaborators transform fashion from the past into original clothing, bags, and accessories that add zest to any wardrobe. The eclectic little shop is a great place to browse and watch Federica at work on her latest creations.

HOUSEWARES
Madera
Campo San Barnaba 2762, tel. 041/522-4181, Mon.-Sat. 10am-1pm and 3:30pm-7:30pm
Madera offers a contemporary range of dining and cooking ware. Local designers produce most of the dishes, utensils, and cutting boards and the owner makes many of the wooden items herself. The style is more Nordic than Venetian, but every piece would be a valuable addition to a kitchen. Nearby is a second store that sells jewelry and accessories with the same artisanal mantra.

MARKETS
Mercatino di Polvere di Ricordi
Campo Sant'Agnese 30123, 7am-7pm
The name of this market translates to "dusty memory market," and it is just that. But it's the good sort of dust, where patient browsers can find hidden gems among a myriad of antiques, old books, prints, silverware, and collectibles. The market only takes place three times a year on the second weekend of March, the first weekend of October, and the last day of November. It's spread around the city and stalls are also set up in the Erberia near the Rialto, Campo San Polo, and Campo San Silvestro.

SAN POLO AND SANTA CROCE
GLASS
Marco Franzato
Santa Croce, Corte Piossi 2176, tel. 041/524-0770, daily 10am-6pm
Marco Franzato is a master glassmaker who has restored the windows of many ancient *palazzi* including Palazzo Ducale. He opened his workshop in 1993. Inside he creates rose glass displays, lampshades, and collectibles. The jewelry is the most accessible in

price and ease of transport, although direct shipping can be arranged. Marco uses a number of techniques to create one-of-a-kind earrings, necklaces, and rings that take shape in the lab at the back of the shop.

MASKS AND COSTUMES
Atelier Pietro Longhi
San Polo, Rio Terà 2608, tel. 041/714-478, Mon.-Sat. 10am-2pm

Atelier Pietro Longhi rents (€160) and sells (€1,500) period costumes. They also tailor original disguises to measure from paintings, photos, comic books, or dreams. It usually takes about a week before you can wear it. Mask also available to buy or rent.

CLOTHING
Altrove
San Polo, Calle Moro 2659a, tel. 041/476-4473, Tues.-Sat. 11am-6pm

If you've ever wanted to dress differently without shocking anyone drop into Altrove. This alternative atelier is off the main shopping drag and provides a fresh take on made-to-measure for men and women. The clothes are geometrical and difficult to categorize other than being oblivious to trends. Textiles, production, and design are all rigorously made in Italy.

Monica Daniele's
San Polo, Calle del Scaleter 2235, tel. 041/524-6242, Mon.-Sat. 9am-1pm and 2:30pm-6pm

Monica Daniele's shop is where adults play dress-up. Monica nearly singlehandedly rescued 18th-century Venetian accessories from fashion oblivion. One item in particular she saved from fashion extinction is the *tabarro,* a wool cloak once commonly spotted on wintery Venetian streets. It comes in blue, black, or gray and

goes well with the extensive range of felt hats on display in the window and around this informal shop.

Piedàterre
San Polo, Ruga dei Oresi 60, tel. 041/528-5513, daily 10am-7pm

Shoes aren't complicated at Piedàterre. The colorful boutique under the arcades of the Rialto has refashioned traditional footwear for the 21st century. The shoes in question are slipper-like and inspired by those once worn by gondoliers and peasants. Today, velvet has been added and recycled tires are used for the soles. They come in all colors for children and adults and make a comfortable summertime walking shoe.

Penny Lane Shop
Santa Croce, Calle Falier 39, tel. 041/524-4134, Tues.-Fri. 9am-noon and 4:30pm-6pm, Sat. 4:30pm-6pm

The high student population may explain the number of funky and vintage clothing shops in the neighborhood, but these small boutiques are for anyone who values retro style and enjoys hunting for new and slightly used hats, bags, and clothing. One of the oldest is the Penny Lane Shop, which stocks colorful northern European brands made from a range of materials. Try on jewelry accessories in the side room dedicated to *haut vintage.*

JEWELRY
Attombri
San Polo, Sottoportico degli Orefici 65, tel. 041/521-2524, Mon. 3:30pm-7:30pm, Tues.-Sat. 10am-1pm and 3:30pm-7:30pm

The arcades leading to the Rialto are the traditional domain of goldsmiths, and many jewelers still work along this busy thoroughfare. The brothers who run Attombri combine traditional metals with contemporary design. They create necklaces, bracelets, and earrings in silver, copper, and glass that are elegant and wearable.

BOOKS
Libreria Mare di Carta
Santa Croce, Fondamenta dei Tolentini 222,
tel. 041/716-304, Tues.-Sat. 9am-1pm and
3:30pm-7:30pm

Venice is the perfect location for a bookshop dedicated to the sea, and Libreria Mare di Carta is lined with nonfiction and fictional tales in which waves are the protagonist. Cristina Giussani is both an accomplished sailor and bookseller who can point you to the right shelf. Most of the literature is in Italian but there's also a great quantity of maps, model boats, prints, and comics that are easily understood.

WOODWORKING CRAFTS
Dalla Venezia Angelo
San Polo, Calle del Scaleter 2204,
tel. 041/721-659, Mon.-Sat. 8am-1pm
and 4pm-8pm

It's easy to pass Dalla Venezia Angelo without a second thought, but if you're interested in how wood gets transformed into miniature objects step inside and let Angelo show you around. He's been keeping the tradition of woodworking alive since 1959 and will gladly explain the dusty workshop where he carves and sands planks of Swiss pine and Tuscan olive into rings and pyramids using a vintage wood-spinning machine that allows him to transform wood into apples and pears. This isn't mass production and prices aren't cheap, but everything is unique and represents a lifetime of dedication.

SPICES
Drogheria Mascari
San Polo, Ruga dei Spezieri 381,
tel. 041/522-9762, Mon.-Sat. 8am-1pm
and 4pm-7:30pm

There are strict rules about the food travelers can bring home, but fortunately the gastronomic goods on offer at Drogheria Mascari will pass customs. This wonderful-smelling shop is full of tempting ingredients like dried porcini mushrooms, sweet paprika, saffron, candied fruits, and mysterious spices. The well-stocked gourmet section also carries truffle-inspired condiments and *mostarda veneta* (Venetian mustard) that elevates meat and cheese.

RIALTO MARKETS

The Rialto is the commercial heart of Venice, and both sides of the bridge have been crammed with activity since the 15th century. The area on and around the bridge feels like one continuous market, with arcades and squares filled with all sorts of businesses that attract locals and tourists alike. The San Polo side is the busier of the two and where the city's main markets are located. **Ruga dei Oresi**, on the northern side of the bridge, was once the domain of jewelers who worked in the small shops lining the arcades, but most have been replaced with boutiques and stalls selling glass, masks, clothing, and souvenirs of varying quality. You can escape the crush of visitors by exploring the alcoves parallel to the main street or by heading north to the nearby **Campo Cesare.** There's a little more breathing room and dozens of kiosks (daily 8:30am-6pm) selling Venetian logoed T-shirts, sweatshirts, and hats in adult and child sizes. **Nicolo** (recognized by his shaved head and good-natured cynicism), like most of the merchants here, offers a discount on multiple purchases. Farther along and facing the Grand Canal are the fish market and produce market.

CANNAREGIO

PAPER GOODS
Moleskine

Stazione Santa Lucia, Fondamenta Santa Lucia 20, tel. 041/740-913, daily 8am-9pm

Want to follow in the literary footsteps of Bruce Chatwin or Ernest Hemingway? Stop in at the local Moleskine branch. The modern shop inside the train station sells more than the famed black diary that made the company famous. You'll also find bags, wallets, e-reader cases, and pens and writing implements with the same unmistakable style.

Tipografia Basso

Calle del Fumo 5306, tel. 041/523-4681, Mon-Sat. 9am-1pm and 2:30pm-6pm, cash only

The smell of ink and paper is the sign you've arrived at Tipografia Basso. Inside the small atelier, Gianni works away on letterpress, lithographic, and offset printers but can always find the time to explain the different printing processes and demonstrate why the old-fashioned way is sometimes the best way. You can buy small prints of Pinocchio and other classic images or order a set of personalized hand-printed business cards.

ANTIQUES
Antichità al Ghetto

Calle Ghetto Vecchio 1133/1134, tel. 041/524-4592, Tues.-Sun. 10am-7pm

You'll find antique lace, purses, pillows, ceramics, and furniture at Antichità al Ghetto. Elisabetta and Giuliano opened their shop in 2006 and have been trading in history ever since. The friendly couple is knowledgeable about the goods they sell and will happily explain the origin and use of any item.

MARKETS
Mercatino dei Miracoli

Campo Santa Maria Nova, tel. 041/271-0022, Mar.-Dec. Sat.-Sun. all day

Venetian flea markets are never shabby and always offer an opportunity to find unique (often antique) Murano glass, lace, silverware, and mixed oddities with loads of historical charm. If you're in Venice on the right weekend that's what you'll find at Mercatino dei Miracoli. Passionate hobbyists and collectors organize this small open-air market in a lovely *campo* where objects of all kinds can be discovered on the second weekend of the month.

CASTELLO

GLASS
Vetreria

Castello 3868, tel. 349/271-3808, €5-30

Vetreria is a fun little shop specializing primarily in jewelry that's made on-site. Prices are reasonable and the style is funky rather than refined. They also custom-make pieces according to your taste and are happy for you to watch while they work.

MASKS AND COSTUMES
Cà del Sol

Fondamenta dell'Osmarin 4964, tel. 041/528-5549, daily 10am-8pm

The walls of Cà del Sol are covered in masks. All the classics are here, including *bauta, columbine,* harlequin, plague, and scores of one-off creations handmade using papier-mâché, leather, ceramic, and iron. The shop has been around since 1986 and helped revitalize the art of maskmaking in the city. It's run by a collective of artisans who patiently answer questions and aren't uptight about allowing customers to try on masks. They organize maskmaking demonstrations and five-day courses, and rent elaborate costumes during *Carnevale*.

Papier Maché
Calle Lunga Santa Maria Formosa 5174,
tel. 041/522-9995, Mon.-Sat. 9am-7:30pm
It takes a while to distinguish between the different mask types, but the quality of the structure and painted detailing is immediately evident at Papier Maché. Four decades of maskmaking experience is on display in the windows of this boutique, which has a large selection of ornate masks with designs you won't see anywhere else. Prices are a little high, but this is the real deal—and perhaps the finest way to keep your identity a secret.

PAPER GOODS
G. L. Pitacco
Ruga Giuffa 4758, tel. 041/520-8687,
Mon.-Sat. 3pm-8pm
Bookbinder G. L. Pitacco specializes in traditional and modern bindings. The little shop stocks diaries, photo albums, and address books of all dimensions. You can also have books bound or repaired. They hand-make sheets of marbleized paper that are different from the Florentine variety; their sheets can also be found at Domino Arte (Castello, Via Giuseppe Garibaldi 1649, tel. 041/523-0090, Fri.-Wed. 1:30pm-7:30pm).

BOOKS
Libreria Aqua Alta
Calle Longa Santa Maria Formosa 5176b,
tel. 041/296-0841, daily 9am-8pm
Books are haphazardly stacked at Libreria Aqua Alta in bathtubs and boats along narrow aisles that would have driven Melvil Dewey crazy. Yet it's hard not to like this bookshop and be absorbed by titles that range in subject and language from architecture to Swahili. Outside near the sleeping literary cats are a collection of vintage postcards, prints, and other paper materials that make unusual gifts.

CLOTHING AND ACCESSORIES
Banco Lotto no.10
Salizada Sant'Antonin 3478,
tel. 041/522-1439, Mon. 3:30pm-7:30pm,
Tues.-Sat. 10am-1pm and 3:30pm-7:30pm
Prison and fashion may seem incompatible, but over the last decade the women's penitentiary in Giudecca has collaborated with local dressmakers to help inmates learn a useful trade. The result is affordable and stylish women's clothing stocked in Banco Lotto no.10 in eastern Castello. You can also find original accessories like bags made from discarded coffee sacks sold for as little as €10.

MARKETS
Mercatino delle Robe da Mar
Via Garibaldi
Venice's most popular market is held several times a year on the first or last Sunday of the month. Mercatino delle Robe da Mar translates to "stuff of the sea market" but that doesn't mean it's only nautical in nature—you'll find everything from antique stamps to used vinyl LPs. It's also a chance to visit one of the lesser-tread parts of the city and discover the eastern tip of Venice.

GIUDECCA

TEXTILES

Fortuny Textile Factory

Fondamenta S. Biagio 805,
tel. 041/528-7697, www.fortuny.com,
Mon.-Fri. 10am-1pm and 2pm-6pm

Giudecca is a long way to go for a shopping spree, and there aren't that many shops to begin with. Yet Venice's longest island does have some industrial gems like the Fortuny textile factory. The long brick building overlooking the canal next to the Stucky wheat mill began producing bolts of cloth in 1921 and still operates today. Though the factory doesn't allow visitors, the showroom does, and it's filled with textiles from the company's past and present. There's also a lovely garden next door that can be visited by appointment.

Recreation and Activities

PARKS AND GARDENS

Grass is rare in Venice and there are few green open spaces. The parks and gardens that do exist are small and simple. They're usually quiet places where tourists have no time to tread and Venetians retreat to push grandchildren around in strollers and read the newspaper.

Giardino Papadopoli

Santa Croce, Fondamenta Papadopoli,
daily 10am-6pm

Giardino Papadopoli is located on an island opposite the train station. It's interspersed with gravel paths that circle a surprising variety of trees and bushes. There's a good playground for little climbers, benches, and a small lawn where you can lie down and forget where you are.

Giardini Savorgnan

Cannaregio, Fondamenta Venier,
daily 8am-6:30pm

On the other side of the Grand Canal, Giardini Savorgnan provides even greater tranquility and a space for street musicians to relax after lunch and toddlers to swing and slide. Like most parks in Venice it doesn't impress in scale or design but it is clean and provides a bucolic break from canals and streets.

Parco della Rimembranze

Castello, Viale IV Novembre, open 24/7,
Sant'Elena vaporetto station

The largest park in Venice is Parco della Rimembranze on Sant'Elena Island at the southern tip of Castello. This is as far from the train station as you can get and well off the tourist radar. It's an everyday park that's well maintained and comes with lagoon views, playgrounds, and shaded walkways. What's also nice is the adjacent neighborhood where residents go about their business seemingly unaware of the rest of the city. There are wide *calle*, several greengrocers, and unadorned bars with tables immersed in green.

Giardini Pubblici

Castello, Viale Giardini Pubblici, Giardini
vaporetto station

The Giardini Pubblici, or public gardens, are nearby over a bridge. These gardens attract art lovers who come to visit the Art Biennale held here on odd-numbered years. The playground has seen better days, but the Paradiso Café near the dock is a nice place to rest a few minutes and has its own little art gallery.

Giardini ex Reali

San Marco, Riva degli chiavone, open 24/7

Closer to the center and just around the corner from Piazza San Marco the Giardini ex Reali provides a tiny refuge from the tourists wandering along the promenade out front. The beech trees and goldfish-inhabited fountains inside this gated garden were part of Napoleon's royal palace and laid out in the late 1800s. There are plenty of empty benches (red seems to be the favorite color for benches in Venice) and the nearby tourist office makes it a strategic spot to plan your next move or spend a few minutes doing nothing.

ROWING

Row Venice

Cannaregio, Sacca Misericordia Marina,
Fondamenta Gasparo Contarini 5540,
tel. 347/725-0637, www.rowvenice.org,
1-2 people €85, 3/€120, 4/€140, daily
10am-4pm

Boats are different in Venice. Shallow canals means most are flat bottomed and rowed standing up to gain maximum visibility. This characteristic led to a particular rowing style, which is practiced in few places outside the city and can be experienced at Row Venice. An Australian expat and her association of 20 female instructors run 90-minute lessons that cost the same as a gondola ride and are twice as fun. Participants learn the basics of navigating a locally made *batellina* vessel, which was once ubiquitous along the canals and looks like a gondola without the regalia. Lessons are conducted

in English and start with a demonstration of basic strokes and a briefing on the rules of Venetian waterways. The group operates off a quiet canal and participants take turns paddling and steering. Wannabe sailors should wear loose-fitting clothes and comfortable shoes.

BOATING

Why sweat on a rowboat when you can relax in a motorboat? It is a somewhat riskier option and some boating experience is preferable, but Venetian maritime laws are surprisingly lenient when it comes to rentals.

Brussa Is Boat

Cannaregio, Fondamenta Labia 331,
tel. 041/715-787, www.brussaisboat.it,
Mon.-Fri. 7:30am-6pm, Apr.-Oct. Sat.-Sun.
8:30am-7pm

No license is required to navigate the small motorboats available from Brussa Is Boat. All you need is a credit card, valid ID, and a desire for adventure.

Daniele or one of his colleagues will familiarize you with the 23-foot pleasure craft and the essentials of Venetian navigation. The *topetta* (traditional flat-bottomed boat) seats six and the 15hp outboard engine is steered from the tiller. The key is to go slow, stay on the right, and avoid busy or narrow canals. This isn't a free-for-all expedition and you can't go anywhere you like. There are seven preestablished itineraries around the lagoon that cover the islands of the Lido (red), Burano (green and purple), and Venice (yellow). That still leaves plenty of exploring to do for an hour (€35 plus tax) or the entire day (€160 plus tax). Fuel is included and reservations should be made in advance during high season. If your nautical skills aren't up to Venetian waterways you can hire someone to do the sailing for you.

KAYAKING

Vaporetto and gondola aren't the only ways of getting around Venice. Adventurous travelers can do their own paddling and discover the city's waterways.

Venice Kayak

Certosa Marina, Certosa Island,
tel. 346/477-1327, www.venicekayak.com,
half day €95, full day €125, vaporetto 4.1
or 4.2

Venice Kayak offers a variety of guided tours for both novices and experienced kayakers. Daily half-day excursions for 2-6 people depart mornings (9:15am-1pm) or afternoons (2:15pm-6pm) from the island of Certosa and crisscross the *sestiere* of Castello and San Marco. Expect about 6 miles (10 kilometers) of paddling in single or double kayaks at a relaxed pace. Full-day tours of Venice and the lagoon islands are also available. Dress with the expectation of getting wet and don't bring a camera unless it's waterproof.

Venice by Water

Cannaregio, Calle Stretta Morosini 5823,
tel. 041/528-0893, www.venicebywater.com

Venice by Water provides short day and night kayak tours that last 30 (€35), 60 (€50), or 120 (€90) minutes. Several combine paddling with breaks for food and drink. All tours are guided and explore lesser-trafficked canals around Cannaregio, Arsenale, and Murano. Kayaks seat two people and are equipped with foot pedals in case you tire.

STAND-UP PADDLE
SUP in Venice

Cannaregio, Fondamenta della Sensa 3320,
www.supinvenice.com, €50-80 per hour

There are many ways to explore Venetian canals, but stand-up paddle is the most fun. If you're an experienced paddler or have decent balance and want to give it a try, head to SUP in Venice. Eliana Argine discovered the sport on a trip to California in 2009 and founded her company nearly as soon as she got back to Venice. She's been enthusiastically leading tours and navigating the city ever since. Routes vary depending on number of participants (max four), weather, tide, and traffic and take one or two hours to complete. Excursions are organized from March to November and comfortable attire is required (no bare chests or bikinis).

SUP in Venice

TOURS
WALKING TOURS

It's inevitable to have questions in Venice and spending an hour or two with someone who knows the answers is essential if you're serious about getting to know the city. There are many guides to choose from now that the certification process has been simplified and guides

FAMILY-FRIENDLY VENICE

kids watching glass being made

Venice is a dream city for kids. It may not have a children's museum or amusement park but it has water, boats, and bridges. Parents can relax knowing there are no cars to look out for and give kids full reign to run around the squares chasing pigeons and playing ball with local youth. There are no limits to the imagination in Venice, and the city delights and stimulates children in ways they will never forget. Unfortunately, parents with babies and young walkers may suffer, as carrying a stroller up and down the city's many bridges is an arduous task. It's easier to use a hiking carrier or stick to the *fondamente* promenades. Although bicycles and other wheeled objects are prohibited in Venice, strollers are allowed.

are allowed to work anywhere in Italy. That means it's more important than ever to check qualifications and ensure your guide is an expert on Venice. If the guide is a native that's even better, and if they can combine facts with passion to make the city come alive that's the best.

There are over 400 licensed guides in Venice and passing the certification exam is not a formality. It takes a combination of historical, artistic, and cultural knowledge as well as excellent language skills. Visitors can choose from group tours organized by the city, private tour companies, and independent guides. While the former costs less, the latter are usually smaller and allow for greater personalization. Whatever you choose,

it's a good idea to have a tour early in your stay so you can become familiar with the city as soon as possible. It will help you appreciate and spot red flagpoles, winged lion, and a thousand other things you could easily overlook. Taking a walking tour is also a unique opportunity to let yourself be led by someone who doesn't need a map and rarely gets lost.

Private certified guides charge a standard €70-80 hourly fee and two-hour tours are recommended. Prices are the same whether two or eight people participate. **Group tours** are cheaper but less personal and can include up to thirty visitors. They start from €30 per person for a 90-minute visit. There are fewer itineraries and most generally focus on the San

Here are some Venice experiences families can share:

- To generate a little fun, just buy a **mask.** Parents can find cheap plastic versions (€2) at souvenir stands and shops around the city. Let children pick their own and walk masqueraded through the streets. Note: Inexpensive doesn't always mean made in China. Low-priced plastic and rough papier-mâché masks are also fabricated in Italy. They come in many varieties and may be tricky to tie.

- There are several **playgrounds** (Giardino Papadopoli, Parco Savorgnan, Giardini Pubblici) equipped with traditional swings, slides, and wooden climbing castles. Toddlers to 10-year-olds will love them.

- All ages will love riding the *vaporetto* **boats** that magically eliminate whining—and are free for all passengers under six.

- Hungry kids? That's not a problem in Venice! The mini portions served mornings and afternoons at *bacaro* **bars** make delicious snacks and may convince fussy eaters to try something new.

- Kid-friendly museums include the **Museo Storico Navale** with its collection of ancient sailing vessels and the **secret dungeons** in Palazzo Ducale.

- **Glassblowing** demonstrations on the island of Murano, along with **bell towers** (Piazza San Marco, Isola di San Giorgio Maggiore, or Torcello), will captivate even the shortest attention spans.

- With a little planning you can also organize **papermaking workshops** and classical concerts for artistically minded adolescents.

- Consider booking a hotel room at kid-friendly **Flora** in San Marco, where strollers, high chairs, and cots are all available at no extra cost, or **La Villeggiatura** in San Polo, where children under nine sleep for free.

Marco area. If you're interested in food, modern art, or anything off the beaten track you're better off with a private guide.

Private Guides

Venice native **Luisella Romeo** (tel. 349/084-8303, www.seevenice.it) got her tour-guide license back when the exam was nearly impossible to pass and included a written and oral test. She was one of 27 guides selected from 800 applicants and it's clear why the moment she starts telling the story of the city. Not only does she know her art and history but she also knows how to make it interesting and absorb visitors with her enthusiasm. Today she runs **See Venice Tours** and provides many different ways to experience the city. Visits cost €75 per hour regardless of group size and two hours with Luisella provides a perfect introduction to Venice.

Sara Grinzato (tel. 345/850-1309, www.guidedvenice.com) is another local who knows her city well and loves sharing her knowledge with visitors. After a couple of hours together you'll see Venice differently and things that made no sense will seem normal. She can customize visits according to your interest in art, food, or shopping, but tours often start with an overview of classic destinations like Piazza San Marco and the Rialto. You can arrange to meet both guides at your accommodation and organize fun treasure hunts for young children and teens.

Free Tours

Venice Free Walking Tour (www. venicefreewalkingtour.com) sounds too good to be true—but isn't. This nonprofit initiative leads 2.5-hour morning and afternoon tours that cover the foundation of the city, traditions, gastronomy, and plenty of facts and figures. Tours start from the old wellhead in Campo Santi Apostoli (Cannaregio) and proceed over a historic two-mile route. Guides are passionate local volunteers who get a kick out of helping curious visitors uncover their city. All tours are conducted in English.

Once you've fallen in love with Venice, you may want to help preserve it, and there are many organizations dedicated to just that. **Save Venice Inc.** (Dorsoduro, Palazzo Contarini Polignac 870, tel. 041/528-5247, www. savevenice.org, Mon.-Fri. 9am-5pm) helps repair and restore the city one painting, sculpture, and *palazzo* at a time. You can go to their office and speak with Leslie or Holly about the organization's activities, visit their library, and follow one of their **self-guided tours** dedicated to art and architecture. Each lasts about 90 minutes and the suggested donation of €20 that goes to funding future restoration projects is appreciated.

BOAT TOURS

Several companies including **City Sightseeing** operate boat tours around Venice. Travelers can compare the options along the **Riva degli Schiavoni** waterfront from where they regularly depart. Journey times and itineraries vary and the biggest advantage compared to public transportation is the assurance of getting a seat. The convenience and widespread availability of *vaporetto*, however, make boat tours nearly superfluous.

Il Burchiello (Padova, Via Porciglia 34, 049/876-0233, www. ilburchiello.it, €55 half day, €99 full day) operates expeditions up the Brenta Canal that connects Venice to Oriago and Padova. Boats depart at 9am from the Pietà water station (Riva degli Schiavoni) near Piazza San Marco on Tuesdays, Thursdays, and Saturdays. The *bateau mouche*-like vessels have air-conditioned interiors, but the best seats are upstairs on the roof deck. It's a slow ride through pretty countryside, with numerous stops to visit palatial estates along the way. Lunch is €22-29 extra and the tour is one-way only. Getting back to Venice from Oriago (half day) by bus or Padova (full day) by train is easy and a good excuse to discover another beautiful city.

CLASSES
COOKING
Gritti Epicurean School

San Marco, Gritti Palace Hotel, Campo Santa Maria del Giglio 2467, tel. 041/794-611, www.thegrittiepicureanschool.com, 9am-3pm, €290

Learn the secrets of Venetian cuisine at the Gritti Epicurean School, where a **half-day class** begins by choosing seasonal ingredients at the Rialto market with chef Daniele Turco. There's time for a *bacaro* break before heading back to the professionally equipped kitchen to prepare a Venetian lunch. It's a practical slicing-and-dicing introduction to local specialties that often includes fish. The class ends with a well-deserved three-course meal. Participants range from two to eight and courses are held twice a month or by request. All ingredients and wine are included in the price.

GLASSMAKING
Mauro Vianello

Santa Croce 2251, tel. 041/520-1802,
mv@glasshandmade.it

Mauro Vianello has been working glass for 30 years and sharing his love for the material for nearly as long. When he's not giving demonstrations he's behind the flame in his small classroom workshop spreading the gospel of glass. Students learn how to manipulate the tools of the Lume rod technique and should be comfortable around fire. Experience welding or operating torches is useful but beginners are welcome too. Classes run one hour per day for a week (€450 plus VAT) or one day (€200 plus VAT) 10am-5pm with a lunch break. By the end of either option you'll be manipulating glass into brightly colored fish, glass candy, and anything else you can imagine. If you don't have time for a course, Mauro also provides 40-minute demonstrations for €30 or for free if you purchase a piece. (Glass seashells are €120 each.) Courses and demonstrations can be reserved by email in advance.

Accommodations

There's nothing like waking up in Venice, though finding a hotel room can be challenging and expensive. The influx of visitors combined with limited space means low season only lasts from November to January, when rain and falling temperatures dissuade travelers. Italians migrate to beaches and second homes in July and August and hotels often charge midseason rates. Occupancy and prices are high the rest of the year. Advance reservations are essential at peak times like *Carnevale* in February, the Venice Film Festival in September, and major holidays.

Fortunately, hotels aren't the only option. B&Bs and self-catering apartments provide convenient alternatives for travelers who enjoy staying with locals or prefer the independent approach. Many religious institutions also offer accommodation at relatively affordable prices. Rooms are clean and simple, but expect a curfew and little charm. The city's hostels (several of which are located on the island of Guidecca) aren't just for youthful backpackers and often include cool décor and convenient services at significantly lower prices.

Whatever option you choose, it will likely be small. Space comes at a premium in a city where most buildings are several hundred years old. There are five-star exceptions, but these are costly and not always stylish. Many rooms around the city suffer from flamboyant furnishings, gilded headboards, and ugly wallpaper. On the bright side, romantic views of canals, rooftop terraces, and secluded courtyards make up for inconveniences like the absence of elevators (rare except in large establishments) or weak Wi-Fi. If stairs are a problem, check what floor you're on before booking.

San Marco has the largest concentration of hotels but can be a hassle to reach with luggage. It's also the busiest *sestiere,* which means that you may prefer staying in more intimate neighborhoods like **Dorsoduro** or **Cannaregio**. Of course, you can always pay a porter to cart your bags up and down the bridges or ride a water taxi to wherever you need to go. Just make sure you settle on a price before setting off and ask reception to organize the return journey. If you have difficulty finding accommodation in Venice the nearby towns of Mestre and Marghera or farther-away cities like Padova or Vicenza are easy commutes by bus, tram, or train.

SAN MARCO

UNDER €100

Hotel Locanda Fiorita

Campiello Novo 3457a, tel. 041/523-4754, www.locandafiorita.com, €90 d

The flowered facade of Hotel Locanda Fiorita looks out onto a miniature square around the corner from the bustle of Campo Santo Stefano. It's a delightful oasis to come home to and hosts Alessandra and Paolo make it even more enjoyable. Rooms have the right amount of baroque along with dark wooden floors, exposed beams, and earth-toned furnishings that soothe the eye. Rooms 1 and 10 each have their own shaded terrace.

Settimo Cielo B&B

Campiello Santo Stefano 3470, tel. 342/636-2581, www.settimocielo-venice.com, €100 d

Settimo Cielo B&B does have flamboyant Venetian style and ornate furniture, but they just seem to work here. This eclectically styled B&B on the edge of Campo Santo Stefano is secluded enough to guarantee a good night's sleep and central enough to reach any *sestiere* in the city in less than 15 minutes. The complimentary breakfast is closer to a banquet than a buffet. The only inconvenience is the stairs for anyone staying on the third floor.

€100-250

Hotel Ai Do Mori

Calle Larga S. Marco 658, tel. 041/520-4817, www.hotelaidomori.com, €150 d

If you don't plan on spending much time in your hotel and want to start the day a block from Piazza San Marco, Hotel Ai Do Mori is the right choice. Besides location, the advantages are price, a friendly staff, and overall spotlessness. Many rooms look out onto the *campanile* and basilica. Those on the lower floors are slightly larger and accommodation gets smaller the closer you get to the cramped attic. Rooms with shared baths are heavily discounted. Breakfast isn't served but there are plenty of bars in the area.

Flora

Calle dei Bergamaschi 2283a, tel. 041/520-5844, www.hotelflora.it, €160 d

None of the 40 rooms at Flora are the same. Each has custom furniture, tapestries, and Murano glass fittings. The hotel gives off a worldly atmosphere and has been run by the same family for over half a century. Children are particularly welcome and strollers, high chairs, and cots are all available at no extra charge. The highlight of the hotel is the lovely garden where breakfast is served and guests relax in bucolic tranquility.

Locanda Orseolo

Corte Zorzi 1083, tel. 041/520-4827, www.locandaorseolo.com, €175 d

If a friendly face is as important as décor and the size of your bathroom doesn't matter, Locanda Orseolo is worth considering. The young staff is eager to please and readily assist guests before being asked. There are several room types, a lovely breakfast area, and a study full of rustic charm.

✪ **GRITTI PALACE HOTEL:** Churchill and Hemingway once rested their heads at this luxurious 15th-century *palazzo* (page 123).

✪ **HOTEL GALLERIA:** This affordable option has helpful hosts, antique furnishings, and views of the Grand Canal (page 124).

✪ **PENSIONE ACCADEMIA:** An affordable, hospitable option in a 17th-century *palazzo* that retains all its charm and boasts a peaceful garden (page 124).

✪ **CÀ DEL FORNO:** Waking up inside a real Venetian home has its advantages, especially if that home is in a 15th-century *palazzo* and belongs to part-time chef Maria Grazie (page 125).

✪ **HOTEL METROPOLE:** No two rooms are alike at this stylish hotel, which has a canal-side entrance and a Michelin-starred restaurant (page 126).

✪ **GENERATOR VENICE:** The coolest hostel in Venice is located in a former granary complete with canal views and free walking tours (page 127).

Hotel Violino d'Oro

Campiello Barbozzi 2091, tel. 041/277-0841, www.violinodoro.com, €200 d

Prices can range widely depending on your view at Hotel Violino d'Oro. If you come during the low season, ask for a room overlooking the *Campiello* or San Marco Canal. You can sometimes find real bargains at this hotel, which is classically furnished in tones of gold, ivory, and blue.

OVER €250
✪ Gritti Palace Hotel

Campo Santa Maria del Giglio 2467, tel. 041/794-611, www.thegrittipalace.com, €415 d

The Gritti Palace Hotel is no ordinary hotel. It's *the* hotel. This is the only 15th-century *palazzo* Churchill, Hemingway, Garbo, Stravinsky, and a long list of 20th-century legends would consider when in Venice. Yes, there are five-star rivals, but the Gritti does luxury without trying. The €36 million restoration in 2013 has only made things better and staying here on the edge of the Grand Canal could become the highlight of your entire trip. It's like entering the home of a Venetian aristocrat, with plush old-world furnishings in every room and a well-mannered staff who know what you want before you do. It's not a bargain but you get everything you pay for and a lot more.

DORSODURO
UNDER €100
Santa Monica

Calle delle Pazienze 2885, www.santamargherita-lodgings.com, €95 d

The Santa Monica is a small guesthouse with six rooms close to Campo Santa Margherita. Each of the rooms has its own bathroom, safe, and minibar. There's a shared cooking corner in the living area on the ground floor where a breakfast buffet awaits every morning. The owners also rent out four apartments (€100-235) of different dimensions in the neighborhood. All are clean and convenient, with Ikea-like furnishings and a bright, homey feel.

€100-200
✪ Hotel Galleria
Rio Terrà Foscarini 878, tel. 041/523-2489,
www.hotelgalleria.it, €150 d

Affordable accommodation overlooking the Grand Canal is hard to come by, but views that won't break the bank are available at Hotel Galleria. Six of the nine rooms in the hotel face the water and all are decorated with functional antique furnishings. Breakfast in bed can be arranged with Luciano and Stefano, who will happily recommend bars or restaurants and gladly recount the history of their city.

✪ Pensione Accademia
Fondamenta Bollani 1058, tel. 041/521-0188,
www.pensioneaccademia.it, €170 d

Pensione Accademia feels like a five-star hotel at a fraction of the price. It's run by the Salmaso family, who live and breathe hospitality and have been welcoming guests for decades. The 17th-century *palazzo* has retained all its appeal and what rooms lack in size they make up for in charm. The communal hall and garden are great for recovering from a day on the streets and the front desk can assist with dinner reservations and theater tickets, as well as arrange for chilled *prosecco* and roses to be waiting upon arrival.

€200-300
Ca' Maria Adele
Rio Terrà Catecumeno 111, tel. 041/520-3078,
www.camariaadele.it, €290 d

Ca' Maria Adele offers a variety of styles and prices. These include ornate deluxe rooms fit for an opera singer and five themed rooms, like the *Doge's* Room (for anyone who likes red) and the Marco Polo Oriental Room.

Hotel Moresco
Fondamenta del Passamonte 3499,
tel. 041/244-0202,
www.hotelmorescovenice.com, €190-290 d

They understand the importance of first impressions at the Hotel Moresco, where the staff is welcoming and prepared to go the extra kilometer for guests. The hotel is a short distance from the train station and can easily be reached on foot or by water taxi. Each of the 23 elegantly furnished rooms have oak flooring, soundproofed windows, and modern bathrooms. The garden and study are pleasant places to relax after a day exploring the city.

OVER €300
Ca' Pisani Hotel
Rio Terrà Foscarini 979a, tel. 041/240-1411,
www.capisanihotel.it, d €200-480 d

Ca' Pisani Hotel mixes modern with art deco design two minutes from the Ponte dell'Accademia. All 29 rooms are decorated with original 1930s furnishings and come in a number of sizes including family rooms and junior suites. The small restaurant and wine bar offer the perfect end to a long day of sightseeing.

SAN POLO AND SANTA CROCE
UNDER €100
Hotel Al Ponte Mocenigo
Santa Croce, Fondamenta
Mocenigo 2063, tel. 041/524-4797,
www.alpontemocenigo.com, €90-140 d

It's not the number of stars that matters, but the experience, and Hotel Al Ponte Mocenigo delivers in that respect. The décor reflects the fact you're in Venice without going over the top, and the little courtyard where breakfast is served is a great spot to start the day. The Grand Canal is a short walk away and there are dozens of good, reasonably priced restaurants nearby.

€100-200
✪ Cà del Forno
San Polo, Calle del Forno 1421a,
tel. 041/523-7024, €120 d

If you're Italian you might recognize Maria Grazie Calò from her former appearances on popular cooking shows; if you're not you'll just be happy she prepares breakfast at Cà del Forno. The B&B she runs on the second floor of a 15th-century *palazzo* near the Rialto is a classic Venetian home with high ceilings, antique furnishings, and oil paintings on every wall. There are three double rooms, two of which can be converted into triples or quads, with private baths and pleasant views. The price is excellent for Venice and the warm welcome is just what you need after a day meandering through the city.

Pensione Guerrato
San Polo, Calle Drio La Scimia 240a,
tel. 041/522-5927,
www.hotelguerrato.com, €150 d

Pensione Guerrato is a one-star hotel with personality. Most of the furniture in this 20-room *pensione* is secondhand, making the 13th-century *palazzo* feel like home. There's a *vaporetto* station five minutes away and plenty of action in the surrounding streets, so it can get loud during the summer when local bars stay open late. Rooms are on the 3rd floor and several overlook the Grand Canal. There's no elevator and Wi-Fi only works in the lobby, but proud owner Roberto Zammattio and his warm and genuine staff make up for any minor drawbacks.

La Villeggiatura
San Polo, Calle dei Botteri 1569,
tel. 041/524-4673,
www.lavilleggiatura.it, €130-165 d

At La Villeggiatura, B&B rooms are as large as hotel rooms. There may not be a great view and the outside of the *palazzo* could use a paint job, but the inside is immaculate and the six rooms on the 3rd floor are spacious (especially Casanova and *Doge*), well decorated, and all come with king-size beds. Rates vary according to the season but children under nine stay for free all year long.

CANNAREGIO
UNDER €100
We Crociferi
Campo dei Gesuiti 4878, tel. 041/528-6103,
www.we-gastameco.com, €80 d

We Crociferi provides student housing inside a former monastery throughout the year and welcomes everyone from July 15 to August 15. It's comfortable, clean, includes breakfast at the adjacent bar and restaurant, and is located on a lovely square. Rooms and apartments have en suite bathrooms with showers, or you can book a bed in a shared room (€40). There's a major *vaporetto* station less than two minutes away that connects the city with the islands of Murano and Burano.

€100-200
Locanda ai Santi Apostoli
Campo Santi Apostoli 4391a,
tel. 041/241-1652,
www.locandasantiapostoli.com, €120 d

Locanda ai Santi Apostoli is a reliable three-star hotel overlooking the Grand Canal. The 11 rooms are located on the third floor of a historic *palazzo* on the main street in Cannaregio that makes finding the hotel and reaching other parts of the city easy. Rooms are large and nicely decorated.

Ponte Chiodo

Ponte Chiodo 3749, tel. 041/241-3935,
www.pontechiodo.it, €125 d

Ponte Chiodo overlooks a canal minutes away from the best *bacari* and nightlife in the neighborhood. The guesthouse provides Wi-Fi, air-conditioning, and breakfast pastries supplied by a local bakery. There's a delightful garden out back, a railless bridge out front, and an owner inside always willing to talk Venice.

CASTELLO

UNDER €100
Istituto San Giuseppe

Ponte della Guerra 5402,
tel. 041/522-5352,
www.sangiuseppecaburlotto.it, €80 d

Istituto San Giuseppe is simple, clean, and guarantees a good night's sleep. This comfortable religious residence with 14 rooms has an early curfew and if you're not back by 10pm you'll have some explaining to do to the monks.

B&B San Marco

Fondamenta San Giorgio Schiavoni 3385,
tel. 041/522-7589, www.realvenice.it, €90 d

The best thing about B&B San Marco are the hosts, Marco and Alice, who go out of their way to welcome guests. The three rooms of this intimate B&B are large and well decorated and have views of rooftops and canals. Only one has an en suite bath, so book ahead if you don't like sharing. Breakfast is served in the kitchen and consists of Nutella, fresh bread, coffee, fruit juice, and homemade surprises.

€100-200
Foresteria Valdese

Calle della Madoneta 5170,
tel. 041/528-6797, www.foresteriavenezia.it,
€140 d, dormitory €35

Foresteria Valdese, one of Venice's religious accommodations, is run by Italian Methodists who converted an 18th-century *palazzo* into a 14-room guesthouse. Rooms range from private doubles with en suite bathrooms and canal views to beds in one of two ground-floor dormitories. These are often filled with schoolchildren and youth groups who are quiet at night but vivacious during the day. There's no curfew, complimentary breakfast is served 8am-9:15am, and multiple-night stays are discounted.

€200-300
✪ Hotel Metropole

Riva degli Schiavone 4149,
tel. 041/520-5044,
www.hotelmetropole.com, €280 d

Hotel Metropole is a stylish hotel a short walk from Piazza San Marco. No two rooms are the same at this hotel, which looks out on the lagoon and has a canal entrance for making dramatic entries. Doubles, suites, and deluxe rooms are decorated with elegant period furnishings, velvet curtains, rare books, and chandeliers. It's all done tastefully and provides a wonderfully romantic atmosphere. The concierge can handle nearly any request including currency exchange, daily newspaper delivery, babysitting, breakfast in bed, and dry-cleaning. The Michelin-starred restaurant inside the hotel serves a modern mix of fusion dishes that confound the eye and surprise the stomach. Tea is served in the bar every afternoon and live music played every evening.

GIUDECCA

UNDER €100

✪ Generator Venice

Fondamenta Zitelle 86, tel. 041/877-8288, www.generatorhostels.com, €16 per bed in shared room, €80 d

Generator Venice is the coolest. The interior of this former granary feels more like a club, and the bar and lounge areas are perfect for recounting Venetian adventures with travelers from all over the world. There are mixed and female-only rooms of different dimensions with modern and comfortable furnishings. Several cozy double rooms are also located in the attic and look out onto the Canale della Giudecca. The hostel offers complimentary Wi-Fi, 24-hour reception, a restaurant, and free daily walking tours of the neighborhood. The buffet breakfast is served 7am-10am but isn't particularly appetizing. You're better off with a cappuccino and pastry from **Majer** (Fondamenta Sant'Eufemia 461, tel. 041/521-1162, daily 9am-11pm) down the Fondamenta Zitelle near the Palanca *vaporetto* stop.

Getting to Giudecca requires a ferry and the 2, 4.1, 4.2, and N serve the island's five stations. A single ticket is €7.50 but you're better off opting for a daily (€20) or multiday pass. Once you ride one *vaporetto* you'll want to ride others and staying on the island won't seem like such a big inconvenience.

Information and Services

TOURIST INFORMATION

TOURIST INFORMATION CENTERS

Venezia Unica (www.veneziaunica.it, tel. 041/2424, daily 9am-6pm for live operators and 24/7 for recorded info) is the city's tourist official department and provides information about transportation, cultural events, and Venezia Unica Cards. You can purchase tickets to many events online, by phone or at one of several tourist offices around the city. The **Info Point** (daily 7am-9pm) outside Santa Lucia train station sells museum and transport passes; if the office is too crowded you can use the automated machines near the Grand Canal. A second **Info Point** (daily 9am-7pm) is located inside Museo Correr in Piazza San Marco.

There are additional offices in Piazzale Roma (daily 9:30am-3:30pm) and inside the arrivals hall at **Marco Polo Airport** (daily 9am-8pm). During the summer an info point also operates on the **Lido** (Gran Viale 6a, daily 9am-noon and 3pm-6pm).

LUGGAGE STORAGE

There's a **luggage storage facility** (www.grandistazioni.it, daily 6am-11pm) in the train station near platform 1 on the right as you enter the station. The first five hours is €6; it's €0.90 for the 6th-12th hour and €0.40 each additional hour after that. There's another baggage depot in Piazzale Roma (tel. 041/522-3590, www.trasbagagli.it, daily 6am-9pm) that charges a flat €5 per item. There are lines most of the day, so if it isn't absolutely necessary skip it. Most hotels will hold bags before check-in and after checkout.

HEALTH AND SAFETY

EMERGENCY NUMBERS

For medical emergencies dial the 118 hotline or the **Guardia Medica Turistica** (Ca' Savio, tel. 041/530-0874), which is dedicated entirely to diagnosing the ailments of visitors. For emergencies requiring police assistance call **112.**

POLICE

Report crimes at the **Police Headquarters** (Ponte della Liberta, tel. 041/271-5511) in Santa Croce near the train station or any of the smaller **precincts** like the one in Castello (Fondamenta San Lorenzo 5053) opposite Campo San Lorenzo. The police emergency number is **113.** Violent crime is low in Venice, and pickpockets are surprisingly rare for a city that attracts so many tourists.

HOSPITALS AND PHARMACIES

If you need a hospital, go to **Ospedale Fatebenefratalli** (Cannaregio, Fondamenta Madonna dell'Orto 3458, tel. 041/783-111, www.fatebenefratelli.it, 24/7) or **Hospital SS Giovanni e Paolo** (Castello 6777, tel. 041/529-4111, www.aulss3.veneto.it). The latter has an emergency room. Make sure to bring your passport and if you or anyone you're traveling with suffers serious injury inform the consulate as soon as possible.

There are plenty of pharmacies around Venice and you'll find one in each of the *sestiere* neighborhoods including **Farmacia Santa Lucia** (Cannaregio, Lista di Spagna 122, tel. 041/716-332, Mon.-Sat. 8:30am-8pm and Sun. 9am-1pm) near the train station and **Farmacia San Polo** (San Polo, Campo San Polo, tel. 041/522-3527, Mon.-Fri. 9am-1pm and

3:30pm-7:30pm, Sat. 9am-12:45pm). Most are located on busy streets and squares, and recognizable by their green neon cross. Take a ticket at the entrance and wait until your number is called.

FOREIGN CONSULATES

Report lost or stolen passports to the **U.S. Consulate** in Milan (tel. 02/290-351, Mon.-Fri. 9:30am-12:30pm). They can also help with any emergencies you may encounter.

LOST AND FOUND

There's always hope if you've lost something in Venice. Objects forgotten on ferries are stored for seven days inside the **lost and found office** (Santa Croce, tel. 041/272-2179, daily 7am-8pm) in Piazzale Roma across the Ponte della Costituzione bridge. After that items are transferred to the **central office** (tel. 041/274-8225, www.comune.venezia.it, weekdays 9am-1pm). The city issues a monthly online list of objects with the date and location they were found. You can also try the **airport lost and found** (tel. 041/260-6436) in the arrivals terminal and the **Vigili Urbani** (Piazzale Roma, tel. 041/522-4576). Found items that aren't retrieved are eventually sold at auction.

COMMUNICATIONS

WI-FI

Venice (www.cittadinanzadigitale.it) has installed wireless infrastructure around the city, Lido, and lagoon islands. Most large squares and major monuments are now covered by over 200 hotspots that provide limited free access. You can supplement this with the **Venezia Unica Card** (www.veneziaunica.it) and 24 hours of connectivity for €5. Many hotels, restaurants, and bars also offer free Wi-Fi access, but if you're feeling nostalgic for a copy shop with Internet access or want some digital photos printed visit **E Copie da Toni** (Castello, S. Lio Calle delle Bande 5645, tel. 041/522-5100, Mon.-Fri. 9:30am-1pm and 3pm-6pm).

Transportation

GETTING THERE

AIR

Aeroporto di Venezia (VCE, Viale Galileo Galilei 30, tel. 041/260-6111, www.veniceairport.it) is a medium-sized airport with runways overlooking the lagoon that guarantee dramatic takeoffs and landings. There are few direct flights from North America and none from Australia, New Zealand, or South Africa, but many connecting flights from across Europe. The newly renovated interior is easy to navigate and lines move quickly. The well-organized arrivals hall provides passengers with clear indications for reaching Venice by bus, taxi, or boat. There's also a **tourist office** where travel cards and maps are available. Wi-Fi access is limited and requires registration. There are few scheduled flights from Rome and none from Florence.

The cheapest connection to Venice from the airport is by **bus.** The **ATVO booth** in the arrivals hall sells **Airport Shuttle** (tel. 042/159-4671, www.atvo.it, €8 one-way and €15 round-trip) tickets and the ride takes 20 minutes. Clearly marked buses are waiting outside and operate daily between 5:20am and 12:20am. Passengers are dropped off in Piazzale Roma, from where you can walk or catch a *vaporetto* ferry.

UK travelers can choose daily departures with EasyJet (www.easyjet.com) and Ryan Air (www.ryanair.com) that often land at Treviso Airport (TSF) 30 minutes by car and an hour on public transport from Venice.

The most exciting way to reach Venice from the airport is by water and you can buy tickets from the same ATVO booth. **Alilaguna** (tel. 041/240-1701, www.alilaguna.it) operates three **ferry** lines (blue, orange, and red) with convenient daily service to stops around the city including San Marco, Rialto, and Guglie. One-way tickets are €15 (€27 round-trip) and allow for one suitcase and one carry-on item with a €3 surcharge for extra bags. Ferries operate daily from 7:45am to 12:20am and there are several departures per hour.

The fastest and most dramatic aquatic entry to the city is by **water taxi,** of which there are a number of private companies to choose from. **Consorzio Motoscalfi** (tel. 041/522-2303, www.motoscafivenezia.it) is a consortium of water taxis that operate 24 hours a day and can drop you off anywhere you like. A ride for up to ten passengers and ten bags to the city is €110. To take either a public ferry or private taxi you'll need to walk to the ferry terminal five minutes from the arrivals hall.

Call **RadioTaxi** (tel. 041/5964, www.radiotaxivenezia.com) or head to their office in the arrivals hall if you prefer arriving by land. Fares from the airport to Venice are fixed at €40. Taxis do not operate within the city; they'll drop you off in Piazzale di Roma near the train station.

TRAIN

Getting to Venice from Rome or Florence is a pleasant journey on board high-speed trains that depart regularly from both cities. Italo (www.italo.it) and Trenitalia (www.trenitalia.it) provide affordable and comfortable service to Venice.

Trains terminate at Santa Lucia station, from where the city is accessible on foot. Exiting Santa Lucia train station and seeing the Grand Canal for the first time is one of the most dramatic entrances you can make in a city. Along the canal front are automated machines and ticket offices selling *vaporetto* passes for travelers wishing to make an immediate aquatic getaway. Otherwise there are three choices: You can turn right toward Piazzale Roma and Dorsoduro, turn left toward Cannaregio, or cross the Ponte degli Scalzi and enter the Santa Croce neighborhood.

From Rome: Italo (www.italo.it) and Trenitalia (www.trenitalia.it) high-speed trains from Rome Termini and Tiburtina stations to Venice take less than four hours and cost as little as €24 if reserved in advance. There are dozens of daily departures.

From Florence: Trains from Florence Stazione Santa Maria Novella station to Venice take less than two hours and cost as little as €16. All high-speed trains headed to Venice from Rome stop in Florence.

CAR

The drive to Venice from Rome or Florence is fairly straightforward and can be undertaken on well-built modern highways. Driving does take longer than riding a train and comes with the added expense of tolls, fuel, and occasional frustration. The journey ends once you've crossed the Ponte della Libertà, where cars must be parked in one of several conveniently accessed indoor garages or outdoor lots. Prices range €24-35 per day and parking may be difficult to find during special occasions like *Carnevale* or the Venice Film Festival. A thrifty alternative is to park in the nearby town of Mestre on the mainland where rates are about half the price and travelers can reach Venice by bus or train in 15 minutes. If you want to save on rental fees, leave the driving to someone else, and make some new acquaintances try Italian car sharing (www.blablacar.it).

From Rome: The route from Rome to Venice is clearly indicated and consists mostly of two-lane highways with a speed limit of 80mph (130kph). Follow signs for Firenze (Florence) along the A1 highway. The journey to Florence is 234 miles (377 kilometers) and takes a little over three hours. Once you reach the city follow the directions below.

From Florence: If you're parked in Florence's historic center, cross the Arno and continue west along the river. You'll eventually see signs for the A1 highway and should follow indications to Bologna. Once you reach that city take the A13 all the way to Padua and complete the journey along the A57 that runs directly to Venice. The entire journey is 162 miles (260 kilometers), a distance that can be driven in two and a half hours.

Part of the journey crosses the Apennine Mountains that run up and down the Italian peninsula and there are many tunnels, curves, and inclines. Be prepared for occasional roadwork and possible traffic jams during the summer. There are several alternative routes in case you prefer a longer and slower drive.

BUS

Passengers arriving by bus are deposited at the **Tronchetto Bus Terminal** on the western edge of the city, the only eyesore in Venice. Fortunately, the efficient **People Mover monorail** (tel. 041/272-7211, www.peoplemover. avmspa.it, daily 7am-11pm, €1.50) shuttles passengers into and out of the city in a couple of minutes and there are continuous departures.

From Rome: The bus journey from Tiburtina station in Rome to Venice lasts an agonizing eight hours, but tickets are cheap (from €16). You can compare fares of Eurolines, Megabus, Baltour, Flixbus, and other operators using the **GoEuro** (www.goeuro.com) travel planner. There are frequent departures for Venice.

From Florence: Flixbus, Eurolines, and Megabus operate from Piazzale Montelungo near Santa Maria Novella station. Journey time is around three hours and one-way tickets start at €14. Buses depart a dozen times per day.

BOAT

You'd think a city surrounded by water is best reached by water, but that isn't always practical. It's true that cruise ships arrive every day and disgorge thousands of passengers, but none of these stop in Rome or Florence. The only other alternative would be hiring a vessel, which is costly and time-consuming. It's best therefore to save the boats for when you arrive.

GETTING AROUND

The two most common ways of exploring Venice are by foot or *vaporetto*. Although it's small you're likely to

Santa Lucia railway station

walk more in Venice than Rome or Florence. When you tire, board a boat and discover the city from a different angle. The canals are full of different types of boats loading and unloading goods and passengers throughout the day. There are three principal modes of water transportation in Venice: *vaporetto, traghetto,* and water taxi.

VAPORETTO

Public transportation is unique, necessary, and rewarding in Venice. It comprises 24 **ACTV** (tel. 041/2424, actv. avmspa.it) ferry lines that are served by *vaporetti* (ferry boats). Each neighborhood has a handful of *vaporetto* stations and digital signs indicate how long commuters must wait for the next boat. *Vaporetti* on the main routes arrive every twenty minutes, so waiting time is minimal. Service is efficient and makes getting around Venice fast and fun. Stations have color-coded maps that can also be downloaded from the ACTV website. Tickets are expensive for tourists (locals pay a different rate) because boats are harder to maintain than buses. They also require a skilled captain to steer and a crew member to help passengers on and off.

Vaporetti are the most common way of getting around Venice. These omnipresent ferries run up and down the Grand Canal, circumnavigate the city, and connect it with outlying islands in the lagoon. Boats come in varying sizes and several seasonal routes are added during the summer. All have indoor seating and the 2, 4.1, 4.2, 5.1, 5.2, 12, and 13 lines have outdoor seats, which you should try to grab.

Always validate tickets upon first usage, enter water stops through the designated entrance, and allow passengers to disembark before boarding. It can get chilly riding *vaporetti* in early spring and late autumn or even at night during the summer, so have a scarf and hat handy.

Tickets can be purchased at larger stations such as Piazzale di Roma just over the Ponte della Costituzione bridge, or outside the train station. There are many booths, as well as automated vending machines, so lines are short. Some newsstands also sell tickets. You can choose from **single tickets** (€8/75 minutes), **24-hour** (€20), **48-hour** (€30), **72-hour** (€40) and **7-day** (€60) passes. These must be validated at the machines outside each station and passengers may be asked to show their passes by controllers who issue on-the-spot fines of up to €100. Once validated for the first time you have unlimited travel possibilities until your time limit runs out. Passes do not cover the ferries that operate to and from the airport, which must be purchased separately. Children under six travel for free and there are discounts for 6-29 year olds with the Rolling Venice Card.

vaporetto

Vaporetti are great fun and riding them without a destination is always a pleasure. If you want to get a good look at Venice, the **4.1, 4.2, 5.1,** and

VENETIAN VOCABULARY

Geography combined with foreign linguistic influences have formed a unique dialect in Venice that's used to describe the city's unusual urban landscape. The faster you absorb this vocabulary the easier it will be to identify different aspects of the Venetian cityscape and appreciate the beauty of Venice.

- *Calle, calleta:* Street, alley, or thoroughfare that can vary substantially in length and width. The former are wider than the latter.

- *Campo, campiello:* Unevenly shaped square of varying proportions. *Campo* means *field,* and these spaces were originally grassy meadows where food was grown and animals grazed. Most have been paved over and today provide visual and physical relief from the narrow *calle.* A *campiello* is a smaller version of a *campo.*

- *Fondamenta:* Any *calle* located next to a canal or *rio. Fondazione* means *foundation,* and these streets helped reinforce the islands and allow for urbanization. They can feature stone or iron railings—or none at all—and have stairs for making getting on and off boats easier. *Fondamente* (plural) are often lined with shops, bars, and restaurants.

- *Ca':* Short for *casa* (house) and used to indicate important residences like the Ca' d'Oro or Ca' Rezzonico. The word is usually followed by a family name indicating the original residents.

- *Corte:* A small dead-end courtyard surrounded by residential buildings. They're generally reached through a *sotoportego* or *calleta* and are the center of micro-neighborhoods where Venetians once spent their days washing, sewing, preparing meals, and socializing.

- *Pietra d'Istria:* Dense, impermeable limestone quarried from the Istria peninsula and an essential material in the construction of Venice. Used to build and decorate *calle,* bridges, canals, churches, homes, and palaces.

- *Rio:* Small canal. There are hundreds throughout the city that function both to enhance communication and permit the tides to flow freely through the city and prevent stagnation.

- *Rio Terra:* Any canal that's been filled in and transformed into a street.

- *Riva:* Wide walkway bordering the Grand Canal or San Marco Canal.

- *Sestiere:* Historic neighborhood or district. There are six in Venice and they are symbolically represented by the six metal strips decorating the prow of every gondola.

- *Sotoportego:* Underpass connecting *calle, campi,* or *fondamente.* These were usually created by removing the ground floor of houses and often contain small shrines or sacred images of the Virgin Mary and other popular saints.

5.2 lines circumnavigate the city and terminate in **Fondamente Nuove** where you can transfer onto larger ferries heading to Murano, Burano, and Torcello. Lines 1 and 2 go up and down the Grand Canal and you can ride either from Piazzale Roma to San Marco or vice versa in under 30 minutes.

Vaporetto are usually crowded in summer and have a capacity of up to 250 depending on the boat. Each line has different hours but service usually starts around 6am and continues until midnight. There's also a night service (N) that runs 11:30pm-5am and serves Grand Canal and Lido stations.

WATER TAXI

Water taxis are the quicker, more expensive way of getting around Venice. These slick motorboats zip passengers along the canals in style. Pickup can be arranged in advance or simply by going to the nearest water taxi station. There are several at Piazzale Roma, Piazza San Marco, and other locations around the city.

Prices depend on distance and time. The fixed price for a one-hour ride for four passengers is €120. You can decide any itinerary you like with your driver and should ask to explore quieter canals. A ride from Santa Lucia station to Piazza San Marco is €60-70 for 1-4 passengers, while a trip to the airport is €100-120. Extra passengers are charged €10 each.

The boats are extremely comfortable and resemble miniature floating limousines, with leather seats, wood paneling, and sunroofs that can be slid open or closed depending on the weather. Water taxis are much smaller than *vaporetto* and are susceptible to waves, especially when going down the Grand Canal or out into the open lagoon. Some drivers will point out interesting sights but most are happy to leave passengers to themselves and periodically check their smartphones.

Boats can be reserved from Water Taxi Venice (tel. 342/106-8412, www.consorziovenezifutura.it) or Acqua Taxi Venezia (tel. 351/202-6881, www.taxiserviceh24.com).

TRAGHETTO

Private gondola rides, which can seat up to six passengers, are expensive (the rate is fixed at €80 for a 40-minute ride), but you can save money by taking advantage of the *traghetti* (gondola ferries, Mon.-Sat. 7:30am-7pm and Sun. 9am-7pm, €2) that operate on the Grand Canal. A ride lasts five minutes and is a fun and practical way to get from one neighborhood to another. Dozens of these ferry points once operated, but today there are only three left—and it's worth riding them all. They can be boarded at the docks near Santa Maria del Giglio opposite the Guggenheim, San Tomà halfway between Ponte dell'Accademia and the Rialto, and next to the covered fish-market near the Rialto. Locals usually stand during the crossing, but you can also sit on the side railing and watch as two gondoliers skillfully oar their way from one bank to the other.

BUS AND TRAM

The only place you'll see buses or trams (€1.50 or €3 on board) in Venice is Piazzale Roma, just over the Ponte della Costituzione bridge from the train station. They are primarily used by locals commuting from the mainland town of Mestre and tourists taking the airport shuttle (€15) but are not for getting around Venice itself. Tickets are available from automated machines near the modern awning in the center of the *piazza* as well as newsstands and *tabacchi* shops.

VENICE'S LAGOON ISLANDS

There are dozens of islands and countless islets in the Venice Lagoon, but Murano, Burano, and Torcello are the most popular destinations. Each has its own distinct personality, and all three can be visited in a day by *vaporetto*. Murano is the closest, largest, and most populated. It's famous for glass and could be mistaken for another, albeit smaller, Venice. The other two islands are farther away and smaller. Burano, known for lace production and cuisine, is a feast for the eyes and stomach. It's covered with brightly painted houses where fishermen

Itinerary Idea 138
San Michele 139
Murano 140
Burano 146
Torcello. 151
The Lido. 154
San Lazzaro
   degli Armeni 158

HIGHLIGHTS

✪ **MURANO'S GLASSMAKING WORKSHOPS:** After visiting the workshops and boutiques of this busy island, where furnaces have been melting sand into glass for centuries, you'll never look at glass the same way again (page 142).

✪ **FONDAMENTA CAO MOLECA:** Burano's brightly colored houses and quiet backstreets are a wonderful respite from the throngs of Venice. This stretch along the island's easternmost canal is a good place to start wandering (page 146).

✪ **BEACHES AND CYCLING ON THE LIDO:** Soak in the nostalgic atmosphere on a beach in the Lido, home to what was once the world's largest beach resort. For more peace and quiet, cycle along the Adriatic on a bike path with panoramic views (page 156).

and skilled lace makers still reside. Torcello is the greenest and least visited, and retains traces of medieval glory and American literary greatness.

Murano, Burano, and Torcello are usually visited in that order, but you can reverse it by starting at the farthest point and working your way back to Venice, or limit yourself to one or two islands. On the way, you'll pass the monumental island of San Michele, with thousands of graves in the cemetery, including those of Stravinsky and Ezra Pound. Afterward, you can explore other parts of the lagoon like the beaches of the Lido, where the Venice Film Festival is held and bike riding is permitted, or the tiny island of San Lazzaro degli Armeni, which is entirely occupied by an Armenian monastery.

PLANNING YOUR TIME

There's only one way of getting around the lagoon and that is by boat. You can take a water taxi or rent a motorboat but the cheapest (and most romantic) way to go is via the *vaporetti* (ferries) that connect all the outlying islands. Unless you're only planning to visit one island, it's worth purchasing a *vaporetto* day pass (€20), as a single trip costs €7 (€14 round-trip). Set off in the morning and make sure to validate your ticket upon first usage. Journeys between islands can take 30-45 minutes and you'll need an entire day to visit them all. *Vaporetto* make scheduled departures every 15-20 minutes 6am-10pm, after which night ferries operate.

The Cannaregio neighborhood in northern Venice is a good place to start a journey. Ferries depart regularly for Murano, Burano, and Torcello from the **Fondamente Nove** water station. You can reach this dock from anywhere in Venice onboard the 4.1 or 4.2 *vaporetto* that circumnavigates the city. The Lido is accessible from Saint Mark's Square and from many stations along the Grand Canal and the Castello neighborhood.

Venice's Lagoon Islands

Map labels:
SP40 · A57 · SS14 · Favaro Veneto · VIA ORLANDA · Tessera · VENICE MARCO POLO AIRPORT · SP40 · SS14 · Campalto · Laguna Veneta · Torcello · Torcello · Mazzorbetto · SEE "BURANO" MAP · Burano · FONDAMENTA CAO MOLECA · SEE "MURANO" MAP · SR11 · PONTE DELLA LIBERTA · GLASSMAKING WORKSHOPS · Murano · Sant'Erasmo · Sant'Erasmo · Portosecco · Lio Grando · Ca' Savio · San Michele · SP42 · SANTA LUCIA STATION · VENEZIA · Venice · PIAZZA SAN MARCO · Le Vignole · Certosa · Punta Sabbioni · VIA FAUSTA · Giudecca · San Giorgio Maggiore · LIDO · La Grazia · San Sèrvolo · San Clemente · San Lazzaro degli Armeni · Lido · Sacca Sessola · Laguna Veneta · ADRIATIC SEA · BEACHES AND CYCLING ON THE LIDO · Lido di Venezia · Poveglia · 0 — 2 mi · 0 — 2 km · Malamocco · © MOON.COM

ORIENTATION

There are hundreds of islands within the Venice Lagoon, most of which are uninhabited. San Michele is one of the closest to Venice and lies to the north, halfway between Cannaregio and Murano, which is made up of seven interconnected islands. Burano is four miles farther to the northeast, and Torcello is a single *vaporetto* stop from there. The Lido is east of Venice and provides a natural barrier against the Adriatic Sea. San Lazzaro degli Armeni is a postage stamp-shaped island off the western side of the Lido with a single dock that's open only during the high season.

Itinerary Idea

ESSENTIAL LAGOON ISLANDS

With one day, you can visit San Michele, Murano, Burano, and Torcello, including stops at a glassmaking studio, an ancient church, and a former Hemingway haunt, before returning to Venice for the evening. Although it's possible to do this circuit in a half-day, it will feel very rushed. Take your time, and dedicate a full day. If you leave around 9am, expect to be back at 5pm. The journey between islands is around two hours. Ferries leave continuously every 15-20 minutes from Fondamente Nove. It's worth making lunch reservations at Burano's Al Gatto Nero before you set out.

1 Hop on the 4.1 *vaporetto* from Fondamente Nove and ride one stop to San Michele, home to a lovely cemetery, Cimitero di San Michele, where thousands of Venetians are buried. Enjoy a little solitude along the gravel, tree-lined paths. Pay your respects to one of the 20th century's greatest composers before heading back to the dock.

2 Continue on to Murano (a five-minute ride), and get off at the first stop. Walk down the Fondamenta Manin past the glass boutiques and head to Vetreria Artistica Emmedue for a glassblowing demonstration.

3 Next, head to Murano's Faro Station, and board the number 12 *vaporetto* to Burano. This 40-minute trip is the longest part of the journey, so make sure to get a window seat to enjoy the ride. You can observe birds nesting in the lagoon and fishers at work.

4 When you arrive in Burano, walk in the opposite direction from where everyone else is going, letting instinct be your guide. There is no wrong turn in Burano, and it's easy to stumble upon craftspeople at work. When you're hungry, grab a canal-side table at Al Gatto Nero, a popular *trattoria* that specializes in seafood and risotto.

5 After lunch, browse the glass jewelry being created at Lumeart a few blocks away and bring home an authentic souvenir made while you watch.

6 Find your way back to the island's only water station (Burano), and board the number 9 or 12 headed to Torcello, 10 minutes away. Walk along the herringbone path all the way to the Ponte del Diavolo bridge. Cross it and take the back way to the island's ancient churches.

7 Climb the *campanile* of Santa Maria Assunta for a panoramic view of the lagoon. (Note that there's no elevator, and it gets windy at the top!)

Lagoon Itinerary Idea

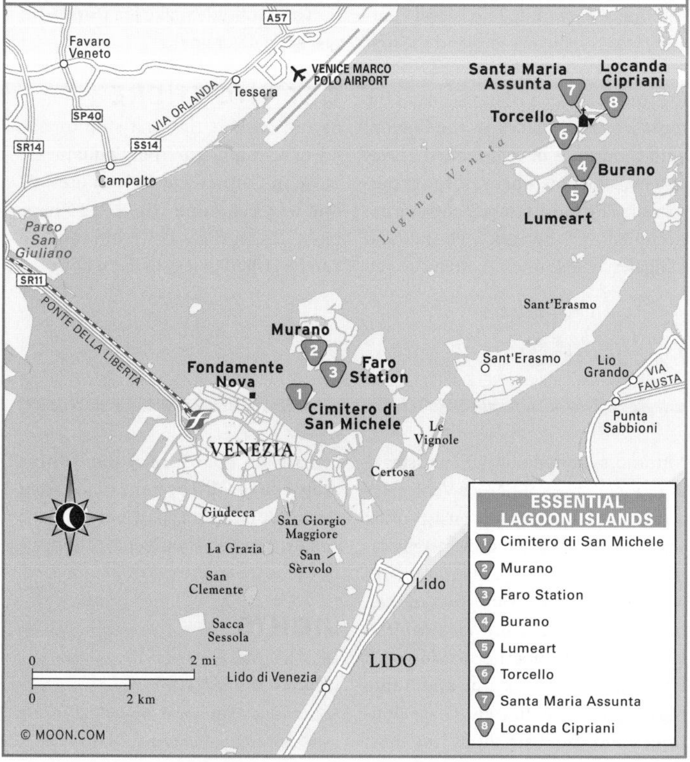

ESSENTIAL LAGOON ISLANDS
1. Cimitero di San Michele
2. Murano
3. Faro Station
4. Burano
5. Lumeart
6. Torcello
7. Santa Maria Assunta
8. Locanda Cipriani

8 On your way back to the Torcello water station (there is only one), stop for an espresso at **Locanda Cipriani**, where Ernest Hemingway once stayed, then enjoy the return journey to the city on the 12 *vaporetto*.

San Michele

The *vaporetto* stop before Murano is San Michele, a cemetery island that will be of particular interest to poets, dancers, and musicians, or anyone looking for a tranquil spot. The Greek Orthodox Cimitero di San Michele is the final resting spot of poet Ezra Pound, Russian ballet impresario Serge Diaghilev, and composer Igor Stravinsky. If you're interested, hop off; if not, keep on sailing.

SIGHTS

CIMITERO DI SAN MICHELE
tel. 041/729-2841, daily 7:30am-4pm, free
Burying the dead has always been a

challenge in Venice and it wasn't until the 19th century that a permanent solution was found. The island cemetery was Napoleon's idea and the first burials occurred here in 1826. Today the square-shaped island is one of the most peaceful places in the lagoon, with thousands of well-tended graves and mausoleums where ashes are preserved. The most famous of these are occupied by Stravinsky, Pound, and Dhigalev, whose tomb is often covered with ballet shoes and roses. Although it may sound grim, the island's vegetation and solitude make it a wonderful place to reflect on life.

GETTING THERE

San Michele is the first stop on the 4.1 or 4.2 *vaporetto* from Fondamente Nove in Cannaregio (10 minutes, €7 one-way, €14 round-trip, €20 24-hour pass). It's on the way to Murano and can be visited in less than an hour.

Murano

Murano, synonymous with glassmaking, resembles a miniature Venice. It's a quarter of the size and consists of six separate islands interconnected by canals and bridges. The Canal Grande di Murano splits the town in two and can be crossed at the Ponte Vivarini iron bridge. On the northern side you'll find the Glass Museum and Santa Maria e Donato church. Glass boutiques and souvenir shops line most of the *fondamente* (embankment). The farther you walk from these, the closer you'll get to the bucolic residential parts of the island, with low-rise housing, pretty pedestrian streets, and vegetable gardens.

The first *vaporetto* stop in Murano is the busiest and that's where most visitors usually disembark to browse the storefronts and discover how glass is blown. From Colonna station (first stop), you can walk up Fondamenta dei Vetrai through the center of town and visit lovely little squares where lunch awaits. The Faro station (second stop) is located near the island's lighthouse and is where ferries heading to Burano regularly stop. If you remain on board until the Venier stop, you can discover the island from the inside out, get a good look at all the canals, and rub shoulders with locals in Campo San Bernardo.

SIGHTS

GLASS MUSEUM
(Museo del Vetro)

Fondamenta Giustinian 8, tel. 041/527-4718, www.museovetro.visitmuve.it, daily 10am-6pm, €10 or Museum Pass

The Museo del Vetro glass museum is organized chronologically, starting with ancient Roman glassware.

Glass Museum

Murano

The pieces on display show how 700 years of Murano glassmaking tradition evolved from the 13th century to the present. There are frequent exhibitions of contemporary artists who use glass in creative ways. The collection is located inside one of Murano's oldest *palazzi* and takes less than an hour to visit.

Guided tours of the Glass Museum are given on Tuesday and Thursday at 2:30pm, followed by a live demonstration (€18) at a local glass school nearby; reserve in advance. Unfortunately, there are no demonstrations inside the museum itself. Occasionally, the museum screens a documentary about glassblowing technique, but you'll get more out of the experience of observing artists at work in the galleries and workshops nearby.

CHIESA DEI SANTI MARIA E DONATO

Campo San Donato 11, tel. 041/739-056, Mon.-Sat. 9am-6pm, Sun. 12:30pm-6pm, free

Unlike most churches in Venice, Chiesa dei Santi Maria e Donato can be circled on foot. It feels like each side is different, and progressive makeovers since 1141 are probably the cause. The Gothic facade is imposing but plain and the only decoration is a relief sculpture of St. Donatus above the entrance. The right side is more impressive, as it is lined with windows set within lovely brick arches that could be mistaken for 20th-century designs. The back of the church, or apse, has

141

Chiesa dei Santi Maria e Donato

double tiers supported by twin arches and intricate brickwork that deserves closer inspection.

The interior is nearly as interesting. Besides the remains of the saint Donato, you'll find a 12th-century mosaic of the Virgin Mary, a Roman sarcophagus, and an incredible marble floor filled with complex geometric designs that look too nice to walk on. Mass is held on Monday, Wednesday, and Friday at 6pm, and Sunday at 11:15am and 6pm.

✪ GLASSMAKING WORKSHOPS

Glass is an important export trade, and not just for the tourists drawn to Murano. The island once housed thousands of glassmakers, and there are still hundreds earning their livelihoods from this ancient craft. Murano glass became renowned for its clarity and color, thanks to a unique combination of ingredients and the skills of its artisans. It's tempting to take photographs of the creations inside, but most shops don't allow photos.

Vetreria Artistica Emmedue

Calle Miotti 12A, tel. 041/736-056, daily 9am-4:30pm

Murano furnaces combine glass selling with glassmaking demonstrations, allowing visitors to witness the magic moment of glass creation. Vetreria Artistica Emmedue puts on demonstrations nearly continuously for groups who arrive by the boatload. Walk through the narrow entrance to the shop and head straight to the back, where bleacher seating has been set up around the furnaces and you can get a close-up look as glass takes shape. Expert artisans all over the island tend to make miniature horses for audiences, and things are no different here. There's usually a brief explanation in several languages, and once the free demonstration is over, visitors are encouraged to ask questions, get a closer look at the tools of the trade, and browse the shop.

Seguso Venice Boutique

Fondamenta Manin 77, tel. 041/527-5333,
daily 9am-1:30pm and 2:30pm-5:30pm

The Seguso family has been blowing glass for 23 generations and keeping their techniques secret since 1397. Inside their Seguso Venice Boutique are vases, glasses, lampshades, and jewels that mix traditions of the past with a desire to innovate and push the boundaries of glassmaking. The showroom (Fondamenta Venier 29) regularly organizes visits to their nearby factory and other glass-related sights.

GLASSMAKING CLASSES

Abate Zanetti School of Glass

Murano, Calle Briati 8b, tel. 041/273-7711,
www.lascuoladelvetro.it , Mon.-Fri. 9am-1pm
and 2pm-6pm

Once you've seen sand heated to a thousand degrees and transformed into glass, you may want to try making some yourself. What looks simple, however, isn't. Most glassblowers have been practicing their craft for decades. To understand what's involved in the process you'll need to go to school, and the best place to do that is the Abate Zanetti School of Glass. Students learn how a furnace functions, and are instructed in the basics of shaping raw

glassmaking on Murano

material through marbling and blowing techniques. Most courses are for beginners and last 20 hours over several days, but there are also weekend courses in lamp working (€400) and glassworking (€480) for groups of 4-10 people. Single-day private lessons (€120) are also available, and participants get to keep their creations.

FOOD

Most restaurants in Murano are located along the busy canals, and Fondamenta Manin and Venier are good places to start reading menus.

Osteria Al Duomo

Fondamenta Antonio Maschio 21,
tel. 041/527-4303, daily 11am-10pm, €12-15

Osteria Al Duomo, across the bridge from Maria e Donato church, is a pleasant refuge from the heat. The neat white facade hides a large shaded garden where diners enjoy fish, meat, or pizza prepared in a wood-burning oven.

La Perla ai Bisatei

Campo S. Bernardo 6, tel. 041/739-528,
daily 11:30am-2:30pm, €6-10

If you venture down the residential back streets of Murano you'll eventually stumble onto La Perla ai Bisatei. This neighborhood *osteria* on a quiet square is popular with locals who come for *cicchetti* and conversation. The menu isn't extensive but includes essentials like *spaghetti alle vongole* (spaghetti with clams) and grilled fish. It's a jovial, family-friendly place where glassworkers come for lunch and a half liter of house wine costs €4.

ACCOMMODATIONS

There are several hotels in Murano, but the majority are of the flowery-wallpaper-and-gold-plated-headboard

VENETIAN GLASS

a glassmaking demonstration

Glassmaking has existed in the Venice region since antiquity and was largely influenced by the Middle East, where the craft originated. Murano officially became the center of production when the Venetian Republic prohibited glassmaking in Venice in 1291 (to avoid fires) and established the island of Murano as the center of production. It was a lucrative business and artisans held a prominent role in society. They were obliged to live on the island, however, and were forbidden to leave without permission for fear they would reveal their secrets to rival cities.

The key to Murano's success was innovation. Glassmakers developed new techniques and designs in the 14th century that found receptive overseas markets. The island produced the highest quality in the world by grinding local quartz with soda ash from the eastern Mediterranean. The formula allowed artisans to create a product that could be tinted by adding ground-up coloring agents that were melted into the glass.

New commercial realities and the influx of tourists have altered the business in recent decades. It's easy to stumble on a demonstration, and many have a zoo-like atmosphere in which the artisan is on display. Still, it's interesting to see glass heated to 1,000 degrees and scooped out of an oven like

type and are in desperate need of a makeover. The best options, if you decide to spend a night on the island, are the B&Bs and residences, which offer just as much service for double the charm.

Villa Lina

Calle Dietro gli Orti 12, tel. 041/739-036, www.villalinavenezia.com, €140-200 d
Villa Lina is five minutes from the Colonna *vaporetto* station, directly on

a canal. The three comfortable rooms inside this pretty pink villa are filled with modern furnishings, and each equipped with air-conditioning, Wi-Fi, minibar, safe, and a surprisingly small TV. It's a B&B that feels like an intimate hotel. Guests have their own keys and can enjoy the enchanting garden after exploring the town. Breakfast is served on the terrace with a distant view of Venice.

molten honey. The heated glass is soft and malleable in the hands of a master, who maneuvers a hollow metal rod until he's satisfied with the lump of fiery glass he's extracted. He then cuts and blows, taking a moment to examine the melting mound until it becomes a recognizable shape (often a vase or a horse) before the amazed eyes of an enthusiastic international audience.

Many expert craftspeople in Murano and Burano utilize the *lume* technique, which involves melting long, thin rods of colored glass into small objects or jewelry. It requires lower temperatures and less space to undertake than traditional glass blowing.

Operators of many of the remaining active furnaces offer demonstrations that are repeated throughout the day. Many of these are free and some involve a small fee. There's usually a brief explanation of the glassmaking process, followed by an artisan skillfully creating a small statuette. Demonstrations last 10-15 minutes, after which visitors are encouraged to visit the adjacent galleries. Prices range widely; it's worth shopping around until you find something you like.

There are dozens of workshops around Murano and throughout Venice where you can watch glass being made using different techniques. Here are some of the best:

MURANO

- **Vetreria Artistica Emmedue:** One of the biggest workshops, with multiple furnaces and ongoing demonstrations throughout the day (page 142).

- **Abate Zanetti School of Glass:** The largest glass school on the island organizes demonstrations and offers courses for anyone who wants to blow their own glass (page 143).

BURANO

- **Lumeart:** A husband-and-wife team who are never too busy to explain the *lume* glass technique while they work (page 148).

VENICE

- **FGB:** Small workshop near San Marco where glass jewelry is continuously being made (page 105).

Maison Volpi

Calle Volpi 39, tel. 333/456-7561,
www.maisonvolpi.it, €120 d

Maison Volpi is a good self-catering option. This single-family home is tucked away in the heart of a residential neighborhood where few tourists wander. The spacious two-story house has bright rooms that are decorated with an abundance of antiques. The luminous kitchen is a cozy place to come home to and looks out on a little garden. The minimum stay is three nights, although the owner will occasionally make exceptions.

GETTING THERE AND AROUND

Murano can be reached from Venice on the 3, 4.1, 4.2, 7, 12, 13, or N *vaporetto* lines. The 3 (daily 6:15am-7:15pm) departs from Piazzale Roma and stops at the train station before heading directly to Murano. The **4.1** and **4.2** (daily 6:10am-11:22pm) circumnavigate Venice and stop in Fondamente Nuove, from which they set off to Murano. All three lines stop at the seven *vaporetto* stations on Murano and take less than 15 minutes to make the crossing. *Vaporetto* tickets cost €7 one-way, €14 round-trip, and €20 for a 24-hour pass.

Burano

Burano, known for its lace production, is a magical island and a pleasant escape from Venice. The photogenic canals and streets are lined with brightly colored houses and shops selling linen, lace, and glass jewelry. Most visitors proceed straight from the ferry dock up Viale Marcello, past a concentration of boutiques. The quieter route is to the left along the lagoon to the first canal that splits the island nearly in half.

There are two other canals to stroll along and many lovely streets to explore, complete with drying laundry and stray cats. A bell tower leans perilously next to the church on Piazza Baldassarre Galuppi, where the Lace Museum is located. Fishing still plays an important role here in both the economy and the gastronomy. There are hundreds of small fishing boats docked along the canals and three small ports. Burano can be circumnavigated in less than an hour, but you may find it hard to leave.

SIGHTS
MUSEO DEL MERLETTO
(Lace Museum)
Piazza Galuppi 187, tel. 041/730-034,
Tues.-Sun. 10am-6pm, €5 or Museum Pass
Burano is really about walking and letting your eyes enjoy the scenery, but if you're passionate about lace, visit the Museo del Merletto. The museum explains the tradition, evolution, and commercial importance of lace with a 40-minute documentary and more than 200 intricate patterns. The highlight is watching the little group of skilled ladies working away on new designs and demonstrating an art that is slowly fading.

GIUSEPPE TOSELLI'S HOUSE
Calle Daffan 339
All the houses on Burano are colorful but Giuseppe Toselli's house stands out. Toselli, or *Bepi* to the islanders, was a former handyman and candy vendor who spent his spare time painting geometric patterns and shapes on his house. The result is something original in an already original town. Although Giuseppe passed away more than a decade ago, he hasn't been forgotten, and his much-loved facade was recently restored.

✪ FONDAMENTA CAO MOLECA
The easternmost canal along Fondamenta Cao Moleca has few shops or restaurants, but it's a good place to appreciate the colorful homes Burano is known for. Locals tell different stories about why the houses are brightly painted, but the most common answer has to do with helping returning fishermen locate their homes through morning fog.

FOOD

It may be impossible to find a bad restaurant in Burano. They're all more or less good and specialize in seafood, which is the most abundant ingredient on the island. Burano's fishermen go out five days a week in search of mullet, sea bream, crustaceans, mollusks, and more. Traditional methods of line and net fishing are still used to supply the island and all of Venice with varieties that you may never have tasted before.

Al Gatto Nero

Via Giudecca 88, tel. 041/730-120, Tues.-Sat. 12:30pm-3pm and 7:30pm-9pm, Sun. 12:30pm-3pm, €12-20

A handful of *trattorie* are concentrated on Via Baldassarre Galuppi, which leads to the only *piazza*, but if you ask locals where to eat most will mention Al Gatto Nero. It's always busy, and the tables overlooking the canal will be occupied unless you arrive early or reserve. Nearly every dish includes fish or crustaceans, and the house appetizer is a wonderful way to start a meal. Firsts are a tempting toss-up between *bigoli in salsa* (thick spaghetti-length pasta in sardine sauce) or the rice and seafood specialty *risotto alla Buranella*. Anyone hungry for more can order a second course of grilled sole, eel, monkfish, cuttlefish, or sea bream. If you can't decide, ask for the *griglia mista* (mixed grill) and taste a little of everything.

Fritto Misto

Fondamenta dei Squeri 312, tel. 041/735-198, daily 9:30am-8:30pm, €12

Fritto Misto is an informal outdoor eatery opposite the ferry landing. Given its location, you might be inclined to avoid it on principle, but that would be unfortunate for your taste buds. The delicately fried

the colorful cottages of Burano

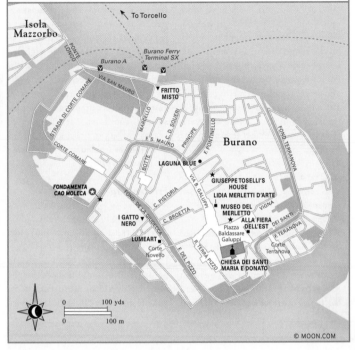

Burano

© MOON.COM

shrimp, calamari, and sardines, served over fries on an edible plate made of bread, are delicious and go great with a cold beer. The menu option includes a drink and a generous plate of lagoon fish for €17. Wait for your order at the counter and then choose a wooden stool in the shade to enjoy the lagoon views.

SHOPPING

Burano isn't commercial in the way Venice can be. Shopping is a relaxed experience with little pressure on buyers. Lace is the obvious purchase, but glass and masks are also available. It's worth seeking out products that are handmade in the little boutiques that dot the island.

GLASS

Lumeart

Via della Giudecca 40,

tel. 041/527-2278, daily 11am-5pm

Although glassblowing is more famous, the *lume* technique of small-scale jewelry making is a common technique in Burano. There are a handful of tiny workshops where artisans melt glass rods (at lower temperatures) into earrings, necklaces, charms, and figurines. Massimo Mauro is one of the veteran glassmakers on the island and has been perfecting the craft since boyhood. The compact corner studio of Lumeart is where his wife sells his creations. It's filled with delicate objects born from his imagination and the tools of his trade.

CLOTHING AND JEWELRY
Alla Fiera dell'Est

Via S. Martino Sinistro 166,
tel. 041/527-2234, daily 10am-6:30pm

Alice dei Rossi couldn't decide between glass, felt, *papier-mâché*, or terra-cotta, so she decided to use them all. She transforms the materials into jewelry and clothes inside Alla Fiera dell'Est, which is painted electric blue on the outside.

LACE AND MASKS
La Stramba

Via San Martino Sinistro 238,
daily 9:30am-6pm

Fabiola creates masks and lace at La Stramba, which doubles as her home. She will happily explain the three types of traditional Venetian masks and show you how they are made.

Lidia Merletti d'Arte

Via Baldassarre Galuppi 215,
tel. 041/730-052, www.dallalidia.com,
daily 9:30am-6:30pm

Lidia Merletti d'Arte is the oldest boutique on the island and only sells local lace. Choose from many different patterns on everything from household linen to handkerchiefs, tablecloths, bedcovers, and nightshirts. There are also several racks of women's and children's clothing. Prices are in line

traditional lace store in Burano

with the time and effort employed by the experienced hands who supply the shop.

FISHING TOURS

Fishing tourism *(pescaturismo)* gives visitors an opportunity to go out with fishermen and discover the day-to-day realities of fishing inside and outside the lagoon. Participants discover the methods for luring different varieties of fish and play an active part in the expedition. Once you're back on shore, you'll learn how the fish you've caught are prepared and cooked before tasting the results of your labor.

fishing boat in Burano

Cooperativo San Marco

tel. 041/730-076,
www.pescaturismoburano.com

Contact Igor at the Cooperativo San Marco to arrange a *pescaturismo* excursion. These usually last 2-3 hours and leave daily at 10am. Boats are open and measure 26-32 feet (8-10 meters) long during the summer; slightly larger, covered boats are used in winter. This initiative, started in 2012 by the cooperative, shares the fishing traditions of the island with visitors. Although it is primarily aimed at larger groups, Igor will happily give you a quote on smaller groups.

LOCAL TIP: TAKE THE BACK ROAD TO BURANO

If you want to take a little detour and arrive in Burano on foot without any tourists, disembark one stop early on the island of Mazzorbo. Turn left from the dock and follow the *fondamenta* along the water until you reach the wooden bridge that connects the two islands.

A fishing tour for four costs around €300. For an extra €25 per person, you can also enjoy a lunch of freshly caught fish.

ACCOMMODATIONS

There are no hotels in Burano and few places to stay. The island is out of the way and not the obvious choice for accommodation, but if you're after tranquility and don't mind being 40 minutes from Venice, Burano can make an enchanting base for visiting lagoon islands. It's also an opportunity to see Burano after all the tourists have gone and the island breathes again.

Laguna Blue

Calle Daffan 431, tel. 041/730-650, €90 d

Laguna Blue is a comfortable, recently renovated B&B in the center of town near the main street. Rooms are clean, modern, and above all, silent. Each comes with an en suite bathroom, but there are no in-room TVs or telephones.

Venissa

Mazzorbo, Fondamenta Santa Caterina 3, tel. 041/527-2281, www.venissa.it, €100-180 d

Venissa is a small estate on the nearby island of Mazzorbo. It's perfect for wine lovers and anyone who isn't in a hurry. The six suites and double rooms combine rustic fittings with contemporary furnishings. All rooms face a small vineyard that was rescued by the owners and now produces a notable white wine. The rural complex is connected to Burano by a pedestrian bridge, so it's only a 10-minute walk from the *vaporetto* station. Guests can choose to dine in the in-house *osteria* or the Michelin-starred restaurant, both of which use ingredients from the on-site fish farm and vegetable garden.

GETTING THERE AND AROUND

There are daily scheduled departures from Fondamente Nuove station in Cannaregio to Burano on the **12** *vaporetto* **line** (€7 one-way, €14 round-trip, €20 24-hour pass). Ferries operate 4:20am-11:20pm and leave every 20-30 minutes. Travel time is 40-50 minutes and there's only one stop in Burano. You can also arrive by **water taxi** from anywhere in Venice. The cost for up to four passengers is €120-130. The entire island is pedestrianized and can be circled in less than an hour.

You can reach other lagoon islands from Burano on foot (Mazzorbo), *vaporetto* (Torcello, Murano), or water taxi. **Water taxis** can be found at the main dock or near the Carabinieri station behind Piazza Baldassarre Galuppi. They can also be reserved by phone (tel. 041/522-2303).

Torcello

Torcello was the first inhabited island in the lagoon and was thriving when Venice was still a backwater. The tide turned and today, there are only 14 permanent residents, a couple of farms, plenty of flamingoes, and a few remaining churches and towers that hint at the island's past. The main canal, lined with a smattering of bars and restaurants, is next to the ferry dock and splits the island in half. There's far less frenzy here than in Venice or on most other islands in the lagoon. Torcello is a good place to get back to nature for a couple of hours, have lunch in a historic restaurant, and reflect on the fragility of civilization.

SIGHTS

Torcello has a single brick road (Strada della Rosina) that runs along a canal and leads to the island's ancient remains. Along the way there are several possibilities for getting sidetracked into the rural scenery. The first is 200 yards (180 meters) from the dock on the left, near the first house. It's a dirt path that leads through grasslands to **Casa Museo Andrich** (tel. 041/735-542, www.museoandrich.com, daily guided visits at 10:30am, 11:30am, 2:30pm, 3:30pm, 4:30pm, and 5:30pm, €15), an informal house museum created by two local artists to display their lagoon-inspired paintings and sculptures.

Continue along the canal (you'll see the *campanile* in the distance) to reach a bridge known as **Ponte del Diavolo** (Devil's Bridge) because it lacks any protective railing. If you want to give tourists the slip, cross the bridge and follow the gravel path to a second wooden bridge. Cross that one and walk left along another canal. You can take the next bridge back to the main route or continue straight toward the bell tower. You may need to make your own path and cross a wooden plank at some point, but you will eventually arrive at a final bridge leading to the historic monuments of the island. All detours are short and take less than 25 minutes to complete.

The historic center of Torcello lies at the end of Strada della Rosina where the canal takes a sharp turn and a dirt path commences. The town once boasted more than a dozen churches, but the only ones standing today are the Basilicas of Santa Maria Assunta and Santa Fosca.

Ponte del Diavolo

SANTA MARIA ASSUNTA

Fondamenta dei Borgognoni 24,
tel. 041/730-119, daily 10:30am-5pm,
€5 or €9 with campanile, free audio guide

Santa Maria Assunta is one of the oldest structures in the lagoon. It was part of a religious complex that included a baptistery, of which the circular foundations are still visible. The Gothic facade consists of 12 receded arches punctuated by a half-dozen windows.

Chiesa di Santa Fosca

It dates from AD 639, but the present building was more or less completed in the first millennium. The entrance is on the right near the ticket office and reveals a simple interior that shows its age. The back wall is entirely covered in Venetian byzantine mosaics of the *Universal Judgment.*

The *campanile* (Tues.-Sun. 10:30am-5pm, €5 or €9 with basilica) is behind the basilica and worth climbing for a view of the island, as well as Burano and Venice in the distance. It's the only tower in the city. There is no elevator, but it's a fun climb. It gets windy at the top, and there's not much room in the narrow corridors along the upper terrace.

Tickets are available from the basilica office. Adjacent to the basilica is the church of Santa Fosca (free), begun in the 12th century. It's vaguely reminiscent of the Basilica di San Marco: a rare example of a Greek Orthodox plan with Byzantine influences.

Underneath the tree in the grassy yard opposite the churches are several well caps and the marble throne on which Attila the Hun is alleged to have sat. The seat more likely served local officials, but it remains a popular photo opportunity nonetheless.

MUSEO PROVINCIALE

Piazza Torcello, tel. 041/730-761, Tues.-Sun. 10:30am-5:30pm, €3

Archaeologists still conduct digs on the island and their finds are stored in the Museo Provinciale opposite Santa Fosca. This small museum houses Greek and Roman antiquities, Etruscan and Paleo-Venetian finds from the estuary, ancient documents, and church treasures.

FOOD AND ACCOMMODATIONS

Locanda Cipriani

Piazza Santa Fosca 29, tel. 041/730-150, www.locandacipriani.com, Wed.-Thurs. and Sun.-Mon. noon-3pm, Fri.-Sat. noon-3pm and 7pm-9pm, €16-24

There are several *trattorie* along the main canal, but Locanda Cipriani is the institution. It was opened in the 1930s by the legendary restaurateur who had already turned Harry's Bar and the Cipriani Hotel into international success stories. The Locanda was more low-key but still attracted postwar VIPs, including Queen Elizabeth, Charlie Chaplin, and Ernest Hemingway, who became friends with Cipriani and wrote *Across the River and Into the Trees* on Torcello. During the summer you can dine outside on the terrace or garden of this elegant hideaway, whose experienced kitchen turns out carpaccio classics and reinterpretations of Venetian favorites.

Eventually, Cipriani added five spacious rooms for overnight guests (two suites and three singles, closed Jan. and Feb., €140 per person). Rooms are classically furnished with hardwood floors, large beds, and pleasant views. The surroundings are romantic and

Locanda Cipriani

often used for wedding receptions, and you can always stop at the bar to savor the past.

Taverna Tipica

Fondamenta dei Borgognoni 5,
tel. 041/099-6428, daily 9:30am-7pm,
€13-18

The first eatery along Strada della Rosina, Taverna Tipica, is a down-to-earth option. It's a casual *osteria* with outdoor dining on wooden tables and benches next to a large grassy field where children play and parents rest. Rice and fish dishes are the mainstays of the menu, which includes *risotto alla Buranella* and *bis di saòr,* both of which can be accompanied with a carafe of great wine.

GETTING THERE AND AROUND

Torcello can be reached on board the number 9 *vaporetto* (€7 one-way, €14 round-trip, €20 24-hour pass) from Burano and via the N night service. Journey time from Burano is seven minutes. and ferries depart every 30 minutes. The schedule is posted at the dock and is worth memorizing or taking a photo of to avoid a wait as you hop from one island to another. The island is best explored on foot, and if you do decide to get off the main walkway, make sure to wear proper footwear—especially if it's been raining.

The Lido

The Lido di Venezia is a thin stretch of land that separates Venice from the Adriatic and made the lagoon possible. The island's original beach bums were 19th-century Romantic writers like Goethe, Byron, and Shelley who were seduced by their surroundings. Their books and poems boosted popularity of the Lido, which became the world's largest beach resort. It still attracts crowds in the summer and provides a nice break from Venice. There's a stylish, laid-back nostalgia about the place and plenty of five-star elegance. Things get really glamorous during the Venice Film Festival when Hollywood and the rest of the film world relocate to the Lido for 10 days in September.

Outdoor dining on the Lido

Most of the island's 17,000 inhabitants live in the northern half of the island closest to Venice and the main *vaporetto* station. The two smaller localities of **Malamocco** and **Alberoni** in the south are quieter and attract fewer visitors. You can reach both by bus or bike. Exploring the Lido is the perfect antidote for tired feet and ochlophobia (fear of crowds).

It's a pleasant place to pedal, lie on the beach, or take a scenic seaside stroll. You can pick up a map of the island along with the summer event calendar at the tourist **Info Point** (Gran Viale 6a, daily 9am-noon and 3pm-6pm, summer only).

Unlike Venice, the Lido allows cars, so be careful when crossing streets and intersections.

NIGHTLIFE

The first beach platforms were built in 1857, followed in 1888 by wooden *capanne* (family beach huts) and luxury hotels not long after. Although some have fallen on hard times and await restoration, others still offer plenty of glamour. Most nightlife is located directly on the beachfront, though many bars close down over the winter months.

Grand Hotel Excelsior

Lungomare Guglielmo Marconi 41,
tel. 041/526 0201,
www.hotelexcelsiorvenezia.com

The Excelsior established the Lido as one of the world's most luxurious beach resorts back in the early 20th century and a recent restyling has helped maintain its premier status. There are two bars inside and you don't have to be a millionaire to enjoy a seaside cocktail here. The **Elimar** (summer 8am-11pm, €6-15) on the ground floor provides indoor and outdoor seating within a cozy pastel setting. The drinks menu includes mocktails, frappés, wine and beer, and a selection of food items served all day long. The **Blue Bar** (daily 10am-midnight) is entirely dedicated to cocktails and has been preparing them for over a century. Bartenders here are all veterans, and watching them prepare the classics or improvise new creations with flare is a lot of fun.

Aurora Beach Bar

Lungomare Gabriele D' Annunzio,
tel. 340/813-2984, daily summer 8am-2am

The Aurora is located next to one of the Lido's free beaches and attracts many bathers after a day of sun. The atmosphere is laid-back, with tables and chairs in the sand and bartenders who operate from a small kiosk. There are DJs on weekends and dancing goes on until dawn.

Bar 9

Via Lepanto 9, tel. 347/030-1575,
daily 9:30am-12:30am

Locals gather all year long at Bar 9 for cocktails and tasty *cicchetti*

(appetizers). The €3 spritz is a steal, and you can sit outside on a pedestrian street near one of the Lido's few canals or inside the brick-lined interior where the owner and his staff keep everyone smiling.

Bagni Alberoni

Strada Nuova dei Bagni 26,
tel. 041/731-029, www.bagnialberoni.com,
daily 8:30am-midnight

You can set up a towel wherever you like or rent a chair from Bagni Alberoni. It's a colorful, laid-back beach club with a simple bar and restaurant where you can order spaghetti with clams or a cocktail. The A bus stops directly out front and there's a good chance of hearing some live music on summer evenings.

Lido Beach

RECREATION AND ACTIVITIES

✪ BEACHES

Lido Beach

Sunbathers will enjoy the long stretch of yellowish sand that lines the entire eastern side of the island. The sand owes its unique hue to the Piave River, which carries sediment from the Dolomite Mountains that contains quartz and magnetic iron. Erosion has become a problem in recent years and the beach narrows considerably the farther away you get from town. In all parts the sea remains shallow for some distance, which makes it a tranquil spot for children and swimmers of all levels. Stroll along the beach to pick your favorite *stabilimento* (beach club), where you can rent an umbrella and *lettini* (lounge chairs).

Paradise Beach

Via Klinger, tel. 335/766-8843,
www.spiaggiaparadiso.it

Lido beaches get crowded in summer and Venetians tend to favor the *stabilimente* (beach clubs) farthest from the Hotel des Bains where tourists congregate. Paradise Beach is at the tip of the island and can be reached on the A bus line. It's favored by families and couples who rent cabins and spend much of their summer enjoying the sun here. It's open to everyone, though, and a lounge chair *(lettino)* and umbrella are €10 for a half day and €15 for the entire day. Front-row spots closest to the sea cost slightly more and sell out by 10am. Wi-Fi is free, a lifeguard is on duty 9am-6pm, and there's a restaurant that's open from breakfast to dinner.

For even more privacy, head to the Alberoni Dunes at the southern tip of the Lido. This part of the island is a WWF sanctuary and is far less populated, with only a couple of beach establishments.

✪ CYCLING

Bicycles aren't allowed in Venice, but cycling is popular on the Lido. The island is flat and great for pedaling. Lido residents do own cars, but islanders drive slowly. The Lido's population triples in size during the summer but most Venetian holidaymakers stick to the beaches and biking is pleasurable year-round.

There's a **bike path** beside Via Sandro that starts at the Lido *vaporetto* station. It changes names but remains the same road and runs the length of the narrow 7.4-mile-long (12-kilometer-long) island. Along the way, you can stop in the pleasant seaside hamlet of Malamocco and have lunch or shop for picnic supplies. The road skirts the lagoon the rest of the way and becomes surprisingly verdant the closer you get to the ferry dock on the southern tip of the island. On the way back, you can ride a different route and follow the eastern coast facing the Adriatic. To take this path turn right on Via Doge Galla at the Malamocco sign just beyond the water-treatment plant and continue until you see water.

There are several rental shops on the main street minutes from the *vaporetto* station.

Lidoonbike

Gran Viale Santa Maria Elisabetta 21b,
tel. 041/526-8019, www.lidoonbike.it,
Mar.-Sept. daily 9am-7pm

You can get Dutch-style singles, tandems, and fun family bikes that seat four at Lidoonbike. Ninety minutes on a standard bike is €5 and comes with a lock. Deposit and ID are required; make sure to read the rules carefully before setting off.

Venice Bike

Gran Viale Santa Maria Elisabetta 79a, tel. 041/526-1490, www.venicebikerental. com, Mar.-Oct. daily 9am-7pm

Just down the block from Lindoon bike, Venice Bike offers similar bikes for similar rates.

SCOOTER RENTALS
Venice Scooter Rental

Via Perasto 6b, tel. 388/888-8842, www.scooterrentvenice.com, daily 10am-7pm

Another fun way to explore the Lido is by scooter or electric bike. Venice Scooter Rental rents both by the hour (€20) or day (€35). No experience is necessary, but you will need a driver's license. You can carry up to one passenger on the light, easy-to-ride 50cc scooters.

HELICOPTER TOURS
Heliair

Aeroporto G. Nicelli, tel. 347/786-0653, www.heliair.it

Venice lacks the hills of Rome or Florence, and even climbing the *campanile* in San Marco doesn't provide a full bird's-eye view of the city. The only way to get that is by helicopter and Heliair, based on the small airstrip at the northern tip of the Lido, can give you instant perspective on the city. The 10-minute tour of the northern lagoon and Venice, which includes a mid-air pause above Piazza San Marco, is €130 per person. Longer excursions are also possible on board Robinson R44 helicopters that seat a maximum of three passengers. The airport can be reached on bus A, or take the 17 *vaporetto* and get off at the

Lido San Nicolò stop. It's only a five-minute walk from there.

GOLF
Circolo Golf Venezia

Lido, Strada Vecchia 1, tel. 041/731-333, Tues.-Sun. 8am-7pm, €97 weekdays, €116 weekends

Some say that when Henry Ford visited Venice in 1928, he asked his aristocratic host where he could play golf. At that time there was no course in the area, but not wanting to disappoint future guests, Count Giuseppe Volpi had a nine-hole course built on the Lido. Circolo Golf Venezia was one of the earliest clubs in Italy and later enlarged to an 18-hole par-72 course near a wild beach where Goethe went to watch the waves. The course is not particularly challenging except on windy days, but it's fun to play and the native flora and fauna along the fairways are appealing. Clubs can be rented for €20 from the pro shop and tee times should be reserved in advance.

GETTING THERE AND AROUND

The Lido lies 10 minutes from Piazza San Marco or 50 minutes from Venice's train station by *vaporetto* (€7 one-way, €14 round-trip, €20 24-hour pass). The main ferry terminal can be reached on the 1, 2, 5.1, 5.2, 6, 10, 14, and N lines. Two smaller stations are located to the north and are served by the 8, 17, and 18, of which the latter two only operate during high season. Another two serve the southern half in summer. The island extends 7.5 miles (12 kilometers) from north to south, and buses A, B, C, N, V, and 11 connect the center with the southern tip near the golf course along two routes.

San Lazzaro degli Armeni

The Isola di San Lazzaro degli Armeni was named for Lazarus, the patron saint of lepers, because a leper asylum was established on the island in 1182. Armenians have been persecuted for centuries and the Republic of Venice gave this miniscule island to a group of monks who were on the run from Turkish forces. The monks set about restoring the island's preexisting church and gradually constructed other buildings, including a library with more than 170,000 ancient volumes and manuscripts. The monastery is still active today in preserving Armenian culture and visitors are welcomed once a day for guided tours of the complex.

SIGHTS

MONASTERO DI SAN LAZZARO DEGLI ARMENI

Isola Di San Lazzaro, tel. 041/526-0104, visitesanlazzaro@gmail.com, Mon.-Fri. 3pm-6pm, free

The convent that the Armenians constructed in 1740 still has an important collection of Eastern art and documents. Known for their hospitality, the priests welcome visitors to their monastery, cloister, print shop, and library. Rare illuminated manuscripts, an 8th-century document regarding rituals, and a 13th-century history of Alexander the Great are among its treasures. A room dedicated to Lord Byron features mementoes and rare books. During the 19th century, Byron was a frequent guest in the convent and stayed in an adjacent room.

GETTING THERE

Vaporetto 20 (€7 one-way, €14 round-trip, €20 24-hour pass) leaves the San Zaccaria water station near San Marco at 3:10pm and arrives at the island's water station at 3.25pm. After a visit, you can continue on to the Lido or return to Venice.

San Lazzaro degli Armeni

PADUA

Padua (Padova in Italian) is a
vibrant university town where Galileo taught and
Giotto introduced the art world to the possibilities of three-dimensional perspective in painting.
Surrounded by canals, Padua has a flat historic
center with cobblestoned streets, unique squares,
and lively markets. Unlike Venice, where tourists outnumber the locals, Padua has a sizable,
youthful population. All over town, you'll see students cycling through this immensely livable city.
After a day of sightseeing, join the locals filling
the bars and squares for happy hour (*aperitivo*).

Itinerary Idea 162
Sights 163
Food 167
Nightlife. 168
Performing Arts 169
Shopping 169
Recreation and
   Activities 171
Accommodations 172
Information and
   Services 173
Getting There 174

HIGHLIGHTS

✪ **SCROVEGNI CHAPEL:** Giotto's three-dimensional frescoes inside this small chapel transformed Western art (page 163).

✪ **BASILICA SANT'ANTONIO:** Padua's most exotic church combines Eastern and Western influences, in the burial place of the city's patron saint (page 165).

✪ **MARKETS:** The picturesque open-air markets at Piazza delle Erbe and Piazza dei Frutti make up Padua's traditional commercial hub (page 169).

This evening ritual, punctuated by the city's trademark *spritz* cocktail, offers a refreshing break and great people watching.

PLANNING YOUR TIME

Less than an hour away by train (or 10 hours by scenic boat ride), Padua is easy to reach from Venice and offers a nice break from the crowds of tourists. This convenient day trip can be combined with excursions to Vicenza or Verona.

You'll need at least 3-4 hours to explore Padua's museums, churches, and markets. Each of Padua's three tourist offices sells the **Padova Card** (tel. 049/201-0020, €16), which is valid for 48 hours from the time it's first used and provides access to 12 museums, including the Scrovegni Chapel, as well as public transportation and discounted admission to many other attractions.

Entry to Padua's most popular site, **Scrovegni Chapel,** must be reserved in advance, as visitor numbers are limited. Many museums are closed Monday. Early risers can maximize their time by visiting **Basilica Sant'Antonio** first, as it opens before most other sights. Morning is also the best time to explore the city's markets, which close at around 2pm on weekdays and 8pm on Saturdays. Markets and many businesses are closed on Sundays.

ORIENTATION

Padua's historic center is small, flat, and pedestrianized, with shaded porticoes that make it perfect for walking or cycling. The train station is a 20-minute walk north of the center, and from Padua Station, Corso Garibaldi leads directly to Cappella degli Scrovegni and the city's most important market squares, Piazza delle Erbe and Piazza dei Frutti, the most animated parts of Padua. Visitors will enjoy exploring the town's many pedestrian streets and the peaceful canals that surround the city.

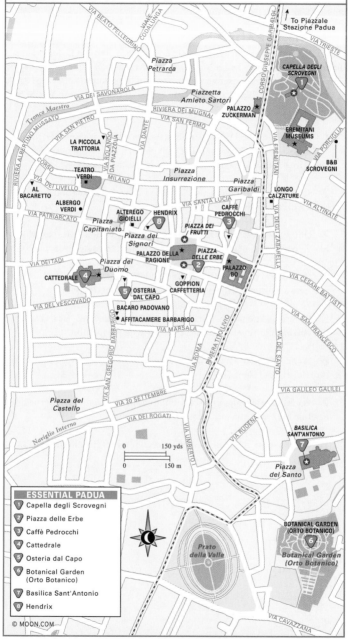

Padua

VIA BEATO PELLEGRINO
VIALE CODALUNGA
VIA TRIESTE
To Piazzale
Stazione Padua
CORSO GIUSEPPE GARIBALDI

Piazza
Petrarca

CAPELLA DEGLI
SCROVEGNI
1

VIA DEI SAVONAROLA

Piazzetta
Amleto Sartori

Tronco Maestro

RIVIERA DEI MUGNAI

PALAZZO
ZUCKERMAN

EREMITANI
MUSEUMS

VIA SAN FERMO

VIA PORCIGLIA

VIA SAN PIETRO

VIA DANTE

B&B
SCROVEGNI

RIVIERA ALBERTINO MUSSATO

LA PICCOLA
TRATTORIA

CORSO VIA DEI LIVELLO

VIA ROLANDO DA PIAZZOLA

Piazza
Insurrezione

Piazza
Garibaldi

VIA FREMITANI

TEATRO
VERDI

MILANO

CAFFÈ
PEDROCCHI
3

LONGO
CALZATURE

VIA DEGLI ZABARELLA

AL
BACARETTO

ALBERGO
VERDI

VIA SANTA LUCIA

VIA ALTINATE

VIA PATRIARCATO

ALTEREGO
GIOIELLI

HENDRIX
8

PIAZZA DEI
FRUTTI

Piazza
Capitaniato

Piazza dei
Signori

PALAZZO DELLA
RAGIONE

PIAZZA
DELLE ERBE
2

PALAZZO
BO

VIA CESARE BATTISTI

VIA DEI TADI

Piazza del
Duomo

CATTEDRALE
4

OSTERIA
DAL CAPO
5

GOPPION
CAFFETTERIA

VIA SAN FRANCESCO

VIA DEL VESCOVADO

BACARO PADOVANO

AFFITACAMERE BARBARIGO

VIA MARSALA

VIA DEL SANTO

VIA SAN GREGORIO BARBARIGO

VIA ROMA

RIVIERA TITO LIVIO

VIA GALILEO GALILEI

Piazza del
Castello

VIA 20 SETTEMBRE

VIA DEI ROGATI

VIA UMBERTO I

Naviglio Interno

BASILICA
SANT'ANTONIO
7

| 0 | 150 yds |
| 0 | 150 m |

Piazza
del Santo

Prato
della Valle

BOTANICAL GARDEN
(ORTO BOTANICO)
6

Botanical Garden
(Orto Botanico)

VIA CAVAZZANA

ESSENTIAL PADUA

1 Capella degli Scrovegni
2 Piazza delle Erbe
3 Caffè Pedrocchi
4 Cattedrale
5 Osteria dal Capo
6 Botanical Garden
  (Orto Botanico)
7 Basilica Sant'Antonio
8 Hendrix

© MOON.COM

PADUA

Itinerary Idea

ESSENTIAL PADUA

For this itinerary, catch an early train from Venice to arrive in Padua around 10am. At least 24 hours before you leave Venice, schedule a morning visit to Cappella degli Scrovegni, as reservations are mandatory. If you follow the steps in this itinerary, you'll probably be ready to hop on a train back to Venice by about 6pm.

1 Ride the blue tram from the train station or walk down Corso Garibaldi to **Cappella degli Scrovegni.** The visit consists of a 15-minute video followed by 15 minutes to view the frescoes inside the chapel.

2 Stroll through the market stalls lining **Piazza delle Erbe** and purchase some fruit for a snack.

3 Order an espresso at **Caffè Pedrocchi,** the city's oldest coffee bar, which has been a favorite of revolutionaries and intellectuals since 1831.

4 Continue west through **Piazza Capitaniato** to the **Cattedrale (Duomo)** and have a look at the frescoes inside the baptistery next door.

5 Enjoy a traditional lunch at **Osteria dal Capo** and sample local favorites like *baccalà alla Veneta* (creamed cod slowly stewed in milk).

6 Wander through a medieval **Botanical Garden** to discover a variety of rare flowers and plants.

7 Pay homage to Padua's patron saint inside **Basilica Sant'Antonio** before heading back to the historic center for happy hour.

8 Order a spritz at **Hendrix** and sip it outside on the city's liveliest square.

Sights

✪ SCROVEGNI CHAPEL
(Cappella degli Scrovegni)

Piazza Eremitani, tel. 049/201-0020, www.cappelladegliscrovegni.it, daily 9am-7pm, reservation only, €13 with entry to Eremitani Museum or Padova Card

A wealthy banker commissioned this small chapel during the Middle Ages, when charging interest was considered a sin. To further absolve his guilt, the banker hired Giotto (1266-1337) to adorn the chapel walls with a fresco cycle depicting the *Life of Christ,* the *Life of the Virgin,* and other religious themes. The result is a masterwork that redefined Western art. Giotto's paintings broke away from traditional styles by portraying humans with emotions inside three-dimensional scenes. The artist's vivid blue backgrounds are filled with radiant biblical characters dressed in vibrant shades of pink, orange, red, and gold. The chapel's architectural elements create a natural pictorial space for Giotto's groundbreaking work. Nowhere is this better demonstrated than in the two panels, known as the **Coretti**, on either side of the altar, where Giotto experimented with perspective and created the illusion of space.

A work this important must be protected from heat, moisture, and dust, which is why getting into the chapel is a little complicated. Reservations are required, and only 25 visitors can be admitted at a time. Tours begin with an informative 15-minute video, followed by a 15-minute visit to the chapel. Multilanguage panels describe the scenes depicted on the walls. If you haven't booked in advance, check for any last-minute availability at the ticket office.

Your ticket to the Scrovegni Chapel also covers entry to the Eremitani Museums and Palazzo Zuckermann.

EREMITANI MUSEUMS

Piazza Eremitani 8, tel. 049/820-4551, Tues.-Sun. 9am-7pm, €10 or Padova Card, free with Scrovegni Chapel ticket

Two small museums are combined within this former monastery. One is dedicated to local archaeological findings, and the other displays medieval art, including an entire multimedia room dedicated to Giotto. Any outstanding questions about the Scrovegni Chapel will be answered here.

The Museo Archeologico archaeological museum contains tombs, coins, statues, and tools used by Paleo-Venetians (Iron Age inhabitants of the Veneto region), Etruscans, and Romans since Padua was founded nearly 3,000 years ago.

The Museo d'Arte Medievale e Moderna medieval museum is dedicated to art created between the 13th and 18th centuries, including works

Scrovegni Chapel

by Tintoretto, Veronese, and Canova. Don't miss the Angel Room, with its militant angel warriors by Guariento, and a Giotto crucifix. The Ovetari Chapel has fragments of Andrea Mantegna's fresco cycle, which was damaged during World War II. Both museums are modern, well lit, and attended by enthusiastic staff members, who are eager to answer questions.

PALAZZO ZUCKERMANN

Corso Garibaldi 33, tel. 049/820-4513,
Tues.-Sun. 10am-7pm, €10 or Padova Card,
free with Scrovegni Chapel ticket

This grand three-story building, which once housed Padua's central post office, is now home to Museo Bottacin and Museo d'Arte Applicate. The first and second floors are dedicated to decorative and applied arts. There are hundreds of objects on display, from 16th-century furniture to 18th-century clothing, ceramic pottery, and jewelry. On the third floor, an extensive coin collection includes ancient Greek, Roman, medieval, and Renaissance currency. Temporary exhibitions are frequently held.

This is a great place to see a large collection of random and unexpected things. There is no showstopper at Palazzo Zuckermann, but the museums will interest anyone who likes antiques. It's just around the corner from the Scrovegni chapel and is included with that ticket, so stop in for a quick visit if time permits.

PALAZZO BO

Via VIII Febbraio 2, tel. 049/827-3939,
www.unipd.it, English tours Mon.-Fri.
10:30am, 12:30pm, 2:30pm, and 4:30pm,
and Sat. 10:30am and 12:30pm, €7

Padua's university was founded in 1222, and it has been the center of the city's academic activity since the 1500s. Inside is the lecture hall where Galileo taught physics, and the wooden anatomy theater where medical students watched autopsies being performed. If you use your imagination, you may be able to conjure what went on inside this renowned university building back when Harvard and Yale were nothing but grassy knolls. There is an air of reverence inside these halls after centuries of study.

The building can only be entered with one of the guided tours that last 45 minutes and are limited to 40 visitors at a time. Tours can be reserved in advance. Itineraries vary during the academic year, depending on which rooms are in use.

PALAZZO DELLA RAGIONE

Piazza delle Erbe, tel. 049/820-5006,
Tues.-Sun. 9am-6:30pm, €4

Palazzo della Ragione (Palace of Reason), which locals refer to as the "salon," is the heart of Padua, where the city's courts were once located and special events are now held regularly. The expansive interior is adorned with frescoes depicting months of the year and the planting, harvesting, and communal activities associated with each season. Informational signagein Italian and English provides details about the massive building, which was constructed in 1218 and separates Padua's two main squares, Piazza delle Erbe and Piazza dei Frutti. Visitors enjoy fine views of the squares from the colonnaded porticoes that run along the exterior of the building.

PIAZZA DEI SIGNORI

Venice dominated Padua for centuries, ruling the city from Palazzo del Capitano in Piazza dei Signori. This government building is rarely open to the public, but the exterior is

Basilica Sant'Antonio

worth seeing, with Venice's winged lion mascots decorating the facade, and another one perched atop a column in front. The Torre dell'Orologio (Astronomical Clock Tower) in the center of the building was inaugurated in 1473 and tells the hour, month, lunar phase, zodiac sign, and position of the planets. Three 45-minute tours of the clock tower are offered in Italian on Friday and Saturday 9:30am-11:45am (free, but donation requested). Pass under the tower's arch to reach the tree-lined Piazza Capitaniato and the Faculty of Arts University, where local students like to hang out.

Piazza dei Signori hosts a market (Mon.-Fri. 8am-2pm and Sat. 8am-8pm) and is lined with cafés and bars that start to get busy in late afternoon.

CATTEDRALE
(Padua Cathedral)
Via Dietro Duomo 5, tel. 049/662-814, Mon.-Sat. 7am-2pm and 4pm-7:30pm, Sat. 7am-7pm, Sun. 8:30am-8pm, free

Michelangelo was one of the designers of Padua's Cattedrale, known simply as the Duomo. Construction on the cathedral began during the 13th century, but the facade was never completed. Inside, look up at the center of the dome, where you'll see *Paradise,* painted in 1375-1378 by Florentine artist Giusto de' Menabuoi. The painting features an array of saints and local celebrities. You'll also find Giusto de' Menabuoi's frescoes of *St. John the Baptist* and *Stories of Mary,* which feature vibrant colors and architectural settings that were modeled on the city.

The Baptistery (tel. 049/656-914, daily 10am-6pm, €3) next door, which is dedicated to St. John, dates from the 12th century. Linger inside to admire the original 14th-century frescoes.

✪ BASILICA SANT'ANTONIO
Piazza del Santo 11, tel. 049/822-5652, daily 6:20am-6:45pm, free

Anthony of Padua wasn't born in the city, but he died here in 1231 and became Padua's patron saint. This

165

Romanesque Gothic basilica is dedicated to him and was built to house his remains. The exterior design was influenced by Eastern architecture, with eight domes and spires that are reminiscent of Byzantine buildings. Donatello's bronze bas-reliefs (1444-1448) along the main altar tell stories from St. Anthony's life, including the *Miracle of the Donkey*, in which the saint convinced the animal to accept a consecrated host instead of grain. The church interior is rich with colorful frescoes by Altichiero and Giusto de' Menabuoi, including a scene of the saint gesturing toward the city. Anthony's tomb, in the north transept, is a year-round destination for religious pilgrims, who flock to the basilica in greatest numbers on June 13, the saint's feast day.

Outside the basilica stands Donatello's bronze statue of the Venetian mercenary Gattamelata, the first equestrian statue of its size cast since the fall of the Roman Empire. On the same square, stop in to **Oratorio di San Giorgio** (daily 9am-1pm and 2pm-6pm, €3), a Romanesque chapel, to see the earliest documented frescoes by Titian.

PRATO DELLA VALLE

Italy's largest square was built in 1775 and consists of an oval island, surrounded by a moat filled with fish and reached by four pedestrian bridges. The grassy area in the center of the island is a favorite retreat, where locals relax under shade trees and shop at the flea market that's held on Saturday 7am-7pm. Statues of the city's illustrious forefathers line the outer perimeter, where street peddlers offer cheap sunglasses and knockoff handbags to passersby.

Prato della Valle

BOTANICAL GARDEN
(Orto Botanico)

Via Orto Botanico 15, tel. 049/827-3939, www.ortobotanicopd.it, summer Tues.-Sun. 9am-7pm, winter Tues.-Sun. 9am-5pm, €10, €5 with Padova Card

Padua's botanical garden was first planted in 1545 and contains more than 3,500 species. Declared a UNESCO World Heritage Site in 1997, the garden holds beauty for casual visitors as well as botanists. Pick up a map at the entrance; information is included, describing the outdoor areas and modern greenhouse, which are organized by tropical, arid, and temperate climate zones. It's a great place to learn about biodiversity. Spring is the best time to visit, as much of the flora is dry and fading by summer. Guided tours (in Italian) depart at 11am and 3pm from the visitor's center.

Botanical Garden

Food

Padua is a great place to eat, and if you're visiting on a day trip from Venice, you'll want to seek out regional specialties. Local cuisine includes a lot of risotto dishes, such as the classic *risotto Padovano*, served with radishes and wild herbs or peas. Thick, spaghetti-like *bigoli* is the local pasta, usually served with *anatra* (duck) ragu. Cod (*merluzzo*) is served in a variety of preparations, and is often accompanied by polenta. In Padua you'll also enjoy lower restaurant prices than in Venice. Note that many restaurants are closed on Sunday.

Wine can be ordered by the glass, carafe, or bottle. Colli euganei rosso is the local red made from a blend of cabernet franc, cabernet sauvignon, merlot, raboso, and barbera grapes. The novello (young wine that's drunk as soon as it's bottled) is ready November 1; rosso d'annata is enjoyed four months after harvest; and rosso riserva is aged two years. The white colli euganei bianco is produced from seven grape varieties and comes in still and sparkling *(spumante brut)* versions.

ITALIAN
Bacaro Padovano
Via S. Gregorio Barbarigo 3,
tel. 049/876-2777, Wed.-Sat. noon-2:30pm
and 7pm-10:30pm, Mon. and Tues.
7pm-10:30pm, €8-11

Bacaro Padovano is a cozy *osteria* and *cicchetteria* (tavern) where you can come for a full meal or just a glass of wine and appetizers. The menu includes classics like *bigoli* with duck ragu, *sarde in saòr* (sweet and sour sardines), and a number of vegetarian options. It's located south of the duomo, on a porticoed street leading to one of the waterways that runs through the city.

La Piccola Trattoria
Via R. Da Piazzola 21, tel. 049/656-163,
www.piccolatrattoria.it, Tues.-Sat.,
noon-2:30pm and 8pm-11pm, €8-11

Padua isn't limited to Venetian food, and if you want to try Sardinian fare, head to La Piccola Trattoria. The waiters in this homey one-room eatery will gladly explain the difference between *malloreddus* and *maccarones* pasta, and enjoy practicing their English. The octopus served with potatoes, green beans, and capers makes a tasty second course. Try capping your meal with Sardinia's popular Mirto berry liquor.

Osteria dal Capo
Via Obizzi 2, tel. 049/663-105,
Mon. 7pm-midnight, Tues.-Sat. noon-2:30pm
and 7pm-midnight, €8-12

Osteria dal Capo has been preparing the same dishes the same way for generations, and no one's complaining. The menu is short but includes all the local favorites, such as baccalà alla Veneta, fegato alla Veneziana (stewed pork or beef liver), and homemade desserts that vary daily. Tables are slightly cramped, but the food is too good for that to matter.

COFFEE
Caffè Pedrocchi
Via VIII Febraio 15, tel. 049/878-1231,
daily 8am-midnight

Neoclassic Caffè Pedrocchi, with its ornate Gothic wing, has been a meeting spot since 1831 and was the scene of student uprisings in 1848. Don't miss its signature coffee drink, *caffè Pedrocchi*, a creamy concoction with a hint of mint, served in a large cup and topped with cacao. Locals come here to relax with a cup of coffee or tea, read the paper, and socialize. The Museum of the Risorgimento and Contemporary Age (tel. 049/878-1231, Tues.-Sun. 9:30am-12:30pm and 3:30pm-6pm, closed Mon. and holidays, €4 or free with Padova Card) upstairs recounts Italy's journey towards unification.

Palazzo della Ragione

Goppion Caffetteria

Piazze delle Erbe 6, tel. 049/657-275, daily 7am-8pm

Goppion is a popular, modern coffee chain with an outlet on Padua's main square. It's a good place to sip cappuccino under the arches facing Piazza delle Erbe or grab a quick cup at the counter, where triangular *tramezzini* sandwiches, fruit smoothies, and healthy snacks are prepared fresh daily.

Nightlife

Venice has had a strong influence on Padua, and here, too, there are *bacari,* bars serving drinks and snacks that are known as *spunciotti* by residents. A spritz cocktail (made with *prosecco*, Aperol, seltzer, and a slice of orange) is the favored happy hour drink, and many bars offer discounts on Wednesdays. In Piazza delle Erbe, Piazza dei Frutti, and Piazza dei Signori, tables are filled from the time the market stalls clear out in the early afternoon until well after dark.

BARS AND *BACARI*

Hendrix

Piazza dei Signori 38, tel. 049/501-0175, daily 5pm-1am, €6-8

Hendrix is a small, laid-back bar with an industrial décor, on one of the city's most happening squares. Tables with umbrellas are set up outside during the summer, and the bar serves great gin and whiskey cocktails all year long. If you've never had a *spritz,* this is the place to get your first taste.

Cantina del Golfo

Via Santa Lucia 91, tel. 049/876-4114, Mon.-Sat. 6pm-2am

Padua's version of a pub is a cozy, brick-vaulted drinking den where choosing a beer isn't easy. Fortunately, the staff is happy to help you make a choice, and the taps have something for everyone. Music is played at just the right volume here, and food is available whenever you get hungry.

Al Bacaretto

Via S. Pietro 105, tel. 391/360-9835, 6:30pm-midnight, €7-10

This tiny bacaro is popular with locals who fill the four tables out front in summer and enjoy spunciotti at the counter inside year-round. These include thin slices of fresh bread covered with creamed cod, smoked salmon, shrimp, sardines, and more. You'll want to try them all! Daily specials are written on a chalkboard, and the friendly owner is happy to translate unfamiliar terms to English.

Performing Arts

Teatro Verdi
Via dei Livello 32, tel. 049/877-7011,
www.teatrostabileveneto.it
Great acoustics and a stunning triple-tiered interior are the hallmark of Teatro Verdi. The Baroque theater was inaugurated in 1751 and contains 700 plush seats that host an opera, dance, and performing arts season, with ticket prices starting at €12.

Shopping

Shopping is most fun outdoors in Padua, where open-air markets sell food, clothing and accessories, housewares, and more. The biggest markets occur on weekdays and Saturdays in Piazza delle Erbe and Piazza dei Frutti, but many other squares around the city have daily or weekly markets. There's also a flea market in Prato della Valle on Saturday 7am-7pm.

For boutique shoppers, Via Santa Lucia is lined with stylish shops. Padua is known for producing women's shoes, including some of Louis Vuitton's designer footwear. Leather goods in general are excellent here.

✪ MARKETS
As you wind your way under the arcades near Palazzo della Ragione, you can step out into either Piazza delle Erbe or Piazza dei Frutti, both of which are home to vibrant open-air markets. Hundreds of locals do their shopping every day among the pretty stalls filled with fresh fruits and vegetables. Browsing and making a few purchases of your own can be great fun. In the afternoon, commerce gives way to café tables and chairs where *aperitivo* is served.

Piazza delle Erbe
Mon.-Fri 8am-1pm, Sat. 8am-8pm
Locals have been buying fruits and vegetables in Piazza delle Erbe for centuries. These days, 52 special stalls (*scariolanti*) with canvas roofs to shield produce from the sun, fill the square. Flowers are sold around the fountain, and vendors calling out the merits of their tomatoes or cherries ensure a spirited atmosphere.

Piazza dei Frutti
Mon.-Fri 8am-1pm, Sat. 8am-8pm
Piazza dei Frutti is home to a mixed food and dry goods market. There

market on Piazza delle Erbe

are 16 stalls selling fruits, vegetables, and local specialties like olive oil and honey. The rest of the square is dedicated to shoes, clothing, and housewares. This is a good place to pick up a souvenir *moka* coffee maker or T-shirt. During the Christmas holidays, homemade ornaments, candles, and sweets are also sold.

JEWELRY
Alterego Gioielli
Piazza dei Signori 26, tel. 049/661-864,
Mon.-Fri. 9:30am-12:30pm and 3:30pm-7pm
Goldsmith Massimo Guerra forms angular, tubular, modern designs in the back of this retro-style boutique. You'll find one-of-a-kind rings, bracelets, and earrings at prices in the range of €30-150.

LEATHER AND SHOES
Longo Calzature
Via Zabarella 97/99, tel. 049/875-6345,
Tues.-Sat. 9am-12:30pm and
3:30pm-7:30pm, Mon. 3:30pm-7:30pm,
shoes €50-100
The window display at Longo Calzature is crammed with Italian-made shoes for men and women. If you venture inside, you'll find many more brands and styles. The salespeople are friendly without being pushy and provide disposable socks in case you're wearing sandals.

Recreation and Activities

CYCLING
BIKESHARE AND RENTALS
Goodbike Padova (www.goodbikepadova.it) is the city's bike-sharing program, with more than 250 bicycles stationed around the historic center. The €25 registration fee is only worth it for visitors who plan to stay at least a few days, or for anyone who really needs a bike on Saturday afternoon or Sunday, when the recommended bike rental offices are closed. To rent by the day, check out **Street Bike** (Via S. Biagio 28, tel. 328/258-5381, Mon.-Fri. 8:30am-12:45pm and 3pm-7pm, €15 per day) or **E-Garage** (Via S. Pietro 118, tel. 347/430-7151, Mon.-Fri. 9am-12:30pm and 3:30pm-7pm, and Sat. 9am-12:30pm, €15 per day). The latter delivers bikes to hotels for free.

BIKE PATHS
There are 75 miles (120 kilometers) of bike paths in and around Padua.

biking in the Giardini dell'Arena

Percorso Arginali
Percorso Arginali is a good option for a biking route. Ride west until you reach the Riviera S. Benedetto canal and follow it south to the Bacchiglione River. The dirt path on the northern bank follows the river for about 1 mile (1.5 kilometers) before heading north and eventually looping back to the historic center. Along the way, you'll pass rural farmland, neat suburbs, and impressive sections of Padua's old city walls. It's an easy ride, and bike maps are available from the tourist office. Percorso Arginali is divided into three sections (blue, yellow, and red) that circle the city with a total length of 6 miles (10 km).

TOURS
Guide Turistiche Padova
Piazza Bardella 3, tel. 049/836-4389, www.guidepadova.it, €120 per group
Guide Turistiche Padova is an association of more than 30 authorized guides who provide classic and personalized tours of the city's monuments. Visits can be reserved online or by contacting guides directly by phone or email. A half-day tour reveals fundamental information about Padua's long history and the nature of its population.

City Sightseeing Padova
www.padova.city-sightseeing.it, €15
City Sightseeing Padova operates two guided bus routes from April to November. Line A (60 minutes) tours the historic center while Line B (45 minutes) heads out to the nearby thermal towns. It's a quick way to see a lot of the city in a little time.

CRUISING THE BRENTA CANAL

The Brenta River has long been an important artery of transportation and commerce for Venice. To take advantage of the fertile plains of northeastern Italy, which supplied the city with rice, wheat, and other essential crops, Venetians dug a network of canals linking the Brenta Canal to Venice's lagoon, and from the 14th century on, wealthy landowning families built villas along these waterways. Andrea Palladio (1508-1580), the most influential architect at the time, created a new style of agricultural estate that was open and undefended. These homes became highly prized, and there was great competition among aristocrats to outdo one another with elaborate mansions and gardens.

VENICE TO PADUA BY BOAT

The best way to see these Palladian villas is by boat on a leisurely cruise from Venice to Padua, and **Il Burchiello** operates tours from Venice to Padua and vice versa. The excursion includes guided tours of **Villa Foscari, Villa Widmann,** and **Villa Pisani,** as well as a lunch break in the town of **Oriago** (€22-29). Il Burchielo also offers half-day tours (4 hours, €65) that don't go all the way to Padua but stop in the town of Oriago and return to Venice, making fewer stops along the way.

If you're using the full-day cruise as a method to travel between Venice and Padua, it's easier to depart from Venice and spend the night in Padua. You can then spend part of the next day exploring Padua before taking a train back to Venice. Luggage sized 75x50x30 centimeters (29x20x12 inches) or smaller can be stored onboard at a cost of €20 per bag. The boat trip is a slow alternative to train travel, but you'll enjoy a choice of comfortable, air-conditioned interiors or outdoor seating with wonderful countryside views, as well as the chance to explore palatial villas off the beaten tourist path.

Accommodations

HOTELS

Affittacamere Barbarigo

Via S. Gregorio Barbarigo 15,
tel. 049/836-4163,
www.affittacamerebarbarigo.it, €60 d

Barbarigo is perfect for travelers looking for a clean, simple room close to the historic center. There's no front desk, spa, or restaurant, just the basics on a quiet street less than 100 meters from the Duomo. Guests have access to a communal kitchen, and there's parking nearby. Check-in is at Albergo Verdi 5 minutes away (noon-midnight).

Albergo Verdi

Via Dondi dall'Orologio 7,
tel. 049/836-4163,
www.albergoverdipadova.it, €100 d

The elevator is so tiny at Albergo Verdi that you might have to send your luggage upstairs without you, but this three-star hotel was remodeled in 2006 to offer more comforts and modern design. The updated rooms and a friendly staff attract university professors and theater performers from Teatro Verdi a few steps away. Each of the 10 double rooms is quiet and

city gate and bridge spanning the Brenta River

IL BURCHIELLO
Via Porciglia 34, Padua, tel. 049/876-0233, www.ilburchiello.it
March-October Mon.-Fri. 9am-6pm
Full-day cruise: 10 hours, €99; half-day cruise to Oriago: 4 hours, €65
Venice to Padua: Tues., Thurs., Sat. departing 8:50am from Pontile San
Zaccaria A (Riva degli Schiavoni), arriving 7pm
Padua to Venice: Wed., Fri., and Sun., departing 8am from Pontile della
Scalinata (Imbarco Portello), arriving 5:30pm

comfortable, and has a hairdryer, TV, and safe.

BED-AND-BREAKFAST

B&B Scrovegni

Via Porciglia 18, tel. 049/661-474,
www.bebscrovegni.it, €100 d

This charming bed-and-breakfast in a remodeled 14th-century building is a favorite with couples. The stylish rooms and self-catering apartments come with private bath, mini bar, and safe. There are nice rooftop views from the upper floors, and a hearty continental breakfast (included in the price) is served in a bright dining area overlooking a small garden. Silvia and Angela at reception welcome guests and make sure everything runs smoothly.

Information and Services

TOURIST INFORMATION

Padua has three **tourist offices.** One is located inside the train station (tel. 049/520-7415, www.turismopadova.it, Mon.-Sat. 9am-7pm and Sun. 10am-4pm); another is at Vicolo Piazzetta Cappellato Pedrocchi 9 (Mon.-Sat.

9am-7pm and Sun. 10am-4pm); and the third is at Piazza del Santo (daily 9am-1pm and 2pm-6pm). Each sells the Padova Card.

LUGGAGE STORAGE

Luggage can be stored at the train station with the Deposito Bagagli (6:30am-6pm, €1 per hour) near track 1. Look for the blue suitcase icon.

Getting There

PADUA GETTING THERE

GETTING TO AND FROM PADUA

Padua is accessible by train or car from Venice, or via a romantic cruise up the Brenta Canal (see p. 172).

TRAIN

Dozens of trains from Venice's Santa Lucia Station stop in Padua throughout the day. Regional service to the city takes 50 minutes and costs €4.25, while high-speed trains run by Italo (www.italotreno.it) or Trenitalia (www.trenitalia.it) take half the time and twice the money (€9.90-15.90). From Verona's Porta Nuova, 50 trains (€7.30-17.90) connect to Padua per day and take 40-80 minutes, depending on the service.

Padua's train station is less than a mile (1.3 kilometers) north of the city center, which can be reached in 20 minutes on foot. There are also buses and a single tramline (€1.30 or €2 onboard for 75 minutes) that are convenient for getting to and from the train station. The No. 5, 10, and 42 buses all stop outside the station and head south down Corso Garibaldi to the historic center. Taxis are also available out front, and a ride to the center is about €6. The last train back to Venice leaves at 11:21pm.

CAR

Padua is 25 miles (40 kilometers) west of Venice and can be reached in 35 minutes by car on the A57/A4 highway. It's straight driving all the way until the Padova Est exit (€2.70). From there, you'll find that directions to the center are clearly indicated.

Verona is 62 miles (100 kilometers) west of Padua; it's a 70-minute drive on the A4 to the Padova Est exit (€5.10).

Parking

There are about a dozen open-air and covered parking lots in Padua. Most are near the train station; follow the signs after you enter the city. The closest one to the historic center is also the most expensive: Park Piazza Insurrezione (Piazza Insurrezione, €3 per hour). There are other lots only a few minutes north that charge less, such as Piazzale Boschetti (€1.70 per hour) and Sarpi (€1 per hour).

VICENZA

UNESCO declared Vicenza (vee-CHEN-zah) a World Heritage Site in 1994, and strolling along its elegant and tidy streets lined with Palladian buildings, you can begin to see why. If you haven't heard of Andrea Palladio you will have by the time you leave Vicenza. Andrea Palladio's designs transformed 16th-century architecture, and Vicenza boasts 30 of his symmetrical masterpieces, including the Basilica Palladiana in the heart of Vicenza, the indoor amphitheater Teatro Olimpico, and the revolutionary Villa La Rotonda on the outskirts of

Itinerary Idea 178
Sights 179
Food and Nightlife 183
Shopping 186
Recreation and
    Activities 187
Accommodations 188
Information and
    Services 189
Getting There
    and Around 189

HIGHLIGHTS

✪ **TEATRO OLIMPICO:** This Renaissance theater, Palladio's final project, is an indoor amphitheater with a ceiling painted like the sky. Visit at 10am or 3pm for a light and sound extravaganza (page 179).

✪ **PALLADIAN BASILICA:** The architect's iconic masterwork is the only Palladio building in town with a rooftop terrace, where you can enjoy drinks with a view (page 180).

✪ **VILLA VALMARANA AND VILLA LA ROTONDA:** These two exquisite villas on the outskirts of Vicenza have lost none of their 16th-century charm (pages 181 and 182).

town. Even if stately columns aren't your thing, Vincenza offers enough bustling squares, one-of-a-kind artisan workshops, and gourmet cuisine to make a visit here memorable.

PLANNING YOUR TIME

Vicenza is an ideal half-day trip from Venice, though you may want to stay longer to explore the array of villas and gardens. It's 46 miles (75 kilometers) from Venice, roughly halfway between Padua and Verona, so if you're traveling from Venice, Vicenza can easily be combined with a visit to one or both of those cities.

The **Museum Card** (Card Musei, €15) includes access to seven sights, including Teatro Olimpico (Olympic Theater), Palladio Museum, and Palazzo Chiericati. It's valid for seven days and can be purchased at the tourist office next to the entrance to Teatro Olimpico, or at info points at Santa Corona, Basilica Palladiana (when open), and the Palladio Museum. Given that a ticket to the theater alone costs €11, the Museum Card is a good deal; you only need to visit one other monument to make it worthwhile. Keep in mind, tickets to Palazzo

Chiericati and Teatro Olimpico are sold at the tourist office in Piazza Matteotti rather than on-site.

Museums in Vicenza are closed Monday, and the Villa La Rotonda interiors are only open Wednesday and Saturday March-November. Several monuments offer audio guides, but you can also download the city's digital **sound tour** (www.vicenzae.org) to learn about individual sights.

ORIENTATION

Vicenza is a small, walkable city with an orderly street pattern. *Contrà* is the locals' word for streets, and all of Vicenza's clean, cobbled lanes are worth exploring. The main artery, **Corso Andrea Palladio,** runs the entire length of the historic center and splits the city in half. The historic center is bordered on three sides by the Retrone and Bacchiglione Rivers. Both are small and nearly dry at the height of summer, but you'll enjoy nice views anytime from bridges like **Ponte San Michele** and **San Paolo,** which lead to less explored areas south of the center. This is also the direction of the Palladian villas, which can be reached on foot, bicycle, or bus.

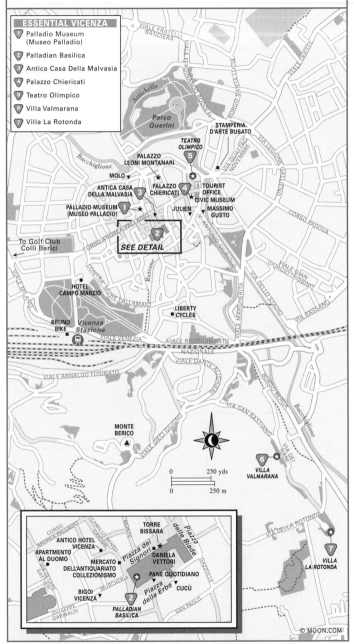

Vicenza

ESSENTIAL VICENZA

1. Palladio Museum (Museo Palladio)
2. Palladian Basilica
3. Antica Casa Della Malvasia
4. Palazzo Chiericati
5. Teatro Olimpico
6. Villa Valmarana
7. Villa La Rotonda

VIALE FRATELLI BANDIERA

Astichello

Parco Querini

STAMPERIA D'ARTE BUSATO

TEATRO OLIMPICO 5

Bacchiglione

PALAZZO LEONI MONTANARI

MOLO ▼

ANTICA CASA DELLA MALVASIA 3

PALAZZO CHIERICATI 4

TOURIST OFFICE

PALLADIO MUSEUM (MUSEO PALLADIO) 1

JULIEN ▼

CIVIC MUSEUM

MASSIMO GUSTO

CORSO ANDREA PALLADIO

SEE DETAIL 2

To Golf Club Colli Berici

CONTRA' DELLE PALLAMAIO

Retrone

HOTEL CAMPO MARZIO

LIBERTY CYCLES

VIALE MILANO

BRUNO BIKE

Vicenza Stazione

VIALE VENEZIA

VIALE RISORGIMENTO NAZIONALE

VIALE ARNALDO FUSINATO

VIALE DANTE ALIGHIERI

MONTE BERICO

VIALE DIECI GIUGNO

VILLA VALMARANA 6

VIA DELLA ROTONDA

VILLA LA ROTONDA 7

0   250 yds
0   250 m

VICENZA

CORSO ANDREA PALLADIO

CAMILLO SENSO

CONTRA' MONTE

ANTICO HOTEL VICENZA

TORRE BISSARA

APARTMENTO AL DUOMO

Piazza dei Signori

MERCATO DELL'ANTIQUARIATO COLLEZIONISMO

MUSCHERIA

Piazza delle Biade

DANIELA VETTORI

PANE QUOTIDIANO

Piazza delle Erbe

CUCÙ

BIGOI VICENZA ▼

GIUSEPPE GARIBALDI

PALLADIAN BASILICA 2

SAN PAOLO

© MOON.COM

Itinerary Idea

ESSENTIAL VICENZA

Plan to arrive in Vicenza by late morning so that you can be at **Basilica Palladiana** just before noon, when the bells in the adjacent tower chime, and at **Teatro Olimpico** by 3pm for the sound and light show. This itinerary takes five or six hours to complete. When you're done, hop a train to your next destination. If you have luggage with you, you can leave it for free at the tourist office in Piazza Matteotti while you explore Vicenza.

1 From Vicenza's train station, walk north up Viale Roma and enter Vicenza through the city gates leading to Corso Andrea Palladio. Turn left on Contrà Porti and step inside the **Palladio Museum** to get to know the architect who reimagined the city.

2 Head south a couple of blocks to the **Basilica Palladiana** and climb to the terrace, where you can look down at the city and market (Tues. and Thurs.) in the square below. Arrive six minutes before noon to hear the bells chime in the adjacent tower.

3 Have lunch at **Antica Casa Della Malvasia,** where you can try the local specialty, *baccalà alla Vicentina* (cod slowly stewed in milk and served with polenta).

4 After lunch, head east to explore one of Palladio's finest buildings, the art-filled **Palazzo Chiericati.**

5 Discover the first covered theater in the world, the UNESCO-listed **Teatro Olimpico,** a few minutes away. Show up for the 3pm digital tour if possible.

6 Walk south for about 20 minutes, following the R. Casarotto pedestrian path and bearing right up Via G. Tiepolo, to **Villa Valmarana.** Explore the interior, painted by Giambattista Tiepolo and his son Giandomenico, along with the surrounding Italianate garden.

7 Head a few minutes farther south to **Villa La Rotonda** (Wed. and Sat., Mar.-Nov. only), Palladio's iconic residence, before heading back to the train station. If you hop on a train for Verona in the late afternoon or early evening, you can be there by dinnertime.

Sights

PALLADIO MUSEUM
(Museo Palladio)

Contra' Porti 11, tel. 044/432-3014,
www.palladiomuseum.org, Tues.-Sun.
10am-6pm, €8 or Museum Card

Given how much Andrea Palladio influenced Vicenza, this museum dedicated to the architect is a good place to start your visit, and you don't have to be an architect yourself to enjoy the scale models, drawings, blueprints, and videos on display. Unlike most of his 16th-century contemporaries, Palladio wasn't concerned with imitating ancient designs; instead, he focused on the use of light, material, and form to create buildings that fit harmoniously within their urban or rural settings. The two-story residence housing the museum was itself built by Palladio, and each of the seven rooms inside is dedicated to a different aspect of his unique style. Various facets of Palladio's genius are explained (in Italian and English) by experts who appear in holographic-like projections.

CIVIC MUSEUM
(Museo Civico Pinacoteca)

Piazza Matteotti 37/39, tel. 044/222-811,
www.museicivicivicenza.it, Sept.-June
Tues.-Sun. 9am-5pm, July-Aug. Tues.-Sun.
10am-6pm, €7 or Museum Card

Palladio began building **Palazzo Chiericati** for a wealthy count in 1551 but it wasn't completed until a century later. Since 1885 this building has housed the Museo Civico Pinacoteca. The museum displays paintings and sculptures from the medieval period through the 18th century, with the majority of works coming from

16th-century Venetian artists. Paolo Veronese, Lorenzo Lotto, Jacopo Tintoretto, Anthony Van Dyck, Jan Bruegel, and Giambattista Tiepolo are all represented. There are also many engravings and sketches by Palladio and others. The museum's basement, which was restored in 2012, contains the kitchens, fireplaces, and storage areas that were used by servants. The villa comprises 16 sumptuous rooms spread out on two floors.

exhibition inside the Civic Museum

TOP EXPERIENCE

✪ OLYMPIC THEATER
(Teatro Olimpico)

Piazza Matteotti 11, tel. 044/320-854,
www.teatrolimpicovicenza.it, July-Aug.
Tues.-Sun. 10am-6pm, Oct.-Jun. 9am-5pm,
€11 or Museum Card

Palladio's final project was arguably his finest. It required transforming a medieval fortress into a Renaissance theater. The ingenious solution he developed was to enclose the existing structure and create an indoor amphitheater inspired by classical Greek and Roman designs. It's the oldest covered theater in the world. The stage consists of an enormous triumphal arch with an elaborate *trompe l'oeil* backdrop depicting the ancient city of Thebes. The frescoed ceiling above the crescent-shaped seating area is decorated with painted clouds and blue sky, giving the impression of being outside.

The theater was inaugurated in 1585 with a performance of *Oedipus Rex*, and it is still used today. Concerts and music festivals are held throughout the year, with ticket prices starting at €30. If you can't attend a special event here, the best times to visit are 10am and 3pm daily, when visitors can participate in an interactive tablet tour and see the stage lit up in a short sound and light display. Tours last 45 minutes and are limited to 70 people at a time. Tickets are available from the tourist office. You can generally count on getting a tour spot if you get there a half hour early.

✪ PALLADIAN BASILICA (Basilica Palladiana)

Piazza dei Signori 36, 044/422-2850, www.museicivicivicenza.it, Apr.-Oct. Tues.-Sun. 10am-1pm and 5pm-8pm, €4

One of Palladio's most important commissions was to renovate the courthouse in the center of the city. He wrapped the preexisting structure in an elegant two-story loggia that has come to symbolize Vicenza and Palladio's connection to the city; a statue of Palladio stands on the western side. Today, exhibitions are held inside the immense second-floor hall, and there are jewelry shops underneath the colonnades at street level.

Olympic Theater

Palladian Basilica

Upstairs is a wonderful terrace with a rooftop bar overlooking the piazza. Drinks are pricier (€5-8) than in the square below, but they come with a delightful view.

Like a number of historic buildings in the Veneto region, the basilica was damaged during World War II, and the remarkable green copper roof had to be entirely replaced. The building is illuminated at night. Tickets include entry to the hall and terrace, but additional fees may be charged for special exhibitions.

TORRE BISSARA

Piazza dei Signori

This 82-meter (269-foot) tower next to Basilica Palladiana dates from 1174 and is the tallest structure in the historic center. It was hit by allied bombs in 1945 and was severely damaged. Restoration took time, and the finished product didn't entirely match the original. The bells were finally returned to the tower in 2005 and play *"Ora Nona"* ("Grandmother's Hour") six minutes before noon and 6pm. The tower is closed to visitors and is best viewed on the western side of the square, where you can see the blue clock façade.

PALAZZO LEONI MONTANARI

Contrà Santa Corona 25, tel. 800/578-875, www.gallerieditalia.com, Tues.-Sun. 10am-6pm, €5

Palazzo Leoni offers an opportunity to view fabulous art inside one of the few Baroque buildings in Vicenza. The permanent collection of this private gallery, a branch of the Galleria d'Italia, is an eclectic mix of ancient Greek ceramics, 16th-century Venetian paintings, and Russian icons. Frequent traveling exhibitions devoted to painting and photography are displayed in elegant frescoed rooms that include a *Last Judgment* by Tiepolo. A free audio guide is available in English and provides interesting descriptions of the art and architecture inside. The museum takes about 45 minutes to visit.

○ VILLA VALMARANA

Via Dei Nani 8, tel. 333/597-3054, www. palazzina.villavalmarana.com, summer daily 10am-6pm, winter daily 10am-4pm, €10

Not only is this estate surrounded by a lovely Italianate garden, its interiors were decorated by two masters

Torre Bissara

of 16th-century painting. The painters also happened to be related to each other: Giambattista Tiepolo painted the main house while his son Giandomenico worked on the forestry. There is a clear generational divide between the brush strokes of the classically minded elder and the free-spirited youth, inspired by everything he saw. The 40-minute tablet tour (€2.50) and video immersion room (€2.50-4) recount the villa's history. Members of the Valmarana family have lived here since 1720, and past A-list guests have included Johann Wolfgang von Goethe, Truman Capote, Salvador Dalì, Peggy Guggenheim, Frank Sinatra, and Albert Camus. There's a small café with outdoor seating and pleasant countryside views.

The villa is a 20-minute walk from center. Head south to Piazzale Fraccon, follow the R. Casarotto pedestrian path, and bear right up Via G. Tiepolo. Alternatively, ride bus 8 to the Via Borgo Berga stop (immediately after the Benza gas station) and continue on foot from there.

✪ VILLA LA ROTONDA

Via della Rotonda 45, tel. 333/640-9237, www.villalarotonda.it, interior Mar. 10-Nov. 10 Wed. and Sat., garden year-round Tues.-Sun., opening hours for both 10am-noon and 3pm-6pm, €10 interior, €5 garden

Palladio created many different building types, but he's most famous for the villas he designed for wealthy local families. There are more than 20 of these summer estates scattered along the Brenta Canal and other waterways that linked provincial cities like Vicenza with Venice. Only La Rotonda, however, has a vaulted

cupola and four facades that are exactly the same. In essence, it's a circle inside a square. Work began in 1567, and the first owner was enjoying the finished residence by 1571. To say it significantly influenced Western architecture is an understatement. The techniques and concept behind its construction have been imitated everywhere from local U.S. courthouses to Thomas Jefferson's home at Monticello (Virginia) and the Capitol building in Washington DC.

Each room is elaborately painted, and *trompe l'oeil* frescoes cover the ceilings. The owners have been careful to preserve antique furnishings and keep the villa in a pristine state. That's probably why they don't open it to the public every day. Photos are not allowed inside.

Villa La Rotonda

La Rotonda is located 600 meters south of Villa Valmarana (a 20-minute walk south of the city center) and can be reached on foot from there by way of Via Valmarana.

MONTE BERICO

Piazzale della Basilica, daily, free

When locals want to admire their city they drive up to the Monte Berico and look out at a panorama of Vicenza from the terrace. It's a 25- to

Monte Berico Basilica

30-minute uphill walk south of the train station along Viale 10 Giugno through a leafy residential neighborhood. The piazza contains a couple pairs of binoculars (€1) to get a detailed view of the skyline and Alps, which are visible most days. Once you're done in the square you can visit the Baroque sanctuary next door; it was built after a local sighting of the Madonna was reported in 1426. The bar on the side of church is nothing special, but it's the only place around for a drink.

Food and Nightlife

Vicenza has more than its share of specialty ingredients and dishes. Typical mixed starter plates include a spicy salami called sorpressa Vicenza (Vicenza surprise), and asiago cheese that comes fresh or aged. Both are Designation of Origin Protected (Denominazione di Origine Protetta, or DOP) and are available at most *trattorie*. First courses include *bigoli con il ragù d'anatra* (pasta with duck ragu), *risi e bisi* (rice and peas), and *pasta agli asparagi bianchi* (pasta with white asparagus). *Baccalà alla Vicentina* is a favorite main course consisting of cod slowly stewed in milk and served with polenta. It's a hearty meal that's perfect in winter but available all year long.

Wines include tai rosso (red) and durello (white), along with spritz cocktails mixed at every bar. For dessert or an afternoon snack there's the dense, delicious, cheesecake-like treat *torta putana* (prostitute cake): leftover bread that's soaked in milk and stuffed with raisins, pine nuts, liquor, and lemon. (Italians have many politically incorrect names for food.) Marostica cherries ripen in early summer and are available from the fruit and vegetable stalls around the city.

ITALIAN
Bigoi Vicenza
Contrà Muschieria 21, tel. 044/402-8459, Tues.-Fri. 11:30am-3pm and 7pm-9:30pm, Sat.-Sun. 11:30am-9:30pm, Mon. 11:30am-3pm, €5

Bigoi Vicenza proves that pasta can be a street food. The concept is simple: Long, soft, freshly made *bigoli* pasta is served in a paper cup and covered with a delicious sauce. Choices include ragu, pesto, *amatriciana* (pasta with bacon-flavored tomato sauce), and the daily specials. There are no seats inside; diners eat outside with a compostable fork. Drinks are available.

Antica Casa Della Malvasia
Contrà delle Morette 5, tel. 044/454-3704, Tues.-Sat. 11:30am-3pm and 7pm-11:30pm, €9-12

This restaurant is a reliable dining spot on a cozy pedestrian street. Sit down at one of the tables outside and wait for a friendly waiter to bring over a menu. It's full of traditional classics, and if you haven't sampled *ragu d'anatra* or *baccalà alla Vicentina* this is a good place to be initiated. The décor inside is rustic and doesn't distract from the strong flavors.

Julien
Contra' Cabianca Jacopo 13, tel. 044/432-6168, Mon.-Sat. 12:45pm-2:45pm and 6pm-11:30pm, Sun. 6pm-11:30pm, €12-14

Vicenza has a dynamic culinary scene considering the size of the city and this

is one of the new entries in town that attracts young hipsters in the mood for on-trend dishes, such as a plate of spicy beef tartar or creamy *cacio e pepe* (cheese and pepper) pasta. You'll find inventive Italian fusion selections within a contemporary atmosphere. It's also a good cocktail and *aperitivo* destination east of the historic center.

Massimo Gusto
Viale Antonio Giuriolo 17, tel. 348/715-3044, Tues.-Sat. 11am-2:30pm and 6pm-10pm, Sun 11am-2:30pm, €15-18

If you have a craving for oysters, squid, sardines, or any other seafood, you'll be satisfied here. The interior design breaks Italian restaurant clichés by steering away from typical rustic décor and could easily belong in New York or Paris. Meals are relaxing and civilized, service is attentive, and tables in the back overlook the Bacchiglione River.

oysters from Massimo Gusto

Molo
Contrà Pedemuro S. Biagio 48, tel. 044/432-7359, Sat.-Sun. 12:30pm-2:30pm and 7pm-11pm, Tues.-Fri. 7pm-11pm, €14-16

There's no menu at Molo, and what you eat depends on what the Sicilian owner and chef of this convivial eatery north of center finds at local markets.

Seasonal ingredients are transformed into a variety of refined fish, meat, and vegetarian dishes that are always good and surprising to the palate. Large first courses like the tuna carbonara leave little room for seconds such as grilled sardines stuffed with roasted zucchini and lemon sauce. There's a nice selection of local wine, and knowledgeable waiters can help with recommendations. Arrive early or make reservations, as tables fill up fast.

BAKERY
Pane Quotidiano
Piazza delle Erbe 3, tel. 320/858-9507, Tues.-Thurs. 8am-2:30pm, Fri.-Sun. 8am-2:30pm and 5pm-10pm, €5

This bakery offers fresh bread in a great location, as well as sandwiches, coffee, and *torta putana* cakes that can be sampled inside or outside at tables facing the city's main square.

WINE AND COCKTAILS
Cucù
Piazza delle Erbe 7, tel. 345/687-6279, daily 10am-2pm, €5-10

This little cocktail bar near the center is a nice place to hang out. There's a long list of wines and beers, and a nice twist on the spritz. Grab one of the stools facing the street and enjoy the scene.

Vicenza by night

Shopping

Clothing boutiques and major chains are clustered along **Corso Andrea Palladio,** but if mass-produced fashion isn't what you're after, it's easy to find artisans doing their thing in workshops around the center. The jewelry tradition in Vicenza goes back a long way, but skilled hands also work iron, wood, ceramics, and vintage printing presses.

JEWELRY
Daniela Vettori

Piazza dei Signori 35, tel. 044/432-3855,
Tues.-Fri. 10am-1pm and 3:30pm-7:30pm,
Sat. 10am-7:30pm

All that glitters in Vicenza is probably silver or gold. More precious metal is bought, sold, traded, and crafted here than in any other Italian city. Jewelers line the colonnades around the Basilica Palladiana, and Daniela Vettori is a good place to commence window-shopping. All rings, bracelets, necklaces, and bracelets are handmade using wax casting and a hammer. Daniela's daughter Margherita recently joined the business, and the two have created a variety of wearable lines based on global influences. Prices start around €35.

ARTISAN
Stamperia d'Arte Busato

Contrà Porta Santa Lucia 38,
tel. 044/451-3525, Mon.-Fri. 9am-6pm

Printing press technology crossed the Alps and reached Veneto in the second half of the 15th century, and dedicated craftspeople are still doing things the original way. Signor Busato is one of them, and watching him spread ink onto lithographs, engravings, or woodcuts is a powerful reminder of one of man's greatest achievements. Very little has changed inside his rustic workshop since it opened more than 70 years ago, and the smell of paper and ink still prevails. All sorts of beautiful images can be chosen and printed on the spot.

Liberty Cycles

Contrà S. Silvestro 30, tel. 044/404-2482,
Mon.-Sat. 8:30am-12:30pm and
3:30pm-7:30pm

You can't rent a bike here, but you can meet Alberto and learn how he transforms unused and unwanted parts into lovely handmade bicycles. There are great shapes and colors on display and lots of imagination that anyone with a fondness for frames, gears, and breaks will appreciate. Alberto is a nice guy who enjoys showing visitors around his workshop.

MARKETS

Outdoor food and clothing markets are essential to daily life in Vicenza, where there's a market going on every day except Monday. On **Tuesday** dry goods are sold in Piazza dei Signori, while

flower market, Piazza delle Erbe

fruits and vegetables are available along Contra' Garibaldi, where you'll find cherries in early summer and seasonal delights all year long. The plant and flower market is held Wednesday in Piazza delle Erbe. Thursday is the biggest market day, with activity in both squares facing Basilica Palladiana and more vendors than usual in surrounding streets. Organic farmers and producers gather in Piazza Matteotti on Saturday. All markets in the city are held from 7:30am to 1pm. On Friday (Via Fabiani) and Sunday (Via Prati) there are neighborhood markets outside the city center.

Mercato dell'Antiquariato Collezionismo e Vintage

Piazza dei Signori, tel. 349/641-0654, www.antiquariatovicenza.it, second Sundays 8am-5pm

On the second Sunday of every month, stalls covered with antiques, collectibles, and vintage objects fill the squares and streets of this spectacular citywide market. The historic center is packed with paintings, curiosities, accessories, and cool oddities. There's tons to browse and friendly sellers who enjoy answering questions.

Recreation and Activities

CYCLING

Vicenza's compact size, smooth cobbled streets, and flatness make it perfect for cycling, and that's how a large portion of the population get around. There are many bike racks, but locals tend to leave their wheels unlocked wherever they happen to be and walk bikes on crowded streets. A bike ride is also a pleasant way to reach the villas outside of town.

RENTALS
Bruno Bike

Viale Milano 138, tel. 330/649-490, Mon.-Sat. 6:30am-8pm, €5 per hour, half-day €10, day €15

Surprisingly there are few rental shops in town, but Bruno Bike is conveniently located inside the train station and rents basic women's, men's, and kids' city bikes. These are perfect for getting around town and to the villas, but they're not suitable for longer treks.

PARKS

Parco Querini

Viale Ferdinando Rodolfi, tel. 044/422-1111, daily 7am-8pm

Vicenza has three large parks close to the historic center, but Parco Querini is the only one with a dedicated jogging and fitness area. It's popular with families who picnic on the lawns in summer, and with kids, who follow the ducks, rabbits, and turtles that roam around the park. There's a small decorative temple on a hill surrounded by water, and clean restrooms nearby.

GOLF

Golf Club Colli Berici

Strada Monti Comunali, tel. 044/460-1780, www.golfclubcolliberici.it, summer daily 8am-9pm, winter daily 8am-5pm, €35-70

Golfers will enjoy this undulating 18-hole course 334 meters above sea level with water hazards, sand traps, and an informal clubhouse. The front nine overlook the Po Valley, offering magnificent views of the Dolomite Mountains, while the back nine extend into a forest of oaks, hornbeams, and chestnut trees. The par 70 is accessible to all levels, and clubs (€20) and carts (€16-38) are available to rent. Green fees vary according to holes played and day. Weekdays are cheaper, and reservations are not required. The club is a 20-minute taxi ride from Vicenza.

Accommodations

HOTELS

Hotel Campo Marzio

Viale Roma 21, tel. 044/454-5700,
www.hotelcampomarzio.com, €95-130 d
Campo Marzio is a convenient hotel with 22 standard and 13 superior rooms a short walk from the train station and the historic center. Superior rooms are modern and elegantly furnished (one has a hot tub and others have showers with hydromassage). Downstairs there's a bar, restaurant, and private parking.

Antico Hotel Vicenza

Stradella dei Nodari 5, tel. 044/4157-3422,
www.anticohotelvicenza.com, €100-150 d
This historic four-star hotel in the heart of Vicenza combines the vintage look and feel of a black-and-white film with modern conveniences and services. Personnel are courteous, breakfast is satisfying, and the antiques are authentic. There's also a lovely roof terrace with excellent views of the city.

APARTMENT

Apartmento al Duomo

Via Cesare Battisti 19, tel. 348/357-7432,
www.appartamentoalduomo.com, €80-100
You can live like a local in this bright, one-bedroom apartment in the center of the city. Gianna, the owner, provides a warm welcome and ensures guests have all they need. If you don't feel like using the kitchen, there are plenty of restaurants, bars, and pastry shops on the streets nearby.

Al Duomo apartment

Information and Services

Tourist Office
Piazza Matteotti 12, tel. 044/432-0854, daily 9am-5:30pm

The tourist office sells the **Museum Card** and provides maps and event info. The office also organizes guided two-hour tours (€10, Italian only) and can set you up with English-speaking guides.

Luggage Storage
There's no luggage storage at Vicenza's train station, but you can stash your luggage for free at the tourist office.

Getting There and Around

GETTING THERE

TRAIN
From Venice's Santa Lucia station, dozens of regional, direct regional, and high-speed trains depart for Vicenza every day. The journey takes 45-75 minutes, depending on the service, and costs €6-15 with **Trenitalia** (www.trenitalia.it).

From Padua's central station, trains depart every 20 minutes for Vicenza. The trip takes 15-30 minutes and tickets are €4.25-€17, depending on the service. Regional and direct regional trains are the cheapest options, and the latter is only a couple minutes slower than high-speed trains. From Verona, there are three or four departures per hour, and the trip can take 25-60 minutes, depending on the service.

The historic center of Vicenza is a 10- to 15-minute walk from the station.

CAR
Vicenza is easily reached via the **A4** highway from Venice (€8.50 toll), Verona (€2.90), and Padua (€2). It's a 43-mile (70-kilometer), one-hour drive from Venice, and half that time and distance from Verona or Padua. The **Vicenza Est** exit leads to the center, and there are a number of clearly indicated parking lots (www.aimmobilita.it). Fees are €0.50 per hour with a €5 maximum daily charge. The historic center is a **ZTL** (limited traffic zone), and a permit is required to enter.

GETTING AROUND
Vicenza is a pedestrian-friendly city and all sights can be reached on foot. Bicycles are another good way to get around and to reach the villas slightly south of the center. A single **SVT Bus** (www.svt.vi.it) ticket is €1.30, or pay €5.20 for a daily pass. Bus number 8 stops near several villas. **Radio Taxi** (tel. 044/492-0600) is on call 24/7 and is useful to reach destinations outside the city.

VERONA

Itinerary Idea 194
Sights 195
Food 200
Nightlife 202
Festivals and Events 203
Shopping 204
Recreation and
    Activities 205
Accommodations 208
Information and
    Services 209
Getting There
    and Around. 209

Verona owes a lot to Shakespeare and two lovesick characters who put the city on the literary map. Thousands of tourists arrive each year intent on finding Romeo and Juliet, only to discover there's a lot more to the city than a balcony and a tragic ending. Verona's status as a UNESCO World Heritage City has nothing to do with fiction, and everything to do with some of the finest ancient monuments outside Rome and medieval fortifications that stretch around the historic center. Yes, you will find a crowded house where Juliet supposedly lived but you can

HIGHLIGHTS

⊕ **ARENA DI VERONA:** Climb the steps inside this perfectly preserved Roman amphitheater, which is nearly as large as the Colosseum (page 195).

⊕ **TORRE LAMBERTI:** Verona's highest tower provides an instant 360-degree view of town (page 197).

⊕ **ADIGE RAFTING:** Floating down the Adige River is a thrilling way to discover Verona from a different angle (page 205).

also discover wonderful bridges, delightful regional cuisine, and an intact Roman amphitheater where concerts are performed all summer long.

PLANNING YOUR TIME

Verona shouldn't be rushed. There's a lot to see and the city is only 75 miles (122 kilometers) from Venice on the same train line as Padua and Vicenza. It makes a good overnight stop after visiting either or both of those cities and can be a multiday base from which to explore Lake Garda, 18 miles (30 kilometers) away.

However long you stay, the **Verona Card** (€18/24 hours or €22/48 hours) will be useful. The card provides access to all the town's museums and monuments, as well as public transportation. It's available at the monuments and museums where it's accepted, at the tourist office (www.tourism.verona.it) in Piazza Bra, and at the newsstand inside Porta Nuova train station. If you buy it at the station, you can start using it right away on any of the buses heading to the center.

Opera lovers flock to Verona during the summer music festival, and hotel rooms and restaurants fill up fast. If your visit coincides with a concert, make your lodging and dining reservations in advance. Also, keep in mind the Arena di Verona closes a couple of hours early on days when there's a performance, and most monuments and museums are closed Monday mornings.

ORIENTATION

Verona's historic center, known as Città Antica, is neatly tucked into a bend of the Adige River. The area is extremely dense, with little green space and long, straight streets that are a result of ancient Roman town planning. The Porta Nuova train station is about a mile (1.5-kilometers) away from the center, a 20-minute walk up Corso Porta Nuova to the Arena and Piazza Bra, where the tourist office is located.

Piazza Erbe is another lively square located a few blocks north of the Arena, in the heart of the city. A market is held here Monday-Saturday 7:30am-8:30pm and occasionally on Sunday. From Piazza Erbe, it's a short walk to the Roman bridge, theater, and panoramic terrace overlooking the city. Basilica di San Zeno Maggiore is slightly west of the center but still easily reached on foot.

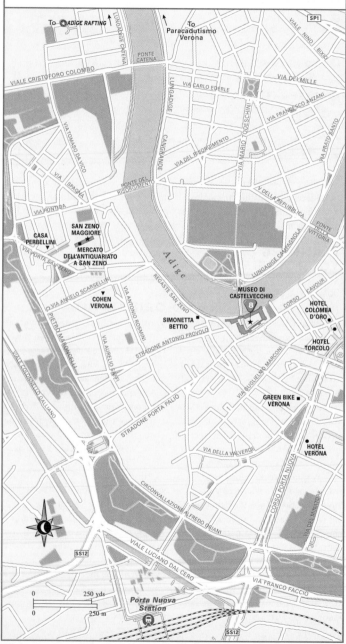

Verona

To ● ADIGE RAFTING ↑

To Paracadutismo Verona

SP1

VIALE NINO BIXIO

PONTE CATENA

LUNGADIGE CATENA

VIALE CRISTOFORO COLOMBO

VIA CARLO EDERLE

VIA DEL MILLE

VIA FRANCESCO ANZANI

LUNGADIGE CANGRANDE

VIA DEL RISORGIMENTO

VIA MARIO TODESCHINI

VIA PRATO SANTO

VIA TOMASO DA VICO

VIA SPAGNA

PONTE DEL RISORGIMENTO

V. DELLA REPUBBLICA

VIA FONTOA

PONTE DELLA VITTORIA

CASA PERBELLINI ▼

SAN ZENO MAGGIORE

MERCATO DELL'ANTIQUARIATO A SAN ZENO

A d i g e

LUNGADIGE CAMPAGNOLA

VIA PORTA SAN ZENO

O VIA ANGELO SCARSELLINI

COHEN VERONA ▼

VIA ANTONIO ROSMINI

REGASTE SAN ZENO

MUSEO DI CASTELVECCHIO

CORSO CAVOUR

8 ★

HOTEL COLOMBA D'ORO ●

PIETRO MARONCELLI

SIMONETTA BETTIO ■

VIA AURELIO FABRI

STRADONE ANTONIO PROVOLO

HOTEL TORCOLO ●

VIALE COLONNELLO GALLIANO

STRADONE PORTA PALIO

VIA GUGLIELMO MARCONI

GREEN BIKE VERONA ■

VIA DELLA VALVERDE

HOTEL VERONA ●

CORSO PORTA NUOVA

CIRCONVALLAZIONE ALFREDO ORIANI

VIA DEL MINATORE

SS12

☾

VIALE LUCIANO DAL CERO

VIA FRANCO FACCIO

0 ——— 250 yds
0 ——— 250 m

Porta Nuova Station

SS12

192

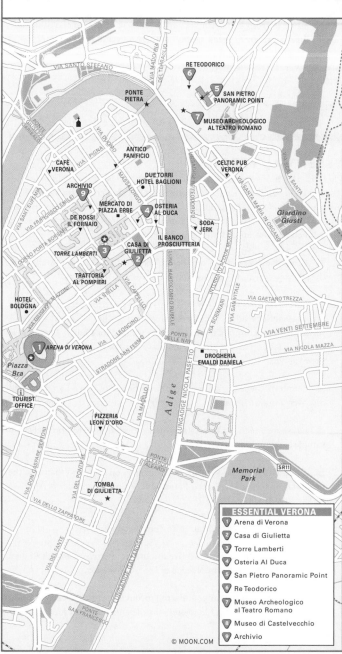

RE TEODORICO
6

5 SAN PIETRO
PANORAMIC POINT

PONTE
PIETRA

7 MUSEO ARCHEOLOGICO
AL TEATRO ROMANO

VIA SANTO STEFANO
VIA MADONNA DEL TERRAGLIO

ANTICO
PANIFICIO

CELTIC PUB
VERONA

CAFÉ
VERONA

DUE TORRI
HOTEL BAGLIONI

ARCHIVIO
9

VIA PIGNA

VIA OLMO

MASSALONGO

MERCATO DI
PIAZZA ERBE

4 OSTERIA
AL DUCA

Giardino
Giusti

DE ROSSI
IL FORNAIO

SODA
JERK

CASA DI
GIULIETTA

IL BANCO
PROSCIUTTERIA

VIA SANTA MARIA IN ORGANO

TORRE LAMBERTI 3

2

TRATTORIA
AL POMPIERI

VIA STELLA

VIA CAFFELLO

LUNG.ADIGE RUBELE

VIA GAETANO TREZZA

HOTEL
BOLOGNA

VIA SAN VITALE

VIA SCHIAVARI

VIA VENTI SETTEMBRE

1 ARENA DI VERONA

VIA LEONCINO

PONTE
DELLE NAVI

VIA NICOLA MAZZA

STRADONE SAN FERMO

Piazza
Bra

DROGHERIA
EMALDI DANIELA

LUNGADIGE NICOLA PASETTO

TOURIST
OFFICE

VIA MAFFEI

Adige

PIZZERIA
LEON D'ORO

PONTE
ALEARDO
ALEARDI

Memorial
Park

SR11

VIA DON GASPARE BERTONI

VIA DEL PONTE

TOMBA
DI GIULIETTA

VIA DELLO ZAPPATORE

VIA DEL FANTE

LUNGADIGE GALVANI ROSA

PONTE
SAN FRANCESCO

© MOON.COM

ESSENTIAL VERONA

1. Arena di Verona
2. Casa di Giulietta
3. Torre Lamberti
4. Osteria Al Duca
5. San Pietro Panoramic Point
6. Re Teodorico
7. Museo Archeologico al Teatro Romano
8. Museo di Castelvecchio
9. Archivio

Overall, Verona is a flat, walkable city, and the only time you may want to hop a bus is from the train station to Piazza Bra, or to reach some of the recreation options outside the city. The Veronetta neighborhood is home to the university and some of the city's best nightlife. It's east of the historic center on the other side of the Adige and reached by crossing the Ponte Nuovo bridge.

Itinerary Idea

ESSENTIAL VERONA

Plan to arrive in Verona early in the day. Better yet, spend the night here after visiting Padua and/or Vicenza, then wake up to this Verona itinerary, which takes around 6-8 hours to complete. If you need to stow your luggage, you can do so in the Verona train station for a small fee. Before setting out for the day, make lunch reservations at Osteria Al Duca for noon.

1 Circle the **Arena di Verona** before going inside. Be sure to walk up to the last row of seats to get a feel for its impressive dimensions.

2 Follow the street signs (and the tourists) to pay tribute to Shakespeare's most romantic creation. Whether she lived here or not, it's easy to imagine Juliet on the balcony of **Casa di Giulietta** waiting for Romeo. Leave a love letter or a lock on the gate nearby and have a quick look inside Juliet's supposed abode.

3 Climb the steps or ride the elevator to the top of **Torre Lamberti** and discover Verona from above.

4 Pause for lunch at **Osteria Al Duca** (reservations recommended) to sample local specialties.

5 Cross Ponte Pietra, Verona's oldest bridge, on foot, and then ride the funicular up to the **San Pietro Panoramic Point** for another perspective on the city.

6 Stop for a coffee or cocktail at **Re Teodorico** nearby.

7 Continue walking downhill five minutes to discover Verona's Roman theater at the **Museo Archeologico al Teatro Romano.**

8 Cross back over the Adige and stroll through the historic center toward the **Museo di Castelvecchio** fortress that defended the city for centuries.

9 Order an *aperitivo* cocktail at **Archivio** before heading back to Venice, or on to your next destination. Alternatively, head back to the Arena to catch a live performance.

Sights

✪ ARENA DI VERONA

Piazza Bra 1, tel. 045/800-3204,
www.arena.it, Jun.-Aug. daily
8:30am-7:30pm, Sept.-May Tues.-Sun.
8:30am-7:30pm, €10 or Verona Card

Verona's Roman arena was built before the Colosseum and is the third-largest amphitheater from antiquity. It could accommodate 30,000 spectators and has been used nearly continuously since its inauguration in 30 AD. It might not look massive from the outside, but once you get inside and climb the steps to the last row, you'll grasp its true dimensions. Depending on when you arrive, there could be a long line at the two ticket booths. The theater is most crowded mid-mornings in July and August, but once you're inside there's plenty of space. Entry comes with an informative pamphlet, and you can wander around the vast interior at your own pace. The corridor leading to the monumental northern entrance is double the height of the others, because it's where ancient elite entered the arena. The best time to see the Arena is during the city's popular opera festival, when spectacular summertime concerts are staged.

Arena di Verona

OPERA IN THE ARENA

Watching international stars perform the world's greatest arias inside **Arena di Verona** (Piazza Bra 1, tel. 045/800-5151, www.arena.it) is unforgettable, even if you don't have a favorite tenor. Tickets in the upper decks can be purchased for as little as €30, or you can splurge and get a comfortable seat near the stage (€150-200). Three or four performances are scheduled each week late June-early September. Concerts start at 9pm and gates open at 7pm. Food and drink are available inside. Show days vary, but there are always performances on Friday and Saturday.

Tickets sell out fast, and it's best to buy them ahead of time online rather than find yourself at the mercy of scalpers. The series often stages productions of full operas or performances by singers such as Placido Domingo. If opera really isn't your thing, though, rock and pop concerts are scheduled throughout the year, too. Pink Floyd, Pearl Jam, Adele, Michael Bublé, and Björk have appeared in the past.

opera performance in the Arena di Verona

CASA DI GIULIETTA

Via Capello 23, tel. 045/803-4303,
Tues.-Sun. 8:30am-7:30pm, Mon.
1:30pm-7:30 pm, €6 or Verona Card

William Shakespeare's *Romeo and Juliet*, set in Verona, catapulted the city to lasting literary fame. Shakespeare himself never visited Verona and is not known to have had any knowledge of this house, which some claim was the home of the famous Juliet. Still, Juliet's alleged house and balcony are major attractions, and for some, whether she existed or not hardly matters.

Myriad couples mill about the small, ivy clad, courtyard below the balcony, leaving romantic messages on walls (bring your own pen and paper to declare your love) and securing love locks on the nearby gate. Inside the house there's a statue of the bard's famous heroine, her supposed bed, and the entrance to the iconic balcony, where everyone wants to stand. It can be a 5- or 10-minute wait to step onto the balcony, which isn't bad for the city's number one photo op. A small souvenir shop sells postcards and *Romeo and Juliet*-related gifts below.

TOMBA DI GIULIETTA

Via Luigi da Porto 5, tel. 045/800-0361,
Tues.-Sun. 8:30am-7:30pm, Mon.
1:30pm-7:30pm, €4.50 or Verona Card

According to legend, Shakespeare's Juliet was buried here, inside the convent San Francesco al Corso. Since the 18th century, it's been a destination for literary pilgrims who come to see an ancient (and empty) tomb. An enterprising official who saw the value in strengthening the city's link with Shakespeare added a bust of the bard during the 1930s. It's possible to leave disappointed if your expectations are too high. Fortunately, the convent is also home to a **fresco museum** that was completely renovated in 2015 and makes a visit more worthwhile.

LOVE LOCKS

While walking around Verona, you may notice small red locks attached to poles, bike racks, bridges, and anything else people can find. When this tradition began is unknown, but couples have been signing and attaching locks throughout the city for decades as a sign of everlasting affection. It's gotten so big, there are now a couple of shops that only sell locks. They're also sold at the souvenir shop facing Juliet's house (€5-13), as well as other shops just around the corner. City officials do periodically remove the locks, but the practice doesn't seem to be discouraged the way it is in other cities. Instead, the city of Verona seems to have embraced its role as the home of lovers from around the world.

✪ TORRE LAMBERTI

Via della Costa 2, tel. 045/927-3027, www. torredeilamberti.it, Mon.-Fri. 10am-6pm and Sat.-Sun. 11am-7pm, €8 or Verona Card

Construction of Verona's tallest tower began in 1172, but it wasn't until 1779 that it reached its modern-day height of 84 meters. Bells, each with a specific purpose that local ears could easily recognize, were added in 1295. The biggest bell called the communal council to their chambers and alerted the town's defenders of foreign threats, while the smallest bell warned of fire and tolled the hours.

There's a great view of Verona from the top of the tower. The stairs are wide and there's plenty of space for visitors going up and down, but if 368 steps sound daunting, take the elevator for €1. Tickets to the tower include entry to the adjacent **Galleria d'Arte Moderna** (http://gam.comune.verona. it) gallery, which contains hundreds of paintings by Italian artists from the late 18th century to the present day.

MUSEO DI CASTELVECCHIO

Corso Castelvecchio 2, tel. 045/806-2611, Tues.-Sun. 8:30am-7:30pm, Mon. 1:30pm-7:30 pm, €6 or Verona Card

Verona was heavily fortified during the Middle Ages, and this castle was an essential part of the city's defenses. Today the ramparts have given way to a museum with a vast collection of medieval, Renaissance, and modern art spread out in 29 rooms.

Torre Lamberti

narrow streets leading to Castel San Pietro

The **video guide** (€4) lasts an hour and offers information about the art and the castle's history. The **Ponte Castelvecchio** bridge, which is attached to the fortifications, once enabled river traffic to be controlled. It's fun to walk across and peer out from the turrets.

PONTE PIETRA

Open 24/7, free

Verona's oldest bridge is located at the northern tip of the historic center. It's been rebuilt many times over the centuries, most recently after the Germans blew it up at the end of World War II. The large blocks of white stone that make up two of the five arches are part of the original Roman construction, while the smaller red bricks used on the other three are from subsequent medieval, Renaissance, and modern restorations. The 92-meter-long bridge is one of the most emblematic features of the city and leads to the archaeological museum, **Museo Archeologico al**

Teatro Romano, and the funicular on Verona's less explored northern bank. The bridge is pedestrian-only and a popular late afternoon hangout with younger locals.

SAN PIETRO PANORAMIC POINT AND FUNICULAR

Piazzale Castel S. Pietro 1, open 24/7, free

Verona extends beyond the historic center, and you can get a better grasp of the city's size and shape if you cross the Adige River at Ponte Pietra and climb up the Scalinata Castel San Pietro staircase to this panoramic

Ponte Pietra at twilight

terrace. It's steep going with great views of the Roman Theater along the way.

It takes 15-20 minutes to walk from Verona's historic center up to the viewpoint. If you don't want to walk, there's also an automated **funicular** (Via Santo Stefano, summer 10:30am-8pm, winter 10:30am-5pm, €1 each way), which is fun to ride and takes you to the top in only five minutes. The funicular departs every 10 minutes. You can take it up and walk down to save energy.

MUSEO ARCHEOLOGICO AL TEATRO ROMANO

Rigaste Redentore 2, tel. 045/800-0360, Tues.-Sun. 8:30am-6:30pm, Mon. 1:30pm-6:30pm, €4.50 or Verona Card

Verona was an important Roman city, and hundreds of ancient statues, mosaics, jewelry, and household objects are contained within this contemporary five-story archaeological museum. Inside, you can discover what daily life was like 2,000 years ago and see what was unearthed at the Arena. Outside, Northern Italy's largest outdoor theater, **Teatro Romano,** can be explored. The theater was built in the first century AD and rediscovered by accident in the late 19th century. Like the Arena, the theater is frequently used to stage summer concerts.

SAN ZENO MAGGIORE

Piazza San Zeno 2, www.basilicasanzeno. it, Nov.-Feb. Tues.-Sat. 10am-5pm and Sun. 12:30pm-5pm, Mar.-Oct. Tues.-Sat. 8:30am-6pm and Sun. 12:30pm-6pm, €3 or Verona Card

Verona's finest Romanesque church is a short walk west of the center. The facade, which was restored in 2018, is adorned with a stained-glass window,

and inlaid sculptures recount biblical stories on either side of the entrance. Inside, an audio guide describes the history of the religious complex, which includes a monastery and works of art that have been added over the centuries. Andrea Mantegna's triptych painting near the altar is the most famous, along with a statue of the smiling San Zeno, considered the patron saint of the city and much loved by locals, on the lateral nave. A crypt on the lower level contains the saint's remains. The tree-lined square outside and Piazza Corrubbio nearby are lined with eateries and make good spots to relax after a visit.

inside San Zeno Maggiore

GIARDINO GIUSTI

Via Giardino Giusti 2, tel. 045/803-4029, Apr.-Sept. daily 9am-8pm, Oct.-Mar. daily 9am-7pm, €8.50 or Verona Card

The 16th-century palace and gardens of Giardino Giusti have attracted esteemed visitors of all stripes, from kings and princes to composers and musicians of the highest caliber. (Grand tour travelers were often wealthy and the gardens were popularized by Goethe, Ruskin, and other writers.) Agostino Giusti, a knight of the Venetian Republic, designed the Renaissance gardens in 1580. The

Giardino Giusti

garden swoops up toward wild woods and links to a series of stone terraces with city views. Highlights here are the rows of cypresses, hidden fountains, and grotto. The palace itself is closed to the public.

Food

Finding a *trattoria* in Verona is easy. They're everywhere and many have been in business for decades, or even centuries in a few cases. Local gastronomy benefits from exceptional ingredients, including rice, wheat, corn, olives, grapes, and an appetizing assortment of fruits and vegetables. Add a little creativity over the ages and the result is dishes like brasato di cavalo (braised horsemeat) stewed in wine and spices, polenta covered in cheese and mushroom sauce, and fresh gnocchi. Every season brings its traditional desserts like the pandoro (golden cakes), invented in the 19th century, and fritole (sweet fritters), which are the harbingers of Christmas and Carnival.

Verona also produces great wines and there are eight DOP (Protected Designation of Origin) zones in the countryside outside the city. Varieties to try include valpolicella and amarone, first bottled in 1940; both are red wines from the plains and hills leading toward the Monti Lessini mountains. Bardolino, another red, is drunk in its novello (new) phase, just a few months after grapes are harvested. Soave, a medieval town south of Verona, gives its name to the local white wine from grapes grown in the Mezzane, Illasi, and Alpone Valleys.

ITALIAN
Osteria al Duca

Via Arche Scaligere 2, tel. 045/594-474,
Mon.-Sat. noon-2:30pm and
6:30pm-10:30pm, tasting menu €20-29

Osteria Al Duca is one of the oldest and most authentic taverns in Verona. It's also very popular, so be sure to reserve ahead of time. Tables are set close together, and the atmosphere is boisterous, with service that's rushed but friendly. There are four tasting menus available. The cheapest option (€20) offers a dozen first and second course dishes to choose from, including bigoli pasta, polenta with snails, and horsemeat in several preparations. Portions are generous and the house wine is cheap. This isn't the most romantic or glamorous place to dine, but you will get a culinary glimpse of what people have been eating in Verona for generations.

Trattoria Al Pompieri

Vicolo Regina D'Ungheria 5,
tel. 045/803-0537, Tues.-Sat.
12:30pm-2pm and 7:30pm-10:30pm,
Mon. 7:30pm-10:30pm, €12-18

This *trattoria* around the corner from Juliet's house has all the trappings of a classic Italian restaurant, from the black-and-white photos on the walls to the green-checkered tablecloths. It's a great place to enjoy a meal, and the uniformed waiters know how to treat guests. Start with a selection of hams or cheeses from the cutting corner and continue with hearty gnocchi and *bigoli* specialties. The wine menu includes hundreds of choices, with local wine particularly well represented.

Il Banco Prosciutteria

Via Ponte Nuovo 7, tel. 045/592-718,
Thurs. noon-2:30pm and 7pm-10:30pm,
Wed. 7pm-10:30pm, €12-17

With a brick vaulted cellar and modern charm, Il Banco Prosciutteria proves that not all eateries are rough and rustic in Verona. The menu is equally contemporary with cured ham and cheese starters and a selection of refined firsts (primi) and seconds (secondi) that you won't find anywhere else. Original creations like wine-infused gnocchi and pesto-flavored tartar make for an exceptional meal.

Casa Perbellini

Piazza San Zeno 16, tel. 045/878-0860,
Tues.-Sat. 12:30pm-2pm and 7:30pm-10pm,
tasting menu €58-149

Gourmet cuisine in a two-star Michelin restaurant comes at a price, but if you want to surprise your palate with unusual flavors, textures, and ingredients, this is the place to splurge. There are three tasting menus in this intimate eatery with half a dozen tables and an open kitchen that gives diners a front-row seat to watch the cooking artistry. Dishes include cauliflower gnocchi, grilled veal tongue, and venison sirloin.

PIZZA
Re Teodorico

Piazzale Castel S. Pietro 1,
tel. 045/834-9903, daily noon-3pm
and 7pm-11pm, €8-12

The best thing about Re Teodorico, located across Ponte Pietra near the archaeological museum, is the city view, which is undoubtedly the best in Verona. Sit on the terrace at sunset for extra magic. The menu includes an interesting selection of gourmet pizzas, salads, and beer. Prices are in line with the location overlooking the city: A plain *margherita* (marinara and mozzarella) pizza here is €8 rather than the €5 or €6 you'd pay at a pizzeria in the center. The restaurant closes between lunch and dinner, but the cocktail bar and terrace, with equally good views, are open 1pm-11pm if you'd like to stop by for a drink.

Pizzeria Leon d'Oro

Via Pallone 10a, tel. 045/803-6658, www.pizzerialeondoro.com, Thurs.-Tues. 12:30pm-2:30pm and 7pm-11pm, and Wed. 7pm-11pm, €5-11

Pizza isn't native to Verona, but if you are craving a Neapolitan style pie, head to Leon d'Oro. There's a large outdoor dining area in an elegant courtyard facing the city walls and plenty of space inside this convivial pizzeria. The highly digestible dough is made with 100 percent OGM-free wheat and is rested 36 hours so that it's easier to roll, tastes better, and has a lighter consistency. German lager and Weiss beer are on tap, and there's also a good selection of bottled beer from Belgium and beyond.

BAKERIES

De Rossi il Fornaio

Corso Porta Borsari 3, tel. 045/800-2489, Tues.-Sun. 7:30am-7:45pm

The de Rossi family has been baking bread since 1947, and their vintage bakery is a great place to sample local loaves and pastries. The *frittelle di mele* (apple fritters) are a specialty and can be ordered along with coffee at the counter in the back.

Antico Panificio

Via Achille Forti 2a, Mon.-Sat. 8am-7:30pm, Sun. 10am-2pm

Bread has been baked here since 1883 and the sign on the outside dates from the 1950s. The inside has been renovated over the years but the passion for bread remains. There are lots of edible souvenirs to take home, and sandwiches are made on the spot for hungry patrons. There are no tables inside and all orders are wrapped to go.

Nightlife

Verona remains lively after dark. There are lots of bars with good *aperitivo* offers around town. University students and young professionals tend to hang out in the **Veronetta** neighborhood on the eastern bank of the Adige River, at places like Soda Jerk and Celtic Pub Verona, while **Piazza Erbe** attracts tourists in search of late-night cocktails.

BARS

Cafè Verona

Via Sant'Egidio 16, Mon.-Sat. 7am-2pm and Sun. 1pm-12am

Aperitivo starts at 6pm at Cafè Verona, and the generous portions of finger food can easily substitute for dinner. Barmen aren't showy but still manage to mix great drinks. Groups of friends gather around marble tables in this dimly lit establishment, where conversation is given precedence over music.

Archivio

Via Rosa 3c, tel. 345/816-9663, Mon.-Sat. 8am-midnight, Sun. 11am-midnight

Cocktails are listed on a mirror inside this small, characteristic bar filled with regulars. The Moscow Mule (vodka, ginger ale, lime juice) is a reliable option and barmen do not skimp on the vodka. They also come up with a monthly special drink, which they're happy to explain. There's no seating inside, but drinking outside in Verona is common practice.

Soda Jerk

Vicolo Quadrelli 5, tel. 045/237-5108, daily 7am-2am

Verona's version of a speakeasy is located in the Veronetta neighborhood, down an anonymous lane on the eastern bank of the Adige River. Just ring the bell below the gold plaque and you shouldn't have any problem getting in, except on weekends when it gets crowded. The cocktail list includes 10 original creations mixed with quality liquors. Each one costs €8 and is served in style.

Celtic Pub Verona

Via Santa Chiara 1, tel. 388/877-1783, Tues.-Sun. 5:30pm-2am

If you're craving Guinness (or any other beer), head to Veronetta and check out this small, wood-paneled

Irish pub, where everyone gets a warm welcome. The taps are filled with lager, bitter, white, and stout, and change weekly. There's a kebab shop next door that may be hard to resist after a couple of pints.

LIVE MUSIC

Cohen Verona

Via Angelo Scarsellini 9a, tel. 045/894-9522, Tues.-Sun. 6pm-12:30pm

There aren't many live music venues in town, but Cohen Verona more than compensates for that. International and local musicians play several times a week, and jazz is the preferred genre. The €15 food-and-concert deal gets you one appetizer and a choice of pasta dishes, including a gluten-free lasagna. You can also forgo the meal and get a concert-plus-one-drink deal for €10. Shows usually start around 9pm at this laid-back club around the corner from Piazza San Zeno, and there's great beer on tap.

Festivals and Events

Verona in Love Festival

Piazza dei Signori, Cortile Mercato Vecchio, and Ponte Pietra, Feb. 14-18

Valentine's Day is extra special in Verona, as the city celebrates with Verona in Love. Throughout the festival, guided tours of the city are given, museums offer discounts, and pop-up kiosks sell chocolates and other sweets. Every year the Juliet Club (www.julietclub.com) awards prizes for the best love letters. The judges are members of the *Segretarie di Giulietta* (Juliet's Secretaries) and the winners get a weekend stay in the city. Letters can be written in any

language and sent by email or post, or dropped off at the club's red mailbox (Corso Anastasia 29). Last year's winners were from Spain, Germany, and Brazil. The film *Letters to Juliet* recounts this tradition and provides a romantic, entertaining introduction to the city.

Estate Teatrale Veronese

Teatro Romano and Corte Mercato Vecchio, www.estateteatraleveronese.it, June-Sept., €18-29

Verona's summer theater and dance festival takes place from June to September. Shakespeare is nearly always represented, along with contemporary dance groups like Momix and Paul Taylor. Every three or four days, there's a show, many of which are held in the Roman theater. From the top seats you can see the stage, Adige River, and the city.

Verona Jazz
Various locations,
www.estateteatraleveronese.it, €20-50
Jazz musicians from around the world converge on Verona every June during this historic festival, now in its 46th year. Tickets are affordable and there are opportunities to meet the players after each performance.

Shopping

Verona's long, pedestrianized streets are well-suited for commerce and are often packed with shoppers. **Via Mazzini, Corso Sant'Anastasia,** and streets around **Piazza Erbe** are filled with local and international boutiques, some of which have been in business for generations. Shops do not close for lunch and many are open on Sunday. There are also plentiful markets selling food and clothing in the city's central squares.

DROGHERIA
Drogheria Emaldi Daniela
Via S. Paolo 6, Mon. 3:30pm-7:30pm,
Tues.-Sat. 9am-12:30pm and 3:30pm-7:30pm
Drogherie are old-fashioned grocery shops that are nearly extinct in Verona. However, this one has been doing business in the Veronetta neighborhood since 1882. It sells spices, herbs, natural beauty products, and candy stored in glass containers behind a vintage wooden counter. The shop itself feels a little like a museum piece, and anything you buy here makes a nice souvenir.

MARKETS
Mercato di Piazza Erbe
Piazza Erbe, Mon.-Sat. 7:30am-8:30pm

Verona's oldest market is held in the city's nicest square, supplying locals with fruits and vegetables, and tourists with wine, olive oil, and Christmas treats during the holidays. There are also stands dedicated to nonedible souvenirs like handmade bags, candleholders, jewelry, and mass-produced T-shirts. Market stalls fill the entire square and remain open all day.

Mercato dell'Antiquariato a San Zeno
Piazza San Zeno, third Saturday of every month 8am-5pm
This market is also known as *Tre A* by locals, in reference to the art, antiques, and artisanal vendors who set up their stalls once per month outside the Basilica San Zeno. This market is popular with collectors of every type, who come looking for furniture, 20th-century curiosities, vintage clothing, and more.

Neighborhood Markets
The *mercati rionali* (neighborhood markets) are the best places to get a feel for local daily life, and pick up some fresh, locally grown produce or inexpensive housewares. Every

a market stall in Piazza Erbe

Porta Vescovo (Wed. and Fri., 8am-5pm) on the eastern edge of Veronetta.

Christmas Market

Piazza dei Signori, Nov. 16-Dec. 26

The holidays transform Verona, and from mid-November to late December, Piazza dei Signori fills up with picturesque wooden huts selling handmade glass, and ceramic ornaments and gifts. There's lots of street food on hand, as well as aromatic *vin brulè* (mulled wine). Cortile Mercato Vecchio courtyard, Piazza San Zeno, and Via Lungadige San Giorgio along the banks of the Adige River also get into the Christmas spirit, and stalls remain open 10am-10pm daily.

neighborhood holds a market once or twice a week. The most lively are Piazza San Zemo (Tues. and Fri., 8am-2pm) facing Basilica San Zemo, Corso Porta Nuova (Fri., 8am-2pm) a few blocks southwest of the Arena, and

Recreation and Activities

CYCLING

In theory, Verona, which is flat and easy to navigate, is a good city for cycling. But in practice there are too many pedestrians walking around the center to make riding practical. If you do want to rent a bike to explore the city, stick to smaller streets or the wider ones flanking the Adige River.

RENTALS

Verona operates a bike-sharing program (tel. 800/896-948, www. bikeverona.it) with 24 stations and the possibility of daily (€2) or weekly registration (€5). The first half hour is free, the second is 0.50, and it's €0.75 per hour after that. The bikes themselves are on the heavy side with low frames and a front basket.

Green Bike Verona

Vicolo Volto S. Luca, tel. 342/022-6438, daily 8:30am-6pm, 4 hours €20, day €30

Green Bike Verona rents sturdy yellow electric bikes, which are perfect for cycling around Verona or longer treks outside the city.

RAFTING
✪ Adige Rafting

Via del Perloso 14a, tel. 339/232-2491, www.adigerafting.it, €25

The Adige River is the second longest in Italy. It originates hundreds of miles north of Verona in the Italian Alps, and it's perfect for rafting. Adige Rafting takes visitors on exhilarating two-hour paddles downriver, past countryside, 12 bridges, and the embankments of the city. Although there are several sections with decent rapids, this 5.25-mile (8.5-kilometer) journey is accessible to all, and guides take

rafting down the Adige River

time to describe sights along the way in Italian and English. Rafts depart from Bottagisio Sport Center (north of the city), which can be reached on bus 11 from the train station in 20 minutes. Outings are organized daily, and reservations are required.

PARACHUTING
Paracadutismo Verona

Aeroporto di Boscomantico, tel. 045/565-332 or 329/548-2858, www.paracadutismoverona.it, Fri.-Sun. 8am-sunset

Verona offers plenty of thrills, but if you want an instant shot of adrenaline and a view of Verona from 2.5 miles (4 kilometers) above the ground, then Paracadutismo Verona is what you need. This parachuting club located at the city's second airport provides tandem jumps with registered instructors. The only requirement is courage. After a 15-minute briefing, you'll be ready to free fall for 60 seconds at a speed of 125 miles (200 kilometers) per hour. Once the parachute cord is pulled, you'll

glide down to earth for several minutes with incredible views of Verona, Lago di Garda, and large swaths of the Veneto region within sight.

To reach the airport take bus 11 from the train station to Via Turbina 15v and follow the signs to the Aero Club Verona on foot. It's a 40- to 45-minute ride on the bus, or about 20 minutes by taxi (€15-20).

FOOTBALL
Stadio Marc'antonio Bentegodi

Piazzale Olimpia, tel. 045/818-6111, www.hellasverona.it, €20-75

Verona is the smallest city in Italy to have two soccer teams in Serie A (Italian first division), which means there's always a game on, whether you support Hellas Verona or Chievo Verona. Both teams play in Stadio Marc'Antonio Bentegodi, an old-style venue that seats 37,000 and is rarely full unless the Juventus football team is in town. Tickets can be purchased on-site, and beer and other refreshments are sold inside. The season runs September to June, and games are usually played on Sunday afternoons. The stadium is a 15-minute bus ride from Piazza Bra on the 11, 12, or 13 lines.

TOURS
WALKING AND CYCLING TOURS
AssoGuide Verona
Via F. Baracca 1b, tel. 045/810-1322,
www.veronacityguide.it
Assoguide Verona is an association of certified guides who run private walking and biking tours. Itineraries look back at the city's Roman, medieval, and Romantic periods. The classic tour is perfect for first-time visitors and covers all the major sights. The cost is €115 for up to 30 people on a 2.5-hour tour. Starting out with a tour of the city will open your eyes to hundreds of details you might otherwise miss.

Simonetta Bettio
Regaste San Zeno 1, tel. 328/028-0174,
www.simonettabiketours.it
Simonetta Bettio combined her love of travel and bikes into a tour company dedicated to Verona and the surrounding Veneto region. Participants get to cross bridges, follow the city's historic walls, and discover lesser known parts of the city in a three-hour tour (€35) that's perfect for cyclists of any ability level. She also offers a Bike and Rafting (€70) experience that's a little bit more challenging. It starts at 9:30am with a bike ride that takes you upstream before rafting down the Adige River. It's

a daylong adventure that lasts seven hours and is offered from March to October. Comfortable shoes and clothing are recommended for both types of tour. Water is provided, but lunch is extra.

BUS TOURS
Bus tours can be handy for travelers with limited time or mobility issues. Of the two options listed below, Trenino is more highly recommended, because groups are smaller, and the tours venture into the narrow streets of the historic center.

Citysightseeing
www.city-sightseeing.it, €20
Citysightseeing operates two lines in Verona. Both stop in Piazza Bra and make hop-on, hop-off loops around the city that last about an hour. Their comfortable double-decker buses run March-October daily 9am-7pm. Buy tickets on board or online. The €20 fee covers the use of these buses for one day.

Trenino Turistico
Via dei Mutilati 3b, tel. 331/250-3312,
www.visitareverona.it, summer daily
10am-7pm, €5
Trenino Turistico takes passengers through the historic center on a ride that's fun for kids and tired adults. It leaves from Piazza Bra and makes a 40-minute circuit without stopping. *Trenino* means little train, but this tour actually uses three open-air carriages that are pulled by a small tractor made to look like a train.

Accommodations

Two major factors affect price and availability of rooms in Verona: trade fairs at the Fiera exhibition grounds and the summer opera season. At those times, rooms are hard to come by (even in the outskirts) and prices rise accordingly.

HOTELS

Hotel Verona

Corso Porta Nuova 47/49, tel. 045/595-944, www.hotelverona.it, €90-120 d

Hotel Verona is centrally located near Porta Nuova train station. Comfortable and modern rooms offer Wi-Fi, fluffy pillows, and well-stocked minibars. The staff is friendly, and bikes are free for guests to use.

Hotel Torcolo

Vicolo Listone 3, tel. 045/800-7512, www.hoteltorcolo.it, €80-120 d

The economical Hotel Torcolo has a small lobby and breakfast area, but rooms are large and traditionally furnished. It's located on a quiet side street, around the corner from the Arena.

Hotel Bologna

Piazzetta Scalette Rubiani 3, tel. 045/800-6830, www.hotelbologna.vr.it, €100-140 d

Near Piazza Bra, Hotel Bologna is cute on the outside and convenient on the inside. Breakfast (included in the room rate) is bountiful, and the buffet is well-stocked even if you wake up late.

Hotel Colomba D'Oro

Via C. Cattaneo 10, tel. 045/595-300, www.colombahotel.com, €150 d

Upscale, traditional Hotel Colomba D'Oro has a lovely lobby and cocktail bar, and its attractive outdoor sitting area is a perfect place to relax after a day exploring the city. Rooms are romantic, and no two are decorated alike. The breakfast buffet (included in the room rate) is abundant, and free parking is available.

Due Torri Hotel Baglioni

Piazza S. Anastasia 4, tel. 045/595-044, www.baglionihotels.com, €180 d

A central location, elegant charm, tasteful furnishings, and superb staff make Due Torri Hotel Baglioni an unforgettable stay in Verona's historic center. The inner courtyard and a terrace with a fabulous view are the icing on the cake. Even if you don't stay here it's worth stopping by for the *aperitivo,* offered daily at 5pm.

Hotel Bologna, Verona

Information and Services

Tourist Office

Via degli Alpini 9, tel. 045/806-8680,
www.turismoverona.eu, Mon.-Sat. 9am-6pm,
Sun. 10am-4pm

The multilingual staff at the tourist office are extremely patient and friendly. They can help find last-minute accommodation, provide the latest event info, and answer questions about the city. This is also the place to pick up the **Verona Card**.

The office is located near the Arena in a nondescript entrance along the city walls; look carefully because it's easy to miss.

Luggage Storage

A left-luggage deposit is available at the Verona train station (daily, 8am-8pm, €6 first 5 hours, €0.90 cents per hour for the next 6 hours, and €0.40 cents per hour after that).

Getting There and Around

GETTING THERE

AIR

Verona Villafranca Airport (VRN, www.aeroportoverona.it) runs a handful of European flights, including daily arrivals from London Gatwick and Stansted, but most overseas visitors fly into Milan or Venice. The **Aerobus shuttle** (€6) operates daily. It leaves every 20 minutes for the train station (5:35am-11:30pm), reaching Verona in about 25 minutes. Taxis are waiting outside the main terminal and can be ordered by calling **Unione Radio Taxi** (tel. 045/532-666) or **Taxi e Autoblu** (tel. 045/858-1403). The ride takes 20 minutes and costs €20-27, depending on the amount of luggage and time of day.

TRAIN

From Venice's Santa Lucia station, dozens of regional, direct regional, and high-speed trains connect to Verona Porta Nuova station daily. It's a 70-minute journey on board

Frecciarossa (www.trenitalia.it, €22.90), 90 minutes on **Regionale Veloce** (direct regional, €9), and more than two hours with the regional (€9) service. The latter two options make stops in Padua and Vicenza.

Verona's **Porta Nuova train station** is about a mile (1.5 kilometers) from the Arena, which marks the beginning of the historic center of Verona, a 20- to 25-minute walk. There are dozens of buses right outside the station, and the 11, 12, 13, 51, and 52 drop passengers off near the Arena.

Taxis are also waiting outside the station to bring passengers to the center, and can be ordered day or night by phoning 045/532-666.

CAR

Verona is a short drive from Venice, Padua, and Vicenza on the A4 highway. It's 70 minutes west of Venice, and there's a €11.50 toll at the **Verona Sud** exit. From there, follow Viale del Lavoro north to the **Parcheggio**

Stazione Ovest (2 hours €2.50, 5 hours €5, or 24 hours €7) or Porta Palio parking lots at the entrance to the historic center. The latter is free, and there's a bike-sharing station on-site; alternatively, it's a 15-minute walk to Piazza Bra.

GETTING AROUND

Verona is walkable, but buses can be handy for getting into town from the train station, or for reaching recreation options outside the city.

BUS

ATV (www.atv.verona.it) tickets cost €1.30 for 90 minutes or €4 for a day pass and can be purchased at the machines or office outside the station. The Verona Card also includes public transportation. It's available at the newsstand inside the train station, and you may want to buy it there to cover your bus ride from the train station into the city.

TAXI

If you need a taxi, call 045/532-666 (radiotaxiverona.it) or download appTaxi from any app store. It allows users to plan journeys, order cars, and pay for taxis directly from a smartphone.

CAR RENTAL

There is a Maggiore (Piazzale XXV Aprile, tel. 045 803 2184, www.maggiore.it, Mon.-Fri. 8:30am-8:30pm, Sat. 8:30am-4pm) car rental office at the train station and an Avis (Via Albere 74, tel. 045/800-6636, www.avisautonoleggio.it, Mon.-Fri. 8:30am-12:30pm and 2:30pm-6:30pm, Sat. 8:30am-12pm) branch 10 minutes away. Both are located near the highway leading toward Lake Garda.

LAKE GARDA

As Italy's largest lake, Garda is known by all as the "king" of Italian lakes, spanning a total area of 143 square miles (370 square kilometers). Sitting halfway between the cities of Brescia and Verona, the lake dominates a fairly large portion of north-central Italy and serves as one of the most popular holiday destinations for Europeans.

The southern end of Garda feels like a piece of Mediterranean paradise at the foot of the Italian Alps, with palm trees and little villages of colorful houses stacked up against one another. As

Itinerary Ideas 215
Peschiera del Garda 217
Desenzano del Garda
  and Sirmione 222
Lazise 231
Bardolino. 236
Malcesine 240
Riva del Garda 246

HIGHLIGHTS

✪ **GARDALAND, PESCHIERA DEL GARDA:** Popular with locals as well as tourists, this amusement park is one of the best-known theme parks in Italy. Thousands visit every year for a full day of roller coasters, thrill rides, themed events, and more (page 218).

✪ **CASTELLO SCALIGERO, SIRMIONE:** This medieval fortress lies directly in the blue waters of Lake Garda. Climb to the top of the towers for an aerial view of the entire castle as well as the surrounding village of Sirmione along the turquoise backdrop of the lake (page 225).

✪ **ISOLA DEL GARDA, SIRMIONE:** This privately owned island with a gorgeous villa is a true example of luxury and elegance with classic Northern Italian style. From March to October, take a guided boat tour and discover the many charms (and uses) of Lake Garda's largest island over the years (page 226).

✪ **PUNTA SAN VIGILIO, BARDOLINO:** Lying less than 4 miles (6 kilometers) north of Bardolino, this small peninsula is one of the most pristine spots on Lake Garda. Visit this natural paradise for a peaceful outdoor experience (page 236).

✪ **MONTE BALDO, MALCESINE:** This towering mountain range serves as the backdrop of Lake Garda's northeastern shore and is easily accessed via a high-tech cable car from the village of Malcesine. At the top, enjoy picturesque aerial views of the northern part of the lake, paraglide down, or hike one of the many trails along the summit (page 241).

✪ **CASCATA DEL VARONE, RIVA DEL GARDA:** The beautiful waterfalls in Varone near Riva del Garda make for one of the most unique experiences in the region. Here you can walk through natural caves to view the falls from the bottom up and feel the clear water pooling at your feet. Likewise, you can view the falls from above, looking down to experience the full length of the falls (page 249).

you head north on the lake, you'll see towering mountains so imposing, they seem to push villages right up against the water.

Lake Garda offers a little of everything, from water sports to amusement parks to historic villas and ancient Roman ruins. The towns dotting its shores are vibrant and charming, with plenty of things to do and see, both indoors and outdoors. More than any other Italian lake, Garda is family-friendly in nature, with plenty of events and activities for children. No matter how long you spend on Lake Garda, you'll never get bored.

ORIENTATION

Italy's largest lake is shaped like an axe with a long handle that covers a large chunk of the country's northern territory. It's 20 miles (32 kilometers) from

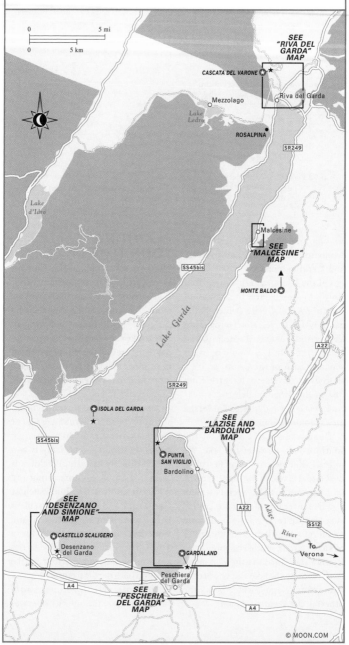

Lake Garda

0 — 5 mi
0 — 5 km

SEE "RIVA DEL GARDA" MAP

CASCATA DEL VARONE ★

Riva del Garda

Mezzolago

Lake Ledro

ROSALPINA

SR249

Lake d'Idro

Malcesine

SEE "MALCESINE" MAP

SS45bis

MONTE BALDO

Lake Garda

SR249

A22

ISOLA DEL GARDA ★

SEE "LAZISE AND BARDOLINO" MAP

SS45bis

PUNTA SAN VIGILIO ★

Bardolino

SEE "DESENZANO AND SIMIONE" MAP

CASTELLO SCALIGERO

Desenzano del Garda ★

A22

Adige River

SS12

To Verona →

GARDALAND

Peschiera del Garda

A4

SEE "PESCHERIA DEL GARDA" MAP

A4

© MOON.COM

- **If you want family-friendly fun:** Head to Peschiera del Garda and spend a thrilling day at Gardaland or the underwater wonder of the Sealife Aquarium.

- **If you want to avoid the crowds:** Stick to Bardolino in the spring or late summer. You'll find a quieter, local vibe, and just north of the village, you'll enjoy the beautiful, nature-oriented Punta San Vigilio peninsula.

- **If you want outdoor recreation:** Spend a day on the water in Riva del Garda, where you can rent kayaks, stand-up paddleboards, sailboats, and more. Alternatively, head to higher altitude by trekking around one of the hiking trails in this mountainous area.

- **If you want an easy trip from Venice:** Peschiera del Garda and Descenzano del Garda can both be reached by train from Venice in less than two hours. Both towns have scenic lakeside walkways and plenty of dining options.

- **If you want a mix of history and nature:** Malcesine is home to an ancient medieval castle overlooking the lake, as well as a huge mountain where you can paraglide from the summit or take a cable car up to the top.

Verona and borders three regions: Lombardy (to the west), Veneto (east), and Trentino (north).

On the lake's eastern shore, from south to north, are the towns of **Peschiera del Garda** (which is the gateway for travelers arriving from Venice and Verona), **Bardolino**, and **Malcesine.** Only a couple of miles separate each of the towns, so it's a short drive, bus ride, or ferry trip from one to the other. Malcesine is near Riva del Garda and **Monte Baldo,** the area's famous mountain range.

Desenzano del Garda, on the southwestern shore of the lake, 9.3 miles (15 kilometers) west of Peschiera del Garda, is one of the biggest towns on Lake Garda. In between Peschiera and Desenzano is the narrow peninsula leading to **Sirmione,** a historic medieval village located in the center of Lake Garda's southern shore.

Riva del Garda is the northernmost town on the lake and one of only two towns (Nago-Torbole being the other) in the Trentino region.

PLANNING YOUR TIME

The best way to plan your time on Lake Garda is to understand what is accessible based on your primary mode of transportation. Traveling by car gives you the luxury of having all of the lake's towns at your fingertips, but roads around the lake get crowded in summer and traffic jams are common. Aim to travel early or leave your car parked and hop on a ferry.

If you're traveling by train, choose a home base of **Desenzano** or **Peschiera,** which are two of the larger towns on the lake, and the only two served directly by train. Peschiera is close to a number of interesting and family-friendly attractions, such as Gardaland and smaller amusement parks, and there are shuttles to and from the train station to the parks, so a car isn't necessary. Buses and ferries are a great way of experiencing the lake and both depart from either town.

Gestione Navigazione Laghi (www.navigazionelaghi.it) operates slow and high-speed ferryboats connecting major towns around the lake. Frequency depends on the season and in summer there are hourly departures. Fares are €3-10 one-way per person based on distance. Day tickets for the lower part of the lake (€23.40) or entire lake (€34.30) are also available. Peschiera del Garda, the main port, is a good place to start a ferry tour.

Give yourself at least **two days** on the lake if you plan to hop between towns, but you can easily fill an entire week here given the diverse range of sights and activities.

Lake Garda is one of Europe's most popular vacation destinations in the summer, so book your accommodations as early as possible if you plan to visit during July or August.

Itinerary Ideas

To maximize your time on Lake Garda, settle into your hotel in **Desenzano del Garda** the night before you begin this itinerary.

DAY 1

1 Start your morning with a hearty breakfast at your hotel, then head to the ferry station to grab a boat to **Sirmione.** Spend your morning exploring the **Scaligero Castle.**

2 Head to the Roman ruins of **Grotte di Catullo** before grabbing a boat back to Desenzano.

3 Have lunch at **La Cambusa,** a small, cozy restaurant off of the lakefront. This spot is known for its robust *tagliere* (cold cut and cheese platter) plates.

4 Walk off lunch by exploring the ruins of **Villa Romana.**

5 Wander the streets of Desenzano, popping into a few local stores. For a break, head to the **waterfront** and grab a seat and a gelato at one of the handful of gelaterias lining the shore.

6 Have dinner at **Molin22,** one of the highest-rated restaurants in Desenzano, serving quality Italian food near the waters of Lake Garda.

7 If you still have energy after a long day of exploring, head to **Coco Beach** for a night of dancing and drinks.

DAY 2

If you have a second day, explore the northern part of the lake in the beautiful town of **Malcesine,** accessible by ferry from Desenzano. Ferries depart hourly, and the journey takes a little over two hours on the catamaran speed boats.

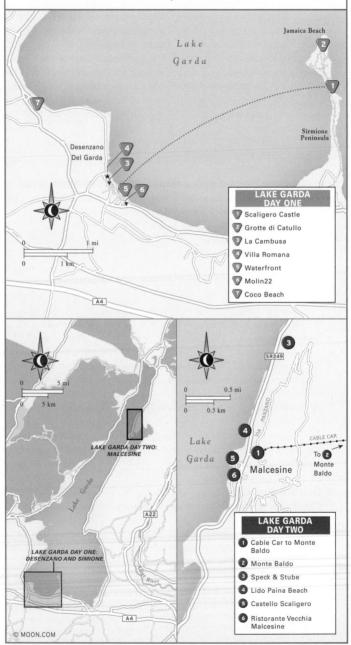

Lake Garda Itinerary Ideas

Jamaica Beach

Lake Garda

2

1

Sirmione Peninsula

7

Desenzano Del Garda

4

3

5 **6**

0 — 1 mi
0 — 1 km

LAKE GARDA DAY ONE

1 Scaligero Castle
2 Grotte di Catullo
3 La Cambusa
4 Villa Romana
5 Waterfront
6 Molin22
7 Coco Beach

0 — 5 mi
0 — 5 km

LAKE GARDA DAY TWO: MALCESINE

Lake Garda

LAKE GARDA DAY ONE: DESENZANO AND SIMIONE

A22

A4

Adige River

3

SR249

0 — 0.5 mi
0 — 0.5 km

Lake Garda

4

5 **1**

6 Malcesine

VIA PANZANO

CABLE CAR

To **2** Monte Baldo

LAKE GARDA DAY TWO

1 Cable Car to Monte Baldo
2 Monte Baldo
3 Speck & Stube
4 Lido Paina Beach
5 Castello Scaligero
6 Ristorante Vecchia Malcesine

© MOON.COM

1 Head straight to the center of Malcesine to grab the cable car up to the peak of Monte Baldo.

2 Once you've reached the top, spend your morning in the sun doing one of the several recreational activities on the mountain, such as paragliding or hiking the Peace Trail.

3 Head back down near the water for a casual, filling lunch of meat and other roasted treats at Speck & Stube.

4 In the afternoon, catch some rays right on the water at the free, public Lido Paina beach. The nearby bar offers drinks, snacks, and gelato.

5 From the beach, walk a little farther to the looming Castello Scaligero for a more in-depth look into the village's history.

6 For dinner, try the locally beloved Ristorante Vecchia Malcesine for a full tasting menu of local flavors. Spend the night in Malescine and catch the ferry back to Peschiera or Desenzano in the morning.

Peschiera del Garda

The colorful resort town of Peschiera del Garda sits on the southeastern corner of Lake Garda, roughly 15 miles (25 kilometers) west of the city of Verona. The town is a wonderfully family-friendly place to visit, with resorts, beaches, and lakeside walkways. Next to Peschiera del Garda is the small village of Castelnuovo del Garda, which is home to Gardaland, one of the most popular amusement parks in Europe. Still, there is plenty of old-world charm to be had in Peschiera, as a stroll through the historic center full of rainbow-hued buildings, local boutiques, and restaurants, will show.

Peschiera falls on the main rail line connecting Venice and Milan, so it is an ideal place to stay for those traveling without a car.

SIGHTS
HISTORIC TOWN CENTER
Bounded by Via Mantova (west),
Via Nencioni (east), the SR11 (south),
and the shoreline (north)

To pass a pleasant hour or two in Peschiera, simply wander around the charming, historic center, which is against a backdrop of sparkling lake waters and ancient Venetian city walls. Enjoy the Mediterranean feel in the air as you browse through clothing boutiques, leather goods shops, family-run restaurants, bars with flower-draped patio seating, and more. Hopping from one establishment to another is a treat in and of itself, as friendly owners welcome you, inviting you to stay as long as you please. Foodies and shoppers are sure to find the perfect souvenir here.

Peschiera del Garda

✪ GARDALAND RESORT AND AMUSEMENT PARK

Via Derna 4, Castelnuovo del Garda, tel. 045/644-9777, www.gardaland.it, July-Sept. daily 10am-11pm, late Mar.-June daily 10am-6pm, adults €40.50, ages 10 and under or 60 and over €34.50

The Gardaland Resort and Amusement Park is Peschiera del Garda's main draw year after year, attracting more than three million visitors since it first opened in 1975. Not only is it Italy's most visited and most beloved theme park, spanning 64 acres (26 hectares), but it is also one of Europe's most popular parks. Sitting on the eastern shore of Lake Garda, the park actually faces away from the lake, and is divided into multiple themed areas, such as Camelot, Arabia, Rio Bravo, and Fantasy Kingdom.

The park offers a variety of rides, including roller coasters, water rides, thrill rides, and scaled down kiddie rides. Roller coaster fans won't want to miss the giant Blue Tornado, with its double inline twist ending, or the Shaman with its double loop and double corkscrew. You'll also find plenty of bars and food stalls in the park selling everything from chocolate-covered waffles to American-style fast food, as well as an Italian cafeteria. The place is packed on weekends and on the special theme nights (especially at Halloween), so visit during a weekday and in the morning if you want to avoid long queues; waits can be up to an hour during peak season.

Gardaland Amusement Park

To make a holiday out of it, you can stay at one of the resorts near the park to receive discounts on park entrances and other package deals: The Gardaland Hotel (www.gardalandhotel.it, €140 per night) or the Gardaland Adventure Hotel (www.gardalandadventurehotel.it, €150 per night). In addition to its regular opening season, the park is open during certain times in October, November, December, and January for special themed events. Official schedules can be found on the website. Purchase tickets online to get a discount (€36 per adult). Kids under 3 feet, 3 inches (one meter) enter free.

To get from the center of Peschiera del Garda to Gardaland, take the SR249 northeast, following the signs to the aquarium along the way. It's a 10-minute drive over 2.5 miles (4 kilometers).

GARDALAND SEA LIFE AQUARIUM

Via Derna 4, Castelnuovo del Garda, 045/644-9777, www.gardalandsealife.it, Apr.-Oct. daily 10am-6pm, €12.50-16

Like many aquariums around the world, the aquarium in Peschiera is a family-friendly, interactive space with both fresh and saltwater creatures from all over the world. For most visitors, the top attraction is walking through the transparent ocean tunnel, completely surrounded by blue waters and hundreds of fish, including sharks. Visitors can also witness daily shark feedings and watch a short film on marine life. Small pools scattered throughout the aquarium invite children to interact with the marine life. There's also a decent restaurant on the property serving quick snacks and drinks. You can purchase an individual aquarium ticket, or buy a combination ticket to Gardaland for €43.50. The aquarium is generally closed during the winter months of November-March, but there are a few days in that period when it is open.

To get from the center of Peschiera del Garda to the aquarium by car, take the SR249 northeast, following the signs to the aquarium along the way. It's a 10-minute drive over 2.5 miles (4 kilometers). Alternatively, you can catch the free shuttle bus from the Peschiera del Garda train station during the park's opening hours. The shuttle departs from both the park and the station every half hour, and the journey takes 5-10 minutes each way.

RECREATION AND ACTIVITIES

BOAT TOURS

Il Pentagono Boat Tours

Central Harbor Peschiera del Garda, Riviera Carducci 1, tel. 340/905-8331, www.pentagonorent.com, Mar.-Oct. daily 9am-6:30pm, deposit €150, €30 per hour

For a little offshore fun, rent a boat from the Il Pentagono boat company, a local group of boatmen who are incredibly friendly and knowledgeable about Lake Garda. Not only do they offer boat rentals, but they also give you the best advice for your tour around the lake. Boats can be rented by the hour or the day, starting at €30 without gas or €50 with gas. During high season, rent a boat for less than four hours with fuel included, so you can avoid the long lines for gas. You can always book a boat by calling in advance. To rent a boat, a deposit is required along with a valid identification card and phone number.

Peschiera del Garda's main port

BEACHES
Braccobaldo Beach

Locality Fornaci, tel. 342/125-4336,
www.pentagonorent.com, daily
9:30am-6:30pm, €6-18

The Il Pentagono boat company also offers private beach access for those wanting to relax on the shores of Lake Garda. Braccobaldo Beach is one of the more unique beaches on the lake because it is dog-friendly. One sun bed for one person and one sun bed for one dog is included in the entry price. Each deck chair comes with an umbrella. During the summer, it's best to book in advance, as there is a limited capacity (total 60 people). Nearby, you'll find a bar serving drinks and snacks, as well as parking and restrooms.

WALKS
Mincio River to Borghetto sul Mincio

To get a taste of the Veronese countryside and the little towns just south of Lake Garda, follow the flow of the Mincio River straight out of the Peschiera and down to the charming riverside village of Borghetto sul Mincio, nationally known for creating delicate handmade tortellini. To make a day of it, start walking in the morning and head to the village by lunch, then fuel up on tortellini and wine before walking back to Peschiera. The paved pedestrian and bike path, which is fairly flat the entire way, follows the river and simply guides you to this little piece of paradise, which is complete with a quiet village church, a water wheel, cobblestone pathways full of Michelin-star restaurants, and local boutiques. The entire walk from Peschiera to Borghetto is roughly 7.5 miles (12 kilometers), which takes a couple of hours each way. You'll walk parallel to the SR249 and eventually onto the SP74 down to the village.

NIGHTLIFE
Bar Al Porto

Riviera Carducci 5, tel. 339/211-5643,
daily 10am-3am, €10-20

Bar Al Porto is a small modern bar that overlooks Lake Garda. Beloved by locals, it stays open late and serves traditional *aperitivo* treats like spritz, chips, olives, and finger foods. This place stays pretty busy in the summertime, and if you swing by just after dinner, you'll observe the bartenders talking to old friends, and diners and drinkers mingling well past midnight. Despite its late-night hours, this is not a club. Rather, it's a cozy local place that's ideal for slowing down and enjoying the night breeze coming off the lake.

FOOD

Marco and Daniela Time

Via Risorgimento 1, tel. 045/755-3582,
www.marcoedanielatime.it, Fri.-Wed.
noon-3pm and 6pm-10pm, €7-12

Beloved by locals and highly rated by travelers, this cozy, casual spot serves Italian comfort food at cheap prices, all with a buzzing atmosphere and great flavors. Whether you order a freshly made Italian meat sandwich, a mixed salad, the pasta of the day, *bruschetta*, or tiramisu, everything is house-made with great care. Stay for a while to soak in the cool vibes. Study the local foodstuffs stocked on the wall-to-wall wooden shelves, and enjoy a local beer from the tap. No need for reservations, but know that this place fills up quickly for lunches and dinners, especially during high season, so come right when it opens.

Osteria Rivelin

Via Milano 1, 045/252-6048, Wed.-Mon.
7pm-10:30pm, Sat.-Sun., noon-2pm, €10-20

This cozy, local joint feels like home the moment you walk in the door, with its low lighting and wooden shelves full of regional wines. The arched brick walls and domed ceiling add to the intimate and relaxed atmosphere. The menu includes local pasta dishes as well as beef filets with truffle, liver, tartare, chicken lasagna, and other baked pasta dishes. Start your meal off with a large plate of cold cuts, cheeses, honeys, and jams paired with a local wine, as bardolino.

ACCOMMODATIONS

Hotel Garden

Viale Stazione 18; 045/755 3644;
www.hotel-garden.it; €64

Located conveniently next to the Peschiera train station, the Hotel Garden is a nice option for those wanting to stay a little bit away from the lake and close to transportation options. The hotel itself is simple yet modern, with a classic American feel. The property includes a bar with patio seating, and the hotel partners with a nearby Italian restaurant to offer meals at discounted rates. Each guest room includes air-conditioning, Wi-Fi, and private bathroom. Continental breakfast and parking are included in the price of each room.

Parc Hotel

Via Paradiso di Sopra, tel. 045/6405-2011,
www.parchotelpeschiera.it, €150

Peschiera's Parc Hotel is a family-friendly, modern, and bright hotel that is beloved by tourists visiting the resort town year after year. The huge complex includes both an indoor and outdoor pool, a wellness center, a restaurant, playground, and many sports areas, including a golf course. Each guest room includes air-conditioning and a private bathroom with a tub. Some rooms also include a balcony overlooking the recreation areas below. A huge buffet breakfast and parking are included in the price of each room.

GETTING THERE

BY CAR

Peschiera is 87 miles (140 kilometers) west of Venice, and the 90-minute journey is entirely on the A4 highway. It's only a half-hour drive from Verona. There's paid public parking near the train station, and once you park, the lake is 10 minutes away on foot.

BY TRAIN

Peschiera del Garda is on the main rail line connecting Venice and Milan, so freccia (high-speed) and regional trains stop here. **Frecciarossa** (www. trenitalia.it) service leaves hourly from Venezia Santa Lucia and tickets are €13.50. Regional trains depart hourly from Verona and reach Peschiera in 15 minutes. Tickets cost €3.45.

GETTING AROUND

The center of Peschiera is entirely walkable, unless you want to get to more remote restaurants or accommodations, or to Gardaland. To get from the center of Peschiera del Garda to Gardaland, take the SR249 northeast, following the signs to the aquarium along the way. It's a 10-minute drive over 2.5 miles (4 kilometers). If you don't want to drive, you can catch the free shuttle bus from the Peschiera del Garda train station during the park's opening hours. The shuttle departs from both the park and the station every half hour, and the journey takes 5-10 minutes each way.

Desenzano del Garda and Sirmione

The town of Desenzano del Garda sits on the southwest corner of Lake Garda, roughly 9 miles (15 kilometers) west of Peschiera del Garda. Since the 1st century, it has been one of the preferred vacation spots for wealthy Veronese and later grew to become a favorite destination for many tourists from Germany, Austria, and Switzerland.

The colorful town has quite a range of things to do and see: Roman ruins and castles at your fingertips, relaxing beaches, fine dining and casual restaurants, plenty of nightclubs, and bars that stay open late. If you plan to spend a night or two here, you can select from more than 25 major hotels and dozens of other accommodation options. Despite it being Lake Garda's most bustling town, Desenzano del Garda is no less charming or beautiful than its smaller sibling villages.

The village of Sirmione, located on a narrow peninsula of the same name that juts up from the southern edge of Lake Garda, is just 6 miles (10 kilometers) northwest of Desenzano. The historic village is known for its park of Roman ruins and beautiful medieval castle, from which you can enjoy aerial views of the lake and peninsula. The vibes of Sirmione are much like those of Desenzano, though its deep history is much more prominent.

ORIENTATION

Desenzano del Garda, located on the southwestern shore of Lake Garda, extends from the far southwestern corner all the way to the Sirmione Peninsula. Despite being one of the largest towns on the lake, it is fairly compact and mostly walkable. Although the town itself has no particular structure (it is not organized by a grid or concentric circles like Milan), if you stick to a few main streets, you won't get lost.

In the northwestern part of town, you can follow Lungolago Battisti along the lakeshore until you reach the Roman Villa. In the middle of town, many streets are strictly pedestrian,

Desenzano and Sirmione

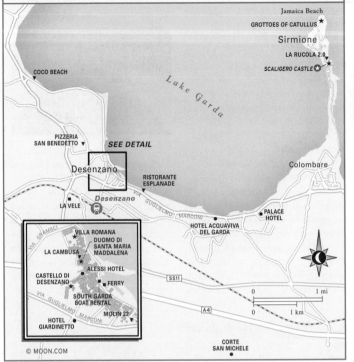

including Via Santa Maria, which runs horizontally through the core of the city center, and along which you will find several bars, restaurants, and shops, including La Vele. The most important churches and *piazzas* are found directly off of this road. If you want to drive across town, use Via Marconi, which runs horizontally through the southern part of the city center. Follow this road straight through several roundabouts then eastward, and you will see signs pointing toward the Sirmione Peninsula, where the town of Sirmione sits 6 miles (10 kilometers) northeast of Desenzano.

If you want to visit Coco Beach, a popular nightspot in Lonato del Garda, follow Lungolago Battisti north until it turns into Via Vo'. The town in which the club is located is only a couple of miles north of the main part of Desenzano.

SIGHTS

DESENZANO DEL GARDA
Cathedral of Saint Mary Magdalene (Duomo di Santa Maria Maddalena)

Via Roma 5, Desenzano del Garda, tel. 030/991-4164, www.duomodesenzano.it, daily 8:30am-6:30pm, free

Sitting in the center of Desenzano is the Duomo Di Santa Maria Maddalena, the town's main cathedral and religious heart. The facade

223

features Baroque-style details, and the inside is full of paintings depicting the life cycle of Mary Magdalene. Inside you'll also notice the immense arched columns and darkly frescoed ceilings, illuminated by the natural light streaming through the grid-like patterned windows. As this church holds frequent Mass services, it's best to remain quiet during your visit so as to not disturb the worshippers.

Villa Romana

Via Crocefisso 22, Desenzano del Garda, tel. 030/914-3547, www.comune.desenzano. brescia.it, Tues.-Sun. 8:30am-7pm, €4
Although the Roman ruins that laid for centuries under Desenzano's city center were not discovered until the 1920s, their origins date back to a villa that was built in the 1st century BC and represents one of the most significant pieces of history in this region.

Villa Romana

At that time, the villa with its piers and moorings overlooked the lake. Since its discovery, the space has been fenced in and gated, and is now surrounded by residential buildings in a tranquil corner of the center of town. You can walk around the covered ruins in less than an hour. You can also read about the history of the villa in English and Italian.

Desenzano's waterfront square

Castello di Desenzano

Via Castello, Desenzano del Garda,
tel. 030/374-8726, www.comune.desenzano.
brescia.it, Tues.-Sun. 10am-12:30pm and
3pm-6pm, €3

Castello di Desenzano, the historic castle overlooking Lake Garda and the town of Desenzano, houses a small museum outlining the history of the 11th-century fortress and its four angular towers. The castle was built with an irregular, rectangular plan, with the gray stone walls slightly crumbling, showing the age of the fortress. Today, you can climb up to the highest tower to reach the panoramic observatory, where you can catch an aerial view of the surrounding town and the southern shore of Lake Garda. You can also walk along the outer walls and towers, and down to the lower level of the castle for a peek at an ancient collection of old military arms. This is a great option if you cannot or do not want to make your way to the castle in Sirmione.

SIRMIONE
✪ Castello Scaligero (Scaligero Castle)

Piazza Castello 34, Sirmione,
tel. 030/2896-5218, www.polomuseale.
lombardia.beniculturali.it/, Tues.-Sun.
8:30am-7:30pm, €6

Castello Scaligero originally served as a fortress during the 13th and 14th centuries. The castle's sturdy walls were built into the lake, along with its three giant towers. Heading up to the towers for the views is a must, as is visiting the boat dock near the water for a better understanding of how the castle functioned when it was in use. The white stone castle, surrounded by the calm, gorgeous turquoise waters of Lake Garda, is one of the most visited and beautiful sights in the area.

Inside the castle, you'll find an exhibit outlining the history and importance of the castle during Roman and medieval times. Descriptive placards are available in several languages, including English. Do not leave without climbing the wooden staircase up to the tower keep for an awesome panoramic view of the castle, village, and the surrounding lake—definitely one of the most breathtaking views you will experience. The elevated walkways that connect the walls and towers also offer an experience that no other castle offers.

Grottoes of Catullus

Piazza Orti Manara 4, Sirmione,
tel. 030/916-157, www.grottedicatullo.
beniculturali.it, Mon.-Sat. 8:30am-7:30pm,
Sun. 9:30am-6:30pm, €8

These Roman ruins at the tip of the Sirmione Peninsula were originally part of a 1st-century Roman villa that overlooked the southern shore of Lake Garda, and today they are part of a large park dedicated to the villa's remains. The park leads you through various levels and sections of the former villa, with signs (in Italian and English) identifying the room you're standing in and its purpose. It's easy to feel the historical impact of this place, how somber and peaceful it is as you

Scaligero Castle

gaze out at the waters of the lake. The best time to visit is a weekend morning or on a weekday, when you'll likely have the place mostly to yourself to wander about at your leisure.

✪ Isola del Garda

San Felice del Benaco, Sirmione,
tel. 328/612-6943, www.isoladelgarda.com,
Mar.-Oct. daily tours, €31-38

Isola del Garda is Lake Garda's largest island and has been used in various ways over the centuries. It's been a pirate's retreat, a Roman burial site, a Franciscan monastery, and fortification for the town. Today, this beautiful island is privately owned by the Cavazza family and is home to **Villa Borghese Cavazza,** a villa surrounded by Italian and English gardens; it's the quintessence of Northern Italian luxury and elegance. The Cavazza family opens their private island to visitors March-October each year. From Sirmione (at the main docking area along the peninsula), you can grab a private boat once a day to and from the island on Tuesday and Thursday. The ride is about a half an hour each way.

Upon arrival to the island you'll be welcomed with a glass of wine. The engaging tour (about two hours) will teach you a great deal about the historical and cultural significance of the island. You'll walk throughout the villa, including the private rooms where much of the elegant and antique furniture is prominently displayed. You'll also be taken through the magnificent gardens, where you'll find groomed hedges and a plethora of fruit trees, including grapefruit, lemon, pear, pomegranate, and caper.

In addition to touring the island

Grottoes of Catullus

from Sirmione, guests can also transfer from other villages along Lake Garda's shores, including Lazise, Bardolino, Manerba, and San Felice del Benaco. An official timetable with prices is available on the island's website.

RECREATION AND ACTIVITIES

BEACHES AND WATER SPORTS

Jamaica Beach

Lago di Garda, Sirmione, daily 24/7, free

If you're looking for a local hangout that is totally free, hit Jamaica Beach for a few hours or for a full day of sun and swimming. There are no frills here; this public spot sits just next to the Grottoes of Catullus in Sirmione, where you'll see locals grab their beach gear and set up camp on the flat rocks near the shallow waters for a full day of fun. Pack a lunch, grab some towels, and set up early, as spots fill up fast in the summer. Simply follow the walking path down from Grottoes of Catullus, where you'll find the flat rocky area as well as a beach bar selling drinks, gelato, and traditional aperitivo food, including olives, potato chips, peanuts, finger sandwiches, and cold cuts.

South Garda Boats Rental

Piazza Ulisse Papa 5, Desenzano Del Garda,
tel. 333/534-7687, www.gardaboatrent.com,
daily 9am-6pm, from €70

Whether you want to rent a private boat or float along on a guided tour of the southern end of Lake Garda, South Garda Boats Rental has you covered. Boats can be rented, with or without a boating license, by the hour or for up to a week at a time, starting from €70 per hour. (Smaller boats with a capacity of up to eight people are available for those without a license.) Insurance and a full tank are included in the price of each hour or day, although additional fill-ups come out of your pocket.

If you don't want to rent a boat but still want an experience on the water, the company offers several private and group boat tours, ranging from romantic sunset cruises with wine and *aperitivo* included to quick, fun tours showing you the shoreline of each southern Garda village. Tours can last anywhere from a couple of hours to an entire day and accommodate up to 28 people per tour. Prices range from €90-450 per boat, but official quotes are given based on the number of people and tour selected.

WALKS

While the southern shore of Lake Garda isn't known for hiking the way the northern part of the lake is, you'll still find a handful of nice, flat trails.

Desenzano to Sirmione

The trail from the center of Desenzano to the village of Sirmione on the Sirmione Peninsula is one option for a walk. Start your journey on the waterfront in the center of town, then continue east along the shore, following the water's edge for nearly 6 miles (10 kilometers) over a course of a couple of hours. Along the way, you'll encounter plenty of bars, restaurants, and benches to stop for a break or simply admire the water at your feet. Once you're in Sirmione, you can turn back and walk the same way that you came, or take a ferry back to Desenzano.

NIGHTLIFE

Coco Beach

Via Catullo 5, Lonato del Garda,
tel. 392/172-1659, www.cocobeachclub.com,
summer daily 8pm-4am, €15-20

Coco Beach is one of Lake Garda's most popular disco clubs. On the weekends, this place is flooded with young locals, mostly aged 20-30, coming for a night of drinking and dancing to popular new music spun by DJs. On Friday and Saturday evening, starting at 9:30pm, you can reserve a dinner table for your group. On Sunday there's a happy-hour buffet starting at 6pm, but the club doesn't come to life until midnight. In the summer, you'll find an interesting mix of locals and international tourists filling the multiple dance floors and beach-style lounge furniture. The first drink is included in the entrance price, with all subsequent drinks costing around €10 each. There is also a restaurant and beach that you can enjoy during the day.

FOOD

CASUAL DINING

Pizzeria San Benedetto

Via S. Benedetto 151, Desenzano del Garda,
tel. 030/999-1976, daily 6pm-11pm, €7-15

For a classic Italian dinner that doesn't break the bank, head to Pizzeria San Benedetto in the center of Desenzano for a traditional pizza and beer combo. The atmosphere is casual, and you can see your pizza being put into the large brick oven as soon as it's made. Pizzas range from simple *margheritas* to those with plenty of toppings, such as sausage, pepperoni, potato, zucchini, and more. Tables can be reserved, which isn't a bad idea on weekends, and pizzas can also be ordered to go.

✪ La Cambusa

Via Canonica 12, Desenzano Del Garda, tel. 342/762-7535, Mon., Tues., Thurs.-Sat. 10:30am-2am, Sun. 10:30am-midnight, Wed. 3:30pm-1am, €15-25

This tiny hole-in-the-wall restaurant sits back from the lake, in a quiet corner in the center of Desenzano, and is known mostly for its robust *tagliere:* plates of local meats, cheeses, honeys, and jams. You really can't have a complete meal here without starting with a *tagliere.* From there, you'll find a small menu of Italian classics, such as lasagna and spaghetti. The cozy and unpretentious atmosphere is accented by mismatched decorations, plates, and mugs. At the front of the restaurant where you pay your bill, you'll find a selection of local products available

an appetizer at La Cambusa

for purchase. Book ahead here in the evenings, as the tables are limited and can fill up.

FINE DINING
Molin22

Via Tommaso dal Molin 22, Desenzano del Garda, tel. 030/991-4437, www.molin22.it, Tues.-Fri. noon-10pm, Sat.-Sun. 10am-11pm, €25-50

Dining on the terrace at Molin22 with a sensational cocktail in hand is one of the hidden treats of Desenzano. The large patio overlooks the blue waters of Lake Garda, and customers come back for the innovative and well-balanced cocktails time and time again. Dishes are classic Italian with a modern twist, so you'll see traditional local ingredients such as Garda olive oil, tomatoes, pasta, and *risotto* mixed with fresh cheeses and asparagus, or paired with black sepia chips or colorful flowers. You can also stop by in the late afternoon for a cocktail at happy hour.

✪ La Rucola 2.0

Strentelle Pass 7, Sirmione, tel. 030/916-326, www.ristorantelarucola.it, noon-10pm daily, €30-70

La Rucola 2.0 is a Michelin-star restaurant known for innovative and modern cuisine that is almost too beautiful and artistic to eat. The flavors of each dish, from the *risotto* with roasted rabbit to the octopus and tuna, are strong and perfectly balanced, composed of the highest-quality ingredients. The atmosphere is modern and upscale without feeling pretentious, and the staff is knowledgeable and attentive. You can opt for the daily fixed menu or order à la carte. Book ahead, regardless of when you're coming, as this place is as popular as it is special.

Carducci Square in Sirmione

Ristorante Esplanade

Via Lario 3, Desenzano Del Garda, tel. 030/914-3361, www.ristorante-esplanade. com, daily 12:30pm-1:45pm and 8pm-10pm, €30-70

Ristorante Esplanade is a great fine-dining spot that offers one of the best views of Lake Garda. Food here is high-quality and beautifully presented, with plates including raw seafood, fresh cheese, homemade pasta, and sensational desserts full of chocolate and fruit. Customers consistently rave about the exceptional, attentive, and friendly service here, with staff well prepared to give you the best experience from start to finish. The ambience leans toward elegant, so dress accordingly and book ahead, and request a table on the terrace for a lulling view of the water.

ACCOMMODATIONS

UNDER €80
Hotel Giardinetto

Via Guglielmo Marconi 33, Desenzano del Garda, 030/914-1228, www. hotel-giardinetto.com/reservation.html, €90

Located in the center of Desenzano is this classic, simple, family-run hotel with free parking and a breakfast buffet included in each room. The exterior is surrounded by colorful plants, and the area is full of restaurants, bars, and shopping. Each room includes a private bathroom with toiletries, air-conditioning, safe, television, and Wi-Fi. For those looking for a comfortable stay without any frills, Hotel Giardinetto is a great choice.

€80-150
✪ Corte San Michele

Località San Michele, 1, Desenzano del Garda, tel. 333/774-9532, www.cortesanmichele.it, €85

This quaint and modern B&B features exposed stone walls and bright guest rooms with handmade quilts, exposed wood-beamed ceilings, and antique furniture. The homemade breakfast each morning is plentiful and delicious, and the property, which is near the lake, includes a peaceful outdoor swimming pool and a large garden. Each room includes air-conditioning, Wi-Fi, and a private bathroom. Parking is included.

Alessi Hotel

Via Castello 3, Desenzano del Garda, tel. 030/914-1980, www.hotelalessi.com, €95

The modern, sleek guest rooms at Alessi Hotel are a nice option for those wanting an upscale feel without emptying their wallets. Located in the center of Desenzano and just a stone's throw away from the shore, the hotel includes an internal courtyard as well as two restaurants, a wine bar, a pizzeria, and a terrace. Each room includes a patio or balcony with a garden or city view, air-conditioning, and a private bathroom. A large breakfast buffet and parking are included.

€150-250
✪ Palace Hotel

Viale F. Agello 114A, Desenzano del Garda, 030/990-2262, www.palacehoteldesenzano.it, €160

This bright and elegant hotel sits

right on Lake Garda, and includes a huge pool overlooking the lake and surrounded by greenery and lounge chairs, as well as a smaller infinity pool. The modern interior is classically furnished, and there's a wellness center with a sauna and Turkish bath as well as a selection of massage treatments. Each guest room includes a private patio with a garden view, air-conditioning, a private bathroom with bathtub, and a small living area. A large, fresh breakfast and parking are included in the price of each room.

Hotel Acquaviva del Garda

Viale Francesco Agello 84, Desenzano del Garda, tel. 030/990-1583, www.termedisirmione.com, €180

Hotel Acquaviva del Garda is just under 2 miles (about 3 kilometers) outside the main part of Desenzano del Garda, so it's a tranquil option for those who have cars and want a relaxing, upscale getaway near the lake. Apart from the modern building and interior, the hotel includes an outdoor pool and a private beach as well as a beautiful, colorful garden with views of the lake and Sirmione. The wellness center includes an indoor pool, a hot tub, sauna, and Turkish bath. Each room includes a balcony with a garden or lake view, air-conditioning, Wi-Fi, and a private bathroom. A large breakfast buffet is included in the price of each room, as is parking.

INFORMATION AND SERVICES

The official **tourist office** in Desenzano (Via Porto Vecchio 34, Mon.-Sat. 9am-noon and 3pm-6pm) is located in the center of town. Here you can grab a free map of the city and learn more about the local attractions,

dining, and accommodation options from the English-speaking staff.

In case of emergencies, you can find the local **questura** (police) office at Via Dante Alighieri 17. You need to press the buzzer outside of the gate to enter the building at any time of day or night, and you can call 118 in case of emergency. The hospital of Desenzano is found at Località Montecroce (030/91-451), and it is open 24 hours.

GETTING THERE

BY CAR

Desenzano is 9.3 miles (15 kilometers) west of Peschiera on the SRll road. Normally it's a 20-minute drive, but there's increased traffic in summer when Italians and northern Europeans holiday in the area.

BY TRAIN

Desenzano falls directly on the main rail line connecting Venice and Milan, which means that both *freccia* (high-speed) and regional trains running between the two cities stop in town. **Frecciarossa** (www.trenitalia.it) trains from Venice reach town in 90 minutes and tickets cost €21.90. Regional trains depart hourly from Verona and reach Desenzano in 25 minutes. Tickets cost €4.45. High-speed service is also available but is triple the price and only 10 minutes faster.

GETTING AROUND

As with every town on Lake Garda, the center of the village is entirely walkable, unless you want to get to some of the more remote restaurants or accommodations.

BY CAR

To drive to the village of Sirmione from Desenzano, follow Via Marconi east, staying straight on the road (it eventually turns into Via Molin, then Viale Agello) until you reach Via Colombare, where you need to turn left to head north into the peninsula. From the center of Desenzano to the village of Sirmione, it's about a 25-minute drive spanning 6.2 miles (10 kilometers).

To reach Coco Beach, follow Lungolago Battisti north until it turns into Via Vo'. The club is only a couple of miles north of the main part of town, which is about a 10-minute drive. While there are a handful of paid parking lots and street parking near the center of town, remember that these lots tend to fill up quickly during high season, so you're more likely to find a spot earlier in the day.

BY BOAT

Traveling by boat is the quickest way to get between Desenzano and Sirmione, if you're without a car. From the Desenzano ferry station in the center of town, you can take a 20-minute ferry, which generally departs for Sirmione every hour 8am-10pm, June- October. A one-way ticket costs around €3 per person. Official fares and timetables can be found at www. navigazionelaghi.it.

Lazise

The colorfully charming lakeside town of Lazise offers everything you could want in a little Italian village: a historic medieval castle, cobblestone streets full of local boutiques, peaceful olive groves, and of course, a long waterfront to stroll up and down. Lazise is positioned between Peschiera del Garda and Bardolino on Lake Garda's southeastern shore, about 6 miles (10 kilometers) north of Peschiera and 3 miles (5 kilometers) south of Bardolino on SR249. If you want to avoid the resort crowd of Peschiera, but still have easy access to the family-friendly attractions and theme parks in the area, Lazise is a good place to stay.

SIGHTS

CASTELLO SCALIGERO DI LAZISE

Via Castello 13, tel. 366/422-3017,
www.tourism.verona.it

Although Scaligero Castle is privately owned and now only open for special occasions, its dominating presence in Lazise is unavoidable. You'll more than likely have to walk through a gate in one of the walls to enter the center of town along the lake. The oldest part of the castle dates to AD 983, but because several dates are inscribed on the castle's walls, we know that it was reconstructed several times and changed hands over the centuries. In the latter half of the 19th century, the current owner built a beautiful green park around the castle to combine his love of nature and history, so you can walk around the public gardens on warm summer afternoons. The stone walls and towers evoke a medieval feel, so stop by for a quick walk around the exterior.

CHURCH OF SAINT NICHOLAS
(Chiesa di San Nicolo)

Via Fontana 5, 8:30am-6:30pm; free
The imposing yet beautiful Chiesa di

Lazise's lakeside promenade

San Nicolo sits lakeside in Lazise, surrounded by local fishing boats floating in turquoise waters. The church was originally built in the 12th century, and an earthquake destroyed part of it shortly thereafter. Today, the old stone edifice gives off ancient and rustic vibes. The **tall bell tower** sticks out on the shoreline, and the interior is much more austere than your average, centuries-old Italian church, with only a handful of pews and frescoes scattered across the walls. However, it's worth a step inside to see an Italian church with a different story than those with golden alters and frescoes covering the walls.

MOVIELAND

Via Fossalta 58, Fossalta,
tel. 045/696-9900, www.movieland.it,
Apr.-Sept. daily 10am-7pm, €22-28

Perched between Peschiera del Garda and Lazise is the small but entertaining Movieland amusement park. Although somewhat overshadowed by the larger and more popular Gardaland, Movieland still holds its own by offering Hollywood-themed rides and attractions, including its own Hollywood mountain. Rides include the Hollywood tower falling roller coaster, the House of Horrors, river rapid rides, and more. The park is extremely family-friendly, offering something for children and adults of all ages, and there are restaurants and food stalls serving mainly Italian foods like pizza, pasta, and gelato. This is a great option if you're traveling by car and you want to skip the long lines at Gardaland. You can also catch a free round-trip shuttle from the Peschiera del Garda train station to this theme park.

RECREATION AND ACTIVITIES

WALKS

Waterfront Walk to Bardolino

If you want to enjoy a peaceful, stress-free stroll along the waters of

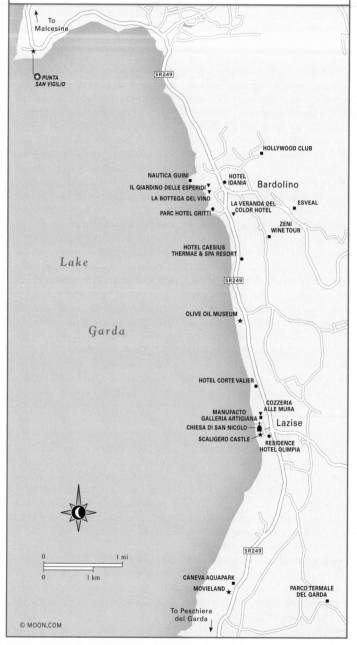

Lazise and Bardolino

To Malcesine

PUNTA SAN VIGILIO

SR249

HOLLYWOOD CLUB

NAUTICA GUINI
IL GIARDINO DELLE ESPERIDI
LA BOTTEGA DEL VINO
PARC HOTEL GRITTI

HOTEL IDANIA

Bardolino

LA VERANDA DEL COLOR HOTEL

ESVEAL

ZENI WINE TOUR

HOTEL CAESIUS THERMAE & SPA RESORT

SR249

Lake

OLIVE OIL MUSEUM

Garda

HOTEL CORTE VALIER

COZZERIA ALLE MURA

MANUFACTO GALLERIA ARTIGIANA
CHIESA DI SAN NICOLO
SCALIGERO CASTLE

Lazise

RESIDENCE HOTEL OLIMPIA

0   1 mi

0   1 km

SR249

CANEVA AQUAPARK
MOVIELAND

PARCO TERMALE DEL GARDA

To Peschiera del Garda

© MOON.COM

Lake Garda, wander away from the shoreline to the middle of Lazise, heading north to Bardolino. The stroll, which is only about 3 miles (5 kilometers), takes around an hour each way, so you can easily fit the walk into a single morning or afternoon, stopping for a glass of wine or lunch at one of the many bars and restaurants along the way. Your path is completely paved and flat the entire way, making it easy for families to complete the journey.

WATER PARK
Caneva Aquapark
Via Fossalta 56, Fossalta, tel. 045/696-9900, www.canevaworld.it, daily 10am-7pm, €22-28

This Caribbean-themed aquapark is one of Lazise's biggest summer hits, complete with thrilling waterslides, diving boards, a lazy river, an adults-only pool, and restaurants and bars to keep you fueled and hydrated all day. With multiple pools and areas to lounge, it's easy to pass an entire fun-filled day beating the heat here. For a thrill, take a ride down either the new SuperSplash or Stukas Boom waterslides, or relax for a while floating along the Windy Lagoon or Lazy River. For those with children, keep in mind that the park gets pretty crowded as the day continues, so come early, grab some lounge chairs, and hang out before the swarm of people arrive to cool down.

If you're not traveling by car, you can catch the free shuttle bus to the Caneva park from the Peschiera del Garda train station. The shuttle runs during the park's opening hours, departing every 30 minutes or so in both directions. Official shuttle timetables can be found on the water park's website.

WELLNESS CENTERS
Parco Termale del Garda
Via Madonna 23, Colá, tel. 045/759-0988, www.villadeicedri.it, daily 9:30am-11pm, €16-24

This public wellness center located at a local villa is one of Lake Garda's most relaxing places to spend an afternoon. The warm thermal pools are sourced from a local spring, with the average water temperature around 34°C (93°F). The park has two small lakes, and within each one you'll find Jacuzzis, jets, waterfalls, geysers, and other hydromassages. The first lake dates back to the 18th century, and the additional lake and the rest of the water features were slowly added on over time. In the villa and around the property, you'll also find a gym, bar, restaurant, and cafeteria, as well as medical spas offering massages and other wellness treatments. When the sun sets and most families go home for the evening, the crowd thins out and the place gets a little more intimate, with lights illuminating the water in the dark.

The best way to reach the wellness center is by car. Follow the SP5 east outside of the center of Lazise for a few kilometers until you reach the Verona Lago Hotel, then turn right following the signs pointing you to the villa and wellness center. Once you reach the small village of Cool, turn right on Via Madonna and continue straight until you reach the parking area for the center. From Lazise, it's a 4-mile (7-kilometer) drive that takes about 10 minutes.

SHOPPING
Manufacto Galleria Artigiana
Vicolo Gafforini 16/18, tel. 347/319-3177, www.manufacto.it, Tues.-Sun. 10am-12:30pm and 3:30pm-7pm

Whether or not you plan to shop

during your time on Lake Garda, if you're in Lazise, stop inside this little treasure of a shop. The entire store is filled with handmade creations from a local goldsmith; here you'll find everything from intricate jewelry to unique decor pieces. You won't find price tags all over the room, as the establishment is just as much a gallery as it is a shop. But if you're looking for a one-of-a-kind souvenir or gift to bring back from Lake Garda, you're sure to find something here.

FOOD
Cozzeria Alle Mura
Via Cansignorio 16, tel. 045/647-0644, www.cozzeria.com, daily noon-2pm, Mon.-Wed. 6pm-10:30pm, €12-30
Come as you are to this casual, laid-back seafood restaurant in the heart of Lazise. The place is beloved by both locals and tourists, with the huge plates of mussels in a tomato broth being the main draw. While you'll find a handful of non-seafood items, it's almost a sin to come here and not get a fish-related dish. You'll find grilled and fried seafood options. The place gets fairly packed in the evenings, especially on the weekends, so book ahead if possible.

ACCOMMODATIONS
Residence Hotel Olimpia
Piazzale Marra 4, tel. 045/758-0123, €130
This simple yet satisfactory hotel consistently garners positive reviews for its high-quality service and staff. The hotel is housed in an old, expanded villa, with classically and minimally furnished rooms and a beautiful outdoor pool in the back surrounded by lawn chairs and palm trees, making an afternoon here feel like you've escaped to a quiet, private corner of paradise. Each guest room includes air-conditioning and private

bathroom. Parking and breakfast are included in the price of each room, and lake access is just outside the property.

Hotel Corte Valier
Via della Pergolana, 9, 045/647-1210, www.cortevalier.com, €170
This modern, luxurious hotel is one of the largest properties in Lazise, complete with a lakeside pool, bar with a terrace overlooking the lake, fine-dining restaurant, and a highly rated spa that includes an indoor pool, Finnish sauna, Turkish bath, and a selection of massage treatments. The hotel sits just outside the center of Lazise, so you're far enough away from the noise of tourist crowds but close enough to walk into town for the day without needing to move your car (free parking is available for guests). Each modern and sleekly decorated room is air-conditioned and equipped with a balcony and private bathroom. A large continental breakfast is included.

GETTING THERE AND AROUND
BY CAR
From Peschiera del Garda, follow the signs for SR249 and head north to Lazise. It's an 8-mile (13-kilometer) drive that takes about 20 minutes. A handful of paid parking lots are available near the center of town, although they fill up very quickly in the summer, so arrive early to find parking or consider finding an accommodation that offers free parking for guests.

BY TRAIN AND BUS
From Verona's Porta Nuova train station, grab the 163, 164, or 185 ATV bus to the center of Lazise. Buses usually depart once an hour 7:13am-7:20pm daily. Tickets can be purchased at the public transit office in the train

station, and generally run between €3-10 one-way. Official timetables and fares can be found at www.atv.verona.it/Linee_e_orari_autobus.

BY BOAT

Public ferries run from Bardolino and Peschiera del Garda to Lazise 8:30am-6:30pm. The trip from Peschiera is about 30 minutes, and from Bardolino, it's about 20 minutes, with fares running €3-10 one-way per person. The ferry station is in the center of the village lakefront. Official fares and timetables can be found at www.navigazionelaghi.it.

Bardolino

The little village of Bardolino is known nationally in Italy for its delicious red wine and high-quality olive oil pressed from locally grown olives. Sitting about six miles (nine kilometers) north of Peschiera on SR249, the small town dates back to at least the early Middle Ages, although human traces from the prehistoric era were once found here.

While walking around town, you'll experience a nice balance of Italy's modern lake life, with the town's rainbow-colored residences, local shops, and restaurants complementing the historic architecture, including the 12th-century city walls and gates that guide you around the city as well as its numerous ancient churches. All of Bardolino can be easily seen in a day, and because there's plenty to do all along Lake Garda's eastern shore, it can serve as a great home base.

SIGHTS
OLIVE OIL MUSEUM
(Museo dell'Olio)

Via Peschiera 54, Cisano, tel. 045/622-9047, www.museum.it, daily 9am-12:30pm and 2:30pm-7pm, free

Owned and operated by a local family, the Olive Oil Museum in Bardolino was opened in 1987 and is the first museum in the world focused on the process of making olive oil. The completely free museum allows visitors to take a look at the step-by-step process of turning olives into oil, including a view of the giant stone mill used to smash the olives. The guides do a great job outlining the importance of olive oil for their region, and explaining how the process has changed over hundreds of years. Video guides are available in English, German, French, Dutch, and Italian. At the end of your museum visit, check out the shop full of olive-related products and purchase a bottle of local extra virgin olive oil or other organic foods.

✪ PUNTA SAN VIGILIO

Via S. Vigilio 17, Garda, tel. 349/939-5748, www.punta-sanvigilio.it, late May-Oct. daily 9:30am-8pm, €3-12

Punta San Vigilio, which is actually about 3.7 miles (6 kilometers) north of Bardolino, is a quiet, green peninsula jutting out into the eastern side of Lake Garda. It's full of cypress trees and olive groves that cover a little less than 2 miles (3 kilometers) of natural space. While locals enjoy spending time here year-round for its tranquility and beauty, it can get particularly busy during summer. The peninsula includes a 16th-century villa that now houses a luxury hotel, a peaceful park with a beach, a swimming pool, and another elegant accommodation option. Regardless of your reason for visiting, you'll enjoy the feeling of being lost in a secluded piece of quiet paradise. While parking directly on the peninsula is limited, there is an hourly paid parking lot nearby, just off the SR249. From the parking lot, it's about a 10-minute walk down a gravel path to the shore.

If you want to spend a few hours at the point, start by taking a walk along the shore of the peninsula to the small port, from which you can see the lake, tall dark trees, and the tumbling mountains in the distance. Bring a towel with you and park yourself near the water for an hour or so under a shady tree with a drink in hand, as you'll find a handful of bars and inns along this walk.

WINERIES
Zeni Wine Tour
Via Costabella 9, tel. 045/721-0022,
www.zeni.it, €5-20, tours on request
For a truly local experience that will enlighten you as to the significance of Bardolino wine culture, book a tour and tasting at the Zeni winery in Bardolino. Call ahead to book your tour, which can be arranged in Italian or English, for up to 10 people. The tour includes a walk through the on-site wine museum, which gives you a detailed history of regional wines and of the winery itself. It also includes a quick walk through the vineyards and other production areas of the site. You'll end the tour with a wine tasting of a Zeni Bardolino bottle of your choice; tour prices may change, depending on your tasting selection. The staff is incredibly affable

and convincingly enthusiastic about what they do, making it a fun way to spend two or three hours of your day. The winery itself is located a couple of miles from the lake; walk from the center of town steadily up the hill to the winery, or book a taxi (try Taxi Bardolino, www.bardolinotaxi.it).

RECREATION AND ACTIVITIES
WALKS
Waterfront Walk to Punta San Vigilio
For a beautiful and relaxing family-friendly stroll, try this waterfront trail. Note that the paved pathway has a very minor incline. From Bardolino, the 3.7 mile (6-kilometer) walk will take about 1.25 hours. The walkway is easy to follow, as you just continue north the whole way until you reach the peninsula, which is marked by signs. You'll also see the way the peninsula extends into the lake. Along the way, you'll find shady areas, benches for resting, bars and restaurants for refreshment, local shops, and more. The walk is short enough to make a round-trip in a full morning or afternoon.

BOAT RENTAL
Nautica Guini
Punta Cornicello Bardolino,
tel. 346/288-6677, www.nauticaguini.it,
daily 9am-7pm, from €40
To enjoy a private boat excursion for up to eight people, this experienced local company rents boats to those with and without licenses. By renting your own boat, you can avoid road traffic and get to other lake towns, such as Sirmione or Punta San Vigilio, much more swiftly. The friendly and professional staff prepares you before departure with all of the information and equipment that you'll need. Boats

can be rented with or without gas, by the hour or day. Each boat includes a GPS system, a sun deck, awning, bathroom, safety equipment, and life jackets (also available in children's sizes). To rent a boat, you'll need a valid identification card as well as a €250 cash deposit. You can book a boat in advance directly on the website.

NIGHTLIFE
Hollywood Club

Via Montavoletta 11, Bardolino,
tel. 045/721-0580, www.hollywood.it,
Wed.-Fri. 8:30pm-4am, €5-35

Hollywood is one of Lake Garda's most popular night clubs; it is definitely the hottest weekend spot for young locals. The multilevel space has low neon lighting, several dance floors, and lounges. The outdoor space is modern and upscale, with small pools and comfortable patio furniture for those who want to enjoy the night air and chat. You'll often find DJs and live pop and house music acts playing here. It also offers a menu of dinner selections for those who want to come early, grab a table, and enjoy a full night here.

SHOPPING
Esveal

Contrada Ceola 19, Bardolino,
tel. 370/724-1618, www.esveal.it, daily
10:30am-12:30pm and 2pm-6:30pm

This small but professional shop sells high-quality organic products sourced from local farms on Lake Garda, including certified organic olive oil that can be bought by the bottle; there's plain olive oil, or oil infused with garlic, orange, lemon, or chili peppers. They also sell traditional limoncello made from lemons grown on local farms. You will find the owners to be

very approachable, and they're fluent in Italian, English, German, and French.

FOOD
ITALIAN
Il Giardino delle Esperidi

Via Mameli 1, Bardolino, 045/621-0477, daily
5pm-11:30pm, Sat.-Sun. 11am-3pm, €20-50

Diners at Il Giardino delle Esperidi are always raving about the flavors here, including baked parmesan and truffles, local meats and fresh lake fish, stuffed pastas, suckling pig, and to-die-for chocolate cake. What's more unique about this place: It's run entirely by women, with a female chef, waitstaff, and hostess. Low lighting illuminates the large wooden cabinets filled with local and national wines. This spot is perfect for a cozy date, but it's also amenable to families.

La Veranda del Color Hotel

Via Santa Cristina 5,
Bardolino, 045/621-0857,
www.ristorantelaverandabardolino.it,
daily 7pm-9:30pm, €20-60

This Michelin-star restaurant epitomizes everything that is fine dining: exquisite flavors, high-quality ingredients, beautifully plated dishes, attentive and friendly staff beaming with pride about their establishment, and an elegant, reserved atmosphere. Yet, despite its reputation as one of the finest dining establishments on Lake Garda, it doesn't feel unapproachable. Try the beef tartare, handmade stuffed pastas, fresh fish, scallops, and more. The dress code is a little more formal than other restaurants in the area, so bear this in mind if you choose to dine here. Be sure to book a table a couple of days in advance, especially during high season.

WINE BARS
La Bottega del Vino

Piazza S. Nicolò 46, Bardolino,
328/701-0914, daily 10am-2am, €5-15

This cozy wine bar in the middle of Bardolino is a hot spot for locals and tourists alike, with a huge selection of both wines and beers, and beautiful *tagliere* plates served from open to close. Select from a handful of plates including a cheese-tasting board, locally sourced cold cuts, *caprese* (salad of tomato, mozzarella cheese, and basil), and more, all served with a large basket of freshly made bread and crackers. Of course, if you're in Bardolino, you can't miss the opportunity to try the well-known bardolino red wine. The bar also has a vibrant, buzzing happy hour and a small selection of sandwiches for those who want an official meal.

ACCOMMODATIONS
Parc Hotel Gritti

Via Gabriele D'Annunzio 1, Bardolino,
tel. 045/621-5011,
www.parchotelgrittibardolino.it, €120

Situated right on the shore of Lake Garda, the Parc Hotel Gritti is one of the more refined, luxurious accommodations in Bardolino, complete with two pools (one indoor and one outdoor), three Italian restaurants and bars, a gym, sauna, Turkish bath, and a selection of beauty treatments from the wellness center. The space is bright and covered in beautiful green trees and vines, with rooms that reflect a balanced mix of antique furniture and modern details. Each guest room is equipped with air-conditioning, Wi-Fi, and private bathroom. A substantial buffet breakfast and parking are included in the price of each room.

Hotel Idania

Via Marconi 18, Bardolino, tel.
045/621-0122, www.hotelidania.com, €140

Situated in the heart of Bardolino, a five-minute walk away from Lake Garda's shores, is this comfortable, classic hotel with an outdoor pool. The hotel is beautifully decorated with classic hotel furniture, and the inviting outdoor areas are bursting with colorful plants, giving the place a more home-like feel than other hotels. Each guest room includes air-conditioning, Wi-Fi, and a private bathroom. A continental breakfast and parking are included in the price of each room.

Hotel Caesius Thermae & Spa Resort

Via Peschiera, 3, Bardolino,
tel. 045/721-9100,
www.hotelcaesiusterme.com, €255

The beautiful and luxurious Hotel Caesius Thermae & Spa Resort is so relaxing that it's tempting to spend your entire Garda holiday on the property. If you're looking for an upscale wellness center situated right on the lake, this is your place. You'll find a gorgeous outdoor swimming pool overlooking the waters of Lake Garda, and a cool and relaxing indoor swimming pool. There are also multiple saunas and Turkish baths, a gym, a tea room, on-site wine cellar, three Italian restaurants and bars, and various relaxing lounge spaces. Each room includes air-conditioning, Wi-Fi, and private bathroom. A large buffet breakfast and parking are included in the price of each room.

GETTING THERE AND AROUND
BY CAR

From Peschiera del Garda follow the signs to SR249 north to Bardolino. The

11-mile (18-kilometer) journey can be made in less than 30 minutes. In summer, it can be faster to take the two-lane SR450 freeway. A handful of paid parking lots are available near the center of town, although they fill up very quickly in the summer, so arrive early to find parking or consider finding an accommodation that offers free parking for guests.

BY BUS
From Verona's Porta Nuova train station, grab the 163, 164, or 185 ATV bus to the center of Bardolino. Buses depart once an hour daily 7:13am-7:20pm. Tickets can be purchased at the public transit office in the train station, and generally run between €3-10 one-way. Official timetables and fares are posted at www.atv.verona.it.

BY BOAT
Infrequent public ferries run from Lazise and Peschiera del Garda to Bardolino 8:30am-6:30pm. The trip from Peschiera is about 45 minutes, and from Lazise it's about 20 minutes, with fares running €3-10 one-way per person. The ferry station can be found in the center of the village lakefront. Official fares and timetables are posted at www.navigazionelaghi.it.

Malcesine

This lakeside town is the perfect mix of history and natural beauty. The 13th-century Castello Scaligero, with its stone exterior and tower, preside over a bustling town teeming with colorful residential buildings, small shops, and restaurants. The town's backdrop, the giant Monte Baldo, is arguably the most well-known and important mountain range in the province of Verona, and is accessible by cable car from the town. For those looking to enjoy the outdoors—whether down by the lake or up in the mountains—Malcesine is a great spot to visit.

Malcesine sits on the northeastern shore of Lake Garda, about 11 miles (18 kilometers) south of Riva del Garda and 18.6 miles (30 kilometers) north of Bardolino.

SIGHTS
SCALIGER CASTLE (Castello Scaligero)
Via Castello, tel. 045/657-0333, www. comunemalcesine.it, daily 9:30am-7pm, €6

It's impossible to spend a day in Malcesine, or simply drive through it, without admiring the medieval Castello Saligero, perched up on a rocky cliff overlooking Lake Garda and the town of Malcesine below. The stone guard tower looms over the rest of the area, serving as an undeniable symbol of the rich history of the Garda region.

The castle is presumed to date back to the Lombard Period (starting from AD 568), but it was destroyed by the Franks in 590 and later rebuilt into its current structure. Although the fortress traded hands many times over

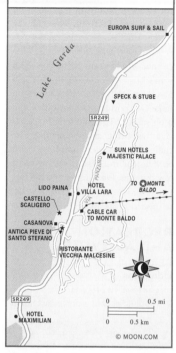

Malcesine

EUROPA SURF & SAIL

Lake Garda

SPECK & STUBE

SR249

SUN HOTELS
MAJESTIC PALACE

VIA PANZANO

LIDO PAINA

HOTEL
VILLA LARA

TO MONTE
BALDO

CASTELLO
SCALIGERO

CABLE CAR
TO MONTE BALDO

CASANOVA

ANTICA PIEVE DI
SANTO STEFANO

RISTORANTE
VECCHIA MALCESINE

SR249

HOTEL
MAXIMILIAN

| 0 | 0.5 mi |
| 0 | 0.5 km |

© MOON.COM

the centuries, it was most notably the home of Alberto della Scala of the important Scaliger family, as well as the Milanese Visconti family.

Today, you can walk through the quiet courtyard and enter the castle, now home to a Natural History Museum (same hours and included in the entrance price to the castle), which gives visitors a multisensory experience of the regional landscape and wildlife. A tour of the castle takes you through several antique-filled rooms, small gardens and courtyards, and a beautiful balcony overlooking the waters of the lake. End your tour by going up to the tower for gorgeous views overlooking the entire town of Malcesine and the serene lake below you.

ANTICA PIEVE DI SANTO STEFANO

Via Parrocchia 14, tel. 045/740-0065, free

This 8th-century church sits on a hilltop overlooking Malcesine, home to what was once a pagan temple and later turned into a Catholic church. Easily reachable by a marked, sloped footpath (or a parallel sloped road) from the central waterfront promenade, the church can be seen over the trees and buildings in town. Inside, the church's white walls are intermittently adorned with framed fresco paintings, with an intricately detailed arched ceiling directing the eyes to a larger colorful fresco above the altar. Given that the church is located off of the lake, many visitors miss it, but it is well worth a few minutes of your time. Consider it a quiet escape from the crowds. Daily Mass occurs here, so make sure to remain quiet as you enter.

TOP EXPERIENCE

❂ MONTE BALDO

The Monte Baldo mountain range is arguably the best known and most beloved among the Veronese, spanning a total of 25 miles (40 kilometers)

Monte Baldo overlooking Lake Garda

between the provinces of Trento and Verona along the northeastern border of Lake Garda. The mountains, primarily made of calcareous rocks, peak at 7,277 feet (2,218 meters). Near the foot of the range, you'll find such Mediterranean flora as olive trees, chestnut trees, and rosemary bushes. Near the top, the earth is very rocky, with wild herbs growing among the stones. Monte Baldo offers many outdoor recreation options, such as hiking and paragliding. There's also the cable car to Monte Baldo, which offers visual rewards and is less physically taxing.

Cable Car to Monte Baldo (Funivie di Malcesine e del Monte Baldo)

Via Navene Vecchia 12, tel. 045/740-0206, www.funiviedelbaldo.it, late Mar.-early Nov. daily 8am-7pm , €10 round-trip

For truly unforgettable and unmatched panoramic views of Lake Garda, the rest of the mountain range, and the towns below, grab the cable car to the top of Monte Baldo from the center of Malcesine. The cable car system itself is one of the most modern and high-tech in the world. Each car has windows on all sides, so you won't miss a single angle. This trip gives you the best aerial views on Lake Garda and gets busy quickly in high season. To avoid long lines, arrive first thing in the morning. The cable car runs every half hour, with each ascent and descent lasting just a few minutes. Once you get to the top, you'll find a small station with a flat, natural viewing area.

RECREATION AND ACTIVITIES

BEACH
Lido Paina

Localitá Paina 49, 24/7, free

This public pebble beach is just north

Malcesine

Malcesine Beach

of the Scaliger Castle and a quick walk from the center of town. The small public park area includes a swimming raft out on the lake, beach volleyball courts, a small skateboard park, and a separate recreation area where you'll usually find little kids kicking around a soccer ball while taking a break from the water. Along the shore, you'll pass several bars and restaurants before you get to the ferry dock, where the beach ends. A large parking lot is located directly next to the beach. Because the beach is public and free, it fills up quickly in the summer, so come stake your spot early in the morning or later in the afternoon to grab a place near the water.

HIKING

San Zeno di Montagna

Via Canevoi, San Zeno di Montagna

For an easy walking trail that avoids the crowds around the cable car on Monte Baldo, start on Via Canevoi in the small village of San Zeno di Montagna, which is reachable by driving about 12.5 miles (20 kilometers) south of Malcesine on the SR249. Follow its entire length of 6.2 miles (10 kilometers) until it circles back around to the starting point. The path takes you through the Sperane pinewood to the small historic mountain village of Lumini, then to the summit

of Mount Belpo in the Monte Baldo range. From there, you'll pass a small adventure park, pass through Dosso Croce (cross on Via Dosso Croce), and wind up back where you started. The entire trip climbs to around 984 feet (300 meters) and usually takes about 2.5 hours to complete. Because it's a fairly easy path—mostly paved or guided by tarmac with minor elevation changes—it's suitable for beginners as well as families with young children. It is open every day of the year without any entrance fee.

Peace Trail
(Sentiero della Pace CAI Path)

Peak of Monte Baldo, near the cable car station

Near the peak of Monte Baldo, you'll find the Peace Trail, part of a significant and historic long-distance path that follows a former World War I military trail. Although the Peace Trail is just a small fraction of the famous E5 long-distance trail that starts in Brittany, France, and passes through Italy, you can hike as much of it as you want, then simply turn back around in the direction from which you came. The dirt path makes for an easy, stress-free trek. To find the trail, exit the cable car and look for posted signs directing you to the Sentiero della Pace CAI path. The trail isn't very steep in this area, but bring water and take general safety precautions when hiking.

ADVENTURE AND WATER SPORTS
Fly2Fun

Via Navene Vecchia 12, tel. 334/946-9757, www.tandemparagliding.eu, €150

If you are an adventure lover and want an unparalleled experience during your stay on Lake Garda, try tandem paragliding off the summit of Monte Baldo and land near the village of Malcesine. Seasoned paragliding professionals in the area have years of experience with this jump and make the entire time both fun and thrilling. The 20- to 40-minute glide down to the foot of the mountain gives you amazing aerial views of Lake Garda and Malcesine below. You'll start your day at the cable car station in Malcesine before catching a car up to the summit of Monte Baldo (the cable car ticket is included in the price of the flight). You'll meet your paragliding pilot at the jumping-off point near the top of the mountain, gear up (wear comfortable clothes and tennis shoes), learn more about the safety and overall experience, and then tandem-jump off the mountain top.

Europa Surf & Sail

Via Gardesana 205, tel. 338/605-3096, www.europasurfandsail.com, Apr.-mid-Oct. daily 9am-6pm, €10-300

From this locally run surf and sailing center on the banks of Malcesine, you can rent stand-up paddleboards, catamarans, wind sails, dinghies, kayaks, and bikes. For beginners, the on-site sailing school offers hourly lessons for windsurfers, and those who want to try the dinghies, catamarans, and stand-up paddleboards. The friendly and professional certified instructors are fluent in English, Italian, and German. All equipment can be rented by the hour or day, and various clothing and protective equipment can be rented as well. The sailing center includes nearby parking, a restaurant and bar, changing rooms, and showers. Equipment can be booked in advance if you call ahead or contact the center through the form on their website.

SHOPPING
Casanova

Vicolo Cieco di Mezzo 13, tel. 045/740-0728, daily 9:30am-12:30pm and 3pm-6pm

This beloved and authentic linen shop in Malcesine is owned and operated by Antonella, a local who infuses all her creations with her own personality and style. Stop in to admire the fabric piled in every which direction and her workstation with simple sewing machine in the center of the store. Her impressive handmade collection of quilts, pillowcases, kitchen linens, and more make nice souvenirs.

FOOD
Speck & Stube

Via Navene Vecchia 139, tel. 045/740-1177, daily noon-11:45pm, €15-25

For a casual, quick bite with giant, filling portions, head to the cafeteria-style Speck & Stube. The German-inspired restaurant serves up plenty of roasted meats, including ribs, rotisserie chickens, hamburgers, and sausages, with sides like french fries, pickles, fresh bread, and prosciutto crudo. The idea is simple: grab a tray and fill it with as much food as you want from the various stations, top it off with a pint of one of the many varieties of beer, pay for your meal at the cash register, then head out to the covered patio for a casual meal in the garden.

✪ Ristorante Vecchia Malcesine

Via Pisort 6, tel. 045/740-0469, www.vecchiamalcesine.com, Thurs.-Tues., noon-2pm and 7pm-10pm €30-80

This upscale local restaurant, popular among locals and tourists, has put itself on the Michelin map for its original and delicious tasting menu. After earning its first star, it continues to receive fabulous reviews for its breathtaking setting overlooking Lake Garda, attentive service, and a seven-course tasting menu complete with perfect wine pairings. While a la carte dishes for both first and second courses are available (such as pasta, *risotto*, and lake fish dishes), stick to the daily tasting menu (about €140 per person, including your choice of paired wine) for a real treat. Dishes from this menu may include beautifully plated shrimp cocktail, asparagus *risotto*, perfectly cooked steak and fish, biscotti, and more. Book a few days in advance for lunch or dinner, and note that the dress code is formal.

ACCOMMODATIONS

Hotel Villa Lara

Via Gardesana 108, tel. 045/740-0411, www.villalaramalcesine.it, €50

Just a short walk outside Malcesine, this small hotel is similar to a B&B and is run by the Benamati family. It features a few simple furnished guest rooms surrounded by a small garden with olive trees and other green plants, giving it a private, cozy feel. Each room comes with either a mountain or lake view from the balcony, as well as a private bathroom and free Wi-Fi. Upon booking, specify if you want meals included during your stay. Breakfast is included in the price of the room, but you can also add dinners for €10-15 extra per room, per evening. There is also parking, and an outdoor pool and Jacuzzi available for guests in the warmer months.

Sun Hotels Majestic Palace

Via Navene Vecchia 96, tel. 045/740-0383, www.sunhotels.it, €200

This beautiful hotel feels like a little corner of paradise. The property is huge and includes several outdoor swimming pools and **gardens**. You'll find it 0.6 miles (1 kilometer) away from the lake and about a mile (2 kilometers) away from the center of town, giving you plenty of privacy away from the crowds. The hotel also has an Italian restaurant and bar, indoor pool, and gym. The guest rooms are spacious and classically decorated. Each is equipped with air-conditioning, Wi-Fi, and private bathroom. A large breakfast buffet is included in the price of each room, as is parking.

Hotel Maximilian

Via Val di Sogno 6, tel. 045/740-0317, www.hotelmaximilian.com, €260

This sleek, modern, and upscale hotel sits right on Lake Garda, with a large outdoor infinity pool and an intimate hot tub surrounded by bright green gardens that open up to beautiful views of the water. Directly below the hotel sits a quiet pebble beach; the hotel has its own sun loungers and lawn area near the lake as well. Each room features modern decor and includes a balcony with either a garden or lake view, air-conditioning, Wi-Fi, and private bathroom. Breakfast each morning and parking are included in the price of the room.

GETTING THERE AND AROUND

BY CAR

Malcesine is 40 miles (65 kilometers) northwest of Verona. The shortest route is an hour and 20 minutes. Take the A22 highway north and exit at Laffi-Lago di Garda Sud. From there follow SP9 to Varesche and take the SP8 west to Garda and the SR249 north to town.

From Peschiera del Garda follow the signs for SR249 and head north to Malcesine. The towns are 34 miles (55 kilometers) apart and the drive takes an hour. A handful of paid parking lots are available near the center of town, although they fill up very quickly in the summer, so arrive early to find parking, or consider finding an accommodation that offers free parking for guests.

BY TRAIN AND BUS

From the Peschiera del Garda station, grab one of the ATV buses running from the train station. Lines 483 and 484 run between Peschiera del Garda, Malcesine, and Riva del Garda. Buses generally depart 6:30am-8:30pm daily, but you can check official timetables and prices at www.atv.verona. it. Tickets, which cost €2.80-4 one-way, can be purchased in the bars or tobacco shops at the Peschiera del Garda train station. You can also ask the staff there for a physical timetable for the buses. Each two-hour trip departs hourly 8:22am-6:52pm daily. Line 27 departs from Desenzano six times a day and reaches Malcesine in less than two hours.

BY BOAT

Infrequent public ferries run from Riva del Garda to Malcesine 8:30am-6:30pm. The trip takes about an hour, with fares running €3-10 one-way per person. The ferry station can be found in the center of the village lakefront. Journey time from Descenzano to Riva is three hours on catamaran speedboats or five hours on slower boats. Ferries leave hourly in summer and at 9am and 9:10am in winter.

Riva del Garda

Sitting at the very top of Lake Garda, Riva del Garda (often just called Riva) is arguably the most beautiful town on the lake. The resort town is a perfect mix of gorgeous natural views, relaxation, recreation, and history, providing enough of each to fill a full, long weekend here. With the giant Italian Dolomites serving as the backdrop, the colorful squares hug the shoreline and bring life to the northern tip of the lake. Riva is unique in that, due to its northern position, you see a true blend of Mediterranean and German cultural influences there, especially in terms of architecture (you'll see more wood-beamed ceilings and cozy inns) and food.

The neighboring village of Arco is just north of Riva del Garda, and although it is not on the lakeshore, it is just as beautiful and historic. The two towns are often seen together by tourists, and both get equally flooded during the summer months. Northern European travelers especially find this area alluring, as it offers a taste of the Mediterranean lifestyle without requiring a drive to the sea.

Other than neighboring Limone Sul Garda to the southeast and Torbole to the southwest, there are few other resort towns in the area, and Riva del Garda is much more isolated than the other resort towns on the southern end of the lake.

ORIENTATION

Riva del Garda sits on the north-western corner of Lake Garda, and is

Riva del Garda

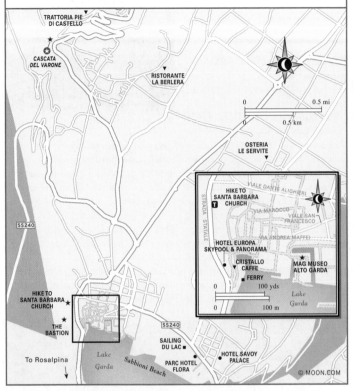

TRATTORIA PIE
DI CASTELLO

CASCATA
DEL VARONE

RISTORANTE
LA BERLERA

OSTERIA
LE SERVITE

0   0.5 mi

0   0.5 km

SS240

HIKE TO
SANTA BARBARA
CHURCH

THE
BASTION

To Rosalpina

Lake
Garda

Sabbioni Beach

SS240

SAILING
DU LAC

PARC HOTEL
FLORA

HOTEL SAVOY
PALACE

VIALE DANTE ALIGHIERI

HIKE TO
SANTA BARBARA
CHURCH

STRADA STATALE

VIA MAROCCO

VIALE SAN
FRANCESCO

VIA ANDREA MAFFEI

HOTEL EUROPA
SKYPOOL & PANORAMA

CRISTALLO
CAFFE

FERRY

MAG MUSEO
ALTO GARDA

0   100 yds

0   100 m

Lake
Garda

© MOON.COM

the lake's northernmost village. The SS240 runs directly through the center of town horizontally, cutting the town almost in half, while the SS45bis runs from north to south along the western edge of town, connecting Riva to Limone sul Garda and Arco. The heart of Riva sits on the western side of town. The historic center (including Catena Square) is completely walkable and many areas nearby are pedestrian-only.

The historic village of **Arco** is a couple of miles north of Riva by a few kilometers if you follow the SS45bis, or you can follow the SS421 north from Riva to Varone and Tenno. Arco is built on a grid, with many squares in the center of the village, and the entire southern edge of town is bordered by the northernmost shore of Lake Garda.

SIGHTS

CATENA SQUARE

Piazza Catena Riva del Garda, 24/7, free

The colorful Catena Square in the heart of Riva is perched right on the lake, with old apartments and restaurants pressed up against one another. Come here to start your morning or end your day with a meal at one of the restaurants or bars here. Sit out on one of the patios, as there's plenty of people-watching to be done here. From Riva, you can also catch a boat to other towns on the lake or head down one of the narrow paths branching off the square for some local shopping.

MAG MUSEO ALTO GARDA

Piazza Cesare Battisti 3A,
tel. 046/457-3869, www.museoaltogarda.it,
daily 10am-6pm, €5

Located in a small medieval castle right on Lake Garda, the Museo Alta Garda is part of the MAG network of museums focused on combining art and history in the Trentino region. The museum is home to a handful of permanent exhibits, including one dedicated to landscape paintings from the 19th century and another to international archaeology from the Copper Age. There are rotating temporary exhibits that focus on more contemporary culture of the region. The museum is also very family-friendly, with

MAG Museo Alto Garda

plenty of educational, creative, and interactive stations and games for children. Come at opening time to beat the crowd, as this place fills up quickly in the summer.

THE BASTION

Mount Rocchetta, tel. 393/905-0379,
24/7, free

Standing tall on a mountain top overlooking Riva del Garda is this historic watchtower, a well-known landmark

Riva del Garda

that has views so beautiful that it's worth the 20-minute hike straight up the mountain to reach it. Built in the earlier part of the 16th century to protect the town, the tower was eventually destroyed by French troops in 1703. Today, the flat viewing area next to the Bastion gives you aerial views of Riva and the northern part of Lake Garda. During the hotter months, bring some water with you and take your time getting up to the landing, as the hike can be tiring. To start your trek, follow the signs for the 404 trail on Via Monte Oro. The trail is mostly gravel and dirt, with steep elevation in some parts, so dress accordingly.

✪ CASCATA DEL VARONE

Cascata del Varone, tel. 0464/521-421, www. cascata-varone.com, daily 9am-5pm, €6

One of the most attractive natural sights near Riva is the gorgeous waterfall of Varone coming from the Magnone River. With two different observation points, you can see the waterfall from the bottom and from higher up. The waterfall is part of a cave, so to get there you have to walk into the cool and tall cavern, along a railed walkway over a clear, calm pool of water. You'll arrive in the lower cave first, which gives you a view from the bottom of the waterfall looking up, before you start the fairly easy climb up the stairs to the upper cave, where you can see the waterfall's full length and admire the beauty of the area. Wear comfortable walking shoes with good traction here, as the waterfall sprays can make the paths slippery.

The waterfall is less than two miles (roughly three kilometers) outside of the city, so you'll need to drive to it from Riva by following the SS421. Parking is available near the entrance of the park. If you're up for it, you can also walk to the waterfall from Riva using the main driving road (pay attention to traffic), with a slight incline for the entire 1.5 miles (2.7 kilometers). The walk takes about 40 minutes from the center of town.

RECREATION AND ACTIVITIES

HIKING

Hike to Santa Barbara Church

If you want stunning panoramic views of Riva and the northern part of Lake Garda while dodging the crowds at the Bastion, hike up to Santa Barbara Church, which was built by miners in 1925 while the town's hydroelectric power plant was also being constructed. The hike can be quite a challenge if you're not used to trekking uphill, as it's on an incline the entire way and often takes at least an hour to get there from the town of Riva, but the views are worth it. Start the hike by following the signs for the 404 dirt trail on Via Monte Oro to the Bastion, and once you're there, continue past it and follow the signs up to the church, which is 620 meters (2,034 feet) above town. Along the way, you'll find two small cafés where you can stop to grab a refreshing drink and take a breather before continuing on the path.

Low Loop 1: From Riva del Garda to Arco

Start from Via Monte Oro in Riva del Garda, https://www.visittrentino.info/en/tour/ gardatrek-low-loop-1-from-riva-del-garda-to-arco_22593453

The Low Loop 1 that starts in Riva del Garda and ends at the castle in Arco is one of the area's most popular trekking trails, as it hits major landmarks and offers gorgeous views of the towns below. Start by following the trail 404 signs from Via Monte Ora in Riva. On the way, you'll walk along the dirt path past the Bastion, the **Romanesque church of San Lorenzo** in Trenno, and **Monte Baone** before reaching the **Arco Castle**. The trail is clearly marked with "GardaTrek Low Loop" signs, but the website listed provides turn-by-turn directions. This 8.6-mile (13.8-kilometer) trail is moderately difficult as you will gain about 1,312 feet (400 meters) in elevation, and it usually takes about six hours to complete.

To get back to Riva after you've completed the hike, you can walk an hour from the castle along the SS45bis from Arco to Riva, or take the Trentino Transporti B861 bus from the Arco bus station (Arco-Autostaz. 38062, Arco) back to Riva, which is about a 20-minute trip. Buses depart 7:23am-8:23pm, with tickets costing around €2 each way.

BEACHES AND WATERSPORTS

Sabbioni Beach

Via Filzi 2, tel. 347/688-7085;
open 24 hours; free

This public piece of well-manicured natural space in the center of Riva del Garda is a family-friendly jack-of-all-outdoor-trades. Here you'll find a pebbled and grassy beach where you can lay out your towels, a basketball court, playground with sandboxes and trampolines, and a floating platform with a slide inside the large, netted swimming zone in the lake. There are plenty of shaded areas in the park, but come early if you want to make a day of it, as the shady spots are claimed quickly. The beach is free and public, and is known for its clear, clean waters. There is a lifeguard on duty during the daylight hours in the summer

months, and showers are available as well. Because the pebbles on the beach become hot, it's a good idea to bring water shoes for getting in and out of the lake. Pack a lunch or snacks if you want to save money, but there is a snack bar serving sandwiches, drinks, and more just next to the park.

Fraglio Vel Riva Sailing School

Via Giancarlo Maroni 2, tel. 046/455-2460,
www.fragliavelariva.it, daily 9am-5pm,
€50-300

Two widely popular water sport activities in the northern area of Lake Garda are sailing and windsurfing. On any given summer day, you'll see dozens of sailboats gliding across the lake. The Fraglio Vel Riva Sailing School owns several of those boats, giving groups of visitors sailing lessons through their official sailing school. The school is divided into two groups: children aged 7-13 and teens aged 14 and older. You can sign up for a daily, weekend, or weeklong course. There are also family packages available. The instructors are local sailors who have been

paddleboats for rent on the Riva del Garda waterfront

teaching the sport for years. You can book a sailing lesson in advance on their website.

Sailing School at du Lac Grand Resort

Du Lac et Du Parc Grand Resort,
Viale Rovereto 44, tel. 046/456-2274,
www.fragliavelariva.it, late Apr.-mid-Oct.
daily 8:30am-6pm, €13-90

If sailing isn't your thing, no worries. The sailing school at the Du Lac Grand Resort offers hourly or daily rentals of both single and double kayaks, as well as stand-up paddleboards. Kayaks can either be rented for one, two, or four hours, or for an entire day. A life jacket for each kayaker is included in the price. Additionally, you can rent a wetsuit for only a few euros more. For a change of pace, you can also rent a stand-up paddleboard hourly, or for two to four hours. For beginners, the school offers two-hour courses daily starting from €35, with the price including a board, wetsuit, life jacket, and a certificate of attendance, as well as instruction from a certified SUP trainer. The school also offers rentals of yachts, bikes, kites, sailboats for leisure or windsurfing, and more. You can book in advance directly using the email form on the website or by calling ahead.

FESTIVALS
Nights of Fairytales (Notte di Fiaba)

Various locations, tel. 046/455-4444, www.
nottedifiaba.it, last weekend of August, free

One of Lake Garda's most family-oriented and diverse experiences is the annual Notte di Fiaba, known as the "Nights of Fairytales." This event takes place during the last weekend of August each year. Over the course of just a few days, the town transforms; even shops and restaurants participate. Each year a different theme is chosen, ranging from classic Disney films such as *The Little Mermaid* or *Aladdin*, to favorite characters such as Sherlock Holmes. Parades and a variety of games are incorporated into each day, as well as storytelling activities and a number of theater performances. The weekend always ends with a giant fireworks show over the waters of Lake Garda. Get there a couple of hours early with plenty of water and some gelato to hold you over while you save your seat for an awesome, up-close view of the show.

FOOD
TRENTINO CUISINE
Trattoria Pié di Castello

Via al Cingol Ros 38, Tenno,
tel. 0464/52-1065, www.piedicastello.
it, Wed.-Mon. noon-2:30pm, Fri.-Sun.
6:45pm-10pm, €10-25

Red meat lovers shouldn't miss this place tucked back into the mountains near Lake Tenno, away from the crowds that gather in Riva in the summertime. Founded at the end of the 19th century, this quiet, family-run restaurant focuses on one main dish: boiled *carne salada* (cuts of beef). In fact, the meat is usually served family style along with a heaping amount of bread, baked beans, and pickled vegetables. While there are other options such as homemade gnocchi and *canederli* (dumplings) in broth, you shouldn't skip the opportunity to enjoy the *carne salada*. To reach Tenno from Riva, follow the Via Molini north until it becomes SS421, then follow the curvy mountain road for about 5 miles (8 kilometers) until you reach the village.

ITALIAN
Osteria Le Servite

Via Passirone 68, Arco, tel. 046/455-7411, www.leservite.com, Apr.-Sept. Tues.-Sun. 5pm-11:30pm, €15-35

Eating under the stringed twinkle-lights on the patio next to a local vineyard at this *osteria* evokes the quintessential feeling of having an authentic homemade Italian meal at an old friend's house. The atmosphere is relaxed and casual, with a friendly staff welcoming you to sit back and enjoy the dining experience. Dishes include *tagliatelle* with ragu, grilled fish and beef, *risotto*, and creamy desserts. This is a place loved by both frequent visitors and locals, so book ahead, as it is only open in the evening.

Ristorante La Berlera

Localitá Ceole 8/B, Riva del Garda, tel. 0464/521-149, www.laberlera.it, Tues.-Sun. 7pm-10pm, Fri.-Sun. noon-2pm, €20-50

A meal at Ristorante La Berlera is worth the higher prices for the setting alone: The restaurant is built into a mountainside. Dishes include homemade stuffed ravioli, roasted octopus, beef stew, and a selection of gelatos and sorbets to finish. The food is plated like artwork, and portions focus on quality over quantity. The attire runs on the formal side. Book at least one day ahead here, especially during high season, and note that the restaurant is roughly two-thirds of a mile (about 1 kilometer) outside of the town center.

CAFÉS AND GELATERIA
Cristallo Caffé

Piazza Catena 17, Riva del Garda, tel. 046/455-3844, www.cristallogelateria.com, daily 7am-1am, €2-10

With plenty of indoor and outdoor seating, this café and gelateria is a hot spot for tourists to cool down during the summer months. It stays open late, so it's ideal for those who want a place to sit and hang with friends late into the night. Gelato flavors range from chocolates to creams to fruity sorbets, and they come in cups, cones, on top of waffles, and inside crepes. A full-service bar is also available, so stop by during opening hours for coffees and pastries in the morning, or an *aperitivo* in the afternoon.

ACCOMMODATIONS
€80-150
Rosalpina

Localitá Pregasina 106, tel. 046/455-4293, www.hotelrosalpina.it, €99

Sitting up in the mountains away from the lake, the Rosalpina hotel is a simple, affordable option for those wanting a little peace and quiet away from the summer crowds, without the frills of fancy resorts. The family-run inn offers unpretentious rooms with classic hotel furniture, each with a balcony. The property includes a small playground and an outdoor pool as well as free parking. Each room comes with a private bathroom and Wi-Fi. The restaurant below serves breakfast as well as classic Italian dinners with local dishes.

Hotel Europa Skypool & Panorama

Piazza Catena 13, tel. 046/455-5433, www.hoteleuropariva.it, €150

Located in the beautiful Catana Square in Riva is the beloved and elegant Hotel Europa, known for its rooftop pool and bar with a terrace affording gorgeous panoramic views of the town and the lake. The restaurant in the hotel serves classic Italian dishes, and a continental breakfast

Riva del Garda's colorful historic center

each morning. Each room includes air-conditioning, Wi-Fi, and private bathroom with toiletries. Parking is included.

€150-250
Hotel Savoy Palace
Via Longa 10, tel. 0464/554-242, www.hotelsavoypalace-lagodigarda.it, €170

In the center of Riva Del Garda is this lovely, bright, large family-friendly resort with a sizable garden, an outdoor swimming pool, and a hot tub. During the day, children can hang out at the kids club, which includes activities and a play area. Each bright and simply furnished room includes air-conditioning, Wi-Fi, and a private bathroom. A large breakfast buffet is included in the price of each room, as is guest parking.

Parc Hotel Flora
Viale Rovereto 54, tel. 046/457-1571, www.parchotelflora.it, €180

Located along the waterfront, the modern and relaxing Parc Hotel Flora is near the beach yet hidden by tall palm trees. The property includes a shaded, heated outdoor pool and a wellness center. Each room is elegantly yet simply furnished, with its own cool color palette. Rooms include air-conditioning, Wi-Fi, and private bathroom. A huge breakfast buffet with fruit, eggs, bacon, and more is included.

INFORMATION AND SERVICES

For assistance during your trip, visit the tourist information office (Largo Medaglie Oro al Valor Militare 5, 046/455-4444, https://gardatrentino.it, 9am-7pm daily) in the center of Riva. The English-speaking staff can provide information on all of the attractions in and around Riva, and give dining and accommodation suggestions. They also offer free maps of the area and other informational booklets.

There's a public hospital (Largo Marconi 2, 118 in case of emergency or 046/458-2629) and a local police station or *carabinieri* (Via Oleandri 10, 118 in case of emergency, or 046/457-6300). Both places are open 24 hours, but note that you'll need to ring the buzzer to enter the *carabinieri* station.

GETTING THERE

BY CAR

Avoid the single lane road around the lake and head north on the A22 highway to get from Peschiara to Lago del Garda. It's a 40-mile (65-kilometer) journey that takes a little over an hour. Exit at Rovereto Sud-Lago di Garda Nord and continue on the SS240 to Garda. The drive from Verona is also on the A22 and takes only slightly longer.

There are several paid parking lots in Riva, but most of the lots near the lake will fill up quickly in the warmer months, so get here as early as you can or consider finding an accommodation that offers parking for guests.

BY TRAIN AND BUS

From the Peschiera del Garda station, catch one of the ATV buses from the train station. Lines 483 and 484 run between Peschiera del Garda, Malcesine, and Riva del Garda. Buses depart daily 6:30am-8:30pm, but you can find official timetables and prices at www.atv.verona.it. Tickets, which cost €2.80-4 one-way, can be purchased in the bars or tobacco shops at the Peschiera del Garda train stations. You can also ask the staff there for a physical timetable for the buses. Each bus trip is about two hours long. Buses depart once an hour 8:22am-6:52pm daily.

BY BOAT

Infrequent public ferries run from Malcesine to Riva del Garda 8:30am-6:30pm. The trip from Malcesine is about an hour, with fares running €3-10 one-way per person. The ferry station is in the center of the village lakefront.

GETTING AROUND

Given that most of the historic center is pedestrian-only, and the town is rather compact, you should take advantage of the beautiful sights on every corner by walking around the village. It generally takes no longer than 15 minutes to get from one end to another on foot. Those who want to visit Arco can take the Trentino Transporti B861 bus between the Riva del Garda bus station (Riva del Garda Autostazione) and the Arco bus station (Arco-Autostazione), a 20-minute trip each way. Buses depart 7:23am-8:23pm (€2 each way).

RAVENNA

Ravenna has the advantage of

being lesser known than Venice, and it's relatively free of long lines of tourists waiting to see its main attraction: early Christian and Byzantine mosaics. Visitors who do make it to this less traveled city are in for a visual, literary, and gastronomic treat. You can pay your respects to Italy's father of poetry and former resident, Dante Alighieri, discover iconic images that have influenced Western art, and taste delicious cappelletti (filled pasta shaped like hats) and piadine (flat bread) wraps.

Itinerary Idea 258
Sights 259
Food 262
Bars and Nightlife 263
Recreation and
    Activities 264
Accommodations 265
Information and
    Services 265
Getting There 266

HIGHLIGHTS

✪ **BASILICA DI SAN VITALE:** One of the greatest works of Byzantine art and architecture ever built in Italy, with the largest and best preserved Byzantine mosaics outside of Constantinople (page 259).

✪ **MAUSOLEO DI GALLA PLACIDIA:** The most stunning mosaics in the city have lost none of their golden shine (page 260).

✪ **CLASSIS MUSEUM:** Ravenna's newest museum vividly explains the city's long history (page 261).

All it takes is a morning or an afternoon to absorb Ravenna's subtle yet powerful splendor.

PLANNING YOUR TIME

Ravenna is a long drive or a three-hour train journey from Venice. Although you can take in the top sights in a half day, there is a lot to see, and Ravenna makes a good overnight destination.

There are three city cards offering discounts and deals, but the most useful is the **Biglietto Cumulativo** (Cumulative Card, €9.50). Valid seven days, it covers the city's five mosaic sights: Basilica di San Vitale, Mausoleo di Galla Placidia, Basilica di Sant'Apollinare Nuovo, Battistero Neoniano, and Cappella di Sant'Andrea. It is not possible to purchase individual tickets, so you must buy the card at participating sights, whether you intend to see one or all the included sights.

On Tuesdays and Fridays in the summer (July-Sept.), you have the additional option of seeing the mosaics on a **Mosaic Night Tour.** The tourist office also offers **guided tours** (€7.50, Italian and English) on Tuesday and Friday at 2pm, and Sundays at 11am.

ORIENTATION

Ravenna's historic center is small and, unlike many Italian cities, is not clearly defined by a river or ancient walls. Streets run straight from the train station, and Viale Farini or Via Carducci are good roads to follow from the station to the historic center. White signs at intersections point the way to major sights, and getting lost is nearly impossible. Some monuments and museums lie a few kilometers to the south of the center and are best reached by bus or bicycle. The seaside is 5.5 miles (9 kilometers) to the east, and there are miles of Adriatic coastline that attract visitors in summer.

Ravenna

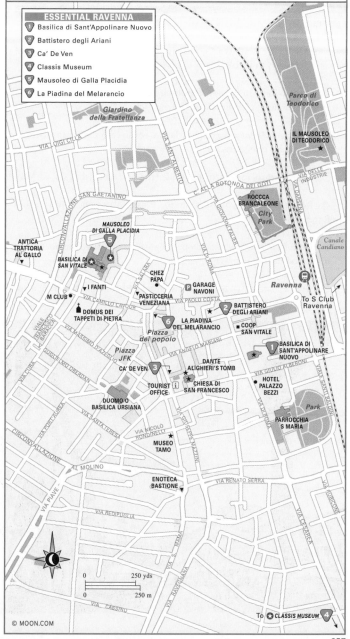

ESSENTIAL RAVENNA

1. Basilica di Sant'Appolinare Nuovo
2. Battistero degli Ariani
3. Ca' De Ven
4. Classis Museum
5. Mausoleo di Galla Placidia
6. La Piadina del Melarancio

RAVENNA

© MOON.COM

Itinerary Idea

This itinerary takes 4-5 hours. Leave your bags in Venice, or make Ravenna an overnight stop and give yourself a little more time to explore the city. You'll want to pick up the **Biglietto Cumulativo** (€9.50) combo ticket at your first stop; it covers entry to all five mosaic sights (individual tickets are not available).

1 Walk to **Basilica di Sant'Appolinare Nuovo** from the train station for an introduction to Ravenna's ancient mosaics.

2 Step inside **Battistero degli Ariani** to see an early Christian portrayal of Jesus and the disciples.

3 Enjoy a hearty cappelletti and grilled fish or meat lunch at **Ca' De Ven.**

4 Rent a bike and pedal south to the **Classis Museum,** to learn about Ravenna's long history.

5 Head back into town and stop at **Mausoleo di Galla Placidia** to gaze upon a ceiling full of mosaics.

6 Grab a *piadina* (flat bread) sandwich at **La Piadina del Melarancio** for the journey back to Venice.

Ravenna's main square, Piazza del Popolo

Sights

BASILICA DI SANT'APOLLINARE NUOVO

Via di Roma 52, tel. 054/454-1688,
daily 10am-5pm, entry only with Biglietto
Cumulativo (€9.50)

With its circular bell tower and red brick facade, this basilica may look simple from the outside, but inside are more mosaics than anywhere else in Italy. Artisans from Constantinople were summoned by Ravenna's rulers to complete much of the interior. They worked side-by-side with local craftsmen and left an indelible mark on the city.

mosaic-covered walls of Sant'Apollinare Nuovo

The walls of the central nave are divided into three horizontal cycles that tell the story of Jesus (top), saints and prophets (middle), and Palazzo Teodorico (bottom). Many images that are familiar features in religious art today, such as the three wise men and Satan, were first depicted here. According to legend, the golden mosaics were darkened to prevent worshippers from being distracted.

BATTISTERO DEGLI ARIANI

Piazzetta degli Ariani, tel. 054/454-3724,
daily 8:30am-6:30pm, €1

This tiny church was built on the orders of Emperor Theodoric for members of his Gothic tribe. It's small and easily overlooked, but the inside dome is stunningly decorated with mosaics depicting the 12 apostles preparing to place crowns of thorns on the head of Christ, who is being baptized by John the Baptist. This iconic Christian image is full of symbolism, which the English-speaking staff is happy to explain. Entry is €1. The ticket machine doesn't give change, but it does accept credit and debit cards.

✪ BASILICA DI SAN VITALE

Via San Vitale 17, tel. 054/454-1688,
www.ravennamosaici.it, Mar.-Oct. daily
9am-7pm, Nov.-Feb. daily 10am-5pm, entry
only with Biglietto Cumulativo (€9.50)

Basilica di San Vitale is one of Ravenna's eight UNESCO World Heritage Sites. The octagonal church, begun in AD 527, has the largest and

Basilica di San Vitale

MOSAIC TOURS

Mosaics are just pretty pictures without someone who can explain how they evolved artistically and what each of the images represents. A guide can explain the intricacies of this ancient craft and how Ravenna came to be the mosaic capital of Italy. The story and symbolism behind the city's mosaics is fascinating and complex, and a tour can help give you an understanding of the big picture.

touring the city with Papavero

MOSAIC NIGHT TOURS
Summertime offers the rare opportunity to see Ravenna's mosaics at night on a **Mosaic Night Tour** (Mosaico di Notte, tel. 054/454-1688, www.ravennamosaici.it, €8.50). From July to September, tours are given on Tuesday and Friday evenings (9pm-10:45pm) at **Basilica di San Vitale** and **Mausoleo di Galla Placidia.** During the day both sites are special, but at night under bright spotlight, the colorful mosaics are even more spectacular.

DAY TOURS
The **tourist office** also gives guided tours (€7.50, Italian and English) year-round on Tuesday and Friday at 2pm and Sunday at 11am.

LOCAL GUIDES
If you can't make one of the tours listed here, consider hiring a local guide like those from **Il Papavero.**

best-preserved Byzantine mosaics outside of Constantinople. Ceilings and walls are covered with golden portraits of Emperor Justinian and Empress Theodora, and images from the Old Testament.

✪ MAUSOLEO DI GALLA PLACIDIA

Via San Vitale 17, Mar.-Oct. daily 9am-7pm, Nov.-Feb. daily 10am-5pm, entry only with Biglietto Cumulativo (€9.50)

The city's oldest mosaics are housed in the Mausoleo di Galla Placidia, built by Emperor Theodoric AD 425-450 for his daughter Galla Placidia. The mausoleum contains many powerful images, particularly *The Good*

Shepherd, which utilizes blue and yellow tiles rarely seen anywhere else. The building was never used for its original purpose, however, as Placidia died in Rome and was buried there. Visiting time is limited to 15 minutes to protect the carefully monitored microclimate inside, and flash photography is prohibited.

CHIESA DI SAN FRANCESCO

Via Guido da Polenta 6, daily 7am-noon and 3pm-7pm, free

The austere-looking Chiesa di San Francesco, near Dante's tomb, is where the poet's funeral is believed to have been held. Hold your breath before you visit the stunning 10th-century mosaics beneath the flooded crypt (it doesn't smell great). It's best to visit early or late, as the church is closed to tourists during Mass.

DANTE ALIGHIERI'S TOMB

Via Alighieri Dante 9, Mon.-Fri. 10am-6pm and Sat.-Sun. 10am-7pm, free

You can sense the serenity and reverence as you approach Dante Alighieri's tomb, in part because of a city ordinance mandating silence in the area and in part because Italians have great respect for their premier poet. Ravenna was the last place Dante lived, and it's where he wrote the final verses of *Il Paradiso* (Paradise), part of his masterpiece *The Divine Comedy*, before his death in 1321. A votive lamp filled with oil from Florence hangs above his tombstone.

MUSEO TAMO

Via Nicolò Rondinelli 2, tel. 054/421-3371, www.tamoravenna.it, Mon.-Fri. 10am-5pm, €4 or €7 with crypt and Domus dei Tappeti di Pietra

After seeing all the mosaics in Ravenna, you may wonder how this ancient art started and want to learn more about making and restoring mosaics. You can dig deeper into the history and process of mosaic making at the city's mosaic museum, located in a deconsecrated church south of the city center. Visitors get a chance to discover ancient Roman and medieval mosaics, and learn how they were made through informative videos and exhibits. Hour-long guided tours (in English) cost €40 per group and can be reserved during museum hours.

DOMUS DEI TAPPETI DI PIETRA

Via Gian Battista Barbiani 16, tel. 05/443-2512, www.domusdeitappetidipietra.

it, daily 10am-6:30pm, €4 or €7 with Museo Tamo and crypt

A €7 cumulative ticket with Museo Tamo allows entry to Domus dei Tappeti di Pietra, an ancient Roman villa. The mosaics on the floors now lie underground, but they're in great condition and a well-designed walkway and good lighting allow perfect viewing. It's worth the 10-minute walk from Museo Tamo. You could also start here and then move on to Museo Tamo, because the Domus is located in the city center. It doesn't take long to visit, and the €2 audio guide is useful for understanding how Roman mosaics were made and used.

IL MAUSOLEO DI TEODORICO

Via delle Industrie 14, tel. 054/454-3724, daily 8:30am-6:30pm, €4

Theodoric the Great ruled over Italy for 33 years and brought peace, tolerance, and wealth to a land that had suffered long periods of chaos after the fall of the Roman Empire. He planned his mausoleum while he was still alive and ordered precious Istrian stone to be used. The resulting 10-sided, two-story structure has a massive roof made from a single block of stone. It's impressive and unique among all the other structures in the city. The inside, however, is rather plain and lacking in decoration.

✪ CLASSIS MUSEUM

Via Classense 29, tel. 054/447-3678, www.classisravenna.it, daily 10am-6:30pm, €7

Ravenna's newest museum was inaugurated at the end of 2018 and tells the city's history from the Etruscans to the Middle Ages. It's located inside an enormous 19th-century sugar factory that's been renovated from top to bottom and filled with archaeological material that brings the city's past to life. There's a lot of focus on mosaics, of course, but you can also learn about the ancient port of Classis, which was the largest on the Adriatic coast. Many of the statues, vases, and everyday objects found nearby are on display here. Panels and interactive exhibits (in Italian and English) help visitors understand the how and why behind the museum's collection.

The museum is about 3 miles (5 kilometers) south of the center. Take bus 4 from the train station or ride a local commuter train from the station one stop south to Classe. It's an easy bicycle ride, and there's a bike lane (Via Romeo Sud) much of the way.

Food

The Emilia Romagna region is famous for food, and Ravenna is part of the reason. Pasta dishes like cappelletti filled with cheese, vegetables, or meat and served in broth or ragu originated here. Long tagliatelle and *strozzapreti* (rough-cut spaghetti-like pasta) are also local creations, and are served with beans or tomato sauce. Grilled meats from locally bred beef and pork are traditional seconds, accompanied by warm piadina (flat bread) and raw vegetables like fennel, radishes, carrots, and celery. The sea is close by and provides a variety of crustaceans and mollusks, along with anchovies and sardines that are breaded and fried.

Every occasion has its dessert in Ravenna, and red wines to sample are sangiovese, trebbiano, and pagadebit.

ITALIAN
✪ Ca' De Ven
Via Corrado Ricci 24, tel. 054/430-163,
Tues.-Sun. 11am-2:30pm and
6:30pm-10:30pm, €10-14
Ca' De Ven is a cavernous winery and restaurant in the center of town that serves traditional meat-and-potato-style dishes. Even the basic *pasta e fagioli* (pasta with beans) is done exceptionally well, not to mention the

cappelletti and *tortelloni.* The house red wine is excellent and *ravioli con marmalade* makes for a sumptuous dessert.

Antica Trattoria al Gallo
Via Maggiore 87, tel. 054/421-3775,
Wed.-Sat. 11:30pm-2pm and 7pm-11pm,
Sun. 11:30am-2pm, €9-13
The family-run Antica Trattoria al Gallo has been cooking pasta *al dente* for nearly a century. The largely vegetarian menu owes nothing to trends; the chef simply uses Italy's best products, and never strays from seasonal ingredients.

STREET FOOD
La Piadina del Melarancio
Via IV Novembre 21, tel. 054/420-1108,
daily 11:30am-10pm, €3.50-5
Piadine are a local invention similar to wraps, but with thicker flat bread and tastier fillings. They can be found all over town, but this popular eatery prepares some of the best. Place your order at the counter in front, get the receipt, and wait for your number to be called. Most customers take their piadina to go but there is seating on two floors inside. Lunchtime is always crowded but service is fast.

Saturday market at Piazza del Popolo

PASTRIES
Pasticceria Veneziana

Via Salaria 15, tel. 054/212-171,
daily 6:30am-8pm, €3-5

To sample Ravenna's famous brioche pastries (Italian-style croissants) and other sweet temptations, visit Pasticceria Veneziana. The modern bakery also serves light sandwiches, fresh juices, and coffee indoors or at a handful of tables on a quiet street near the center.

Bars and Nightlife

You will find a couple of bars and cool hangout spots in Ravenna, but overall this is a sleepy town. Most of the partying around here happens at the nearby beaches.

BARS
I Fanti

Via Manfredo Fanti 9A,
tel. 054/435-135, daily 6pm-1am

This popular brick-lined, low-lit bar near Ravenna's main pedestrian thoroughfare serves an extensive selection of wines and comfort food. It makes an excellent end-of-day destination, and the young, energetic staff puts newcomers immediately at ease. The weekday afternoon happy hour starts at 6pm and includes a solid buffet.

Enoteca Bastione

Via Bastione 29, tel. 054/421-8147,
daily 7pm-4am

When locals are thirsty, they head to this laid-back, friendly bar for beer, cocktails, and wine. There's seating at the wooden counter in front of an impressive row of taps, and a back room has TV screens tuned to football

263

games on weekends. The kitchen prepares generous-sized burgers with fries and stays open late.

S Club Ravenna

Via Zara 48, tel. 054/459-0219, daily 6pm-2am

Ravenna's industrial zone starts behind the train station and has been undergoing redevelopment for the past decade. Some of the coolest late-night locales are here, such as this popular *aperitivo* hangout facing the canal. There are lots of tables outside, and the eclectic interior has a bohemian air. Patrons are a friendly bunch, and frequent musical events attract a young crowd.

Recreation and Activities

CYCLING

Bikes are everywhere in Ravenna. The city's flat paving and cycle paths make it a good place to ride. Bikes can also come in handy to reach more distant destinations such as the Classis Museum and the seaside.

Coop San Vitale

Piazza Farini Luigi Carlo, tel. 054/437-031, Mon.-Fri. 9am-5pm

Bikes can be rented from Coop San Vitale right outside the train station, by the hour (€3), half-day (€10), or day (€15).

Garage Navoni

Vicolo Padenna 13, tel. 054/421-2534, daily 7am-8pm

Garage Navoni, a short walk from the train station, provides simple city bikes for €5 per half day and €10 per full day. Bikes come with locks and all you need to rent is an ID.

TOURS

Il Papavero

Via Cavour 114, tel. 054/43-0101, www.guide-ravenna.com, three hours €110

This tour guide cooperative has been operating for more than 20 years. Guides are locals who know their city backward and forward. Their enthusiasm shows, and the three-hour tour that includes all the major sights is an eye opener.

Accommodations

HOTELS

Hotel Palazzo Bezzi

Via di Roma 45, tel. 054/436-926,
www.palazzobezzi.it, €85-130 d

This modern four-star hotel has bright, elegant rooms and lots of extras like a small gym, day spa, and billiard room. There's a quiet courtyard where breakfast is served and a terrace upstairs with panoramic views of the city. Parking is 100 meters away.

BED-AND-BREAKFAST

✪ Chez Papa

Via Pellegrino Matteucci 14,
tel. 054/421-7705, www.chezpapa.it, €95 d

Chez Papa is a poetic B&B in a Liberty-style building with three suites and three double rooms. Each room is named after a French literary great and has its own soothing beige decor. All rooms come with minibar, satellite TV, safe, and Wi-Fi. Common areas include a delightful garden, veranda, and relaxing reading room. The location is perfect for visiting the center of Ravenna.

PALAZZO

M Club

Piazza Baracca 26, tel. 054/437-538,
www.m-club.it, €100-130 d

Located in the historical center near the mosaics, M Club offers five color-coordinated rooms in five different colors, all in a refurbished 15th-century palazzo. You'll be surrounded by luxury.

Information and Services

TOURIST OFFICE

Piazza San Francesco 7, tel. 054/435-755,
www.turismo.ra.it, Mon.-Sat. 8:30am-6pm,
Sun. 10am-4pm

The **tourist office** is centrally located and a good first stop. The helpful staff can offer the latest event information, arrange guided tours, and provide useful free maps. Their **Talking Ravenna app** is available from app stores and uses geolocalization to enhance your experience with interactive descriptions, images, and augmented reality that make it easier to understand the city and how it once looked.

SERVICES

A lost-and-found service operates from the city government headquarters in an office called **Servizio Economato** (Via Mafalda di Savoia 14, tel. 054/448-2152). The central police station is at Via Rocca Brancaleone 1 (tel. 054/448-2999).

The main hospital is **Ospedale Santa Maria delle Croci** (Via Randi 5, tel. 054/428-5111). There are several pharmacies in Ravenna called Farmacie Comunale, and they take turns staying open 24 hours. There's one near the train station at Piazza Farini 6 (tel. 054/421-2835).

Marina di Ravenna beachfront

The soft, golden-sand beaches near Ravenna are long and wide, stretching for miles on the Adriatic coast. The limpid blue water and sandy bottom make these beaches perfect for splashing about. The sea is easy to reach from Ravenna by bus or bike, and you can have lunch, sunbathe, windsurf, walk, or cycle around here for hours or an entire day. The area is mostly pristine, once you pass the industrial zone and refineries, and pine forests (which were planted to drain swamps and provide shade) run parallel behind many of the beaches. It gets hot around here during the summer and beach clubs dotting the coast are busy early May-late September. They're all equipped with restaurants and bars, lounge chairs, and umbrellas (€10-15 per day), and many offer activities like beach volleyball and sailing.

MARINA DI RAVENNA AND PORTO CORSINI

Beach action is centered around the seaside towns of **Marina di Ravenna** and **Porto Corsini**. Both were founded in the 1930s and are filled with two-story housing on pine tree-lined streets. They're fun towns to explore on foot or a bicycle. Marina di Ravenna is the busier of the two, with hundreds of small pleasure boats bobbing in its harbor.

There are **public toilets** (€0.50) in Piazzale Aldo Moro and Piazza Resistenza but you can also generally walk into any bar, order a coffee at the counter, and use the restroom.

Getting There

CAR

Ravenna is 90 miles (144 kilometers) south of Venice. To get there, drive south from Venice on the SS309, a scenic, one-lane state road that skirts the coast. There are no tolls along the way and lots of small parking lots once you arrive. Some are free while others charge a €1 hourly rate paid at automated machines. The drive takes a little over 2 hours.

RECREATION AND ACTIVITIES

You can rent windsurfing gear and other types of boards from **Adriatic Wind Club** (Via Teseo Guerra 25, Porto Corsini, tel. 054/444-8222, www.adriaticowindclub.com). There's also a dike where you can walk 437 yards (400 meters) out into the sea; it's a great place to feel the power of the sea and clear your mind. There's a public beach nearby, and if you keep walking north along the sand, you'll pass beach clubs every 50 yards (46 meters) until you reach the **River Lamone,** 2 kilometers (1.25 miles) from the Adriatic Wind Club. Along this part of the coast is a long swath of pine forest that was planted back when Mussolini was in power.

MARINA ROMEA

Past the Adriatic Wind Club are the suburban town of Marina Romea and the **Piallassa Baiona wetlands** (Marina Romea, www.parcodeltapo.it, 24/7, free). This protected area is home to a number of wooden cabins built on short docks called *capani da pesca*. Traditionally, a big net in the front of a cabin is lowered into the water and then raised at the right moment to capture fish that periodically swim in from the sea. **Museo NatuRa** (Via Bollana 10, Cervia, tel. 054/452-8710, www.atlantide.net, Tues.-Thurs. 9:30am-1pm and Fri.-Sun 9:30am-6pm, €3) gives tours of the wetlands, offering visitors a chance to watch exotic nesting birds and discover where Italy's founding father, Giuseppe Garibaldi, once hid. The **Capanno Garibaldi** (Via Baiona 192, Porto Corsini, tel. 054/421-2006, free, hours vary but usually 9am-5pm on most days) cabin is a faithful reconstruction of the hut where he stayed briefly while he was on the run from Austrian forces that occupied the area in the 1840s. The original hut burned down in 1911.

FOOD

Balneario Malaika (Viale Italia 46, Marina Romea, tel. 054/444-6368, www. balneariomalaika.com) is a secluded lunch stop in Marina Romea with a varied menu and dishes like spaghetti alla chitarra allo scoglio and fritto misto (fried calamari, shrimp, and sardines). You can get back to enjoying the beach afterward, or maybe join a pickup volleyball game with locals.

GETTING THERE AND AROUND

The seaside is easy to reach from Ravenna. You can reach Marina di Ravenna (70 and 75 bus) and Porto Corsini (90 bus) on buses that depart regularly from Ravenna's train station. The ride takes about 20 minutes, and the first option is more scenic. From Marina di Ravenna, hop on the ferry (€1, departures every 10 minutes all year) nearby to cross the canal and reach Porto Corsini. You can walk or bike to get to Marina Romea from Porto Corsini.

TRAIN

The journey by train from Venice takes about three hours and requires a transfer in Bologna. There are two departures per hour, and one-way tickets cost €14-35, depending on the service.

The station in Ravenna is walking distance from the historic center, which is served by the 1, 2, 3, 4, 5, and 8 buses (€1.30 for a single journey or €5.50 for a day pass). Bus tickets are available from all newsstands, and taxis are stationed out front. Taxi di Ravenna (www.taxidiravenna.it, tel. 054/433-888, €6-10 to center, €15-20 to beach) operates day and night.

ESSENTIALS

Getting There 268
Getting Around 271
Visas and Officialdom 273
Food 275
Shopping 279
Accommodations 280
Conduct and Customs . . . 281
Health and Safety 284
Travel Tips 285
Tourist Information 291
Italian Phrasebook. 292

Getting There

AIR

AIRPORTS

Venice's **Aeroporto di Venezia** (VCE, Via Galileo Galilei 30, tel. 041/260-6111, www.veniceairport. it) is a medium-sized airport with a handful of direct flights to North America and many connections to cities throughout Europe. From the

airport, travelers can reach Venice by train, bus, ferry, or water taxi.

Milano Malpensa is Italy's second busiest airport with direct flights from cities across the world. The airport is connected to Milano Centrale train station by bus and rail. Journey time is around 50 minutes. Milano Linate is the city's second airport, with daily connections to London, Dublin, and most European capitals.

Verona Villafranca Airport (VRN, www.aeroportoverona.it) has a handful of European flights, including daily arrivals from London Gatwick and Stansted, but most overseas visitors fly into Milan or Venice.

AIRLINES
Flying From North America

There are more than 50 daily nonstop flights from the United States to Italy, and most land in Rome. Alitalia (www.alitalia.com) operates many of these and flies Boeing B777s and Airbus A330s to the capital from Boston, New York, Miami, and Toronto. Delta (www.delta.com), American (www.aa.com), United (www.united.com), and Air Canada (www.aircanada.com) also serve Rome from major cities in North America. There are a handful of direct flights to Venice with Alitalia, American, or Delta; all depart from New York or Philadelphia. There are direct flights to Milan from New York/New Jersey, Miami, Atlanta, and Toronto.

Flying from Europe

There are hundreds of connecting flights from London, Paris, and Amsterdam with Air France (www.airfrance.com), British Airways (www.britishairways.com), or KLM (www.klm.com). Low-cost airlines like Vueling (www.vueling.com), Ryanair (www.ryanair.com), and EasyJet (www.easyjet.com) also fly to Venice from many European capitals. Aer Lingus (www.aerlingus.com) operates flights from Dublin airport, which is equipped with a U.S. immigration office. Passengers are screened in Ireland and bypass customs when returning to the United States.

Alitalia operates most domestic flights, with five daily departures between Rome and Venice. Flight time is around an hour and tickets are inexpensive when purchased in advance.

Vaporetto outside the Venice Airport

Flying from Australia and New Zealand

Getting to Italy from down under is a long journey and there are no direct flights to Rome, Venice, or Milan. Quantas (www.qantas.com), Emirates (www.emirates.com), and Etihad (www.etihad.com) operate daily departures from Sydney, Melbourne, and Perth. Most flights require a transfer in Dubai or Abu Dhabi and total travel time is around 22 hours. China Southern (www.csair.com) is often the cheapest option but requires one or two stops in China and can take up to 40 hours. Travelers from Auckland can transfer in Australia with the above airlines or fly Qatar (www.qatarairways.com), Korean Air (www.koreanair.com), and Emirates on single-stop flights with transfers in Hamad, Seoul, or Dubai.

Flying from South Africa

Travelers from Durban, Capetown, and Johannesburg can reach Rome, Venice, or Milan with Ethiopian Airlines, Qatar, Emirates, KLM, Lufthansa, and Turkish Airlines, each of which requires a transfer in its respective hub. Alitalia offers direct flights (10 hours) between Johannesburg and Rome.

TRAIN

European train networks are well integrated, but getting between countries by rail can still take a long time. There are many trains from northern European cities to Venice. Single tickets can be purchased through www.trenitalia.it; if you are on a European vacation and visiting many countries, purchase a rail pass from Eurail (www.eurail.com) or Rail Europe (www.raileurope.com).

Over the past decade successive Italian governments have invested billions in an expanding network of high-speed tracks that have drastically reduced journey times between Italian cities. Today, traveling between Milan or Rome and Venice is fast, easy, and convenient. There are two operators. The state-owned Trenitalia (www.trenitalia.com) and private Italo (www.italo.it) both provide frequent daily departures between all of these cities. The Trenitalia Frecciarossa (red arrow) service is slightly more expensive and operates more trains, making it

Santa Lucia train station in Venice

popular with business travelers; tourists generally prefer Italo, which sends a monthly newsletter with discount codes. Both companies use the same tracks and leave from the same stations. Regional and high-speed trains stop in Padua, Vicenza, Verona, and Peschiera del Garda. Prices for the latter are more expensive and not much faster as the distances between destinations are small.

Italian high-speed trains are modern, clean, and equipped with Wi-Fi, electrical outlets, leather upholstery, snack machines, and bar cars. Tickets can be purchased online or at train stations from automated machines or service booths. The Italo website is easier to navigate and if you sign up for the newsletter you'll receive advantageous offers every month. There are several levels of comfort on board but even standard seating is adequate.

BUS

Buses are an inexpensive alternative to trains or cars. Half a dozen companies operate between Rome, Milan, and Venice. Eurolines (www.eurolines.com), Flixbus (www.flixbus.com), and Megabus (www.megabus.com) provide similar service on buses that seat around 40 passengers. One-way tickets rarely exceed €20 and depots are located near train stations. Most intercity buses leave from **Termini** or **Tiburtina** station in Rome, **Stazione Centrale** in Milan, and **Santa Lucia** in Venice. All are equipped with restrooms and baggage storage. There are stops along the way, and bus travel takes two or three times as long as train service.

CAR

The **Schengen Agreement** removed border controls between members of the European Union and made travel hassle-free. Ongoing concerns about immigration, however, have led some governments to reinstate checks. Entering Italy from France, Switzerland, Austria, or Slovenia isn't a problem, but leaving Italy can be trickier as border officials check incoming vehicles.

As many highways in northern Italy are at high altitudes, snow and fog in winter can lead to delays. Millions of Northern Europeans head south during the summer, and traffic near crossing points such as the Brenner Pass and Ventimiglia is heavy throughout July and August. The 2018 Genova bridge collapse along the A7 highway will disrupt traffic to and from France until it is rebuilt. Smaller roads that cross the Alps are best driven during the day at low speeds.

Getting Around

GETTING AROUND VENICE

Venice is a walking city. It is entirely off-limits to cars except for dedicated lots near the station, which are linked to the center by a light-rail system. Bicycles and mopeds are banned from Venice and wouldn't be very useful even if they weren't. The city's hundreds of bridges and stairs make these forms of transport impractical.

VAPORETTO

Public transit in Venice is made up of more than 20 **ACTV** (actv.avmspa. it) ferry lines (*vaporetti*) that circumnavigate the city and connect it to islands around the lagoon. Tickets and travel passes must be **validated** upon first use at validating machines near ferry landings. Controllers do occasionally check passengers and will fine anyone without a ticket. Daily and multiday travel cards are available and can be more convenient and cheaper than repeatedly purchasing single tickets.

EXPLORING OUTSIDE VENICE

DRIVING

Rental cars are available from a half-dozen agenices located in Piazzale Roma. From there it's an easy drive

view from a *vaporetto*

over the Ponte della Liberta bridge to the mainland.

Italy's highways (*autostrade*) are generally very good. Drivers collect tickets at booths as they enter the network and pay tolls in cash or credit, based on distance traveled, upon exiting highways. The 310-mile (500-kilometer) journey from Rome to Venice costs €39 and there are dozens of rest stops along the way. Autostrade (www.autostrade.it) manages highways and provides real-time traffic information in English. Signage should be familiar to drivers from around the world; however, there's a much greater use of yield, and roundabouts are frequent in urban areas. To review the rules of the Italian road, visit the Italian Office of Tourism (www.italia.com). From Milan take the A35 highway east to the A4 and on to Venice. The 165 miles (265 kilometers) can be covered in slightly less than three hours.

You'll need a passport and a driver's license if you plan on renting a moped or car. (Specify automatic transmission if you're unfamiliar with manual.) An international driver's permit is not required to rent a car, but you may need one to make use of Italian car-sharing services, and it can help you avoid confusion if you're pulled over. It's available from AAA (www.aaa.com) for $20. The minimum driving age in Italy is 18. Police and *carabinieri* (military police) frequently set up control posts along roads and randomly stop cars. The blood alcohol limit in Italy is 0.5, which is lower than in the U.S. and UK (both 0.8) but on par with most European nations.

Car Rentals

Cars can be rented from Europcar (www.europcar.com), Sixt (www.sixt.com), Maggiore (www.maggiore.com), Hertz (www.hertz.com), and other companies upon arrival at the airport in Venice or from rental offices located near Venice's central train station.

Skyscanner (www.skyscanner) and Kayak (www.kayak.com) can help find the best rental prices. Always get the maximum insurance. Anything can happen on Italian roads, and if you observe cars carefully you'll notice a high percentage of dents. Many streets are partially pedestrianized, and it's easy to find a spot on the outskirts and walk or ride a bus to the center.

You can avoid renting and try Italian car-sharing with Bla Bla Car (www.blablacar.it), which connects passengers with drivers traveling throughout Italy. Prices are €15-30, depending on distance. Knowing some Italian is necessary to navigate the website.

Parking

Paid parking lots and garages are available on the outskirts of all the destinations outside Venice in this book. Street parking is harder to find, and there's a good chance of being fined if unpaid or expired. White lines mean spaces are free of charge, blue is €1per hour, and yellow is off-limits. Payment stations are located at regular intervals on most streets, and street parking is free on Sunday.

TRAIN

Trenitalia (www.trenitalia.it) operates all commuter, regional, and intercity trains throughout Italy. Tickets are inexpensive, and train interiors have a romantic wear and tear about them. Tickets can be reserved in advance, but frequent service makes it as easy to purchase at the time of departure.

BUS

Public buses are useful for getting between the towns of Lake Garda and making short trips within cities. They are not the best option for reaching Padua, Vicenza, or Verona from Venice and are usually slower and as expensive as train service. However, for those who want to travel by bus, **Flixibus** connects Venice with Padua, Vicenza, and Verona. There are 22 departures a day and one-way tickets start from €5.

TAXI AND RIDE-HAILING APPS

Taxi fares in the mainland cities are relatively high and are calculated according to time and distance. Weekend and night rates are higher. Drivers don't expect tips but fares can be rounded up to the nearest euro. If you use **Uber** (www.uber.com) at home you can keep doing so in Italy, although fees are often higher than standard taxis. Note that taxis and Uber do not operate in Venice.

Visas and Officialdom

PASSPORTS AND VISAS
United States and Canada

Travelers from the United States and Canada do not need a visa to enter Italy for visits of 90 days or less. All that's required is a passport valid at least three months after your intended departure from the European Union.

European Union/Schengen

Citizens from all countries belonging to the European Union or the Schengen Area can travel to Italy visa-free. The United Kingdom will remain a full member of the European Union until its exit is finalized in early 2019. UK visitors will not need a visa but will be charged €7 for ETIAS authorization valid three years beginning in 2021. Travelers from the United Kingdom are advised to visit www.gov.uk/foreign-travel-advice for up-to-date travel information.

Australia and New Zealand

Visas are not required for Australian or New Zealand citizens visiting Italy for 90 days or less within any 180-day period in the Schengen Area (European Union). New Zealanders aged 18-30 can apply for a special working holiday visa at the Italian Embassy in Wellington.

South Africa

Visas are required for South African citizens to visit Italy and can be obtained through **Capago** (tel. 087/231-0313, www.capago.eu). The application process begins online and requires stopping into one of the visa application centers located in Cape Town, Durban, Sandton, and Pretoria. Getting a visa takes two weeks and there is a fee.

EMBASSIES AND CONSULATES

Lost or stolen U.S. passports can be replaced at the **United States Embassy** (Via Veneto 119a/121, tel. 06/46741, www.italy.usembassy.gov,

Mon.-Fri. 8:30am-noon) in Rome. Proof of citizenship and a photo ID are required. Replacements are issued on the spot and cost €135. In addition to assisting with missing passports, the U.S. Embassy in Rome can help travelers deal with medical or legal emergencies. There's also a **consulate** (Via Principe 2, tel. 02/290-351, Mon.-Fri. 8:30am-noon) in Milan and **consular agency** (Marco Polo Airport, tel. 041/541-5944) in Venice. Citizens with after-hours problems can contact the embassy at any time by calling 055/266-951. The embassy and consulates are closed during Italian and U.S. holidays. For bureaucratic questions before arriving to Italy call the **U.S. Department of State** (tel. 1-888/407-4747 from the United States or 1-202/501-4444 from any other country, Mon.-Fri. 8am-8pm EST).

The **British Consulate** (Via S. Paolo 7, tel. 02/723-001) in Milan can assist travelers throughout Northern Italy.

The **Canadian Embassy** (Via Zara 30, 800/2326-6831, Mon.-Fri. 8:30am-noon) handles all citizen services and is located northwest of the historic center in Rome. Canadians can also contact the **consulate** (Piazza Cavour 3, tel. 02/6296-4238, Mon.-Fri. 9am-1pm) in Milan. The **Australian** (Via Antonio Bosio 5, tel. 06/852-721), **New Zealand** (Via Clitunno 44, tel. 06/853-7501, www.nzembassy.com), and **South African** (Via Tanaro 14, tel. 06/852-541, www.lnx.sudafrica.it) embassies are also located in Rome. Australia (Via Borgogna 2, tel. 02/776-741) and South Africa (Vicolo San Giovanni Sul Muro 4, tel. 02/885-8581) also operate small offices in

Milan. None of these countries has offices in Venice.

CUSTOMS

Travelers entering Italy are expected to declare any cash over €6,000 and are prohibited from importing animal-based food products into the country. Duty-free imports for passengers from outside the European Union are limited to one liter of alcohol, two liters of wine, 200 cigarettes, 50 cigars, and 50 milliliters of perfume.

Bags are likely to be heavier upon leaving Italy than when you arrive, so it's worth noting that U.S. citizens are limited to $800 worth of goods deemed for personal use. Anything over that amount must be declared and will be taxed. Fresh fruit and vegetables, cheese, and animal-based products are not allowed into the United States. Further details regarding what can and cannot be imported into the country are available from the **U.S. Department of State** (www.state.gov).

Canadian regulations are fairly lenient and allow cheese, herbs, condiments, dried fruits, baked goods, and candies; for a complete list, visit the **Canadian Border Services Agency** (www.cbsa-asfc.gc.ca). Australian regulations are particularly stringent and customs officers go to great lengths to avoid contamination. All fruit, vegetables, and meat products are forbidden. Fake designer goods will also be confiscated and may lead to a fine. If you're in doubt, consult the **Australian Department of Immigration and Border Protection** (www.border.gov.au).

Italians have their own way of doing things—especially when it comes to food. Here's how to blend in with locals:

- **Embrace a light breakfast.** Forget about eggs and bacon. Sidle up to locals at the nearest bar and order a cappuccino and a pastry.

- **Know the coffee culture.** Italians drink coffee at specific times. Cappuccinos are rarely ordered after noon or in restaurants, and should never accompany or immediately precede a meal. Espressos are ordered at the end of lunch and/or dinner, and during midday or midafternoon breaks.

- **Skip the salt and olive oil.** Salt, olive oil, and Parmesan aren't meant to be added to food and won't appear tableside, so don't search for them.

- **Forget about eating on the go.** Italians eat standing at bars and sitting at restaurants, but you'll rarely see them eating while they walk. The only exception is gelato, which makes strolling through historic streets even better.

- **Accept the slowness.** Service may be slower than you're used to. It might be hard to get the waiter's attention, or the second bottle of wine may never arrive. Just remember the sun is probably shining and you are in Italy. A little patience along with good-natured persistence will ensure a pleasant time. Frustration won't.

Food

There are all sorts of places to eat in Italy, and travelers should attempt to experience as many of these as possible. When choosing where to eat, avoid restaurants where staff actively encourages you to enter and menus are displayed in more than three languages. Authentic establishments attract Italians and are not located next to major monuments. Generally, however, it's hard to have a bad meal in Italy, and if food looks good it usually tastes good as well.

ITALIAN EATERIES

RESTAURANTS

The most common sit-down eateries are *trattoria, osteria,* and *ristorante.* The first two have humble origins and are cheaper than a *ristorante.* The typical *trattoria* serves local dishes within a rustic atmosphere. The best have been in business for generations and have a devoted local following. Service can be ad hoc, and waiters are not overly concerned with formality. An *osteria* is similar but has fewer items on the menu and rarely strays from tradition. A *ristorante* will be more expensive and elegant, perhaps with uniformed waiters, an extensive wine cellar along with a sommelier, and fine table settings. Menus often diverge from tradition and combine flavors in novel ways. All three types of eateries are open for lunch and dinner, and continuous service throughout the day is rare.

STREET FOOD

The most popular street food in Italy is pizza, which is available on demand at *pizza al taglio* (pizza by the cut) shops from midmorning onward.

The pizza inside these standing-room-only shops is baked in large rectangular tins. There are a dozen varieties waiting to be cut, and customers randomly line up to order whatever they like. Slices are weighed and reheated if necessary, and they can be eaten immediately or wrapped up for future consumption. Payment is usually made at a dedicated cashier.

Markets are another good destination for tasty fast food from morning to early afternoon.

BAKERIES AND *PASTICCERIA*

Fornaio (bakeries) open before dawn and remain busy until midafternoon. There's one in every neighborhood, and they supply locals with all types of bread, buns, and sweets. You'll also find cakes, cookies, tarts, pastries, white or red pizza, and unique specialties served during holidays. Most items are priced by the kilo and purchased for takeaway. *Fornaio* can be crowded in the morning, and some use numbered ticketing systems to avoid confusion.

Pasticceria shops are entirely dedicated to sweets and keep roughly the same hours as bakeries. They prepare cookies, tarts, and cakes along with an array of smaller finger-sized pastries that Italians serve as midafternoon snacks (*merenda*) or offer to visiting friends. Some *pasticceria* serve coffee.

COFFEE BARS

Coffee bars and cafés open nearly as early as bakeries and provide different services throughout the day. In the morning they supply locals with espressos or cappuccinos and **cornetti** (breakfast pastries), which are either plain or filled with cream, jelly, or chocolate. *Cornetti* rarely exceed €1 and are a cheap and tasty way to start the day. Most bars are supplied by bakeries, but some have their own ovens.

By midmorning, coffee bars trade sweets for triangular *tramezzino* and *panini* sandwiches stacked behind glass counters. These cost €2-4 and can be eaten at the counter or table, or taken away. Larger bars provide *tavola calda* (lunchtime buffets) with a selection of first- and second-course dishes. It's hard to spend more than €15 for a complete meal with water and coffee.

Bars usually operate on a "consume now, pay later" policy with a dedicated cashier off to one side who calculates checks. Counter service is slightly cheaper and always faster, and that's where most locals do their eating and drinking. There's a big difference between neighborhood bars and those overlooking heavily touristed squares like Piazza San Marco, where the **cafés** are far more elegant and may have been around for centuries. Prices are higher in major squares, although the food is more or less the same as what you'd find on a narrow side street. However, those higher prices come with a view, and the tables outside are usually filled with tourists.

Venice is different from other Italian cities in many ways, and the city has developed its own particular type of eatery. Venetian *bacari* serve bite-size slices of bread topped with vegetables, meat, or fish called *cicchetti*. These creative and inexpensive appetizers are accompanied by wine or beer from late morning until early evening. *Bacari* interiors are rustic, seating is limited, and service is friendly.

GELATERIE

Gelaterie (gelato shops) are nearly as common as bars in Italy and stay open late during the summer. They specialize in gelato and sorbet, which come in countless flavors. The best are made on the spot with seasonal ingredients, while less passionate owners cut corners by using preservatives and compressed air to give gelato bright colors and gravity-defying forms. Gelato is priced by the scoop and served in a cone or cup. Clerks will ask if you want *panna* (whipped cream) at no extra cost.

MENUS

Italian menus are divided into courses with an established order. *Antipasti* (starters) are the first things you'll see and can be as simple as *bruschette* (toasted bread topped with tomatoes) or *fiori di zucchini* (fried zucchini flowers stuffed with anchovies). The point of *antipasti* is to relieve hunger and prepare stomachs for the meal to come. House starters *(antipasto della casa)* are a safe culinary bet and usually include plates of local cold cuts and cheeses that are meant to be shared.

The *primo* (first course) can be pasta, *risotto*, or soup. There are hundreds of traditional pasta shapes, all of which are combined with particular sauces that include vegetables, meat, or fish. This is a chance to get adventurous. Rice is as common as pasta in Venice and is usually served with seafood.

Many people surrender after the first course, and that's a shame. If you need help getting through a three-course meal, order a *mezzo porzione* (half portion) and leave room for the *secondo* (second course). It consists of meat or fish and is the gastronomic main event. Let waiters know if you want meat rare *(al sangue)*, medium rare *(cotta)*, or well done *(ben cotta)*. Unless you order a *contorno* (side dish), your steak will be lonely. *Contorni* usually consist of grilled

vegetables or roasted potatoes and are listed at the end of the menu along with desserts and drinks.

Restaurants often have a separate wine menu and daily specials that waiters will translate when possible. Food is relatively inexpensive in Italy and a satisfying three-course lunch or dinner with dessert and coffee runs around €25-40 per person.

DRINKS

Italy has hundreds of natural springs, and Italians drink more mineral water per capita than any other country in the world. The first question waiters often ask is the type of *acqua* (water) you want. You can choose between *frizzante* (sparkling) or *naturale* (still). A liter costs around €3 and sometimes there's a choice of brands. *Acqua di Nepi* is one of the oldest Roman waters and reputed to aid digestion. That's not to say *acqua del rubinetto* (tap water) is bad. It's regularly tested by authorities and is safe to drink.

It's difficult to find a restaurant that doesn't have a decent wine list. Many eateries have a separate wine menu that includes local, regional, and international bottles. House wine is also available and generally very drinkable. It can be ordered by the glass or in different-sized carafes. Geography and a cooler climate make Veneto suitable for growing white grapes, and the region is renowned for its sparkling *prosecco*. A glass of house wine is €3-4, a half carafe €4-6, and a full carafe €8-10. Prices are nearly always indicated on menus, but if they're not—or if a waiter brings you a bottle—ask the price before indulging.

Most Italians end lunches with an espresso and occasionally conclude dinners with a *digestivo* (digestif).

PRODUCE CALENDAR

Italians eat according to the seasons, which means you won't find cherries in winter or kiwis in summer. What you will find is fresh and grown locally. To get an idea of what's in season, visit an open-air market like Campo della Pescheria in Venice. Consult the list below to make sure what you're ordering is ripe.

Spring	Summer	Fall	Winter	Year-Round
artichokes	eggplant	pumpkin	pumpkin	carrots
asparagus	zucchini	white and black truffles	artichoke	endive
green beans	turnips	cabbage	cauliflower	dried beans
fava beans	radishes	mushrooms	broccoli	lettuce
new potatoes	peas	cauliflower	winter melons	leeks
cauliflower	cucumbers	broccoli	Brussels sprouts	celery
broccoli	fava beans	Roman broccoli	radicchio	spinach
cabbage	green beans	chestnuts	oranges	potatoes
zucchini	peppers	grapes	mandarins	chicory
tomatoes	mushrooms	figs	clementines	apples
kiwi	cherries	oranges	grapefruit	pears
strawberries	prunes	mandarins	kiwi	lemons
medlars	peaches	clementines		
peaches	apricots	grapefruit		
	figs			
	melons			
	wild berries			
	tomatoes			

The latter are high-grade alcoholic spirits that are reputed to help digestion. The most famous of these is *grappa*, which is served in a small glass and sipped. **Soft drinks** are available but not very common on restaurant tables.

SEASONAL SPECIALTIES

Locals can tell the date by what's on display inside bakeries and *pasticcerie*. Most seasonal specialties revolve around sweets, which are prepared during major holidays.

The weeks preceding Christmas transform grocery and supermarket shelves, with entire aisles devoted to chocolate, nuts, dried fruit, and *pandoro* cakes made from flour, eggs, butter, and sugar. During *Carnevale*, fried pastries are the gastronomic excess of choice. Easter wouldn't be the same for Italians without *colomba* (dove) cakes topped with almonds and granulated sugar. All are available in bakeries and supermarkets.

New Year's meals nearly always include lentils, which are eaten for good luck, along with *cotechino* (pig's foot). Christmas lunches involve fish while roast lamb is a feature of Easter menus. Season influences what you'll find on tables the rest of the year. Italian diets are regulated by the harvest, and the produce available at outdoor markets varies throughout the year.

HOURS

Restaurants are typically open 12:30pm-2:30pm for lunch and 7:30pm-10pm for dinner. Most close one day a week and many take an extended break in August or January.

Reservations aren't usually necessary, but to guarantee a seat at popular eateries, it's wise to arrive early or late. Bakeries open before sunrise and close in the midafternoon, while coffee bars remain open all day long, and pizza and gelato shops stay open late. Italians tend to eat later in summer when they wait for the sun to set and temperatures to fall.

TIPPING

Tipping is neither required nor expected in Italy. Most restaurants include a €1-3 surcharge *(coperto)* for bread, utensils, and service per customer. Waiters earn a decent living but no one refuses money, and leaving €3-5 behind after a good meal is one way to show appreciation. The other way to express gastronomic gratitude is with words. Italians are proud of their cusine and compliments are always welcome. Customers at coffee bars often leave a low-denomination coin on the counter.

Shopping

The majority of family-owned shops are dedicated to one thing and one thing only. This can be a single product like shoes, hats, books, clothing, or furniture, or materials like leather, ceramics, paper, or glass.

Most businesses are small and have few employees. Luxury boutiques are concentrated around major monuments like Piazza San Marco.

SHOPPING ETIQUETTE

Italians entering a shop (or bar) nearly always greet assistants with *buongiorno* or *buonasera* (good morning/ good afternoon). Most shop owners and employees are not overbearing and welcome browsing. They're happy to leave shoppers alone; however, they are professional and helpful once you demonstrate interest in an item and will happily find your size or explain how something is made. When leaving a store say *grazie* (thank you) or *arrivederci* (good-bye) regardless of whether you've made a purchase.

BARGAINING

Shopping in Italy is a chance to practice your negotiating skills and discover the thrill of haggling. Price can be theoretical at souvenir stands, flea markets, antique stalls, and even smaller shops, where no one will be offended if you ask for a *sconto* (discount). If a price sounds too high, it probably is—and can likely be lowered.

SHIPPING ITEMS HOME

Don't worry if something that's larger than your suitcase catches your eye. Stores, especially Venetian ones selling glass, are accustomed to tourists and can arrange for shipment directly to your door. Expect to pay up to 10 percent of the purchase price for home delivery.

SALES

January and September are the best times to shop in Italy. All stores begin the official sale season in unison during these months and windows are plastered with discounts. Every price tag should contain the original and sale price. Check items carefully before buying and don't hesitate to try clothes on, as Italian sizes generally run smaller and fit slightly differently. The sale season lasts four weeks, but most of the good stuff and sought-after sizes disappear after 10 days.

HOURS

Italy has its own unique rhythm, and nowhere is that more evident than in shops. Family-owned stores and smaller businesses nearly always close between 1pm and 3pm. Many also close on Sunday and on Monday mornings. Larger stores and those located in heavily trafficked streets have continuous hours. Businesses in the Venetian Jewish ghettoes observe Sabbath and shut down from sunset Friday until sunset on Saturday.

Accommodations

HOTELS

Italian hotels are graded on a system of stars, from one to five. How many stars an establishment has depends on infrastructure and services. Criteria varies from region to region but most three-star hotels are quite comfortable. Reservations can be made online and most hotels have multilingual websites. A passport or ID card is required when checking in, and early arrivals can usually leave luggage at the front desk. Many smaller hotels operate a "leave the key" policy in which keys must be left and retrieved whenever guests enter or leave the accommodation.

Large international chains like Hilton (www3.hilton.com), Sheraton (www.starwoodhotels.com), and Best Western (www.bestwestern.com) all operate in Italy, along with budget accommodations like Ibis (www.ibis.com) and Mercure (www.mercure.com). Service may be better and rooms slightly larger in these hotels, but they often lack character and might as well be located anywhere in the world.

Many travelers will enjoy a richer experience if they stay in smaller boutique or family-operated hotels that have managed to retain their charm.

Valuables are best carried or deposited in a hotel safe if available. In addition to the room rate, expect to be charged a city hotel tax of €1-5 per guest or per day, depending on the number of stars and accommodation type. It's a small price to pay to wake up in Venice.

HOSTELS AND PENSIONI

Hostels (ostelli) aren't just for young travelers: There's no age limit to staying in them. They provide clean, affordable accommodation, and many are less sparse than you might expect. Most include single, double, and quad options in addition to classic dormitory-style rooms. A bed costs around €20 per person and may include breakfast. The best thing about hostels, however, is the ambience. They're filled with travelers from all over at various stages of round-the-world adventures. Bathrooms are often shared, although many also have private rooms with en suite baths. Italian hostels are overseen by the Associazione Italiana Alberghi per la Gioventù (tel. 06/487-1152, www.aighostels.it).

Pensioni are small, lower-grade accommodations that are usually family-run. Rooms are clean and functional, although you may be required to share a bathroom. They're often located near train stations or city centers in large buildings that may not have elevators. Some enforce curfews and it's best to check at the front desk (if there is one) before heading out for the night.

CAMPING

Venice has campsites that remain open April-September. Facilities usually include a bar or restaurant, showers, and telephones. Camping in Venice requires a bit of a commute. Equipment can be rented if you've forgotten your tent, and bungalows are sometimes available. For a full list of sites visit the Italian Campsite Federation (tel. 05/588-2391, www.federcampeggio.it).

B&BS AND APARTMENTS

Italy has experienced a B&B boom over the past decade and the country now offers thousands of options. It allows you to stay with local residents and gain an insider's perspective.

To really live like a local, rent an apartment and get an instant native feel. Short-term rental is especially convenient for families and groups of traveling friends. Not only are prices lower than many hotels, but staying in an apartment allows you to call the mealtime shots and relax in a home away from home. Airbnb (www.airbnb.com) and VRBO (www.vrbo.com) are good places to start apartment hunting. Hometogo (www.hometogo.com) searches more than 250 international and local rental sites.

Conduct and Customs

LOCAL HABITS

Italians are attached to their habits and especially those related to food. Mealtimes are fairly strict and most eating is done sitting down at precise hours. Locals generally eat a light breakfast and save themselves for lunch and dinner, which are served at 1pm and 8pm. You won't see many Italians snacking on the subway or bus or walking while they eat. Meals are usually divided *alla Romana* (Dutch) between friends but no one will take offense if you offer to pay. Rounds of drinks are not offered as they are in the United States; groups of colleagues each buy their own. Drinking in general is done over a meal rather than with any intention of getting drunk, and displays of public drunkenness are rare.

Most of the things considered rude outside Italy are also considered rude in Italy. One exception is cutting in line, which is a frequent offense. Italian lines are undisciplined and if you don't defend your place by saying *scusi* or coughing loudly you may be waiting all day for a cappuccino or slice of pizza. Fortunately,

- **Ciao** [ch-OW] This world-famous word is an informal greeting that means both hello and good-bye. It's used between friends or once you have gotten acquainted with someone.

- **Buongiorno** [bwon-JUR-no] / **Buonasera** [bwo-na-SEH-ra] The first means hello (or literally, good day) and the latter good afternoon. These are formal variations of *ciao* and the first words to say when entering a restaurant or shop.

- **Scusi** [SKU-zee] is an invaluable word that sounds very much like its English counterpart: excuse me. It can be used whenever you want to get someone's attention, ask for something, or need to excuse yourself.

- **Per Favore** [PEAR fa-VOR-eh] / **Grazie** [GRA-zee-eh] are pillars of Italian politeness. *Per favore* is useful when ordering at a bar or restaurant and can go at the beginning or end of a sentence (*un caffé per favore* or *per favore un caffè*). Once you've been served something it's always polite to say *grazie*.

- **Dov'è...?** [doe-VAY...?] The Italian phrase for *where* can save you from getting lost. Just add the location to the end and do your best to comprehend the answer. *Scusi, dov'e San Marco?*

- **Parli inglese?** [par-LEE in-GLAY-zay?] should only be used as a last resort, but if you must it's more polite than launching directly into English.

number dispensers are used in post offices, pharmacies, and deli counters. Personal space in general is smaller than in Anglo-Saxon countries, and Italians tend to use their hands as well as words to emphasize ideas.

GREETINGS

Italians are exceptionally sociable and have developed highly ritualized forms of interaction. Daily exchanges with friends and acquaintances often involve physical contact, and kisses on both cheeks are common. Bars and squares are the urban settings for unhurried conversation, which is a normal part of everyday Italian life. The proliferation of the cell phone has fueled the passion to communicate, and in some cases has led to an overreliance that can be witnessed on public transportation and sidewalks of Italian cities.

Kissing is how Italians demonstrate respect, friendship, and love. The practice is as Italian as pizza. The most common form is the double cheek kiss. It can be uncomfortable for the uninitiated but no one will impose it on you, and a handshake is equally acceptable. If you observe carefully you'll see women kissing women, women kissing men, men kissing women, men kissing men, and everyone kissing children.

Kisses are exchanged at the beginning and end of most social encounters. An Italian man introduced to an Italian woman (or vice versa) will exchange kisses. Men will shake hands with each other and women may kiss or shake hands. Non-Italians can greet however they please. While citizens of other countries tend to exchange good-byes quickly, Italians love to linger. The time between verbal indication of departure and actual physical departure can be surprisingly long and is generally spent discussing the next day and making preliminary plans for a future meeting.

ALCOHOL AND SMOKING

Legislation regarding alcohol consumption is relatively relaxed. Alcohol can be purchased in supermarkets, grocery stores, and specialty shops all week long by anyone over 18, and consumed in public. Most locals are not prone to excessive drinking, and public drunkenness is rare.

Smoking has been banned in bars, restaurants, and public spaces since 2005, and if you want to take a puff you'll need to step outside or request an outdoor table. Although there is a high percentage of smokers in Italy, that number is falling, and laws regarding nonsmoking areas are respected. Cigarettes are sold at specialized *tabacchi* shops for around €5 a pack. Venice is particularly serious about keeping the city clean, and smokers can be fined for throwing cigarette butts into canals or streets.

DRUGS

Italy's position in the center of the Mediterranean, coupled with the country's 4,971-mile (8,000-kilometer) coastline, makes drug smuggling difficult to eradicate. There are major markets for heroin, cocaine, hashish, and synthetic drugs imported by sea from South America, North Africa, the Balkans, and Afghanistan. That said, it's very rare to be offered drugs in Italy during the day and the hardest drug you're likely to be offered at night is hashish (a substance derived from cannabis and mixed with tobacco). Most dealers aren't threatening and will take no for an answer. Discos and nightclubs are more likely to be the scene of cocaine or amphetamines, which kill their share of Italian teenagers every year. Marijuana and hashish are classified as light drugs and are illegal but have been decriminalized since 1990. Personal use in public will not lead to arrest but may bring about a fine or warning. It's not worth the risk, and there's enough perfectly legal wine to go around. Harder drugs such as cocaine, heroin, ecstasy, LSD, and so on are all illegal.

DRESS

Italians like to look good. Even if the standards of formality have fallen in recent years, locals of all ages remain well groomed and careful about appearance. It's not just the clothes that are different but the way Italians wear clothes and the overall homogeneity that exists on city streets. Women are elegant, men well fitted, and even retirees look like they're wearing their Sunday best. It's easy to differentiate locals from tourists, who are blissfully unaware of the fashion faux pas they are committing. Tourists can usually be spotted a mile away: They're the ones wearing the baseball caps, white socks with sandals, and khaki shorts. Fitting in means paying a little more attention to how you look and may require some shopping to acquire Italian style.

AT PLACES OF WORSHIP

Most churches have a dress code, which is often posted outside. Revealing too much flesh may result in being denied entry. Knees, shoulders, and midriffs should be covered. Do not expect to enter St. Mark's wearing flip-flops, miniskirts, above-the-knee shorts, or cut-off T-shirts. The same rules apply to some museums and monuments.

Entry may be restricted during mass and a certain amount of decorum (maintaining silence, refraining from eating and drinking, and acting in a respectful manner) should be observed at all times. Photography is usually allowed but rules vary. Flash photography is not permitted inside some churches and museums where light can damage delicate frescoes.

Health and Safety

EMERGENCY NUMBERS

In case of a medical emergency, dial 118. Operators are multilingual and will provide immediate assistance. The U.S. Embassy (tel. 06/46741) and British Embassy (tel. 06/4220-0001) offer their citizens phone access any time for matters regarding illness or victimization of any sort. Carabinieri (112), police (113), and the fire department (115) also operate around-the-clock emergency numbers.

CRIME AND THEFT

Italian cities are safe, and muggings and violent crime are rare. Still, it's best to travel in pairs late at night and be aware of pickpockets at all times. Most petty criminals work in teams and can be quite young. Youth often beg for change at traffic intersections or on church steps and supplement that income by playing music on subways, recycling scrap metal, and dumpster diving.

Crowded train stations and subways are ideal places for thieves. It's best to keep wallets and other valuables in a front pocket or locked in a hotel safe. Leave jewelry, smartphones, and cameras out of sight and always count your change before leaving a store. Make a photocopy of your passport and other vital documents and call your credit card company immediately if your wallet is stolen. If you are the victim of a pickpocket or have a bag snatched, report it within 24 hours to the nearest police station. You'll need a copy of the police report (*denuncia*) in order to make an insurance claim.

MEDICAL SERVICES

Italian medical and emergency services are relatively modern and have been ranked second in the world by the World Health Organization. First aid can be performed by all public hospitals and urgent treatment is entirely free of charge. A symbolic copayment is often required for treatment for a non-life-threatening issue, not to exceed €30. The emergency medical service number is 118. If you can't wait, go directly to the *pronto soccorso* (emergency room) located in most hospitals.

Vaccines are not required for entering Italy, but a flu shot can prevent unnecessary time in bed if you're visiting in winter.

PHARMACIES

Pharmacies are recognizable by their green neon signs, and they're plentiful in city centers. Many operate nonstop hours and remain open during lunch. If a pharmacy is closed, you can always find a list of the closest open ones posted in the window. Pharmacists can be very helpful in Italy and provide advice and non-prescription medicine for treating minor ailments. You'll also find practical items such as toothbrushes, sunscreen, and baby food along with automated prophylactic vending machines out front.

SECURITY

Security in Italy has tightened considerably since the 2015 Paris attacks and there is a greater police and military presence at airports, train stations, and around major monuments. The new measures are most evident in Rome, where churches, museums, and other popular destinations have adopted new entry procedures involving metal detectors and the depositing of backpacks and oversize bags in cloakrooms. Security around French and U.S. embassies, schools, and cultural associations has also been bolstered and will remain so for the foreseeable future.

There haven't been any terrorist attacks in Italy since the 1980s, and the country has kept a low profile compared to other allies that have actively intervened in Middle Eastern affairs and become the target of terrorist groups. That could always change, and travelers concerned about security can register with the **Smart Traveler Enrollment Program** (www.step. state.gov) to receive the latest alerts and allow the U.S. embassy to contact them in case of emergency.

Travel Tips

MONEY

CURRENCY

The euro has been Italy's currency since 2000. Banknotes come in denominations of €5, €10, €20, €50, €200, and €500 (which is currently being phased out). Denominations are different colors and sizes to facilitate recognition. Coins come in €0.01, €0.02, €0.05, €0.10, €0.20, €0.50, €1, and €2 denominations; these also vary in color, shape, and size. The euro is used in 19 nations across Europe, and each country decorates and mints its own coins. Take time to familiarize yourself with the different values, and count your change after each purchase for practice.

CURRENCY EXCHANGE

Fluctuation between the dollar and euro can have a major impact on travel budgets, and so can exchange fees and transaction fees. Over the last decade exchange rates haven't favored U.S. travelers, but since 2014 the dollar has strengthened considerably, and one dollar is now worth roughly €0.85. There are several options for obtaining euros. You can exchange at your local bank before departure, use private exchange agencies located in airports and near major monuments, or simply use ATM machines in Italy. Banks generally offer better rates but charge commission, while agencies charge low commission but offer poor rates. Exchange machines give you another option, and automated exchange machines operate inside many bank branches. Look for the *cambio* (exchange) sign in bank windows. When changing money, request different denominations and count bills at the counter before leaving.

ATMS AND BANKS

ATM machines are easy to find and are located inside or outside all Italian banks. They accept foreign debit and credit cards, and exchange rates are set daily. Before withdrawing cash in Italy, ask your bank or credit card company what fees they charge. Most have an international processing fee that can be a fixed amount or a percentage of the total withdrawal. Charles Schwab is one of the few financial institutions that does not charge either. Italian banks also charge a small fee for cardholders of other banks using their ATMs.

The maximum daily withdrawal at most banks is €500. ATMs provide instructions in multiple languages. Be aware of your surroundings when withdrawing cash late at night or on deserted streets. If the card doesn't work, try another bank before contacting your bank back home. Italian banks are generally open weekdays 8:30am-1:30pm and 2:30pm-5:30pm. They often have lockers at the entrance for storing keys, coins, and anything else that might activate the metal detectors at the entrance.

DEBIT AND CREDIT CARDS

Before your departure, inform your bank and/or credit card company of your travel plans, as many will block cards after unexpected foreign activity.

Debit cards are a ubiquitous form of payment in Italy, and recent legislation meant to encourage cashless transactions has removed monetary limits. You can therefore buy a coffee, museum ticket, or a pair of shoes with Maestro- or Cirrus-equipped cards. Newsstands are about the only place that don't accept plastic, and cash-only restaurants are rare. Most Italian smart cards use a chip-and-PIN system. If your card requires old-fashioned swiping, you may need to alert cashiers.

Credit cards are also widely accepted. Visa (tel. 800/877-232) and MasterCard (tel. 800/870-866) are the most common. American Express (tel. 06/4211-5561) comes a distant third, and Discover is unknown. Cards provide the most advantageous exchange rates, and a low 1-3 percent commission fee is usually charged on every transaction.

SALES TAX

The Italian government imposes a value-added tax (IVA) of 22 percent on most goods. Visitors who reside outside the European Union are entitled to tax refunds (www.taxrefund.it) on all purchases over €155 within stores that participate in the tax-back program. Just look for the Euro Tax Free or Tax Free Italy logo, have your passport ready, and fill out the yellow refund form. You'll still have to pay tax at the time of purchase but are entitled to reimbursement at airports and refund offices. Forms must be stamped by customs officials before check-in and brought to the refund desk, where you can choose to receive cash or have funds wired to your credit card. Lines move slowly and it's usually faster to be refunded at private currency exchange agencies such as Forexchange (www.forexchange.it), American Express (www.americanexpress.com), Interchange (www.interchange.eu), or Travelex (www.travelex.com) in Venice. They facilitate the refund process for a small percentage of your refund. All claims must be made within three months of purchase.

COMMUNICATIONS

TELEPHONES

To call Italy from outside the country, dial the **exit code** (011 for the U.S. and Canada) followed by **39** (Italy country code) and the number. All large Italian cities have a 2- or 3-digit **area code** (041 for Venice) and numbers are 6-11 digits long. Landline numbers nearly always start with a zero, which must be dialed when making calls in Italy or calling Italy from abroad. Cell phone numbers have a 3-digit prefix (347, 390, 340, etc.) that varies according to the mobile operator and numbers are 10 digits long total.

To call the United States or Canada from Italy, dial the 001 country code followed by area code and number. For collect calls to the United States dial 172-1011 (AT&T), 172-1022 (MCI), or 172-1877 (Sprint).

Numbers that start with 800 in Italy are toll-free, 170 gets you an English-speaking operator, and 176 is **international directory assistance.** Local calls cost €0.10 per minute and public phone booths are slowly disappearing. Fees for calling cell phones are higher.

Cell Phones

Your smartphone will work in Italy if it uses the GSM system, which is the mobile standard in Europe. All iPhones, Samsung Galaxy, and Google Nexus devices function, although rates vary widely between operators. Voice calls to the United States can vary from as much as $1.79 (Verizon) to $0.20 (T-Mobile) per minute, depending on your plan. Most companies offer international bundles that include a certain amount of text messaging, data transfer, and voice traffic. If you don't want any unexpected bills, compare offers and choose one that meets your needs.

You can also purchase a SIM card in Italy at any mobile shop and use it in your phone. Wind (www.wind.it), Tim (www.tim.it), and Vodafone (www.vodafone.it) are the most common operators, with stores in all three cities and at airports. This option will require a passport or photo ID and may take a little longer, but it can be the cheapest and useful if you plan to make a lot of domestic and international calls.

If your phone doesn't use GSM you can rent or buy one in Italy. Rentals are available at the airport but are expensive. New phones are a cheaper option and available from the European telecom operators mentioned above. A basic flip phone can cost as little as €29 and be purchased with prepaid minutes. ID is required and some operators have special deals for foreign travelers.

You can save on telephone charges altogether if you have access to Wi-Fi. Many hotels and bars have hotspots, and using FaceTime, Skype, or other VOIP operators is free.

Pay Phones

The advent of cell phones has led to a steady decline of public pay phones. Those still standing operate with coins or phone cards that can be purchased at *tabacchi* or newsstands. Ask for a *scheda telefonica* (phone card), which can be inserted into a slot in the telephone.

WI-FI

Getting online in Italy is easy. Venice's Wi-Fi network makes it simple to stay connected throughout a journey, and access is free. However, registration is required and there are time and traffic limits. Both Trenitalia and Italo train operators provide on board Wi-Fi, as do most Italian airports and hotels.

POSTAL SERVICES

Francobolli (stamps) for standard-size postcards and letters can be purchased at *tabacchi* shops. Larger parcels will require a trip to the post office. **Poste Italiane** (tel. 800/160-000, www.poste.it) offices are yellow, and larger branches are usually open weekdays 8:30am-7:30pm and Saturday 8:15am-12:30pm. Grab a numbered ticket at the entrance and prepare for a short wait. A postcard to the United States costs €0.85 as long as it doesn't exceed 20 grams and remains within standard dimensions. The cost of sending letters and other goods varies according to weight; such items can be sent *posta prioritaria* (express) for a couple euros extra. Mailboxes are red and have slots for international and local mail. Travel time varies and it can take weeks for a postcard to reach its destination.

Stamp collectors may be disappointed, as most post office clerks slap computerized stickers onto correspondence. However, there is a special philatelic branch in Venice (Fondamenta del Gaffaro 3510, tel. 041/522-1614, Mon.-Fri. 8:20am-1:35pm and Sat. 8:20am-12:35pm) dedicated to collectors.

WEIGHTS AND MEASURES

Italy uses the **metric system.** A few helpful conversions: 5 centimeters is about 3 inches, 1 kilogram is a little over 2 pounds, and 5 kilometers is around 3 miles. **Celsius** is used to measure temperature, and 20°C (68°F) is a good air-conditioning setting inside hotels and cars. Summers often break the 35°C (95°F) barrier, and it's best to stay indoors when it does.

Italy is on **Central European Time,** six hours ahead of the U.S. East Coast and nine of the West Coast. Military/24-hour time is frequently used. Just subtract 12 from any number after midday so that 1300 becomes 1pm and 2015 is 8:15pm.

Italians use commas where Americans use decimal points, and vice versa. That means €10,50 is 10 euros and 50 cents, while €1.000 is a thousand euros. Italians order dates by day, month, and year, which is something to remember when booking hotels and tours.

ACCESS FOR TRAVELERS WITH DISABILITIES

Special-needs travelers may find life in Venice challenging. Italy is not especially accessible to the blind or wheelchair-bound, and sidewalks can be narrow and uneven. One positive is that many museums and monuments are free for special-needs travelers and their companions.

Venice may seem impenetrable to special-needs travelers, but 70 percent of the city is actually accessible to all. The city has created a bridge-free itinerary with descriptions in French and English along with a useful accessibility map that highlights options for avoiding urban barriers. Both can be downloaded online (www.comune.venezia.it) or picked up from the **city for all office** (*citta per tutti,* San Marco, Ca' Farsetti 4136, tel. 041/274-8144, Thurs. 9am-1pm) or other tourist offices around the city. Raised **tactile pavements** for the visually impaired have recently been installed along many canals and several flat footbridges and nonslip ramps are set up along key routes. Wheelchairs can be rented from health care stores (Sanitaria ai Miracoli, Cannaregio 6049, tel. 041/520-3513 or Farmacia Morelli, San Marco 5310, tel. 041/522-4196), and up to four at a time are allowed on *vaporetto* lines 1 and 2. Users and companions benefit from reduced fares (€1.50) on all public transportation. There are seven fully accessible public toilets within the city and one in each of the major outlying islands. Museums are free for disabled travelers.

Traveling between cities by train is convenient for anyone with reduced mobility. Italo (tel. 892929, www.italo.it) goes to great lengths to accommodate passengers. Seat numbers and other signage are written in braille, and two seats in car 8 are reserved for wheelchairs. These are located next to restrooms and snack machines designed for maximum accessibility. In-station assistance can be arranged up to one hour before departure at Venezia Santa Lucia station daily 8am-10pm. Trenitalia (tel. 800/906-060) provides similar services and assistance.

TRAVELING WITH CHILDREN

Italians go crazy for kids, and if you're traveling with a baby or toddler expect people to sneak peaks inside the stroller or ask for the name, age, and vital statistics of your child. Restaurants and hotels generally welcome young travelers, and some high-end accommodations offer baby-sitting services for parents who want to sightsee on their own. Many restaurants have children's menus, and most have high chairs. Half-size portions

(*mezza porzione*) can also be requested for small appetites.

Tickets to museums, amusement parks, and public transportation are discounted for children under 12, and are free for kids under 6. Trenitalia has several offers geared toward families, who can save up to 20 percent on high-speed rail tickets. Italo has similar deals and toddlers sit on laps unless an extra seat is reserved. Trains are roomy and give kids plenty of space to roam or be entertained by the landscape outside. There are diaper-changing facilities, and Italo has a cinema car with eight high-definition screens playing family-friendly movies.

Italian tots are used to taking naps, and a midafternoon break back at the hotel can prevent evening tantrums. Parents may want to intersperse fun and high-octane activities with visits to monuments and museums. Most parks are equipped with playgrounds and Venetian beaches provide a pleasant break from city streets. It's hard for kids not to love Italy and involving them as much as possible in the journey will help leave an impression they'll never forget.

FEMALE AND SOLO TRAVELERS

Women attract the curiosity of Italian men whether traveling alone or in groups. For the most part advances are good-natured and can simply be ignored. If you do feel threatened, enter a shop, bar, or public space. Should harassment persist, call the police (113) and remain in a crowded area. At night, it's best to avoid unlit streets and train stations. If you must pass through these areas, walk quickly and keep your guard up. Having a cell phone handy is a wise precaution, and periodically keeping in touch with family back home never hurts. Hotels often go out of their way to assist single travelers and will be happy to order a cab or make reservations whenever necessary.

SENIOR TRAVELERS

Italy has a high average life expectancy (83) and median age (46), which makes gray hair a common sight and visiting seniors feel young again. There's also a general respect for older people, who are an integral part of economic and social life.

Seniority has benefits. Anyone over age 65 is entitled to discounts at museums, theaters, and sporting events as well as on public transportation and for many other services. A passport or valid ID is enough to prove age, even if these are rarely checked. **Carta Argento** (Silver Card) is available from **Trenitalia** for over-60s traveling by train and provides a 15 percent discount on first- and second-class seating. The card costs €30 but is free for those over 75. It's valid for one year and can be purchased at any train station. **Italo** offers anyone over 60 a 40-percent discount on all first-class train tickets.

Italy gets very hot in the summer so it's important to remain hydrated and avoid peak temperature times. You'll also walk a lot, so take frequent breaks and join bus or ferry tours whenever you need a rest. If you take medication, bring as much as you need, as prescriptions can be hard to fill.

LGBTQ+ TRAVELERS

Italians in general are accepting and take a live-and-let-live approach. It's not uncommon to see same-sex couples holding hands today and the sexual preferences of emperors and Renaissance artists are all well known. Violence against LGBTQ+ travelers is rare, although cases of physical and verbal harassment do occasionally make headlines.

Italian homosexual couples have benefited from the same civil union status as heterosexuals since 2016. Italy was one of the last European countries to enact such legislation, doing so more than 20 years after Denmark. Still, it was a big step, and a sign Italian society (or the Italian government) is open to change.

TRAVELERS OF COLOR

The face of Italy has been changing since the 1980s, and the country has become increasingly diverse, with communities of Eastern Europeans, Asians, South Americans, and Africans contributing to the cultural mix. Ethnic minorities no longer turn heads, and if any Italians are surprised to find you in their bar, hotel, or restaurant they certainly won't show it. Blatant discrimination is rare, but if you think you've been refused service based on race, report the incident to local police or *caribinieri*, who treat all acts of racism seriously.

Tourist Information

TOURIST OFFICES

Each of the destinations in this book has a tourist office where city travel cards, maps, and event information can be obtained. Hours vary but most are open daily nonstop from 9:30am until 6pm during the peak summer season. Staff are multilingual and can help reserve local guides, order tickets, or get directions. Offices are located in airports, train stations, and near major sights such as Piazza San Marco in Venice.

LOST AND FOUND

Hopefully you'll never need an *oggetti smarriti* (lost and found), but they do exist in Italy. All airports have dedicated offices at baggage claim. If you forget something on board a Trenitalia train, contact the passenger assistance office located Venice's **Santa Lucia Station** (6am-9pm). Italo has fewer staff inside stations but you can call **Italo Assistance** (tel. 892/020, daily 6am-11pm) for help finding things. Fortunately, objects lost on high-speed trains have a high recovery rate.

MAPS

Maps are available at Venice's tourist offices, for a small fee. They are also sold at newsstands and bookstores. Examine the selection carefully and choose a map that's easy to read, easy to fold, and small enough to store conveniently. Paper quality varies; some maps are laminated and come with sight descriptions on the back. Once you have a map, try to orient yourself and memorize major landmarks and rivers. Studying maps and memorizing the layout of each city beforehand will make getting around easier once you arrive.

Finding the name of a street you're standing on is simple, but finding that same street on a map can be tricky. Often, it's quicker to locate a *piazza* or a nearby cathedral, museum, or monument. Also, asking for directions is the best way to start a conversation with a stranger and learn something new. Sometimes it's best to put a map away and rely on your senses to navigate.

Italian Phrasebook

Most Italians have some knowledge of English, and whatever vocabulary they lack is compensated for with gesticulation. It can, however, be more rewarding to attempt expression in the melodic vowels of Dante rather than succumb to the ease and familiarity of your own language.

Fortunately, Italian pronunciation is straightforward. There are seven vowel sounds (one for *a, i,* and *u,* and two each for *e* and *o*) compared to 15 in English, and letters are nearly always pronounced the same way. Consonants will be familiar, although the Italian alphabet has fewer letters (no j, k, w, x, or y). If you have any experience with French, Spanish, Portuguese, or Latin you have an advantage, but even if you don't, learning a few phrases is simple and will prepare you for a linguistic dive into Italian culture. Inquiring how much something costs or asking for directions in Italian can be a little daunting, but it's also exciting and much more gratifying than relying on English.

PRONUNCIATION

VOWELS

a	like *a* in *father*
e	short like *e* in *set*
é	long like *a* in *way*
i	like *ee* in *feet*
o	short like *o* in *often* or long like *o* in *rope*
u	like *oo* in *foot* or *w* in *well*

CONSONANTS

b	like *b* in *boy,* but softer
c	before e or i like *ch* in *chin*
ch	like *c* in *cat*
d	like *d* in *dog*
f	like *f* in *fish*
g	before e or i like *g* in *gymnastics* or like *g* in *go*
gh	like *g* in *go*
gl	like *ll* in *million*
gn	like *ni* in *onion*
gu	like *gu* in *anguish*
h	always silent
l	like *l* in *lime*
m	like *m* in *me*
n	like *n* in *nice*
p	like *p* in *pit*
qu	like *qu* in *quick*
r	rolled/trilled similar to *r* in Spanish or Scottish
s	between vowels like *s* in *nose* or *s* in *sit*
sc	before e or i like *sh* in *shut* or *sk* in *skip*
t	like *t* in *tape*
v	like *v* in *vase*
z	either like *ts* in *spits* or *ds* in *pads*

ACCENTS

Accents are used to indicate which vowel should be stressed and to differentiate between words that are spelled the same.

ESSENTIAL PHRASES

Hi Ciao
Good morning Buongiorno
Good evening Buonasera
Good night Buonanotte
Good-bye Arrivederci
Nice to meet you Piacere
Thank you Grazie
You're welcome Prego
Please Per favore
Do you speak English? Parla inglese?
I don't understand Non capisco
Have a nice day Buona giornata
Where is the bathroom? Dov'è il bagno?

Yes/No Sì/No

TRANSPORTATION

Where is…? Dov'è…?

How far is…? Quanto è distante…?

Is there a bus to…? C'è un autobus per…?

Does this bus go to…? Quest'autobus va a…?

Where do I get off? Dove devo scendere?

What time does the bus/train leave/ arrive? A che ora parte/arriva l'autobus/treno?

Where is the nearest subway station? Dov'è la stazione metro più vicina?

Where can I buy a ticket? Dove posso comprare un biglietto?

A round-trip ticket/a single ticket to… Un biglietto di andata e ritorno/ andata per…

FOOD

A table for two/three/four… Un tavolo per due/tre/quattro…

Do you have a menu in English? Avete un menu in inglese?

What is the dish of the day? Qual è il piatto del giorno?

We're ready to order. Siamo pronti per ordinare.

I'm a vegetarian. Sono vegetariano

May I have… Posso avere…

The check please? Il conto per favore?

beer birra

bread pane

breakfast colazione

cash contante

check conto

coffee caffè

dinner cena

glass bicchiere

hors d'oeuvre antipasto

ice ghiaccio

ice cream gelato

lunch pranzo

restaurant ristorante

sandwich(es) panino(i)

snack spuntino

waiter cameriere

water acqua

wine vino

SHOPPING

money soldi

shop negozio

What time do the shops close? A che ora chiudono i negozi?

How much is it? Quanto costa?

I'm just looking. Sto guardando solamente.

What is the local specialty? Quali sono le specialità locali?

HEALTH

drugstore farmacia

pain dolore

fever febbre

headache mal di testa

stomachache mal di stomaco

toothache mal di denti

burn bruciatura

cramp crampo

nausea nausea

vomiting vomitare

medicine medicina

antibiotic antibiotico

pill/tablet pillola/pasticca

aspirin aspirina

I need to see a doctor. Ho bisogno di un medico.

I need to go to the hospital. Devo andare in ospedale.

I have a pain here… Ho un dolore qui…

She/he has been stung/bitten. È stata punta/morsa.

I am diabetic/pregnant. Sono diabetico/incinta.

I am allergic to penicillin/ cortisone. Sono allergico alla penicillina/cortisone.

My blood group is…positive/ negative. Il mio gruppo sanguigno è… positivo/negative.

NUMBERS

0 zero
1 uno
2 due
3 tre
4 quattro
5 cinque
6 sei
7 sette
8 otto
9 nove
10 dieci
11 undici
12 dodici
13 tredici
14 quattordici
15 quindici
16 sedici
17 diciassette
18 diciotto
19 diciannove
20 venti
21 ventuno
30 trenta
40 quaranta
50 cinquanta
60 sessanta
70 settanta
80 ottanta
90 novanta
100 cento
101 centouno
200 duecento
500 cinquecento
1,000 mille
10,000 diecimila
100,000 centomila
1,000,000 un milione

TIME

What time is it? Che ora è?
It's one/three o'clock. E l'una/sono le tre.
midday mezzogiorno
midnight mezzanotte
morning mattino

afternoon pomeriggio
evening sera
night notte
yesterday ieri
today oggi
tomorrow domani

DAYS AND MONTHS

week settimana
month mese
Monday lunedi
Tuesday martedi
Wednesday mercoledi
Thursday giovedi
Friday venerdi
Saturday sabato
Sunday domenica
January gennaio
February febbraio
March marzo
April aprile
May maggio
June giugno
July luglio
August agosto
September settembre
October ottobre
November novembre
December dicembre

VERBS

to have avere
to be essere
to go andare
to come venire
to want volere
to eat mangiare
to drink bere
to buy comprare
to need necessitare
to read leggere
to write scrivere
to stop fermare
to get off scendere
to arrive arrivare
to return ritornare

to stay restare
to leave partire
to look at guardare

to look for cercare
to give dare
to take prendere

Index

A

Abate Zanetti School of Glass: 143, 145
Accademia, Galleria dell': 17, 39, 54, 56
accessibility: 288-289
accommodations: 280-281; Lake Garda
    221, 229, 235, 239, 245, 252-253; Padua
    172-173; Ravenna 265; Venice 121-127;
    Venice Lagoon/Islands 143-144, 150,
    152-153; Verona 208; Vicenza 188
activities: see recreation
Adige River: 191, 205-206
Adriatic Coast: 266-267
Aeroporto di Venezia: 25, 129, 269
air travel: 25, 129-130, 209, 268-270
Al Bottegon: 39, 77, 80, 87
Al Gatto Nero: 138, 147
Al Timon: 87, 89
alcohol laws: 283
All'Arco: 42, 85
amusement parks: 212, 218-219, 232, 234
Antica Casa della Malvasia: 178, 184
Antica Pieve di Santo Stefano: 241
Antiche Carampane: 77, 84
aperitivo: see bars and nightlife, food
appetizers: see cicchetti, food
Arco: 247, 249-250
Arco Castle: 250
Arena di Verona: 12, 22, 191, 195, 196
Arsenale: 38, 71
ATMs: 286
attire: 283-284

B

Bacareto da Lele: 85, 87
bacari: 8, 38, 86-87, 119, 168-169
banks: 286
Bardolino: 214, 232 234, 236-240;
    map 233
bargaining: 279
bars: see drinking, nightlife
Basilica di San Marco: 8, 17, 33, 37, 46-47
Basilica di Santa Maria Gloriosa Dei
    Frari: 38, 61
Basilica di Sant'Appolinare Nuovo:
    258, 259
Basilica di San Vitale: 256, 259
Basilica Palladiana: 21, 176, 180-181
Basilica Sant'Antonio: 20, 160,162,
    165-166

Basilica Santa Maria della Salute: 57
Basilica Santi Giovanni e Paolo: 70
Bastion, The: 248
Battistero degli Ariani: 258, 259
beaches: Lake Garda 220, 226, 242-243,
    250; Lido 136, 156; Ravenna 266-267
Beccafico: 77, 78
Bibliotheca Marciana: 46, 51
biking: Lido 136, 156; Padua 171; Ravenna
    264; Verona 205, 207; Vicenza 187
Blue Bar: 77, 97
boat tours: Peschiera del Garda 219;
    Venice 120
boat travel: Brenta Canal 172-173;
    Lake Garda 231, 236, 240, 246, 254;
    Venice 131
boating: Lake Garda 237-238; Venice
    116-117
bookstores: 110, 112, 114
Borghtto sul Mincio: 220
Botanical Garden: 162, 166
Bottega del Tintoretto: 43, 68
Braccobaldo Beach: 220
Brenta Canal: 15, 20, 172-173
Bridge of Sighs: 49
budgeting: 28
Burano: 18, 19, 137, 146-150; map 148
bus travel: 270-271, 273; Venice 129, 131,
    134; see also specific place

C

Cà del Forno: 123, 125
Cà del Sol: 107, 113
Ca' d'Oro: 69
Ca' De Ven: 258, 262
Ca'Mancana: 107, 109
Ca'Pesaro: 37-38, 65
Ca'Rezzonico: 58
cable car, Monte Baldo: 12, 23, 217, 242
Caffè Florian: 77, 79
Caffè Pedrocchi: 162, 167
Calesela dell'Occhio Grosso: 76
Calle del Bastion: 39, 103, 109
Calle della Chiesa: 103
Calle di Ca'Zusto: 76
Calle Frezzaria: 105
Calle Ghetto Vecchio: 68
Calle Stretta: 76
Calleta Varisco: 76

Campanile di San Marco: 50
campi: 53, 133
camping: 281
Campo Cesare: 112
Campo di Ghetto Nuovo: 43, 66
Campo S. Agnese: 53
Campo San Lorenzo: 53
Campo San Polo: 53, 65
Campo Santa Margherita: 37, 42, 58, 95
Campo Santa Maria Formosa: 53
Campo Santo Stefano: 17, 39, 52-53
Canal Grande (Grand Canal): 17, 39, 65-66
canals: 7, 72-73
Caneva Aquapark: 234
Cannaregio: 38, 65-69; accommodations 121, 125-126; food 88-90; map 67; nightlife and entertainment 97-98; shopping 113
Cantina do Mori: 42, 77, 84, 87
Capanno Garibaldi: 267
Cappella degli Scrovegni: 11, 20, 160, 162, 163
car travel: 28, 271-272; Venice 130-131; *see also specific place*
Carnevale: 102-103
Carnival masks: 33, 107; Burano 149; Venice 104, 105-106, 109, 111, 113-114, 119
Casa di Giulietta: 22, 196
Casa Museo Andrich: 151
Cascata del Varone: 212, 249
Casino di Venezia: 98
Castello (Venice neighborhood): 38, 69-72; accommodations 126; food 90-91; map 70; nightlife 98-99; shopping 113-114
Castello di Desenzano: 225
Castello Scaligero: 23, 212, 217, 225, 240
Castello Scaligero di Lazise: 231
Catena Square: 247-248
Cathedral of Saint Mary Magdalene: 223-224
Cattedrale (Duomo), Padua: 162, 165
cell phones: 287
Chiesa dei Redentore: 38, 74-75
Chiesa dei Santi Maria e Donato: 141-142
Chiesa della Madonna dell'Orto: 42, 64, 68
Chiesa di San Francesco: 260-261
Chiesa di San Giorgio Maggiore: 58-59
Chiesa di San Giorgio dei Greci: 70-71
Chiesa di San Nicolo: 231-232
Chiesa di San Polo: 65
Chiesa di San Rocco: 42, 63-64
Chievo Verona: 206

children, traveling with: 118-119, 289
Christmas Market: 205
Church of Saint Nicholas: 231-232
cicchetti: 8, 33, 86-87; *see also* food
Cimitero di San Michele: 18, 138, 139-140
Cini Foundation: 59-60
Civic Museum: 178, 179
Civilita di Venezia: 51
classes: 120-121
Classis Museum: 256, 258, 261-262
clothing/apparel: *see* shopping
Coco Beach: 215, 227
coffee: *see* food
Colonna station: 140
communications: 128, 287-288
concerts: 93-94, 96, 97, 99; *see also* live music
conduct: 281-283
consulates: 128, 273-274
cooking classes: 120
Correr Museum: 43, 51
Corso Porta Nuova: 205
Costituzione: 37
CoVino: 43, 90
crafts: 104, 112
credit cards: 286
crime and theft: 284
cuisine: *see* food
currency: 285; *see also* money
customs (behavior): 281-283
customs (international entry): 274
cycling: *see* biking

DE

Da Nico: 77, 81
Dante Alighieri's Tomb: 261
debit cards: 286
department stores: *see* shopping
Desenzano del Garda and Sirmione: 23, 214, 215, 222-231; map 223
dining: *see* food
disabilities, travelers with: 288-289
discounts/sales: 279-280
Doge's Palace: 9, 17, 33, 37, 48-49
Domus dei Tappeti di Pietra: 261
Dorsoduro: 37, 54-60; accommodations 121, 123-124; food 80-81, 84; map 55; nightlife 94-96; shopping 109-110
Duomo di Santa Maria Maddalena: 223-224
entertainment 94-96; shopping 109-110
drinking: 28, 277-278; *see also* nightlife
driver's license: 28
drug laws: 283
electricity/electrical devices: 24, 29

embassies and consulates: 128, 273-274
emergencies: 24, 128, 284
entry requirements: 24, 273; *see also* travel documents
Eremitani Museums: 163-164
etiquette: 21, 279, 281-283
events: Lake Garda 251; Venice 99-103; Verona 203-204
exchange rates: *see* money
Eurail: 270

F

fall: 24
family travel: 118-119, 289
Faro Station: 138, 140
female travelers: 289-290
ferries: 129; *see also traghetto, vaporetto*
Festa del Redentore: 74, 100
festivals and events: Lake Garda 251; Venice 99-103; Verona 203-204
FGB: 105, 145
fish market (Rialto): 18, 42, 61, 113
fishing tours: 149-150
Flora: 119, 122
Florence, traveling from: 130
Fondaco dei Turchi: 60
Fondamenta Cao Moleca: 136, 146
Fondamenta dei Vetrai: 140
Fondamente della Misericordia: 18, 38, 42
Fondamente Nuove: 38, 133, 136
Fondamente Zattere: 37
food: 28, 82-83, 275-279; dining tips 75, 275; Lagoon 143, 147-148, 152-153; Lake Garda 221, 227, 235, 238, 244-245, 251-252; Padua 167-168; Ravenna 262-263; Venice 75-91; Verona 200-202; Vicenza 183-185
football/soccer: 206-207
funicular: Monte Baldo 12, 23, 217, 242; Verona 198
Funivie di Malcesine e del Monte Baldo: 12, 23, 217, 242

G

Galleria dell'Accademia: 17, 39, 54, 56
Galleria Internazionale d'Arte Moderna: 65
Gardaland: 212, 218-219
Gardaland Sea Life Aquarium: 219
gardens: *see* parks
gas, costs: 28
gelato: *see* food
Generator Venice: 123, 127
Giardini ex Reali: 116
Giardini Pubblici: 115-116

Giardini Savorgnan: 115
Giardino Giusti: 199-200
Giardino Papadopoli: 115
Giotto: 163-164
Giudecca: 38, 73-75; accommodations 127; food 91; map 74-75; nightlife 99; shopping 115
Giuseppe Toselli's House: 146
Glass Museum: 140-141
glass/glassmaking: 10, 18, 33; Venice 104, 105, 109, 110-111, 113, 119, 121; Lagoon 136, 140-141, 142-143, 144-145, 148
glossary of terms: 133
golf: 157, 187-188
gondola: 7, 28, 72
Grand Canal: 17, 39, 65-66
greetings: 282
Gritti Palace Hotel: 93, 123
Grottoes of Catullus (Grotte di Catullo): 215, 225
Guggenheim Foundation: 33, 56-67
guides, private: 119

H

health and safety: 128, 284-285
Hellas Verona: 206
Hendrix: 162, 168
hiking: Monte Baldo 23, 243; Riva del Garda 249-250
history: 36
hospitals and pharmacies: Venice 128; *see also specific place*
hostels: 280-281; *see also* accommodations, *specific place*
hotel bars: *see* nightlife and entertainment
Hotel Galleria: 123, 124
Hotel Metropole: 123, 126
hotels: 28, 280; *see also* accommodations, *specific place*
hours of operation: 24, 25, 278-279, 280

IJK

I Musici Veneziani: 94
Il Burchiello: 20, 120, 172-173
Il Papavero: 260, 264
Imperial Apartments: 51
information and services: Lake Garda 230, 253-254; Padua 173; Ravenna 265; Venice 127; Verona 209; Vicenza 189
international driver's permit: 28, 272
Interpreti Veneziani: 93-94
Isola del Garda: 212, 226
Isola di San Giorgio: 17, 38, 39, 58
Isola Sant'Elena: 71-72

Italo: 130, 270
itineraries: 17-23; Lagoon 138-139; Lake
    Garda 215-217; Padua 162; Ravenna
    258; Venice 39-43; Verona 194-195;
    Vicenza 178
Jamaica Beach: 226
Jewish Ghetto: 66-67
kayaking: 117

L

La Cambusa: 215, 228
Lace Museum: 146
La Fenice Opera House: 37, 51, 93
La Piadina del Melariancio: 258, 262
La Villeggiatura: 119, 125
lace: 104
Lake Garda: 19, 23, 211-254; map 213
lakeside villages: 214
Lazise: 231-236; map 233
Le Stanze del Vetro: 60
LGBTQ+ travelers: 290
Lido: 19, 137, 154-157
Lido Beach: 156
Lido Paina: 23, 217, 242-243
live music: Verona 203; see also concerts
local guides: Ravenna 260
local, travel like a: 21
Locanda Cipriani: 18, 139, 152-153
lost and found: 291; Venice 128
love locks: 197
Low Loop 1: 249-250
luggage: 28
luggage storage: Padua 174; Venice 127;
    Vicenza 189
Lumeart: 138, 145, 148

MNO

Madonna dell'Orto: 42, 64, 68
MAG Museo Alto Garda: 248
Majer: 39, 91
Malamocco: 156
Malcesine: 23, 214, 215, 240-246; map 241
maps, travel: 291
Marina di Ravenna: 266-267
Marina Romea: 267
markets: Padua 160, 165, 169-170; Venice
    61, 108-109, 110, 112-113, 114; Verona
    204; Vicenza 186-187
masks: see Carnival masks
Mausoleo di Galla Placidia: 256, 258, 260
Mausoleo di Teodorico: 261
measurement system: 288
medical services: 284
menus: 277
Mercatino dei Miracoli: 113

Mercatino delle Robe da Mar: 114
Mercatino di Campo San Maurizio:
    108-109
Mercatino di Polvere di Ricordi: 110
Mercato dell'Antiquariato a San
    Zeno: 204
Mercato dell'Antiquariato Collezionismo
    e Vintage: 187
Mercato di Piazza Erbe: 204
metric system: 288
Milan, traveling from: 271
Milano Linate: 269
Milano Malpensa: 269
Mincio River: 220
mobile phones: 287
Molin22: 215, 228
Monastero di San Lazzaro degli
    Armeni: 158
money: 24, 285-286
Monte Baldo: 12, 23, 212, 214, 217, 241-242
Monte Baone: 250
Monte Berico: 182-183
mosaics/mosaic tours (Ravenna): 14,
    256, 260
Movieland: 232
Murano: 18, 19, 140-146; map 141
Museo Archeologico al Teatro
    Romano: 199
Museo Archeologico Nazionale: 51
Museo Civico Pinacoteca: 178, 179
Museo Correr: 43, 51
Museo d'Arte Orientale: 65
Museo dell'Olio: 236
Museo del Merletto: 146
Museo del Vetro (Glass Museum): 140-141
Museo di Castelvecchio: 197-198
Museo di San Marco: 47
Museo Ebraico: 68
Museo NatuRa: 267
Museo Provinciale: 152
Museo Storico Navale: 38, 71, 119
Museo Tamo: 261
Museo di Storia Naturale (Museum of
    Natural History): 60
museums: 25, see also specific museum/
    museo
Musica Palazzo: 94
Naval Museum: 38, 71, 119
Nicolo: 112-113
night tours, mosaics: 14, 256 260
nightlife: Lake Garda 220, 227, 238; Lido
    154-155; Padua 168-169; Ravenna 263-
    264; Venice 91-103; Verona 202-203;
    Vicenza 185
Olive Oil Museum: 236

Olympic Theater: 15, 21, 22, 176, 178, 179-180
opera: Padua 169; Venice 93-94, 98; Verona 196
Oriago: 172
Orto Botanico: 162, 166
Osteria al Squero: 81, 87
Osteria dal Capo: 162, 167
outdoor recreation: *see* recreation

PQ

packing: 28-29
paddleboarding: 117
Padiglione Delle Navi: 71
Padua: 19, 20, 159 174; map 161
Padua Cathedral: 162, 165
Pala d'Oro: 47
Palanca ferry station: 38, 74
Palazzo Bo: 164
Palazzo Chiericati: 178, 179
Palazzo della Ragione: 164
Palazzo Ducale (Doge's Palace): 9, 17, 33, 37, 48-49
Palazzo Grassi: 53
Palazzo Leoni Montanari: 181
Palazzo Mocenigo: 60-61
Palazzo Zuckermann: 164
Palladian Basilica: 21, 176, 180-181
Palladian villas: 20
Palladio, Andrea: 5, 54, 74, 172, 175, 179-180, 182
Papier Maché: 107, 114
parachuting: 206
Paradise Beach: 156
paragliding: 12, 23, 217, 243-244
Parco della Rimembranze: 115
Parco Querini: 187
Parco Termale del Garda: 234
parking: 28
parking: 272
parks and gardens: Venice 115-116; Verona 199-200; Vicenza 187; *see also specific place*
Pasticceria Rizzardini: 18, 42, 88
Peace Trail: 217, 243
Pensione Accademia: 123, 124
pensioni: 280-281; *see also* accommodations, *specific place*
performing arts: Padua 169; *see also* concerts, opera, theater
Peschiera del Garda: 214; 217-222; map 218
pharmacies: 284-285; *see also* health and safety
phones: 287

phrases/phrasebook: 282, 292-295
Piallassa Baiona wetlands: 267
Piazza Capitaniato: 162, 165
Piazza dei Frutti: 169-170
Piazza dei Signori: 20, 164-165
Piazza delle Erbe: 20, 162, 169
Piazza San Marco: 17, 37, 39, 43, 46, 103
Piazza San Zemo: 205
pizza: *see* food
planning tips: 17
planning tips: 24-27
planning tips: Lagoon 136; Lake Garda 214-215; Padua 160; Ravenna 256; Verona 191; Vicenza 176
playgrounds: 119
police: 128
Ponte Castelvecchio: 198
Ponte degli Scalzi: 37
Ponte del Diavolo: 138, 151
Ponte Pietra: 198
Porto Corsini: 266-267
postal services: 288; *see also* information and services, *specific place*
Prato della Valle: 166
produce: 278
produce market: 61, 113
Punta della Dogana: 37, 53, 57
Punta San Vigilio: 212, 236-237
Quaderia picture gallery: 51

R

rafting: 191, 205-206
Rail Europe: 270
Ravenna: 19, 255-267; map 257
recreation: Lake Garda 219-220, 226-227, 232, 234, 237-238, 249-250; Lido 156-157; Padua 171; Ravenna 264; Venice 115-121; Verona 205-207; Vicenza 187-188
Redentore Church: 38, 74-75
restaurants: *see* food
Rialto Bridge: 18, 33, 38, 42, 54
Rialto markets: 61, 112-113
ride-hailing: 273
Rio Terra Lista di Spagna: 38
Ristorante Vecchia Malcesine: 23, 217, 244-245
Riva degli Schiavone: 38, 71
Riva del Garda: 214, 246-254
River Lamone: 267
Roman arena: Verona 195
Rome, traveling from: 130, 271
rowing: 116
Ruga dei Oresi: 112

S

Sabbioni Beach: 250
safety: 128, 284-285
sailing: 250-251
St. Mark's Basilica: 8, 17, 33, 37, 46-47
St. Mark's Square: see Piazza San Marco
sales tax: 286
San Giorgio Church: 70-71
San Giorgio Island: 17, 38, 39, 58
San Lazzaro degli Armeni: 137, 158
San Lorenzo Church: 250
San Marco (Venice neighborhood): 37, 43;
    accommodations 121, 122-123; food
    76-80; map 44-45; nightlife 92-94;
    shopping 105-109
San Michele: 137, 139-140
San Pietro Panoramic Point: 22, 198
San Polo and Santa Croce: 37-38, 60-65;
    accommodations 124-125; food 84-
    88; map 62; nightlife 96-97; shopping
    110-111
San Stae: 61
San Tomà: 72
San Zeno di Montagna: 243
San Zeno Maggiore: 199
Sant'Elena Island: 71-72
Santa Barbara Church: 249
Santa Fosca: 152
Santa Lucia Train Station: 38
Santa Maria Assunta: 138, 151-152
Santa Maria del Giglio: 72
Santa Maria Formosa: 53
Santa Maria Gloriosa Dei Frari: 38, 61
Santa Sofia: 72
Scaligero Castle: 23, 212, 217, 225, 240
scooters: 157
Scrovegni Chapel: 11, 20, 160, 162, 163
Scuola Grande di San Rocco: 18, 38, 62-
    63, 64, 69-70
scuole/schools: 66
seasonal food: 278
seasons: 24-25
security: 285
senior travelers: 290
Sentiero della Pace CAI Path: 217, 243
services: see information and services
shipping: 279
shopping: 279-280; Lagoon 148-149; Lake
    Garda 234-235, 238, 244; Padua 169-
    170; Venice 103-115; Verona 204-205;
    Vicenza 186-187
sightseeing passes: 24, 26, 30-31, 46
Sirmione: 214, 215; see also Desenzano
    del Garda and Sirmione

small streets, Venice: 76
smoking laws: 283
solo travelers: 289-290
souvenirs: see crafts, shopping
Speck & Stube: 217, 244
spring: 24
Squero San Trovaso: 58
Stadio Marc'antonio Bentegodi: 206-207
stand-up paddle: 117
stationery: see shopping
Strada Nuova: 18, 37, 38, 42, 103
summer: 24
SUP in Venice: 42, 117
Synagogue: Venice 68

T

taxis: Venice 129-130; Vicenza 189; Verona
    209, 210
taxis: 273
Teatro Goldini: 93
Teatro La Fenice: 37, 51, 93
Teatro Malibran: 98
Teatro Olimpico: 15, 21, 22, 176, 178,
    179-180
Teatro Romano: 199
Teatro Verdi: 169
theft: 284
time zone: 24
Tintoretto: 36, 48, 51,52, 54, 57, 59, 62-63,
    64, 68, 69, 75, 164, 179
tipping: 279
Tomba di Giuletta: 196
Torcello: 18, 19, 137, 151-153
Torre Bissara: 181
Torre dell'Orologio: 43, 50-51
Torre Lamberti: 191, 197
Toselli, Giuseppe: 146
tourist information: 291; Lake Garda 230,
    253; Padua 173-174; Ravenna 265;
    Venice 127; Verona 209; Vicenza 189
tours: Lagoon 149-150, 157; Padua 171;
    Ravenna 14, 260, 264; Verona 207;
    Venice 117-120; see also specific sight
traghetto: 7, 28, 72, 134
train travel: 28, 270, 272-273; Venice 130;
    see also specific place
trams: 134
transportation: 268-273; Venice 129-134;
    see also specific place
travel documents: 28; see also visas
travel tips: 285-290
travelers of color: 290
Treasury (St. Mark's Basilica): 47
Trenitalia: 27, 130, 270, 272

V

vaporetto: 7, 26, 28, 33, 73, 119, 132, 271
VAT: 286
Venetian glass: see glass/glassmaking
Venice: 32-134; map 34-35
Venice Biennale: 38, 101
Venice Film Festival: 100
Venice Jazz Club: 96
Venice lagoon/islands: 18, 135-158; map 137
Venice Music Project: 96
Venitian cuisine: 82-83
Venier: 140
Verona: 19, 190-210; map 192-193
Verona Villafranca Airport: 25, 209, 269
Vetreria Artistica Emmedue: 138, 142, 145
Via Santa Lucia: 169
Vicenza: 19, 21-22, 175-189; map 177
Villa Borghese Cavazza: 226
Villa Foscari: 172
Villa la Rotonda: 22, 176, 178, 182, 183
Villa Pisani: 172
Villa Romana: 215, 224

Villa Valmarana: 22, 176, 178, 181-182
Villa Widmann: 172
vinerie: 10, 95
Vino Vero: 77, 87, 89
Virtuosi di Venezia: 94
visas: 24, 273; see also travel documents

W

walking tours: Venice 117-119; Verona 207
walks: Lake Garda 220, 227, 232 234, 237; see also hiking
water sports: Lake Garda 226-227, 243-244, 250-251; Venice 116-117
water taxis: 129, 134
weights and measures: 288
wellness centers: 234
Wi-Fi: 128-129, 287-288
windsurfing: 267
wine/wineries: 10, 83, 95, 237, 239; see also nightlife
winter: 24
women travelers: 289-290
workshops: 38

List of Maps

Venice

Venice: 34–35
Venice Itinerary Ideas: 40–41
San Marco: 44–45
Dorsoduro: 55
San Polo and Santa Croce: 62–63
Cannaregio: 67
Castello: 70
Giudecca: 74-75

Venice's Lagoon Islands

Venice's Lagoon Area: 137
Lagoon Itinerary Ideas: 139
Murano: 141
Burano: 148

Padua

Padua: 161

Vicenza

Vicenza: 177

Verona

Verona: 192–193

Lake Garda

Lake Garda: 213
Lake Garda Itinerary Ideas: 216
Peschiera del Garda: 218
Desenzano and Sirmione: 223
Lazise and Bardolino: 233
Malcesine: 241
Riva del Garda: 247

Ravenna

Ravenna: 257

Photo Credits

Acknowlegments

This book would not exist without the talent and dedication of an extraordinary editorial team. I am grateful to Grace Fujimoto in acquisitions for giving me the opportunity to work on this series, Nikki Ioakimedes for overseeing the project from concept to completion, Kat Bennett for her wonderful maps, Lucie Ericksen in design, Crystal Turnau and Katie Mock in marketing, Ravina Schneider in administration, Barbara Schultz in copyediting, and Lindsey Davison, who contributed the Lake Garda chapter.

My favorite part of writing a guidebook is talking to people, and everyone I met along the way was friendly and generous with their time. No one illustrated that more than Franco Possocco, the Grand Guardian of the Scuola di San Rocco, and his associate Giuliano Zanon, who recounted dozens of antidotes about Venice. Federica from Palazzo Grassi kindly provided entry to her art galleries and Samuel Gianotte shared his knowledge about the city. Also instrumental were talks with certified guide Luisella Romeo, Eliana Argine of SUP in Venice, and Jane Caporal, founder of Row Venice. Elena and Letizia from the Verona Tourist Office were extremely helpful, as was Davide Cocchio of Adige Rafting. I am grateful to Giancarlo Busato, Massimo Scopel, Gianna Pedino, Giulio Valmarana and Giada in Vicenza, and the Papavero guides of Ravenna who helped me discover their city.

Final thanks go to Emma, Sacha, and Alessia, who endured my absences and supported me throughout the journey. *Moon Venice & Beyond* is dedicated to them and to curious travelers everywhere.

Alexei Cohen
Rome, Italy

MAP SYMBOLS

═══	Expressway	○	City/Town	ⓘ	Information Center	♠	Park
▭▭▭	Primary Road	◉	State Capital	🅿	Parking Area	⚓	Golf Course
▭▭▭	Secondary Road	◉	National Capital	⛪	Church	✚	Unique Feature
▭▭▭	Unpaved Road	◎	Highlight	🍇	Winery	◤	Waterfall
▭▭▭	Trail	★	Point of Interest	🚪	Trailhead	Λ	Camping
▭▭▭	Ferry	•	Accommodation	🚆	Train Station	▲	Mountain
▭▭▭	Railroad	▼	Restaurant/Bar	✈	Airport	⛷	Ski Area
▭▭▭	Pedestrian Walkway	■	Other Location	✈	Airfield	〰	Glacier
▤▤▤	Stairs						

CONVERSION TABLES

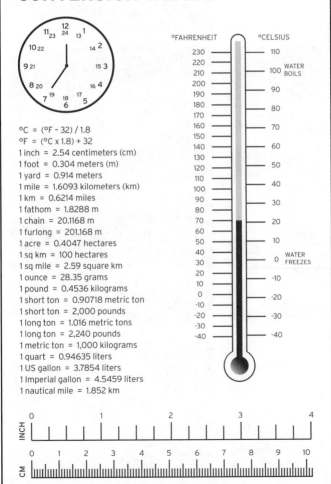

°C = (°F - 32) / 1.8
°F = (°C x 1.8) + 32
1 inch = 2.54 centimeters (cm)
1 foot = 0.304 meters (m)
1 yard = 0.914 meters
1 mile = 1.6093 kilometers (km)
1 km = 0.6214 miles
1 fathom = 1.8288 m
1 chain = 20.1168 m
1 furlong = 201.168 m
1 acre = 0.4047 hectares
1 sq km = 100 hectares
1 sq mile = 2.59 square km
1 ounce = 28.35 grams
1 pound = 0.4536 kilograms
1 short ton = 0.90718 metric ton
1 short ton = 2,000 pounds
1 long ton = 1.016 metric tons
1 long ton = 2,240 pounds
1 metric ton = 1,000 kilograms
1 quart = 0.94635 liters
1 US gallon = 3.7854 liters
1 Imperial gallon = 4.5459 liters
1 nautical mile = 1.852 km

MOON TRAVEL GUIDES TO EUROPE

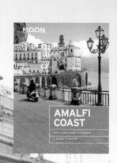

MOON

AMALFI COAST

With Capri, Naples & Pompeii

LAURA THAYER

MOON

BARCELONA & MADRID

JESSICA JONES

MOON

CAMINO DE SANTIAGO

SACRED SITES,
HISTORIC VILLAGES,
LOCAL FOOD & WINE

BEEBE BAHRAMI

MOON

CROATIA & SLOVENIA

SHANN FOUNTAIN ALTIOUR

MOON

EDINBURGH, GLASGOW & THE ISLE OF SKYE

MOON

ICELAND

JENNA GOTTLIEB

MOON

IRELAND

CAMILLE DeANGELIS

MOON

NORMANDY & BRITTANY

With Mont-Saint-Michel

CHRIS NEWENS

MOON

NORWAY

DAVID NIKEL

MOON

PORTUGAL

CARRIE-MARIE BRATLEY

MOON

PRAGUE, VIENNA & BUDAPEST

JENNIFER D. WALKER
AUBURN SCALLON

MOON

ROME, FLORENCE & VENICE

ALEXEI J. COHEN

GO BIG AND GO BEYOND!

Copenhagen & BEYOND
MICHAEL BARRETT

DAY TRIPS, LOCAL SPOTS,
STRATEGIES TO AVOID CROWDS
EXPLORE COPENHAGEN AT YOUR OWN PACE

These savvy city guides include strategies to help you see the top sights and find adventure beyond the tourist crowds.

Florence & BEYOND
ALEXEI J. COHEN

DAY TRIPS, LOCAL SPOTS,
STRATEGIES TO AVOID CROWDS
EXPLORE FLORENCE AT YOUR OWN PACE

Milan & BEYOND
WITH THE ITALIAN LAKES

DAY TRIPS, LOCAL SPOTS,
STRATEGIES TO AVOID CROWDS
EXPLORE MILAN AT YOUR OWN PACE

Venice & BEYOND
ALEXEI Z. COHEN

DAY TRIPS, LOCAL SPOTS,
STRATEGIES TO AVOID CROWDS
EXPLORE VENICE AT YOUR OWN PACE

OR TAKE THINGS ONE STEP AT A TIME

LONDON WALKS
SEE THE CITY LIKE A LOCAL

PARIS WALKS
SEE THE CITY LIKE A LOCAL

ROME WALKS
SEE THE CITY LIKE A LOCAL

Gear up for a bucket list vacation

MOON

TRIP OF A LIFETIME

ANGKOR WAT

MOON

BARCELONA & MADRID

JESSICA JONES

MOON

ICELAND

JENNA GOTTLIEB

MOON

TRIP OF A LIFETIME

GALÁPAGOS ISLANDS

MOON

TRIP OF A LIFETIME

MACHU PICCHU

MOON

MOROCCO

MOON

NEW ZEALAND

MOON

NORWAY

MOON

TRIP OF A LIFETIME

PATAGONIA

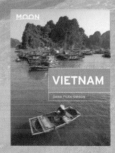

MOON

VIETNAM

DANA FILEK-GIBSON

MOON

USA NATIONAL PARKS

THE COMPLETE GUIDE TO ALL

59 PARKS

BECKY LOMAX

MOON

CAMINO DE SANTIAGO

SACRED SITES,
HISTORIC VILLAGES,
LOCAL FOOD & WINE

BEEBE BAHRAMI

MOON VENICE & BEYOND
Avalon Travel
Hachette Book Group
1700 Fourth Street
Berkeley, CA 94710, USA
www.moon.com

Editor: Nikki Ioakimedes
Copy Editor: Barbara Schultz
Graphics and Production Coordinator: Lucie Ericksen
Cover Design: Faceout Studios, Charles Brock for Handbooks
Interior Design: Domini Dragoone for Handbooks
Moon Logo: Tim McGrath
Map Editor: Kat Bennett
Cartographers: Karin Dahl, Moon Street Cartography, Erin Greb, Kat Bennett
Proofreader: Elina Carmona

ISBN-13: 978-1-64049-069-7
Printing History
1st Edition — July 2019
5 4 3 2 1

Text © 2019 by Alexei J. Cohen
Maps © 2019 by Avalon Travel.

Front cover photo: gondola in Venice © Good Vibrations Images / Stocksy.com
Back cover photo: Piazza delle Erbe, Verona © Xbrchx | Dreamstime.com
Inside cover photo: Cathedral of San Marco, Venice © Zoom-zoom | Dreamstime.com

Printed in China by RR Donnelley